E. A. Kremer,
Wadsworth Ohio
Oct-11-1907

W. B. Hinsdale

OHIO ANNALS.

HISTORIC EVENTS

IN THE

TUSCARAWAS AND MUSKINGUM VALLEYS,

AND IN OTHER PORTIONS OF

The State of Ohio.

ADVENTURES OF POST, HECKEWELDER AND ZEISBERGER.
LEGENDS AND TRADITIONS OF THE KOPHS, MOUND BUILDERS,
RED AND WHITE MEN.

Adventures of Putnam and Heckewelder, founders of the State.

LOCAL HISTORY, GROWTH OF OHIO IN POPULATION, POLITICAL POWER, WEALTH AND INTELLIGENCE.

IN ONE VOLUME, 367 OCTAVO PAGES, ON TINTED PAPER, ENGLISH CLOTH.

EDITED BY

C. H. MITCHENER,

Of the New Philadelphia (Ohio) Bar.

DAYTON, OHIO:

THOMAS W. ODELL, Publisher.

1876.

Printed by W. D. BICKHAM, Dayton, Ohio.

INTRODUCTORY.

GENERAL SUMMARY OF EVENTS—A HISTORICAL PANORAMA OF OHIO.

This volume is dedicated to the Press. Passing over the geological and pre-historic portions, and coming down to the historic column, the State of Ohio presents one of the grandest series of panoramic scenes in history.

SCENE I.

Post's cabin in 1761—He gets from the Indians fifty steps square for God's farm—He returns in 1762 with Heckewelder, and enters the cabin singing a hymn.

SCENE II.

Zeisberger preaching to Netawatwes and the Indians, who give him land for curing small-pox, and privilege to establish mission at Big Spring.

SCENE III.

Heckewelder and twenty-two canoes arrive at Schoenbrunn with Indians, and all go to putting up buildings.

SCENE IV.

Simon Girty at Schoenbrunn urging converts to join the English side in revolution.

SCENE V.

Captain White Eyes rebutting Pipe's speech at Goshocking—Heckewelder rides from Fort Pitt to Coshocton and calms the Delawares.

SCENE VI.

Pipe and the Monseys and Wyandots go over to the British—Return to Salem and drive off missionaries and Indians to Sandusky.

SCENE VII.

Zeisberger and Heckewelder taken to Detroit and tried for treason, while Indians return to valley for corn.

SCENE VIII.

Girty over on Monongahela urging the borderers to go and kill the Indians and burn their towns—March of Williamson to Gnadenhutten with his men—Murder of ninety-six Indians.

SCENE IX.

Girty at Sandusky urging Indian warriors to revenge the death of their kindred—Warriors start on their raids to the border.

SCENE X.

Organizing of Crawford's rangers, and march towards Sandusky—Stop at Schoenbrunn—Crawford in a dream sees Ann Charity and her skeletons—His march onward—Indian towns abandoned--Indians attack and defeat his army—Crawford captured and burned—Army back at Schoenbrunn—Williamson in his dream sees Ann Charity on her return pass Schoenbrunn with her skeletons, guarded with warriors carrying the scalps of Crawford's men—Her appearance at Gnadenhutten—Buries skeletons and scalps—Ann disappears—Great Spirit moves up and down the valley—The ruins for fifty miles—Four hundred Indians repass the Big Spring—God and Mannitto appear; after cursing the valley, dry up the spring and disappear to fight it out on another line.

SCENE XI.

Zeisberger and converts in the wilderness among the snows and dangers for seventeen years.

SCENE XII.

Putnam and his men land at Marietta; settlement thereat—Indian treaty—Brandt and his two hundred warriors at Duncan's falls—He is visited by Louisa St. Clair, who conducts him to the governor's house—Seeks her to wife—Is repulsed by the governor, and returns to his camp crazed in love.

SCENE XIII.

Harmar marches to the Maumee—His defeat—St. Clair renews the fight—His defeat—Indians around Marietta, at the forts, and declare no white man shall plant corn in Ohio—Scenes at Marietta—Wayne comes—Marches to the Maumee, and his victory—Return of peace—Ohio settled by white men.

LAST SCENE.

Death and burial of Putnam and Heckewelder—Tableaux of the great State covered by three million of inhabitants—Owning twenty-three hundred million dollars of property—Paying twenty-three million dollars taxes—Riding on five thousand miles of their own railroad, within her borders—Supporting twelve thousand common schools, two hundred colleges and academies—Three hundred and fifty newspapers and periodicals printed in the State, with two million readers.

In conclusion the editor asks the commendation of the press, by inserting this summary in their papers.

CONTENTS.

CHAPTER VIII.

CHAPTER IX.

CHAPTER X.

CHAPTER XI.

CHAPTER XII.

CHAPTER XIII.

LEGENDS AND TRADITIONS.

HISTORICAL CORRECTIONS AND ERRORS.

There being a distance of one hundred and sixty miles between the editor and type-setters, he was unable to see revised proofs, consequently errors have intervened. He calls attention to the most prominent for the reader to correct:

On page 14, read "who," after "lawgiver;" page 16, read "the tribes," instead of "they;" page 37, "Whitewoman," should be "Walholding;" page 56, "present," should be "original;" 63, "between" read "about;" 65, read "recover," instead of "receive;" 74, read "and the fact," after "plains;" 147, after "from," read "the scenes of;" 159, after "north-west," read "and;" 181, read "vowed," for "avowed;" 189, after "preach," put a "period," and omit "quotation marks;" 217, read "1762" instead of "1792;" 242, read "1781, instead of "1789;" 275, read "valleys," for "counties;" same page, read "Callender, a relation of," before the word "General;" 289, add "Lewis D. Campbell, Vice-President;" 291, read "William T. Bascomb," instead of "Josiah Hartzell;" 298, read "south," instead of "north;" 305, after "valley," read "who came after 1800;" 320, fill first dash, "1819;" second, "80 odd;" pages 321 &c., death-roll, in some cases the death may have been in the latter part of the year before, or the forepart of the year after the one given; 324, read "four thousand," instead of "four hundred," 322, read "1853," instead of "1653;" read "Saffer" as "Laffer," Kinsey, as Knisely, Trupp, as Trapp, Nepart, as Neighbor, Langhead, as Laughead, Nugill, as Nugen, &c.; page 346, read "ten per cent.," instead of "six; same page, read "$10 per head," instead of "$5;" 351, after "Joseph W. White," read "1863 to 1865;" 347, for "mame," read "name;" 353, read "G. W. Hill," after "B. F. Nelson," &c.

In Appleton's Cyclopedia, of sixteen volumes, which occupied the time and scrutiny of a dozen editors several years, it is stated on page 349, of volume 6, that "British frontiersmen," massacred the ninety odd Christian Indians at Gnadenhutten in 1782. These murderers were Williamson's American borderers, aroused to fury by the murders committed by Indians under pay of the British at Detroit, and Simon Girty's band of colonial renegades.

In Evert's Atlas of Stark County, 1875, it is stated that in 1802 there were five thousand Delaware warriors on the Tuscarawas in a distance of eight miles south of Massillon. All the warriors of all the tribes in Ohio did not number five thousand at that time. The Delawares had less than six hundred warriors at Wayne's victory in 1794—the confederated tribes numbering about two thousand. In Harrison's fight with Tecumseh the confederated tribes were less than two thousand. But such errors of fact and the types will occur.

CHAPTER I.

GEOLOGICAL STRUCTURE OF OHIO.

Before noting the coming of men into these valleys, it may be well to refresh the memory as to the geological structure of Ohio.

Going *down* the geological column of the globe, especially as regards North America, the geologist observes the evidence of it having been a molten mass, its surface a sea of fire, and the air nought but sulphurous gas. That after a countless period a crust formed, the air cooled over it, and moisture following, the first rain began to wash a young world.

The turbid waters seeking an outlet through the crevices in the crust caused explosions and earthquakes, ending in upheavals of igneous rocks into continents, and the subsidence of the waters into oceans.

This is the whole story of the action of water in the first, or Eozoic age, when there was no life, according to the elder geologists, but modern discoveries indicate the existence of organized life in that age.

Then came the ages of time classed as:

The Silurian, or age of Mollusks;

The Devonian, or age of Fishes;

The Carboniferous, or age of Plants and Trees;

The age of reptiles; the age of animals, and last the age of man. Omitting the eras, periods, and epochs, in Ohio is found peat and alluvium in the age of man: beaches, terraces, iceberg drift, glacial drift, forest bed and clay in the strata belonging to the age of animals; in the age of reptiles, strata wanting: in the carboniferous age, coal, conglomerate rock, limestone, minerals; in the Devonian age, water-lime, saline rock, shale, and all the rocks found in the Niagara, Clinton and Cincinnati groups; as known to geologists, making twenty-four kinds of strata, repeated many times as in the coal veins. These, as all others, show the action of water as the master force in their formation and deposition, demonstrating the great fact that the sea covered Ohio, sometimes partially, and sometimes entire, sufficiently long to produce all these stratifications, each in turn, and the several series collectively in their turn.

Colonel Whittlesy, of the first geological corps of Ohio, many years ago, estimated the stratas to extend in depth 3566 feet, since which time, by the aid of science, this depth has been increased, but when it is considered, as claimed by some, that each inch of coal counts 2,000 years, it is beyond computation, or human comprehension, to fix the period of all these formations and deposits.

Taking an expanded view of the continents, the geologists find at the bottom of the column minerals, rocks, and limestone, and in the waters, mossy, spongy debris, shells, and coral. Higher up they find in addition sandstone and the ores, and in the waters plants and fishes. Ascending still they find in addition (to gold, silver, iron, and lead,) marble, slate, tin and copper, and in the waters reefs of coral, fossil fishes, and sharks, of great dimensions. Ascending still they find strata of all the rocks and minerals, including dead forests, and plants, converted to coal. Also clay beds, shale, shell beds, fossils, lignite, cement, marl, buhr and building stone, sedimentary sand and gravel, with evidence that mammoth animals roamed over the land, and monsters of the deep swam in every sea long before the age of man.

THE STORY OF ANIMALS.

Among animal and reptile remains found in North America and Europe are mammoths, mastodons, tapirs, carnivores, reindeer, the dinothere—a combination of elephant and whale—two-horned rhinoceros, tigers, lions, bears, hyenas, four times their present size. The ichthyosaurus, forty feet in length with paddles like a whale, and eyes the size of a man's head—the iguanodon, a gigantic reptile, body as large as an elephant—the megalosaurus, a monster reptile seventy feet long—the teleosaurus, a slender reptile, thirty feet, jaws opening six feet—the hadrosaur, a species of kangaroo, twenty feet long—the cimoliasaur, a monster serpent forty feet, are some of the issue of land and water in the ages before man, whose remains have been found by geologists in Europe and America.

In Ohio, the mastodon and elephant roamed. Near Massillon, Ohio, there was dug up in the year 1832, as stated by a gentleman in the Clearfield Banner of that year, two large tusks, measuring each nine feet six inches in length, and eight inches in diameter, being two feet in girth at the largest ends. The outside covering was as firm and hard as ivory, but the inner parts were decayed. They were found in a swamp, about two feet below the surface, and were similar to those found at Big-bone lick, Kentucky, the size of which animal, judging from the bones found, was not less than sixty feet in length. Each tooth of the creature found in Kentucky weighed eleven pounds.

In December, 1868, a Mr. Kennon, of Fairview, Ohio, on the edge of a creek, five miles from the Muskingum River, and ten miles south-east of Zanesville, found a bone of the foreleg, and tooth of a mastodon. The tooth weighed seven pounds and four ounces, and the bone of the leg, or knee, was over two feet in length, and thirty inches in circumference. They were found projecting out of the bank, about four feet below the surface of the land, and near the water. From calculations made at the time, these remains were judged to have belonged to an animal twice the size of a full-grown elephant, and were exhibited by the finder to the junior publisher of this book, and other persons in Cambridge, Ohio, at the time, and taken to the home of Mr. Kennon for preservation.

Other remains of animals of like huge dimensions have been found in these valleys, and elsewhere in the state. Professor Newberry says that in Cuyahoga County numerous portions of the skeletons of elephant and mastodon have been found in the gravel and sand of the Cleveland plateau. In other parts of Ohio they are found in the forest-bed and in the overlying portions of the drift, as well as in the peat marshes that belong to the present geological epoch. Hence it may be concluded that the elephant and mastodon continued to inhabit portions of what is now Ohio from the time when the ancient soil accumulated.

Professor Gilmore says:

"In the summer of 1870, a partial skeleton of a mastodon was found in a swamp in Auglaize County, Ohio. The bones were found in natural juxtaposition and in such shape as to leave no question that the animal was mired and died in the place where he was found. The lower halves of the legs were nearly upright, and in proper relative position, though somewhat sprawled. The bones of the feet were perfectly preserved, together with the distal portion of the lower shaft bones. The upper ends of these bones were somewhat decomposed. The bones of the body and head lay in a crushed and fragmentary condition, about eighteen inches from the surface. Ribs, tusks, vertebra and teeth were in proper place, and the latter were well enough preserved to identify the specimen as an adult and rather large individual of *mastodon giganteus*. The legs being thrust in the mud were best preserved. The body exposed to the air decomposed rapidly, and let the bones fall to the surface of the bog, where they were but partially protected. The overlying peat has been formed since the deposition of the skeleton. The swamp had been cut by some farmers in making a broad ditch, and before drainage had become so firm as to be sparsely covered by trees. There can be no question, however, that the creature lived and died long after the deposition of the drift on which the marsh deposits rest."

THE STORY OF FISHES.

Of fish, the remains of twenty different species have been found in the Ohio coal measures and corniferous limestone. In the waverly group of stone in Southern Ohio, in sediments of the carboniferous age have been found large fish beds; and in Lucas, Delaware, Cuyahoga, Medina, Portage, Summit, Jefferson, Warren, and many other counties, including those of the Muskingum and Tuscarawas valleys, fossil remains of fish, salamanders, and sharks have been found in the shales, coal, and limestone rocks, some of which have been traced back by geologists to their respective Carboniferous and Devonian seas, in accordance with the stratas in which found, these stratas serving with comparatively unerring correctness, to indicate the corner stones of geological time.

It is claimed that the oldest fish remains found in America are those in the carboniferous limestone of the Devonian age, but in Europe fish remains reach down to the Upper Silurian limestones, which in Ohio, are the Cincinnati group, and therein will yet be found these remains.

It is supposed that the first submergence of the Eozoic continent resulted in the deposit of the group of Lower Silurian limestone, which after standing countless ages, the Lower Silurian sea was withdrawn, and succeeded by land surfaces without stratification. Afterward the land was again submerged, the sea reaching nearly as far as before. In the advance, continuance and retreat of the waters of the second submergence, the Upper Silurian strata was deposited, made up in part of the Clinton, Niagara, and Helderberg limestones, from the remains of animals that inhabited the Upper Silurian sea. When the waters again retreated to the ocean basins that have always been sea, and remained millions of years, they again came back in the Devonian submergence, and were filled by hordes of monsters more formidable than the sharks of our day. When the Devonian retreat of seas took place, all the group of great scale armored and bucklered fishes departed, never to return, but when the next or carboniferous submergence took place sharks abounded in great numbers, and reigned as monarchs of the ocean world, while along the shores and in the lagoons of the coal measures, after the retreat of the carboniferous seas, were found the "ganoids," a small glittering scale armored fish which abounded in great numbers. Also amphibeans, many of which were aquatic, and carniverous salamanders not unlike those of this day, but of great dimensions. Some were slender, snake-like without limbs, and from which is traced a connected chain from the ganoids through the amphibeans up to reptiles of our day, for after the retreat of the carboniferous sea, all the space between the Mississippi and Atlantic was left dry land, and never since entirely submerged, and along the lakes and rivers of the Canadian continent, the ganoids of the coal period have continued to exist to the present time.

FORMATION OF THE PLAINS AND BOTTOMS.

Professor Volney says that in 1796, the spring freshet in the Great Miami caused that stream to form but one with the St. Marie, and that he passed over in a boat from the one river which runs into the Ohio, to the other which runs into Lake Erie. The Muskingum, which runs into the Ohio, also at that day communicated by means of the

Tuscarawas, and of small lakes in the present Summit and Stark Counties, with the Cuyahoga, which flows into Lake Erie, and in Volney's day, in the ordinary stages of water in the Cuyahoga, Tuscarawas, and Muskingum, boats passed from the Ohio into Lake Erie with but a very short (if any) portage by land. The recession of waters from the ancient shores of the Muskingum, Tuscarawas, and other streams, forming as we see at this day, first, second, and third stages of flats of land, bear out Mr. Volney in his theory that the Ohio being barred up at one period, burst asunder its barriers little at a time, and in the course of ages the drainage exposed first the plains and then the bottom lands for the use of man. The celebrated Mr. Schoolcraft, in one of his works, while speaking of the tracks two human feet imprinted in a limestone rock, says, "May we not suppose a barrier to have once existed across the lower Mississippi, converting its immense valley into an immense interior sea," and are not the great northern lakes the remains of such an ocean? And did not the demolition of this ancient barrier enable this powerful stream to carry its banks, as it has manifestly done, a hundred miles into the gulf of Mexico? "If," as remarks Professor Priest, "the Mississippi, in bursting down its barriers, drove the earthy matter one hundred miles into the sea, it may well be supposed that if all that space, now the gulf, was then a low tract of country, as its shores are so now, that it was overwhelmed while the higher parts of the coast, now the West India Islands, are all that remain of that doomed country," while on the other hand all that vast expanse of land embraced in Ohio, and other States between northern lakes and the gulf, were drained by degrees, as is shown along the ancient shores of our rivers.

STORY OF THE HILLS, MOUNTAINS, ETC.

During the great submergences of the different ages the action of the waters through fissures on the fire-heated and igneous rocks beneath caused upheavals, forming hills and mountains, and they in turn as the seas retreated produced our valleys and rivers, in efforts of the waters to follow and mingle with the retiring oceans, back in their more ancient basins of carboniferous, Devonian, Silurian, and Eozoic times. But the God of nature, to preserve his works from destruction by the too rapid and all-powerful action of the waters when in motion, seems to have interposed ridges and hills across the valleys and rivers, as terraces, barriers, and water sheds, to prevent the land surface from wastage in washing, and excavating too quickly the rivers, valleys, and gorges.

Thus pent up for ages, these immense back waters produced in turn cold, and that snow, ice, glaciers, with icebergs hanging as pendants at their bottoms, grasping in their freezing embrace bowlders, drift, and rocks, which when a barrier gave way in time in front of the pent up element, by erosion, the glaciers and bergs moved south, the one levelling the land surface, while the other dropped its bowlders, drift, and rock into chasms, gorges, and rivers, as they melted away, thus preparing the earth for the future habitations of men.

ORIGIN OF THE NAMES "MUSKINGUM" AND "TUSCARAWAS."

The Tuscarawas and Muskingum rivers, meandering through parts of Summit, across the counties of Stark, Tuscarawas, Coshocton, Muskingum, Morgan, and Washington, form the valleys called by those names. In early times the valleys and the two rivers were known only as the "Muskingum," but when the whites came the name

"Tuscarawas" was given to all that portion between the dividing ridges in the present Summit County, and the town of Coshocton, near which the Walhonding River intersects the Tuscarawas, and form the Muskingum, which empties into the Ohio at Marietta. In Indian language it was "Mooskingom" or "Elk's Eye."

The name "Tuscarawas" is said by some writers to have been derived from the Tuscarora tribe of Indians, originally in North Carolina, but who it is claimed came to New York State, and became part of the six nation confederation, and afterward some of the tribe wandering west to the Ohio valley, gave their name to the locality of their hunting grounds, and the "a" being substituted for "o" in the spelling, *Tuscarawas* became the historical name the whites gave the river and valley. But as early historians make no mention of the Tuscarora tribe of North Carolina ever having settled in the valley, it is probable that the definition given by Heckewelder is the correct origin of the word. He says Tuscarawas in English means "old town," and that the oldest Indian town in the valley was called "Tuscarawa," being situated near the present Bolivar.

ORIGINAL NAMES OF THE OHIO.

In 1672, a map—attributed to La Salle—calls the Ohio by the Iroquois name of "Olighin Sipon," or, as called by the Ottowas, "The Beautiful River."

A map of 1687 calls it "Dono," or "Albacha" (Ohio or Wabash). A Dutch map of 1708 calls it "Oubach." A map of 1710 makes the Ohio and Wabash one river, and calls it "Oho." In 1711 it is called "Ochio." In 1719 it is called "Saboqnungo," and after that the French named it "Labelle," or beautiful river, and the name finally settled down to the word "Ohio."

THE WATER SHED OF OHIO.

Professor Newberry traces the water shed dividing the basin of Lake Erie from the waters of the Ohio. "This water shed," says Newberry, "forms a range of high lands that slope by long and easy descent to the Ohio." "The trough of the Ohio is excavated in a plain, and the somewhat striking features which it presents are all the result of the erosion of this plain, which, still unbroken, forms the larger part of our area. North from the Ohio the plateau has been excavated to form the broad valleys of the Miami, the Scioto, and the Muskingum." "Our topographical features may therefore be described as those of a plain slightly raised along a line traversing it from north-east to south-west, and worn in the lapse of time by the draining streams into broad valleys." "On a line drawn from Cincinnati to Marietta we begin in the excavated valley of the Ohio, four hundred and thirty-two feet above the ocean, and one hundred and thirty-three feet below the surface of Lake Erie." Going east the summit is reached of the divide between the Miami and Scioto five hundred and fifty-three feet above Lake Erie. The Scioto valley is bordered on the east by a divide which separates the waters of the Scioto from the Hocking about six hundred feet above Lake Erie. Between Athens and Harmar there is a divide separating the valley of the Hocking from that of the Muskingum, which latter has an altitude at its mouth of one hundred and thirty feet above Cincinnati, or about the level of Lake Erie, and reaches northwest to Massillon, in Stark County, where the Tuscarawas has an altitude of three hundred and thirty feet above Lake Erie, part of which is accounted for by the fact ascertained by borings at Canal Dover and other points that the Tuscarawas has been filled up and now runs nearly two hundred feet above its rocky bed of the carboniferous age—an age which involved the extermination of all plant and animal life, and the formation of coal.

Beginning with another line of observation, and running from the west margin of Ohio through Darke, Mercer, Logan, Delaware, Knox, Coshocton, Tuscarawas, Carroll, and Jefferson to Steubenville, Newberry premises that the great divide separating the waters of Lake Erie from the waters of the Ohio has an altitude, on the line dividing Darke and Mercer counties, of six hundred feet above Lake Erie, while in the valley of the great Miami it is but two hundred and eighty feet, and in Logan County nine hundred and seventy-five feet above Lake Erie, the highest point of land in Ohio above the lake. Proceeding east through Delaware, the altitude is less than three hundred feet, and in Knox County the divide between the Scioto and Muskingum is in some places eight hundred feet above Lake Erie. From Coshocton the line of observation runs in the valley of the Tuscarawas an east and west course to Uhrichsville, thence to Steubenville, passing the divide separating the waters of the Tuscarawas from those of the Ohio at an altitude of eight hundred feet above Lake Erie at some points, and on reaching Steubenville the altitude is but seventy-six feet above the lake, showing the ancient bed of the Ohio far below the present stream.

A third line from the northwest corner of the State of Ohio, to the Pennsylvania line in Trumbull County, crosses the great divide in the north-east portion of the State, and in the north and west at Elyria, Monroeville, Fremont, Napoleon, &c., it crosses streams flowing toward the lake in valleys which in depth bear no comparison with those of the rivers draining the southern slope of the divide. These differences in the two slopes of the water shed are accounted for thus: After the ice had retired from the southern part of the State, the lake basin was still occupied by a glacier which reached far beyond the present lake basin, and when that ice sheet moved from the north-east toward the south-west, it planed down the surface north of the water shed, filling the old channels of the draining streams, producing a level plain, and that after the ice had left all Ohio, the water for ages covered all north of the great divide, which became the shore of the great fresh water sea, while the slope south of the divide was exposed to surface erosion, and covered more deeply with earthy sediments.

Hence the later theory is that the Ohio and all its tributaries—Muskingum, Tuscarawas, Scioto, &c.—have been running in nearly the same valleys they now occupy ever since the carboniferous age.

That the water shed kept back the lake waters of Erie north, while the draining streams of the Tuscarawas, Muskingum, &c., in eastern Ohio, and the Scioto, Miami, &c., in the west, collected the overflow of the water shed, and the rain fall below, carrying them to the Ohio, and it in turn emptying them into the Mississippi, which discharged them into the sea; and in Indiana and other States the waters were kept back by like barriers, and drained by their rivers in like manner as the Ohio and Mississippi.

But that both these great streams had barriers barring them up for ages, as Volney and Schoolcraft respectively suggest, there can be no doubt. When they gave way, such was the flow of pent up waters that here, in these valleys, the Tuscarawas and Muskingum cut their channels deep through all the coal veins to rock bottoms, at some points nearly two hundred feet below the present river beds, and in Indiana where Fort Wayne stands, a large river flowing to the lake, and which Newberry says, "never had a name, and no man ever saw," ceased to flow north, and disappeared, as its ancient shores now tell. In the South they have a tradition of a "sunken land," overwhelmed by the elements from the north in ages past—as has happened in our time by fire and sword—and the reader of this story of water may stop and ponder on the coincidence, while further reflecting on the geological fact, that the drainage of the land he lives in cost all that drowned country now lying at the bottom of the Gulf of Mexico.

LEGEND OF THE KOPHS.

At the time of a deluge in the Psychozoic era, the western continent was subjected to the same submergence as was the eastern continent, except that portions of the elevated regions were not covered by water, a fact which is corroborated by the most learned geologists of the present and past centuries. On these elevated regions existed a race approximating to human beings, in that they had powers of locomotion on two feet like man, and similar powers to move on all fours like animals. Their muscular power was equal to the gorilla of this day, and their intellectual power equal to that of man. Their stature was that of the largest of the human race, when standing erect, and when moving on hands and feet, were the size of the largest of the Koph tribe alluded to in the second book of Kings. It is related that one of the tribe was captured and presented to King Solomon, as one of the curiosities of the land of Ophir, by one of that monarch's captains, on his return therefrom with a vessel having for cargo a full load of gold. On one of the monuments of King Thosmes of Thebes, was also found a representation of a Koph in his animal posture, having every appearance of a beardless face, but covered with a coat of long hair from the top of his skull downward to his rump, fitted by nature in folds to his body like unto the cowl and gown of a priest of modern times when he stood erect.

Such were the race of ante-deluvians spared on this continent by the deluge, and on the subsidence of the waters they re-appeared on the table lands along the banks of lakes and streams, and procured a precarious living by the net and sling, in part, and by clubs and stones, their weapons of war, until they were exterminated by a more civilized race.

Another legend is, that when the nomadic Indians reached this continent, about seven hundred years after the flood, and before the birth of Christ, about fourteen hundred and forty years, they found access thereto through Asia and Europe to the Mediterranean, thence by the Canary Islands over a large continent, the size of Africa, stretching from those isles across to what is called the West Indies at this day. These were the outermost shores of the American continent, and the sea now known as the Gulf of Mexico did not exist, but instead thereof all that space was a fruitful and prolific land.

LEGEND OF THE ISRAELITES PEOPLING THIS CONTINENT.

A tradition exists that the Israelites first peopled America. It is a biblical fact that ten of the tribes of Israel were taken north and west about seven hundred years after the flood, or fourteen hundred years B. C. It is a geological fact that the Canary Islands were once a part of the outer rim of the land connecting the eastern with another continent, and that the West India Islands of this day were once the outer fringe of land connecting the western continent with another, and it is handed down in tradition, that a continent did exist in the intervening space of the size of Africa as known at this day. The tradition is given in Washington Irving's Life of Columbus, volume 3, page 401, as follows:

"The island Atalantis is mentioned by Plato in his dialogue of Timæus Solon, the Athenian lawgiver, is supposed to have traveled into Egypt. He is in an ancient city on the Delta, the fertile island formed by the Nile, and is holding converse with certain learned priests on the antiquities of remote ages, when one of them gives him a description of the island of Atalantis, and of its destruction, which he describes as having taken place before the destruction of the world. The island he was told had been situated in the western ocean, opposite to the Straits of Gibraltar. There was an easy passage from it to other islands, which lay adjacent to a large continent, exceeding in size all Europe and Asia. Neptune settled on this island, from whose son, Atlas, its name was derived, and he divided it among his ten sons. His descendants reigned here in regular successions for many ages. They made irruptions into Europe and Africa, subduing all Lybia as far as Egypt, and Europe to Asia Minor. They were resisted, however, by the Athenians, and driven back to their Atlantic territories. Shortly after this there was a tremendous earthquake, and an overflowing of the sea, which continued for a day and a night. In the course of this the vast island of Atalantis, and all its splendid cities and warlike, nations were swallowed up and sunk to the bottom of the sea, which, spreading its waters over the chasm, formed the Atlantic ocean. For a long time, however, the sea was not navigable on account of rocks and shelves, of mud and slime, and of the ruins of the drowned country."

CHAPTER II.

ANCIENT HISTORY IN STARK, TUSCARAWAS, COSHOCTON, MUSKINGUM, MORGAN, AND WASHINGTON COUNTIES.

The early history of the valleys of the Tuscarawas and Muskingum belong to the six river counties of Washington, Morgan, Muskingum, Coshocton, Tuscarawas, and Stark, equally, as it was up and down these valleys they principally ranged, from the Cuyahoga to the Ohio. The eastern counties and the counties west can also justly claim that they, too, are indirectly interested in whatever took place between the red and white men in the six valley counties named. But as the enumeration of incidents of the other counties would necessitate details disproportionate to the size in which this volume is gotten up, it is determined to speak of the tribes who made their homes, and performed their principal evolutions in what is now the six counties named, with an occasional digression into other territory.

As part of the earliest aboriginal, and mound, and cave history of Stark County, the reader will find interesting details touching the supposed cave dwellers in the northern portion, and of Post's efforts to establish a mission in the southern portion, while he was in the service of the Pennsylvania Colony, 1761–2.

As part of the history of what is Tuscarawas County will be found in Gist's journey in 1750, Schoenbrunn and other settlements in 1772–3, and the massacre in 1782.

As part of the history of Coshocton County will be found the events of Boquet's expedition in 1764; the Delaware capital in 1774–5; the settlement at Lichtenau, &c., and General Brodhead's campaign of 1780.

As part of the history of Muskingum County will be found Dunmore's war in 1774; the Waketomeka campaign, and incidental Indian fighting.

As part of the history of Morgan County will be found the Indian slaughter at Big Bottom, and other incidents of Indian warfare.

As part of the history of Washington County will be found St. Clair's campaign, erection of Fort Harmar, Harmar's campaign, fights with the Indians about Marietta, &c.

As regards the residue of Indian historical events they apply to other counties also, or, in other words, form State history.

STORY OF THE CAVE DWELLERS IN STARK.

Circumstantial evidence leads to the conclusion that cave dwellers were the first inhabitants of Ohio, and that they appeared at the head of the valleys under consideration in this volume.

Colonel Charles Whittlesy, president of the Northern Ohio Historical Society, in his publication of an exploration along the Cuyahoga from its source to its mouth, discloses the fact that he found artificial habitations made in the rocks forming the sides of the river, which, though narrow, has cut a channel down the northern side of the dividing ridge between that river and the Tuscarawas. In places the chasm made is deeper than the stream is wide at its head, and on the sides were caves containing bones of animals, and of men, showing that they were once inhabited by human beings.

General Bierce, in his history of Summit County, corroborates from personal examination the statements of Colonel Whittlesy as to the caves, and he further relates that in Green township, formerly of Stark County, now of

Summit, on the east side of the Tuscarawas, great numbers of stones were found by the white settlers of Stark County on an elevated plateau. They varied from four to six feet in circumference, and were elevated slightly above the land surface, with a comparatively even surface on the top, on which it is supposed sacrifices of human beings or of animals were made to appease the wrath or propitiate the favors of some ancient god or gods. Near by is the old Indian trail, used by the Indians in passing from the Sandusky country to the Ohio, along the ridge, but no evidence was found about these stone altars, either in calcined bones of burnt prisoners, or of charred wood, or Indian implements, to indicate that the altars had been made use of for any purpose by the modern race of Indians, and in the absence of other evidence the conclusion is that the altars were erected by the ancient race who domiciled in the caves, and were probably the first of mankind in Ohio.

Passing down the Cuyahoga, Colonel Whittlesy found earth-works and evidences of a later race than the cave dwellers above, and further on toward the lake he found what approaches to regular fortifications, evincing a still higher civilization than the earth-workers above, but he leaves his readers to form their own conclusions, he simply giving the facts he uncovers.

What are the conclusions therefrom forced on the mind? Why, that first there was a race, who not knowing the use of tools, and who lived in caves among rocks, and piled up loose stones to worship or use in worship. Second, a race who could move earth with implements, and erect earth defences, or piled up earth into great mounds for burial, sacrificial or military purposes. Third, a race who worked stone and earth with other improved implements into regular fortifications, and places of abode or worship. Fourth, the race of red men who came after, and kicked down the stone altars, and earth-works, struck fire from a flint, burned all they could of the ancient fortifications, using only for themselves the bow and arrow, stone hatchets and stone arrows, with bark canoes, and thongs of animal hides for fishing and hunting purposes, while the mounds of the ancients were left unharmed as places of lookout, or of burial for their chiefs and warriors. As to who the supposed "cave dwellers" were, and from whence they came, will never be satisfactorily settled.

But three important geological facts when put together renders it an easy task to conjecture their origin. First, it is beyond contradiction that certain portions of this continent are the oldest portions of the earth's surface, and contain its Eozoic crust, without evidence of marine beds, or other proofs of submergence by any floods since that day. Certain areas in northern New York, Canada, Labrador, and west of the Mississippi, in Missouri, Arkansas, Dakota, Nebraska, &c., remain as in Eozoic time.—*See Dana's Geology, page* 135, 136, 137, *and* 138. Second, from the Mississippi River to the Atlantic Ocean no sea has entirely overflown this land since the close of the carboniferous age—the age that produced the plants and forests, out of which coal was formed. Third, at the time the carboniferous sea disappeared, the water shed holding back the mass of waters of the lake existed, and on which dry land first appeared in Ohio. This water shed traversed the State from south-west to north-east, in the direction of the Canadian and New York highlands.

Mr. Atwater, the antiquarian, in his work on the antiquities of America, holds to the opinion that the people who put up stone altars, earth-works, and fortifications, commenced their work at the head of the northern lakes, thence along their borders into what is now western New York, thence in a south-western direction, following rivers to and down the Ohio and Mississippi, thence to the city of Mexico, as now known, where they had their central seat of power, and from which locality radiated colonies into what is now known as South America, and other countries.

MOUND BUILDERS IN STARK AND TUSCARAWAS.

Following down the valley, the history of a later race is written, as shown by their mounds and earth-works, found near Massillon, Navarre, and Bethlehem, in Stark County, and near Bolivar, New Philadelphia, and New Comerstown, in Tuscarawas Counties.

Zeisberger, when he stopped in 1771 at the Big Spring, two and one half miles south-east of New Philadelphia, the spring since called Schoenbrunn (or fine spring), found on the plain above it the clearest evidences of an amphitheater, or circular earth-work, rimmed at the edge with the thrown up earth, and close by on the bank he found three mounds or tumuli of the ordinary height of scriptural mounds, satisfying him that the race who constructed them were more warlike and better acquainted with making defensive positions than the Indians of his day.

Across the river, on the west bank, and nearly opposite the eastern part of the present New Philadelphia, and not a a mile from its court house, are the remains—now obliterated from view, but twenty years ago plainly discernible—of an earth-work or moat, extending in a semi-circular form around the river front of an old cornfield, as the Indians called it, and which had been used prior to the advent of the Christian Indians (in 1772). They were unable to give any account of it, other than that of an old Indian, who came to the mission; and who claimed to be descended from a nation who inhabited this territory many hundreds of years, and were driven away to the south-west by a more ferocious race of men from the north. He had a tradition that his ancestors knew some of the arts, as known to the missionaries—that they were a peaceful people, and devoted much of their time to the worship of deities—that wherever a sufficient number sojourned for a time they constructed works of defence, and for worship, and sacrifice. A short distance from this ditch or moat was a mound on higher ground, on the summit of which large trees were growing when the first white settlers reached the valley. Partial excavations made many years ago exhumed arrow heads, dust as of earthen-ware that had been burnt, and the calcined dust of bones supposed to be human, from which the mound was judged to be the sepulcher of a noted person of the by-gone times, and has never been opened since.

Near the town of New Comerstown, and on the bank of the Ohio Canal, below Port Washington, were found, when the canal was being constructed, the remains of earth-works and earth forts, similar to those discovered higher up the river. What is the more remarkable in this connection, is the fact that although stone was abundant near all the earth-works of those early colonists who constructed them, yet none appears to have been used, whether from religious prohibition, or inability to utilize the rocks of the river hills.

THE ANCIENT RACE AT COSHOCTON, MOUND, ETC.

In the county of Coshocton, as we pass west on the Pan-Handle Railroad, and just before crossing the Muskingum River, two miles, or thereabouts, from the county seat, is seen to the right a large plain in the river bend, of several hundred acres, and on the east bank of the river, a few hundred yards from the bridge, a large mound thirty or forty feet high, with trees thereon. In its vicinity, Zeisberger settled Lichtenau, in 1776, and he was attracted to the spot from the numerous evidences of an ancient race having been buried there, more civilized than the Indians of his day. The missionaries have left but meager details of what they there found, but enough to clearly prove that the inhabitants understood the use of the ax, the making of pottery, and division of areas of land in squares, &c. In a large grave-yard, which covered many acres, human bones or skeletons were found, less in stature than the average Indian by a foot and a half. They were regularly buried in rows, heads west and feet east, as indicated by the enameled teeth in preservation, so that the disembodied spirits on coming out of the graves would first see the rising sun, and make their proper devotional gestures to their great Spirit or God. From approximate measurement this graveyard contained ten acres, and has long since been plowed up and turned into cornfields. The race of beings buried there averaged four feet in height, judging from the size of the graves, and layers of ashes. Estimating that twenty bodies could be buried in a square rod, this human sepulcher, if full, would have contained over thirty thousand bodies, and the ordinary time required to fill such a graveyard, would not be less than five hundred years, in a city the size of Coshocton of the present day, assuming that the generations averaged thirty-three years of life. One skeleton dug up from this grave-yard is said to have measured five and one half feet, and the skull to have been perforated by a bullet. The body had been dismembered, and iron nails, and a decayed piece of oak were found in the grave.

On the farm of a Mr. Long, about fifteen miles south-west of St. Louis, was found, many years ago, an ancient burying ground, containing a vast number of small graves, indicating that the country around had once been the seat of a great population of human beings, of less than ordinary size, similar in every respect to those found near Coshocton. But on opening the graves they found the skeletons deposited in stone coffins, while those at Coshocton bore evidence of having been buried in wooden coffins. After opening many of the graves, all having in them skeletons of a pigmy race, they at length found one, as at Coshocton, denoting a full developed large sized man, except in length, the legs having been cut off at the knees, and placed along side the thigh bones. From this fact many scientific men conjectured that there must have been a custom among the inhabitants of separating the bones of the body before burial, and that accounted for the small size of the graves. The skeletons, however, were reduced to white chalky ashes, and therefore it was impossible to determine whether such a custom existed or not.

A custom is said to have existed among certain tribes of the western Indians to keep their dead unburied until the flesh separated from the bones, and when the bones became clean and white they were buried in small coffins. The Nanticoke Indians of Maryland had a custom of exhuming their dead, after some months of burial, cutting off from the bones all the flesh and burning it, then drying and wrapping the bones in clean cloths, and reburying them, and whenever the tribe removed to new hunting grounds the bones of their dead were taken along. It is known that this tribe removed to western Pennsylvania, and portions of them came to the Muskingum valley with the Shawanese. Zeisberger had two Nanticoke converts at Schoenbrunn, and one of whom (named Samuel Nanticoke) affirmed—as tradition goes—that this pigmy grave-yard at Lichtenau was their burying ground, and contained the bones of their ancestors, carried from one place to another for many generations, and found a final resting place in these valleys, when their posterity became too weak, from the wastage of war, to remove them elsewhere.

THE MOUND AND FORT BUILDERS IN THE COUNTIES OF MUSKINGUM, MORGAN, WASHINGTON, AND OTHER LOCALITIES.

In the year 1826, an English traveler named Ash visited the ancient mounds and forts on the Muskingum, and made some explorations of them. The party procured guides and workmen at Zanesville, and proceeded west five miles from that place, where mounds, barrows, forts, and ramparts of great variety and form were found, which then showed plainly their magnitude and magnificence. The works were of triangular form, and occupied almost the whole surface of a large plain that is bounded by ranges of high hills. The first excavation made was into a large barrow, which was found at the southern end of the group. At a depth of three feet from the surface the shovelers struck a fine mould, and under this were regular layers of flat stones, which had evidently come from the hills in the vicinity. Under the stones were the remains of human frames, placed in rows with a flat stone between them. The bones were in a very advanced state of decay, and instantly crumbled into powder when exposed to the air. A careful calculation satisfied the party that this mound or barrow contained at least two thousand skeletons. In one of the little compartments was found a stone pipe, carved to represent a bear's head, and some pieces of fine pottery.

The party next opened a large flat mound, situated near the center of the group, upon which nothing was growing but a multitude of different kinds of wild flowers. After throwing off the top of this mound to a level with the plain, nothing was found to indicate that it contained any remains. As the party were about to leave it and move to another, one of the men carelessly jumped from the outer bank into the excavation for a spade, when the ground gave way under all of them, and they went down about three feet. Upon examining further it was found that a platform of decayed timbers had given way, which covered a hole measuring four feet by seven, and four feet deep. After considerable digging with the expectation of finding bones, the spades struck hard substances, which proved to be round stones like bodies, nine inches in diameter, and weighing about twenty pounds each. They resembled a mortar shell in size and general appearance, but upon being scraped with sharp instruments the surface became yellow like gold. At this discovery the workmen became almost wild with joy, believing that their fortunes were in their grasp. Upon consultation it was agreed to cover up the "diggings," take one of the "nuggets," and return to Zanesville to test it.

After having arrived at the town a private room was secured, in which the party gathered to witness the trial by fire. A few moments after being placed in the fire the ball turned black, filled the place with a sulphurous odor, and then burst into ten thousand fragments. The inmates rushed from the house pell-mell into the street, and gazed upon each other in mutual wonder and astonishment. After the smoke cleared away they found their gold ball to be nothing more than a sort of metal called sprite or pyrites, composed of sulphur and iron, which abounds in the valley hills.

On the banks of a creek on the west side of the Muskingum, in Morgan County, were found numerous small mounds, the bases of which were composed of hard burned bricks about five inches square, and on the bricks were charcoal cinders mixed with particles of calcined bones of human frames. The general shape and size of the mounds showed that the bones had been first burned on the brick altars, and afterward covered with earth to protect them and mark the spots. One of these mounds was over twenty feet square, and the bricks plainly showed the action of the fire. This mound was covered with large trees, some of which were ascertained to be at least five hundred years old. Lying on the ground were found trees in a state of decay that had fallen from old age. From a minute calculation of the age of the fallen trees and those yet standing, it was found that the mound was at least a thousand years old.

In Washington County, four miles from the mouth of the Muskingum, and not far from that stream, was found an eminence, evidently the work of human beings, the summit of which was flat, and the sides covered with growing trees. An excavation on the top of this eminence failed to disclose any stones or other marks which might lead to the supposition of its being a place of interment for the dead. The land thereabout was undulating, but not sufficiently hilly to obstruct a view from this mound for several miles, which goes far to prove it a place for observation. It is reasonable to suppose that these eminences—there were others found in the vicinity—were the posts for lookouts or sentinels, from which an advancing foe could be seen in time to prepare for an attack. They may have been used as points on which to kindle beacon fires in the night time, such as were used on the heights of Scotland in the times of Bruce and Wallace, or those of the Persians, who in this way worshiped the Oramaze, the god who made all things.

On the west side of the Muskingum, a short distance further north, and on the banks of a small creek which empties into the river, skirted by hills, were found traits of a large number of people having once lived there. On each side of the creek were semi-circles of a huge rampart, containing at least three acres. The remains of two stone abutments were discovered directly opposite each other, on the banks of the creek, and at the center of the circle, which established the fact of there having been a bridge connection between the two forts. The timber which grew on the ramparts and within the inclosure was large and of great age, some trees being seven feet in diameter.

Some distance further up the creek were found a great number of mounds, in regularly formed circles, and cut in two by the creek, or the large circle down the stream. At some distance back from the creek were two large mounds, about twelve feet high. They were composed principally of stone from the creek banks. Heavy timber grew on these mounds also. Here had been placed the remains of the people who inhabited the towns inclosed within the large circles. From all this it is highly probable that the mounds forming the circles were the dwelling places of the ancient race that inhabited these places.

On the east side of the Muskingum, on an elevated plain, about half a mile from the Ohio, were found a large fortification, or town, nearly a mile in circumference. One large fort was almost square in shape, and contained about forty acres, surrounded by a rampart of earth about eight feet high and twenty-four feet wide at the base. Three openings or gateways were on each side, the largest being the center one on the side facing the river. From this outlet was a road formed of two parallel walls of earth about two hundred feet apart. These walls were twenty feet high on the inside, five on the outside, and forty in width at the base. The road descended gradually toward the low ground near the river, which probably reached the ends of the walls when the works were constructed. Inside of this fort, at the north-west corner, was an oblong elevated square one hundred and eighty feet long, one hundred and thirty-two broad, and nine high, level on the summit, and nearly straight on the sides. Near the south wall was also an elevated square, one hundred and twenty by one hundred and fifty feet, and eight feet high, similar to the other, excepting that instead of an ascent to go up on the side next to the wall there was a hollow way, ten feet wide, leading twenty feet toward the center, then rising with a gradual slope to the top. This was thought to have been a secret passage. A third elevated square was in the south-east corner, and measured fifty by one hundred feet, with ascent at the ends ten feet wide. In addition to this forty acre fort was one containing twenty acres, with a gateway on each side, and at each corner was a circular mound. A short distance from this smaller fort was a conical mound, over one hundred feet in diameter at the base, and thirty feet high. Around it was a ditch four feet deep, fifteen wide, and defended by a parapet four feet high, through which was a gateway twenty feet wide. In one corner of the outside wall of the great fort was a reservoir, twenty-five feet in diameter, with its sides raised above the level four feet. It was thirty feet deep and tapered to a point at the bottom like a funnel.

On the west side of the Muskingum, Mr. Ash found an eminence which commanded a fine view of Marietta and the rivers, up and down, displaying a great distance along the narrow valley of the Ohio. After an inspection of this place it was believed to have been once occupied as a point of observation, or a strong hold. The summit denoted artificial construction, and was oval in shape, being twenty-three by forty-five feet. Around the base was a wall of earth which was too much decayed to calculate its size when built. A heavy growth of timber grew over the whole. Upon closer examination a small hole or orifice was found below the roots of a large tree which grew on the very summit. Several flat stones were removed from around the hole, when other larger ones appeared below, and under these a bed of river sand a foot deep. Upon removing the sand a hollow paved with flat stones came into view. These being removed another bed of sand was found, and under it another bed of stones neatly fitted together. Under these was what seemed to be a lot of mats in a great state of decay, the dust of which being blown off revealed a beautiful tesselated pavement of small, colored stones; the color and stones arranged in such a manner as to express harmony and shades, and portraying at full length the figure of a man, at the feet of which was a snake coiled up. The body of the figures was composed of dyed woods, bones, &c., which crumbled into dust at contact with the air. The colors of the stones were white, green, blue, and spotted red and white. The whole was affixed in a thin layer of sand, and fitted together with nice precision. Under this was the remains of a skeleton, at least seven feet in length. By the side of the skeleton was found an earthen vessel or urn, in which were several bones and some white sediment. The urn appeared to have been made of sand and flint, and when struck would ring like glass. It held about two gallons, and had a top of the same material. Among other things found were a stone ax, twenty-four arrow points, some beads, a large conch shell, decomposed like chalk, some shreds of cloth and hair, brass rings, upon which were characters engraved, resembling Chinese.

Ancient remains exist at Circleville, also near Chillicothe, Portsmouth, on the Little Miami, at Cincinnati, on the north bank of Paint creek, along the Ohio, near Lebanon, on the Huron River, at the junction of all the rivers along the Mississippi, on the Illinois River, on the Wabash, opposite St. Louis, down at Baton Rouge, and from the Atlantic to the Missouri, &c.

AN ANCIENT MOUND NEAR DRESDEN.

Samuel Park, Esq., who delivered an address in 1870 before the Pioneer Association of Licking County, on the Antiquities of Franklin, Muskingum, and Licking counties, related among other facts the following: "Elder John Smock, a citizen of Perry County, Ohio, aged seventy-one years, and for fifty-one years a citizen of Muskingum county, says when twenty years old he was burning charcoal near Dresden, and with several others had the curiosity to open a mound eight feet high, about one mile north-east of Dresden. On doing so, they found in the middle of the mound, on a level with the surrounding plain, five human skeletons lying in a radiating position with their feet toward the center. With the bones were a large number of flint arrow points, some of them seven inches long, and they appeared to have been deposited in a wooden box, entirely decayed. They also found a stone hammer, shaped like a shoe-hammer, with a groove around the middle, instead of an eye through it. Also a blue marble pipe, eight inches long, one and a half inches wide, a half inch thick, with the bowl in the middle of it. There were three orifices drilled through to the bowl from each end. Mr. Smock said he had often smoked through each of the six orifices. The pipe was nicely executed and ornamented. A brass kettle was also found, of three gallons capacity, bruised and flattened by the weight of earth upon it. There was also found an ax of four pounds weight, long and narrow bit, badly rusted, but showed the iron and steel when ground to a smooth surface." Mr. Park, in commenting on this mound, remarked, "here were found several articles lying in juxtaposition at the bottom of this ancient tumulus that evidently belong to ages not less than three thousand years apart, and with the mode of burial representing several nations."

FORTS AND MOUNDS IN LICKING COUNTY.

Professor Park spent much time visiting and examining mounds and fortifications in Licking County, in the vicinity of Newark, and the townships adjacent. Of mounds in that county there are about one thousand, three hundred of which had not been opened as late as 1870. Some of those opened had no human bones or articles in them; others had bones, remains of pottery, hatchets of stone, &c. Of the fortifications, of which there were many, eight had not been examined as late as 1870. Of those examined nearly all were constructed with the moat or ditch inside the wall. Many were small, not exceeding two hundred feet in diameter, while others inclosed many acres, inside the walls, which ranged from eight to thirty feet in height, made of stone, unburned brick, and earth, in true military form. The Licking County Agricultural Society's grounds are located in one of the largest ancient mound-fortifications, which incloses forty acres of land, and Mr. Park concludes that in it was probably a massive temple or palace of a ruling prince, who ruled over a city having a population equal to that of the whole State of Ohio at the present day.

The professor, after a full investigation, arrives at no definite conclusion as to the origin of these ancient Americans, but thinks their origin may be traced to the general dispersion from the plains of Shinar, and that the state of civilization to which they attained was not borrowed from any other division of the earth, but was the natural growth and development of their own system of mental culture.

LEGEND OF THE NORTHMEN, ETC.

It is evident that the men who erected the forts at the mouth of the Muskingum knew the mechanic arts, while those who erected the earth-works in Coshocton and Tuscarawas, and the stone altars in old Stark County, at the head of the river Tuscarawas, knew but little of those arts. Who they were and whence they came has been the study of antiquarians for nearly a century. One writer claims that America was peopled as early as the time of the siege of Troy. Another insists that in the time of Alexander the Great, his ships touched and landed some of his subjects on the American continent. A third argues that the Roman ships that carried Cæsar's army to Gaul, were of such huge dimensions that the soldiers had to jump into the sea to reach the land, and therefore those ships could cross the ocean in safety, and land the Romans on this continent. A fourth presumes that the Greenlanders, Scandinavians, Icelanders, &c., reached the continent by reason of the numerous islands then in the Pacific and other seas. The Northmen have a tradition that Lief, Biorn, and Eric, each visited this country at different periods between A. D. 700 and A. D. 1000. Welsh writers give a tradition from Powell's history of Wales, that Prince Modoc sailed the second time from his country toward this continent with ten ships and was never heard of afterward. But that tribes of Indians have been found in the far West who speak a language in unison with the Welsh dialect is a well established fact, and the further fact that scraps of ancient Welsh armor have been found at several localities, and among others at the falls of the Ohio, has led antiquarians to believe that Modoc's ships being wrecked on the American coast, portions of their crews wandered among the Aborigines, and in the course of time became Indians. It has been lately avered that the Modocs of Washington territory, speaking as they do a language approximating the Welsh, were descendants of Welsh colonists.

LA SALLE ON THE MUSKINGUM—TWO HUNDRED YEARS AGO.

Robert Cavalier La Salle was born in France, 1635, educated for the ministry, came to Canada, 1667, renounced his contemplated cloister life, and plunged into the wilderness to make a name as an explorer. After crossing Lake Erie in a small trading-boat of his own, he penetrated the wilderness in many directions, following the sources of the Mississippi and its tributaries, and also tracing other rivers. In 1667, he and a companion were among the Senecas, in New York State, seeking guides to lead them to the Ohio, and country of the Shawanese. They gave him a Shawanee prisoner for some hatchets and clothing, and learning the route he intended to take,—up Lake Erie and down the Miamies, they told him of a shorter route to the Ohio. If we take the map, we find a shorter route to the Ohio by leaving the Lake of Cats (Erie) more easterly than the Miami or Maumee, then going up the more easterly stream (Cuyahoga), crossing a short portage (the summit portage of this day), then down a branch of another river (the Tuscarawas), thence down a large river (the Muskingum) with few rapids in it for one hundred miles to the Oubach (Ohio).

There is no data to show that La Salle followed that route, but the facts that he had a Shawanee guide, and wanted to go to the Shawanese country, and the Ohio, by the nearest route, is strong presumptive evidence that he followed these rivers to Marietta, and from that point ascended and descended the Ohio. But here his record is lost for nearly three years, during which his friends had no trace of La Salle. It is in evidence, however, that he did examine the Ohio and its tributaries, and the three lost years may have been taken up in so doing, for a map was made in 1672 supposed to be from data of La Salle. The whole length of the Ohio is laid down with the name it now bears on this map. Whether he reached the Muskingum at its source or at its mouth—he was on it beyond a doubt—and being there it can readily be perceived that a man of his cast of mind would not have left the valley until he had examined the mounds, earth-works, and fortifications at Marietta, Zanesville, Newark, and other points along the Muskingum and branches described in the preceding chapter of this book. This would have taken up much of his lost three years, for such a prolific territory touching the ancient Americans had not then been found in his travels.

He afterward returned to Canada, and in process of time wandered down the Mississippi, took possession of the whole country in the name of France, and called it Louisiana. Returning to Quebec in 1683 he sailed for France, came back to Canada, organized another expedition and reached Texas, where he charged one of his expeditionists with murdering his son, and this man shot the father also. Thus perished one of the four great explorers whose portraits now grace the walls of the rotunda at the city of Washington.

Mr. Pierre Margry, of Paris, said to be a descendant of La Salle, has unpublished maps and documents of the great explorer, which have been given to the United States, and will soon be published according to a plan which originated with the Historical Society of Northern Ohio, of which Charles Whittlesy, Esq., is president, and who has published a letter to him from Mr. Margry, containing an extract of one of La Salle's unpublished letters indicating the Maumee and Miami as the route he took to reach the Ohio in 1669. The original extract in French was sent to F. Parkman, Esq., of Jamaica Plain, Massachusetts, author of the publication called "Discovery of the Great West," and who had therein described the Alleghany as the natural route from the Senacas—Onondaga—country to the Shawanese country by way of the Ohio.

In a late letter by the writer of this article to Mr. Parkman, the route by Cuyahoga, Tuscarawas, and Muskingum, was suggested as the probable one taken, and an opinion asked of him. His answer is subjoined:

"JAMAICA PLAIN, August 4, 1875.

"C. H. MITCHENER, ESQ., New Philadelphia, Ohio:

"*Dear Sir:* Returning home yesterday, after an absence of several weeks, I found your letter of July 23.

"In the obscurity which covers La Salle's movements after he left the Lulpitians in 1669, it is not possible to state any thing with confidence as to the course he took to reach the Ohio. The only account that seems to me to deserve to be admitted as evidence is that contained in the unpublished memoir of 1678, of which I have given an account in the 'Discovery of the Great West.' On page 20, *note*, I have printed the only passage which throws any light on the matter. By this it appears that he went by way of Onondaga, whence he seems to have reached and descended the Alleghany.

"What he may afterward have done is at present a matter of conjecture. The extract of one of his letters to which you allude,—meaning as I infer the passage sent by Mr. Margry to Colonel Whittlesy,—is too obscure and self-contradictory to afford safe ground for any conclusion. It is, moreover, without date.

"I have some hope that I may hereafter find the means of answering your questions more satisfactory.

"Yours Respectfully, F. PARKMAN."

From the above Mr. Parkman adheres to his published theory, though not confidently. From the Onondaga country in New York, the seat of ancient power of the Five or Six Nations, to the Shawanee country of Ohio, is about five hundred miles by way of the Cuyahoga, Tuscarawas, and Muskingum; by way of the Alleghany, including the meanderings of the Ohio, over six hundred miles, and by way of the Maumee portage over seven hundred miles. In going south or west the Indians took the shortest route, as did the mound builders before them, and the buffaloes before them.

La Salle, in the absence of positive proof to the contrary, may be considered as following the old trails, when he explored the Ohio two hundred years ago.

OHIO AS PART OF FRANCE.

As early as 1535 the territory called New France, embracing about all the land west of the Ohio, was roamed over by the Jesuits, gaining the friendship of the Indians, and planting the catholic cross in the name of the Holy Father. Such was their success, that in one hundred years their beads and rosaries became as potent to the red man as they have to his white brother in all lands.

In 1713, by the treaty of Utrecht, Louisiana belonged to France, and extended from the gulf to the northern lakes.

In 1748 the treaty of Aix-la-Chapelle quieted French title for a time to this great area, and her forts erected at Niagara in 1726, and at Presqueisle, (signifying peninsula, at the present Erie, Pennsylvania,) and at Le Boeuf, (signifying place of buffaloes, Erie County, Pennsylvania,) frowned upon all trespassers from the dominions of his Britanic majesty in the East.

In 1749 some traders found on the Ohio buried a leaden plate, which they stole and sent to the colonial authorities, containing this inscription in French:

Literal Translation.—"In the year 1749, reign of Louis XV., King of France, we, Celeron, commandant of a detachment sent by monsieur, the marquis of Galissoniere, commander-in-chief of New France, to establish tranquility in certain villages of these cantons, have buried this plate at the confluence of the Ohio and of Po-ra-Da-Koin, this 29th of July, near the river Ohio, otherwise Beautiful River, as a monument of renewal of possession which we have taken of the said river, and of all its tributaries, and of all the land on both sides, as far as to the sources of said rivers,—inasmuch as the preceding kings of France have enjoyed (this possession), and have maintained it by their arms and by treaties, especially by those of Riswick, Utrecht, and Aix-la-Chapelle."

In this same year, the French becoming alarmed at the boldness of English traders from the eastern colonies, in venturing into the Ohio country, sent armed forces thereto to drive them back, and in January, 1750, the Pennsylvania colonial governor informed the council that the past summer a French captain, Celeron, with three hundred French and some Indians, had entered the Ohio valley to reprove the Indians for their friendship to the English, and for suffering the English to trade with them.

JOURNAL OF CHRISTOPHER GIST'S TRIP DOWN THE TUSCARAWAS—SEVENTEEN HUNDRED AND FIFTY.

The English colonies of Pennsylvania and Virginia had licensed traders to traverse this French territory, four of whom had been seized as early as 1749 as trespassers, and were carried as prisoners from the banks of the Ohio into Canada, under charges of tampering with the Indians and endeavoring to seduce them to convey to the English rights in land for powder, lead, and whisky.

Under a deed obtained by the colonies of Pennsylvania, Virginia, and Maryland from some Iroquois chiefs for "all the land beyond the mountains," twelve Virginians, among whom was George Washington, in the year 1748, procured from the king of England, through the governor of Virginia, a grant for half a million acres of land, on both sides of the Ohio River, and between the Monongahela and Kenawha rivers. Of this grant, two hundred thousand acres was to be located at once, one hundred families to be put thereon in seven years, and a fort built sufficient to protect them. The company was called the "Ohio Land Company." They immediately sent out a surveyor, by the name of Christopher Gist, to explore the country, and find the best land. He left the Potomac River, in Maryland, in October, 1750, crossed the Ohio near Pittsburg; thence to the mouth of

Beaver River; thence crossed the country and reached the Tuscarawas River on the 5th of December, at a point opposite the present town of Bolivar. On the 7th he crossed over to an Indian village, and found the Indians in the French interest. Following the river south, he reached another Indian town on the 14th, near the junction of the Tuscarawas and White Woman. This town contained about one hundred families, a portion in the French, and a portion in the English interest. Here he met Andrew Montour, a half breed, and George Croghan, an English trader, who had his head-quarters at this town. In his journal, Gist says:

"When we came in sight of the town we perceived English colors hoisted on the king's (chief's) house, and at George Croghan's. Upon inquiring the reason, I was informed that the French had lately taken several English traders, and that Mr. Croghan had ordered all the white men to come into this town, and had sent runners to the traders of the lower towns, and that the Indians had sent to their people to come and counsel about it.

"Monday, December 17.—Two traders, belonging to Mr. Croghan, came into town and informed us that ten of his people had been taken by forty Frenchmen and twenty Indians, who had carried them with seven horse loads of skins to a new fort the French were building on one of the branches of Lake Erie.

"Tuesday, 18.—I acquainted Mr. Croghan and Mr. Montour of my business with the Indians, and talked much of a regulation of trade, with which they were pleased, and treated me very well.

"Tuesday, 25.—This being Christmas day, I intended to read prayers, but after inviting some of the white men, they informed each other of my intention, and being of several persuasions, and few of them inclined to hear any good, they refused to come; but one Thomas Burney, a blacksmith, who is settled there, went about and talked to them, and then several of the well-disposed Indians came freely, being invited by Andrew Montour. The Indians seemed to be well pleased, and came up to me and returned me their thanks, and then invited me to live among them. They were desirous of being instructed in the principles of Christianity; that they liked me very well, and wanted me to marry them after the Christian manner, and baptize their children, and then they said they would never desire to return to the French, or suffer them or their priests to come near them more, for they loved the English, but had seen little religion among them.

"Wednesday, 26.—This day a woman that had long been a prisoner and had deserted, being retaken and brought into town on Christmas eve, was put to death in the following manner: They carried her without the town and let her loose; and when she attempted to run away, the persons appointed for that purpose pursued her and struck her on the ear on the right side of the head, which bent her flat on her face to the ground. They then struck her several times through the back with a dart to the heart; scalped her, and threw the scalp in the air, and another cut off her head. Thus the dismal spectacle lay until evening, and then Barney Curran desired leave to bury her, which he and his men and some of the Indians did just at dark.

"Friday, January 14, 1751.—One Taaf, an Indian trader, came to town from near Lake Erie, and informed us that the Wyandots had advised him to keep clear of the Ottowas, (a nation firmly attached to the French, living near the lakes,) and told him, that the branches of the lakes were claimed by the French, but that all the branches of the Ohio belonged to them and their brethren, the English, and that the French had no business there, and that it was expected that the other part of the Wyandots would desert the French and come over to the English interest, and join their brethren on the Elk Eye (Muskingum) creek, and build a strong fort and town there.

"Wednesday, 9.—This day two traders came into town from among the Pequantices (a tribe of the Twig Twees), and brought news that another English trader was taken prisoner by the French, and that three French soldiers had deserted and come over to the English, and surrendered themselves to some of the traders of the Picktown (Pipetown), and that the Indians would have put them to death to revenge their taking our traders; but as the French had surrendered themselves to the English, they would not let the Indians hurt them, but had ordered them to be sent under the care of three of our traders, and delivered at this town to George Croghan.

"Saturday, 12.—Proposed a council; postponed; Indians drunk.

"Monday, 14.—This day George Croghan, by the assistance of Andrew Montour, acquainted the king and council of this nation (presenting them with four strings of wampum) that their roggony (father) had sent, under the care of the governor of Virginia, their brother, a large present of goods, which were now landed safe in Virginia, and that the governor had sent me to invite them to come and see him, and partake of their father's charity to all his children on the branches of the Ohio. In answer to which one of the chiefs stood up and said that their king and all of them thanked their brother, the governor of Virginia, for his care, and me for bringing them the news; but that they could not give an answer until they had a full or general council of the several Indian nations, which could not be until next spring; and so the king and council, shaking hands with us, we took our leave.

"Tuesday, 15.—We left Muskingum and went west five miles to the White Woman Creek, on which is a small town. This white woman was taken away from New England when she was not above ten years old by the French Indians. She is now upward of fifty; has an Indian husband and several children. Her name is Mary Harris. She still remembers that they used to be very religious in New England; and wonders how the white men can be so wicked as she has seen them in these woods.

"Wednesday, 16.—Set out south-west twenty-five miles to Licking creek. The land from Muskingum is rich and broken. Upon the north side of Licking creek, about six miles from its mouth, were several salt licks or ponds formed by little streams or drains of water, clear, but of a bluish color and salt taste. The traders and Indians boil their meat in this water, which, if proper care is not taken, will sometimes make it too salt to eat.

"Saturday, 19.—Arrived at Hockhocking, a small town of Delawares.

"Sunday, 20.—Traveled twenty miles south-west to Maguck, another small Delaware town near the Scioto."

After exploring the Scioto bottoms, Gist and his party proceeded to Shawnee town, at the mouth of this stream.

"Here we arrived on the 28th, and fired our guns to alarm the traders, who came and ferried us over the Ohio. This town is situated on both sides of the river, and contains about three hundred men. They are great friends to the English interest. In the evening a proper officer made a public proclamation, that all the Indian marriages were dissolved, and a public feast was to be held for three succeeding days, in which the women, as their custom was, were to choose again their husbands. The next morning early the Indians breakfasted, and afterward spent the day in dancing until evening; when a plentiful feast was prepared. After feasting they spent the night in dancing. The same way they spent the two next days until evening. The men dancing by themselves, and the women in turns, around fires, and dancing in their manner and in the form of the figure eight, about sixty or seventy of them at a time. The women, the whole time they danced, sung a song in their language, the chorus of which was:

> "I am not afraid of my husband,
> I will choose what man I please."

The third day, in the evening, the men, being about one hundred in number, danced in a long string, following one another, sometimes at length, at other times in the figure of an eight, quite around the fort, and in and out of the house where they held their councils, and the women, standing together as the men danced by them, and as any of the women liked a man passing by, she stepped in and joined in the dance, taking hold of the man's blanket whom she choose, and then continued in the dance until the rest of the women stepped in and made their choice in the same manner, after which the dance ended, and they all retired to consummate."

Gist and Croghan proceeded on to the falls of the Ohio, and thence returned home by way of North Carolina.

In 1752 he appeared at Logstown, fourteen miles below Pittsburgh, where the English and Indians had met for a "big talk," the English claiming "all the land beyond the mountains," under the Lancaster treaty of 1744, and the Indians claiming that they only ceded their lands to the warrior's road, at the foot of the Alleghanies.

WASHINGTON AND GIST.

In 1753, Colonel George Washington took Mr. Gist with him as a companion, and journeyed on foot to Fort La Bouef (near present city of Erie, Pa.,)—and in his journal, Washington says: "I took my necessary papers, pulled off my clothes, and tied myself up in a watch-coat. Then I took my gun in hand, and pack on my back, in which were my papers and provisions. I set out with Mr. Gist, fitted in the same manner, on Wednesday, the 26th of December. The day following, just after we had passed a place called *Murdering Town*, we fell in with a party of French Indians who had lain in wait for us. One of them fired at Mr. Gist or me, not fifteen steps off, but missed. We took the fellow into custody and kept him until about nine o'clock at night, then let him go, and walked on the remaining part of the night, without making any stops, that we might get the start so far as to be out of reach of their pursuit next day, since we were well assured they would follow our track as soon as it was light. We continued traveling the next day until quite dark, and got to the river, which we expected to have found frozen, but it was not. The ice I suppose had broken up above, for it was driving in vast quantities. There was no way for getting over but on a raft, which we set about building with but one poor hatchet, and finished just after sun-setting. This was a whole day's work; we next got it launched, then went aboard and set off, but before we were half over we were jammed in the ice in such a manner that we expected every moment our raft to sink, and ourselves to perish. I put out my setting pole to try to stop the raft, when the rapidity of the stream threw it with so much violence against the pole that it jerked me out into ten feet water, but I saved myself by catching hold of one of the raft logs. Notwithstanding all our efforts we could not get to the shore, but were obliged, as we were near an island, to quit our raft and make for it. The cold was so severe that Mr. Gist had all his fingers and some of his toes frozen, and the water was so shut up that we found no difficulty in getting off the island in the morning, and went to Mr. Frazier's. As we intended to take horses, and it taking some time to find them, I went up to the mouth of *Youghiogany* to visit Queen Aliquippa. I made her a present of a watch-coat and bottle of rum, the latter of which she thought the better present of the two. Tuesday, January 1st, left Frazier's, and arrived at Mr. Gist's house at Monongahela. The 6th we met seventeen pack-horses with materials and stores for a fort at the forks of the Ohio (now Pittsburg). The day after we met some families going out to settle, and this day arrived at Wells Creek (now Cumberland).—[*The above is abridged from Marshall's Life of Washington.*]

The effort of this land company, as developed by the trip of Mr. Gist into the Ohio valley, to get a foothold west of the Ohio, aroused the French government, and in 1753 that government took the initiative in erecting a line of forts from the lakes to Louisiana, to protect its interests and keep back the English from occupying French territory. Colonel (afterwards General) Washington was dispatched by the Virginia government to demand information of the French, as to the object of the French troops which had arrived at Presque Isle on their way to the Ohio. As soon as he returned to Virginia, that colony raised and sent troops to the Ohio; but before they arrived the French had erected a fort at Logstown, fourteen miles below Pittsburgh, surprised a block-house of the Ohio company at that place, seized their skins and goods, and killed the English traders except two. The Virginia troops arrived at the junction of rivers above, established a post, but, before finishing it, were surprised and captured by a French force, which immediately erected Fort Duquesne, in 1754, and thus a war was begun between England and France. In 1755, General Braddock was sent out with an English army to recapture the place, but was met by the combined French and Indian forces,—the latter numbering five hundred warriors from the Muskingum, Scioto, and Sandusky, —and defeated.

[*Note.*—In regard to this defeat, General Morris said it was owing to the want of care and caution in the leaders, who held in great contempt the Indian mode of fighting. Washington says the dastardly behavior of the regular troops exposed the whole army. In spite of every effort they broke and run like sheep from the Indians. Colonel Burd says the enemy kept behind trees and logs and cut down the troops as fast as they advanced. The colonial soldiers asked to be allowed to take to trees and fight, but General Braddock called them cowards, and struck some who attempted to tree and fight. It is said of two brothers, named Tom and Joseph Faucett, who had spent their lives in Indian fighting, that Braddock struck Joseph Faucett down with his sword, for taking to a tree. Tom Faucett seeing this aimed at and shot Braddock in revenge. Braddock was buried in the middle of the road, and wagons made to pass over it to hide the grave from the Indians, and marks made on trees to enable his friends to tell where he lay. In 1823 some men repairing this road found his bones with his military trappings, which were sent to Peale's museum, Philadelphia.]

Braddock's defeat assured peace for a time to all the French interests in "New France," west of the Ohio, and opened up the border country of Virginia and Pennsylvania to the murdering incursions of the savages from the west, who penetrated into the heart of each colony, and carried back to our valleys the scalps of the English colonists by scores during 1755, 1756, and 1757.

In 1758, expeditions were sent out by the colonial governments of Pennsylvania and Virginia, to recapture Fort Duquesne, and penetrate the Indian territory. In November, Colonel Washington, and the force with which he was connected, came near the fort, when it was set fire to, and abandoned by the French, and taken possession of by the English, who rebuilt and named it Fort Pitt, after William Pitt, the great English statesman, by whose statesmanship the war was brought to a conclusion, and France, in 1760, yielded to England as well all of Canada as the territory west of the Ohio.

Thus we are justified in saying that the Ohio Land Company, in sending Mr. Gist down these valleys in 1750, to "*find the best lands*," was one of the remote causes of that great European war, which ten years later lost France her principal possessions in America, and, at a period still later, procured for the American colonies a general by whose wisdom England also lost her possessions in the colonies.

CHAPTER III.

CAPTIVITY OF COLONEL JAMES SMITH, IN THE VALLEYS.

Colonel James Smith, a citizen of Pennsylvania, was surprised near Bedford in May, 1755, and taken prisoner by two Delaware Indians. He was lodged at Fort Duquesne at the time of Braddock's defeat, and witnessed barbarities practiced upon prisoners taken in that battle, having himself to run the gauntlet, and submit to tortures more cruel than death itself. He was then taken to an Indian town called *Tulhillas*, on the White Woman, about twenty miles above the forks (or north of Coshocton), inhabited by Delawares and Mohicans, where he remained some months, and underwent the ceremony of being made an Indian. His account of it and other ceremonies is here given from his published narrative, illustrative of the manners and customs of the inhabitants of this territory one hundred and twenty years ago. He says:

"The day after my arrival at the aforesaid town, a number of Indians collected about me, and one of them began to pull the hair out of my head. He had some ashes on a piece of bark, in which he frequently dipped his fingers, in order to take the firmer hold, and so he went on, as if he had been plucking a turkey, until he had all the hair clean out of my head, except a small spot about three or four inches square on my crown; this they cut off with a pair of scissors, excepting three locks, which they dressed up in their own mode. Two of these they wrapped around with a narrow beaded garter made by themselves for that purpose, and the other they plaited at full length, and then stuck it full of silver brooches. After this they bored my nose and ears, and fixed me off with ear-rings and nose jewels; then they ordered me to strip off my clothes and put on a breech-clout, which I did; they then painted my head, face, and body, in various colors. They put a large belt of wampum on my neck, and silver bands on my hands and right arm; and so an old chief led me out in the street, and gave the alarm halloo, *coo-wigh*, several times repeated quick; and on this, all that were in town came running and stood around the old chief, who held me by the hand in the midst. As I at that time knew nothing of their mode of adoption, and had seen them put to death all they had taken, and as I never could find that they saved a man alive at Braddock's defeat, I made no doubt but they were about putting me to death in some cruel manner. The old chief holding me by the hand, made a long speech, very loud, and when he had done, he handed me to three young squaws, who led me by the hand down the bank, into the river, until the water was up to our middle. The squaws then made signs for me to plunge myself into the water, but I did not understand them;—I thought that the result of the council was, that I should be drowned, and that these young ladies were to be the executioners. They all three laid violent hold of me, and I for some time opposed them with all my might, which occasioned loud laughter by the multitude that were on the bank of the river. At length one of the squaws made out to speak a little English (for I believe they begun to be afraid of me) and said, '*no hurt you;*' on this I gave myself up to their ladyships, who were as good as their word; for though they plunged me under water, and washed and rubbed me severely, I could not say they hurt me much.

"These young women then led me up to the council house, where some of the tribe were ready with new clothes for me. They gave me a new ruffled shirt, which I put on, also a pair of leggins done off with ribbons and beads, likewise a pair of moccasins, and garters dressed with beads, porcupine quills, and red hair—also a tinsel laced cappo. They again painted my head and face with various colors, and tied a bunch of red feathers to one of those locks they had left on the crown of my head, which stood up five or six inches. They seated me on a bear-skin, and gave me a pipe, tomahawk, and polecat-skin pouch, which had been skinned pocket fashion, and contained tobacco, killegenico, or dry sumach leaves, which they mix with their tobacco,—also spunk, flint, and steel. When I was thus seated, the Indians came in dressed and painted in their grandest manner. As they came in they took their seats, and for a considerable time there was a profound silence—every one was smoking, but not a word was spoken among them. At length one of the chiefs made a speech, which was delivered to me by an interpreter, and was as follows:

"My son, you are now flesh of our flesh, and bone of our bone. By the ceremony which was performed this day, every drop of white blood was washed out of your veins; you are taken into the Caughnewago nation, and initiated into a warlike tribe; you are adopted into a great family, and now received with great seriousness and solemnity in the room and place of a great man. After what has passed this day, you are now one of us by an old strong law and custom. My son, you have now nothing to fear; we are now under the same obligations to love, support, and defend you, that we are to love and defend one another; therefore, you are to consider yourself as one of our people."

At this time I did not believe this fine speech, especially that of the white blood being washed out of me; but since that time I have found that there was much sincerity in said speech; for, from that day, I never knew them to make any distinction between me and themselves in any respect whatever until I left them. If they had plenty of clothing I had plenty; if we were scarce, we all shared one fate.

"After this ceremony was over, I was introduced to my new kin, and told that I was to attend a feast that evening, which I did. And as the custom was, they gave me also a bowl and wooden spoon, which I carried with me to the place where there were a number of large brass kettles full of boiled venison and green corn; every one advanced with his bowl and spoon, and had his share given him. After this, one of the chiefs made a short speech, and then we began to eat.

"The name of one of the chiefs in this town was Tecanyaterighto, alias Pluggy, and the other Asallecoa, alias Mohawk Solomon. As Pluggy and his party were to start the next day to war, to the frontiers of Virginia, the next thing to be performed was the war dance, and their war songs. At their war dance they had both vocal and instrumental music—they had a short, hollow gum closed at one end, with water in it, and parchment stretched over the open end thereof, which they beat with one stick, and made a sound nearly like a muffled drum,—all those who were going on this expedition collected together and formed. An old Indian then began to sing, and timed the music by beating on this drum, as the ancients formerly timed their music by beating the tabor. On this the warriors began to advance, or move forward in concert, like well disciplined troops would march to the fife and drum. Each warrior had a tomahawk, spear, or war-mallet in his hand, and they all moved regularly toward the east, or the way they intended to go to war. At length they all stretched their tomahawks towards the Potomac, and giving a hideous shout or yell, they wheeled quick about, and danced in the same manner back. The next was the war song. In performing this, only one sung at a time, in a moving posture, with a tomahawk in his hand, while all the other warriors were engaged in calling aloud '*he-uh, he-uh*,' which they constantly repeated while the war song was going on. When the warrior that was singing had ended his song, he struck a war-post with his tomahawk, and with a loud voice told what warlike exploits he had done, and what he now intended to do, which were answered by the other warriors with loud shouts of applause. Some who had not before intended to go to the war, at this time were so animated by this performance, that they took up the tomahawk, and sung the war song, which was answered with shouts of joy, as they were then initiated into the present marching company. The next morning this company all collected at one place, with their heads and faces painted with various colors, and packs upon their backs, they marched off, all silent, except the commander, who, in the front, sung the traveling song, which began in this manner: '*hoo caugh-tainte heegana*.' Just as the rear passed the end of the town, they began to fire in their slow manner, from the front to the rear, which was accompanied with shouts and yells from all quarters.

"This evening I was invited to another sort of dance, which was a kind of promiscuous dance. The young men stood in one rank, and the young women in another, about one rod apart, facing each other. The one that raised the tune, or started the song, held a small gourd or dry shell of a squash in his hand, which contained beads or small stones, which rattled. When he began to sing, he timed the tune with his rattle—both men and women danced and sung together, advancing toward each other, stooping until their heads would be touching together, and then ceased from dancing, with loud shouts, and retreated and formed again, and so repeated the same thing over and over, for three or four hours, without intermission. This exercise appeared to me at first irrational and insipid; but I found that in singing their tunes, they used *ya ne no hoo wa ne, &c.*, like our *fa sol la*, and though they have no such thing as jingling verse, yet they can intermix sentences with their notes, and say what they please to each other, and carry on the tune in concert. I found that this was a kind of wooing or courting dance, and as they advanced, stooping with their heads together, they could say what they pleased

4

in each other's ear, without disconcerting their rough music, and the others, or those near, not hear what they said.

"Shortly after this I went out to hunt, in company with Mohawk Solomon, some of the Caughnewagas, and a Delaware Indian that was married to a Caughnewaga squaw. We traveled about south from this town, and the first night we killed nothing, but we had with us green corn, which we roasted and ate that night. The next day we encamped about twelve o'clock, and the hunters turned out to hunt, and I went down the run that we encamped on, in company with some squaws and boys to hunt plums, which we found in great plenty. On my return to camp I observed a large piece of fat meat; the Delaware Indian that could talk some English, observed me looking earnestly at this meat, and asked me, '*what meat you think that is?*' I said I supposed it was bear meat; he laughed, and said, '*ho, all one fool you, beal now elly pool,*' and pointing to the other side of the camp, he said, '*look at that skin, you think that beal skin?*' I went and lifted the skin, which appeared like an ox-hide; he then said, '*what skin you think that?*' I replied that I thought it was a buffalo hide; he laughed, and said, '*you fool again, you know nothing, you think buffalo that colo?*' I acknowledged I did not know much about these things, and told him I never saw a buffalo, and that I had not heard what color they were. He replied, '*by and by you shall see gleat many buffalo: he now go to gleat lick. That skin not buffalo skin, that skin buck-elk skin.*' They went out with horses, and brought in the remainder of this buck-elk, which was the fattest creature I ever saw of the tallow kind.

"We remained at this camp about eight or ten days, and killed a number of deer. Though we had neither bread nor salt at this time, yet we had both roast and boiled meat in great plenty, and they were frequently inviting me to eat when I had no appetite.

"We then moved to the buffalo lick, where we killed several buffalo, and in their small brass kettles they made about half a bushel of salt. I suppose this lick was about thirty or forty miles from the aforesaid town, and somewhere between the Muskingum, Ohio, and Scioto. About the lick was clear, open woods, and thin white-oak land, and at that time there were large roads leading to the lick, like wagon roads. We moved from this lick about six or seven miles, and encamped on a creek.

"Though the Indians had given me a gun, I had not yet been permitted to go out from the camp to hunt. At this place Mohawk Solomon asked me to go out with him to hunt, which I readily agreed to. After some time we came upon some fresh buffalo tracks. I had observed before this that the Indians were upon their guard, and afraid of an enemy; for, until now, they and the southern nations had been at war. As we were following the buffalo tracks, Solomon seemed to be upon his guard, went very slow, and would frequently stand and listen, and appeared to be in suspense. We came to where the tracks were very plain in the sand, and I said, it is surely buffalo tracks; he said, '*hush, you know nothing—may be buffalo tracks, and may be Catawba.*' He went very cautious until we found some fresh buffalo dung; he then smiled, and said '*Catawba can not make so.*' He then stopped and told me an odd story about the Catawbas. He said that formerly the Catawbas came near one of their hunting camps, and at some distance from the camp lay in ambush; and in order to decoy them out, sent two or three Catawbas in the night past their camp, with buffalo hoofs fixed on their feet, so as to make artificial tracks. In the morning, those in the camp followed after these tracks, thinking they were buffalo, until they were fired on by the Catawbas, and several of them killed; the others fled, collected a party and pursued the Catawbas; but they, in their subtlety, brought with them rattlesnake poison, which they had collected from the bladder that lies at the root of the snake's teeth; this they had corked up in a short piece of a cane stalk; they had also brought with them small cane or reed, about the size of a rye straw, which they made sharp at the end like a pen, and dipped them into this poison, and stuck them in the ground among the grass, along their own tracks, in such a position that they might stick into the legs of the pursuers, which answered the design; and as the Catawbas had runners to watch the motion of the pursuers, when they found that a number of them were lame, being artificially snake bit, and that they were all turning back, the Catawbas turned upon the pursuers and defeated them, and killed and scalped all those that were lame. When Solomon had finished his story, and found that I understood him, he concluded by saying, '*you don't know, Catawba velly bad Indian, Catawba all one devil, Catawba.*'

"Some time after this I was told to take the dogs with me and go down the creek, perhaps I might kill a turkey; it being in the afternoon, I was also told not to go far from the creek, and to come up the creek again to the camp, and to take care not to get lost. When I had gone some distance down the creek, I came upon fresh buffalo tracks, and as I had a number of dogs with me to stop the buffalo, I concluded I would follow after and kill one; and as the grass and weeds were rank, I could readily follow the track. A little before sundown I despaired of coming up with them; I was then thinking how I might get to camp before night. I concluded, as the buffalo had made several turns, if I took the track back to the creek, it would be dark before I could get to the camp; therefore I thought I would take a nearer way through the hills, and strike the creek a little below the camp; but as it was cloudy weather, and I a very young woodsman, I could find neither creek nor camp. When night came on, I fired my gun several times and hallooed, but could get no answer. The next morning early, the Indians were out after me, and as I had with me ten or a dozen dogs, and the grass and weeds rank, they could readily follow my track. When they came up with me, they appeared to be in a very good humor. I asked Solomon if he thought I was running away, he said, '*no, no, you go too much clooked.*' On my return to camp they took away my gun from me, and for this rash step I was reduced to a bow and arrow for nearly two years. We were out on this tour for about six weeks.

"When we returned to the town, Pluggy and his party had arrived, and brought with them a considerable number of scalps and prisoners from the south branch of the Potomac. They also brought with them an English Bible, which they gave to a Dutch woman who was a prisoner; but as she could not read English, she made a present of it to me, which was very acceptable.

"When they killed a buffalo they would lash the paunch of it round a sapling, cast it into the kettle, boil it and sup the broth. They were polite in their own way, passed but few compliments, and had but few titles of honor. Captains or leaders were the highest titles in the military line, and in the civil line chiefs or old wise men. No such terms as sir, mister, madam, or mistress, but in their stead, grandfather, father, uncle, brother, mother, sister, cousin, or my friend, were the terms used in addressing one another. They paid great respect to age, and allowed no one to attain to any place of honor among them, without having performed some exploit in war, or become eminent for wisdom. They invited every one that came to their houses or camps to eat, as long as they had anything to give, and a refusal to eat, when invited, was considered a mark of disrespect. In courting, it was common for a young woman to make suit to a young man, and the men generally possessed more modesty than the women. Children were kept obedient, not by whipping, but by ducking them in cold water. Their principal punishment for infractions of their laws or customs was degradation. The crime of murder was atoned for by liberty given to the friends or relations of the murdered to slay the murderer. They had the essentials of military discipline and their warriors were under good command, and punctual in obeying orders. They cheerfully united in putting all their directions into immediate execution, and by each man observing the motion or movement of his right hand companion, they could communicate the motion from right to left, and march abreast in concert, and in scattered order, though the line was a mile long. They could perform various military maneuvers, either slow or fast, as they could run. They formed the circle in order to surround the enemy, and the semi-circle if the enemy had a river on one side of them. They could also form the large hollow square, face out and take trees; this they did, if their enemies were about surrounding them, to prevent being shot from either side of the tree. Their only clothing when going into battle was the breech-clout, leggins, and moccasins. Their leaders gave general orders by a shout or yell in time of battle, either to advance or retreat, and then each man fought as though he was to gain the battle himself. To ambush and surprise the enemy, and to prevent being ambushed and surprised themselves, was their science of war. They seldom brought on an attack without a sure prospect of victory, with the loss of few men, and if mistaken, and likely to lose many men to gain a victory, they would retreat, and wait for a better opportunity. If surrounded, however, they fought while there was a man alive, rather than surrender. A Delaware chief, called Captain Jacobs, being with his warriors surrounded, took possession of a house, defended themselves for some time and killed a number of the whites. When called on to surrender, he said, 'he and his men were warriors, and they would all fight while life lasted.' Being told that they would be well used if they surrendered, and if not, that the house would be burned over their heads, he replied that he 'could eat fire,' and when the house was in flames he and his men marched out in a fighting position and were all killed."

Smith remained in the Muskingum country until October, when he was taken to the country bordering on Lake Erie, where he remained with the Wyandots hunting and fishing for several years. In 1760 he accompanied a war party into Canada, which was captured. The prisoners were confined at Montreal four months, when they were exchanged. Smith then returned to his home in Pennsylvania. He afterward accompanied Boquet's expedition to the Muskingum as a guide. He served as colonel of a Pennsylvania regiment in the revolutionary war, and subsequently removed to Kentucky, and served in the legislature of that State.

CAPTIVITY OF JOHN McCULLOUGH.

In July, 1756, John McCullough, then a lad, was taken by some Delaware Indians in what is now Franklin County, Pennsylvania, and carried into captivity beyond the Ohio. He remained with them eight years. In his narrative of adventures, he relates that a great prophet appeared among the Indians on the Tuscarawas about two years after he (McCullough) had been taken, which would be about 1758. This prophet was of the Delaware nation—had certain hieroglyphics representing the probation human beings were subject to on earth, and the happiness or misery of a future state. While exhorting his hearers he wept like a child, and told them the only way to purify themselves from sin, was to take certain emetics and abstain from carnal knowledge of the different sexes—that as fire was not pure that was made by steel, they should quit the use of fire-arms, and when they wanted fire, should produce it by rubbing two sticks together, as they had done before the white people found out their country. He professed to have his instructions from a higher power called Keesh-she-la-mil-lang-up, who *thought* the red man into being. McCullough states that he knew a company of the followers of the prophet, who had secluded themselves for two years—had quit the use of fire-arms, and lived in accordance with his rules, firmly believing that by so doing they would be able to drive the whites out of the country. But while the prophet and his followers were endeavoring to spirit the white people away, others betook themselves to a more speedy way of getting rid of them. They fell upon a number of traders at Mahoning, and after killing them took their beaver-skins and set off for a trading post on the Tuscarawas, in the vicinity of the present village of Bolivar. An old Indian named Daniel, cautioned the traders not to buy the skins, assuring them that the skins belonged to some murdered traders. They however purchased the furs through fear. The same evening old Daniel assured them they would all be killed by daylight next morning, which prediction was verified, and in the destruction of this trading establishment was frustrated for a time the second attempt of the English colonists to effect a settlement in the Tuscarawas valley.

CHRISTIAN POST'S FIRST VISIT TO THE TUSCARAWAS, SEVENTEEN HUNDRED AND SIXTY-ONE.

The governor of the Pennsylvania Colony induced Rev. Christian Frederick Post, a Moravian missionary, to visit the Indians on the Ohio and its tributaries and deliver peace messages to them. He reached the Ohio in 1758, and the Tuscarawas in 1761, and on its north bank, in present Stark County (near the present Bolivar), erected the first house built in Ohio by white men, except such cabins as were put up by traders and French Jesuits. It is yet indicated by the chimney stones. Post having performed the business intrusted to him, returned to Bethlehem, and being impressed with the belief that he could convert the red men to Christianity, he again returned to the Tuscarawas in 1762, accompanied by John Heckewelder, another missionary of the Moravian church. They arrived in May at the spot whereon Post had erected his cabin in the year previous, and proceeded to mark out about three acres of ground, and clear the same, for a corn-field. The Indians, who had a large village on the opposite side of the river, about a mile south of Post's cabin, became alarmed when they saw the sturdy oaks of the forest falling by the ax of the white man. They sent word to Post to desist, and summoned him to appear before them at their council house the next day, when the great chiefs of the nation, with Tamaque (king beaver) at their head, would announce their decision, as to whether or not he should be permitted to go on clearing his field. Mr. Post was prompt in his attendance at the council house, when the speaker, in the name of the council, delivered to him the following address: (See Heckewelder's Narrative, page 61).

"Brother: Last year you asked our leave to come and live with us, for the purpose of instructing us and our children, to which we consented; and now being come on, we are glad to see you.

"Brother: It appears to us that you must since have changed your mind, for instead of instructing us or our children, you are cutting trees down on our land. You have marked out a large spot of ground for a plantation, as the white people do everywhere; and by and by another, and another, may come and do the same; and the next thing will be that a fort will be built for the protection of these intruders, and thus our country will be claimed by the white people, and we driven further back, as has been the case ever since the white people first came into this country. Say! do we not speak the truth?"

Post had been a missionary among the Iroquois as early as 1745—was well acquainted with the language, manners, and customs of the Indians—had endured great hardships, and endangered his life many times in behalf of the religion he was now about to preach on the banks of the Tuscarawas. Instead of being intimidated by the reproachful address just delivered to him, he replied to it in the following words, as reported by Heckewelder:

"Brothers: What you say I told you is true, with regard to my coming to live with you, namely, for the purpose of instructing you; but it is likewise true, that an instructor must have something to live upon, otherwise he can not do his duty. Now, not wishing to be a burden to you, so as to ask of you provision for me to live upon, knowing that you have already families to provide for, I thought of raising my own bread, and believed that three acres of ground was little enough for that. You will recollect that I said to you, that I was a messenger from God, and prompted by him to preach and make known his will to the Indians (heathen), that they also, by faith, might be saved, and become inheritors of his heavenly kingdom. Of your land I do not want one foot; neither will my raising a sufficiency of corn and vegetables off your land for me and my brother to subsist on, give me or any other person a claim to the land."

Post having retired for the purpose of giving the chiefs and council time to form an answer; this done, they again met, when the speaker thus addressed Mr. Post:

"Brother: Now as you have spoken more distinctly, we may, perhaps, be able to give you some advice. You say that you are come at the instigation of the Great Spirit, to teach and to preach to us. So also say the priests at Detroit, whom our Father, the French, has sent among his Indian children. Well, this being the case, you, as a preacher, want no more land than one of those do, who are content with a garden lot for to plant vegetables and pretty flowers in, such as the French priests also have, and of which the white people are all fond.

"Brother: As you are in the same station and employed with those preachers we allude to; and as we never saw any one of those cut down trees and till the ground, to get a livelihood, we are inclined to think, and especially as these, without laboring hard, yet look well, that they have to look to another source than that of hard labor for a maintenance. And we think that if, as you say, the Great Spirit wants you to preach to the Indians, he will cause the same to be done for you as he causes to be done for those priests we have seen at Detroit. We are agreed to give you a garden spot, even a larger spot of ground than those have at Detroit. It shall measure fifty steps each way; which, if it suits you, you are at liberty to plant thereon what you please."

To this proposition, Heckewelder says, Mr. Post agreed, and on the following day the lot was stepped off by one of the chiefs, named Captain Pipe, fifty steps square, stakes drove in at the corners, and Post went on with his work again. An Indian treaty being appointed at Lancaster that summer, Mr. Post prevailed upon a number of the Indians to attend with him, leaving Mr. Heckewelder at the missionary station, to instruct the Indian children. In a short time after Post's departure it became known to Heckewelder that the Indian nations were again taking up arms, at the instigation of the French, against the English. His situation became very critical, but he found means of sending a letter to Mr. Post, at Lancaster, and receiving an answer, in which Post advised him to leave the country lest he should be murdered. In October he set out with some traders for Pittsburg, and on the way met Mr. Post, accompanied by Alexander McKee, Indian agent, and apprised them of the dangers of going to the Indian town. McKee was going out to receive and provide for the white prisoners promised to be given up at the Lancaster treaty, and Post, considering himself safe under the protection of the Indian agent, they disregarded Heckewelder's counsel and pushed on, but soon returned, McKee without any prisoners, and Post only saved his life by flight through the woods. The same winter a number of traders were murdered by the Indians, and had it not been for the prudence of Heckewelder, both he and Post would have fallen a sacrifice. Thus ended the first attempt of the Moravians to convert to Christianity the heathen of the Tuscarawas valley.

Roundthaler, the biographer of Heckewelder, gives the following facts touching Heckewelder's stay at the Tuscarawas (near the present Bolivar), in 1762. After being thirty-three days on the way, he and Post arrived at Tuscarawas (the Indian town), on the Muskingum, and entered the cabin Post had built the year before, singing a hymn.

The cabin stood about four rods from the stream, on the east side of the river. No one lived on that side, but on the west side, a mile down the stream, resided a trader named Thomas Calhoon. Farther south was the Indian town called Tuscarawas, of about forty wigwams. A mile still farther down the stream a few Indian families had settled. Eight miles above the cabin was another Indian village. [This was probably on or near the site of the present Bethlehem, in Stark county]. Wild ducks were in abundance, but then having no canoe, Post and his companion had to wait until they flew near the shores to shoot them. Wild geese were still more difficult to get. Pheasants and squirrels were worthless in the summer. Of fish they had plenty, but the manner in which they were forced to prepare them, rendered them disgusting; so Post and Heckewelder lived principally upon nettles, which grew in abundance in the bottoms. They resolved to make a canoe, and having finished one, used it to procure game and to bring down cedar wood from up the river for the purpose of making tubs and other articles for the Indians.

After Post left, Heckewelder was compelled to hide his books to prevent the Indians seeing him reading or writing, they believing that whenever the whites were engaged in reading or writing, it was something concerning their territory, and that the writing of the whites was the cause of robbing them of their lands. Having got a canoe, he was enabled to bring down five and six ducks at one shot, but the Indian boys borrowed and lost his canoe before many days. The nettles becoming too hard to eat, Heckewelder waded the river and went to the cabin of the trader, Calhoon, to procure something to eat.

In a short time the wife of the chief Shingash died, which was announced by the most dismal howlings of the women of the town. Heckewelder, Calhoon, and four Indians carried her to the grave. The body was covered with ornaments, painted with vermillion, and placed in a coffin, at the head of which a hole had been made, that the soul might go in and out. On arriving at the grave, the deceased was entreated to come out of the coffin and stay with the living. The coffin was then lowered, the grave filled up, and a red pole driven in at its head. A great feast was then made and presents distributed around, Calhoon and Heckewelder each receiving a black silk handkerchief and a pair of leggins. For three weeks a kettle of provisions was carried out every evening to the grave to feed the departed spirit on its way to the new country. Mr. Calhoon invited Heckewelder to come and stay with him, which he finally did on account of sickness.

Post had not been gone three weeks when it was circulated that he never intended to return, and that his sole purpose in coming there was to deliver the Indian country into the hands of the whites. The Indians said the tribe would not permit him to return if he wished to do so, and Heckewelder was then warned by friendly Indians to leave the country. One afternoon one of Calhoon's men called for Heckewelder to lock his door and come over immediately to Calhoon's, which he did. Calhoon told him that an Indian woman had come and requested him to take the other white man from his cabin, that he was in danger there. The next morning two of Calhoon's men went over to the cabin, found it broken open, and from appearances two Indians had waited there all night to kill Heckewelder. He never saw his cabin again. King Beaver advised him to hasten his departure out of the country or his life would be taken. He was three weeks on the way to Fort Pitt, being worn down with the fever. After recovering he proceeded on to Bethlehem, Pennsylvania.

TRADITIONAL HISTORY OF THE LENAPE, OR DELAWARES.

Heckewelder, in his history of the Indian nations, records a tradition of the *Leni Lenape*, placing them on the western part of the American continent, from whence they migrated eastward, and arriving at the Mississippi or "River of Fish," they joined forces with the *Mengwe*, otherwise called *Mingoes*, or *Iroquois*, and afterward "Five" or "Six Nations." Discovering the country east of the Mississippi to be inhabited by a powerful nation of stout men, who had large cities on the principal rivers, the Delaware, Potomac, Susquehanna, and Hudson, well fortified, entrenched, and ditched, the Lenape (since called Delawares), and Iroquois or Mingoes, asked leave to pass through the country eastward, which being granted by the *Alligewe* or Alleghany Nation, they penetrated east over the Alleghany mountains, but the *Alligewe*, seeing their great numbers, withdrew the permission to pass through; whereupon a war ensued between the Lenape and Mingoes, or Iroquois, or Monseys, on one side, and the *Alligewe* on the other, which finally terminated in the extirpation of the Alligewe, and their forts, cities, and entrenchments fell into possession of the conquerors, known as the Lenape and Mengwe, or Delawares and Iroquois.

They lived as friends for hundreds of years, but feuds having arisen among them, the Lenape took possession of the lands watered by the Hudson, Potomac, Delaware, and Susquehanna, and the *Mengwe* took possession of the lands along the great lakes. The lands along the Delaware became the center of the Lenape possessions, but the whole of that nation did not settle there, many remaining west of the mountains, and on the Mississippi, and some beyond that river. Those of the Lenape or Delawares, who reached the Atlantic coast, divided into three tribes, two of which, the Turkey and Turtle tribes, settled between the coast and mountains, and extended their settlements beyond the Potomac, south. The third tribe, *Wolf*, or *Minsi*, afterward corrupted into *Monsey*, lived back of the two other tribes, and being the most warlike, watched the movements of the *Mengwe* or Iroquois, and in course of time extended their settlements to the Hudson on the east, and west beyond the Susquehanna, and north as far as the heads of that river and the Delaware, while south they penetrated portions of New Jersey, and along the Lehigh, in Pennsylvania.

From these three tribes, in the course of time, sprung many others who took tribal names, and located in different localities, but all looked up to the Lenape as parent tribe, and it was proud to call all these collateral tribes, such as the *Mahiccani* or Mohican, the Nanticokes, &c., grandchildren.

Becoming thus very powerful, the Mengwe or Iroquois, along the great lakes and St. Lawrence, began to be fearful of the Lenape power, and sought to weaken them, by involving the Lenapes in a war with the Cherokees of the south. To effect which they killed a Cherokee, and laid a Lenape war club by his side, then charged the murder on the Lenape tribe. This exasperated the Cherokees to war against the Lenape, but the trick being exposed the Cherokees and Lenape united to exterminate the deceitful Mengwe or Iroquois. About that time the French landed in Canada, and the Iroquois being hemmed in by the French on one side, and the Lenape or Delawares on the other side, sought peace, and proposed a confederacy called the "Five Nations Confederacy" for the purpose of driving out the French from their country. This was between the fifteenth and sixteenth century, and the Delewares and Iroquois, after many battles between themselves, effected peace and established the confederacy. The crafty Iroquois then proposed to the Delawares to abstain from war with the French, and appear as mediators between the French and Iroquois, as a measure of Indian diplomacy. The Delawares in good faith accepted the trust as neutrals and peace-makers, or as the Iroquois termed it, they became *women* for the good of the confederacy. The *Mahiccani* or Mohicans, relatives of the Delawares, were also ensnared into becoming *women*, and were bound not to go to war, but act as peace-makers between the Iroquois and their enemies.

The Delawares having accepted their new functions a feast was celebrated, and all the nations invited thereto, including delegates of the Dutch emigrants who had settled in what is now New York. The ceremony over, of being placed in the situation of "the women," the Delawares became cousins of the *Mengwe*, and the Mohicans became nephews, the hatchet was buried, and it was agreed that if any nation attacked the Delawares the Mengwe should repel them. The peace belt was laid across the shoulders of the peace-makers, and all foreboded future tranquility.

But no sooner had the Mengwe or Iroquois vassalized the Delawares into the humilitating position of women, than they began their machinations to destroy their power. They induced the Cherokees to declare war, and march against the Delawares, at the same time sending runners to their camps advising them of the approach of the Cherokees, and promising to assist the Delawares in their expulsion. Instead of rendering such assistance, they reproached the Delawares in the face of the enemy as "women," as cowards, and held back from the fight until the Delawares were overpowered and defeated, when the Mengwe at once assumed to be their superiors, avowing that they had conquered and reduced them to vassalage. These avowals were made to the English and other Europeans who by this time had planted colonies along the Atlantic coast, and in a few years had such effect as to induce the latter to believe them. The Delawares and their kindred tribes were yet sufficiently strong to have crushed out the treacherous Iroquois, but their attention was attracted by the landing of Europeans along the Atlantic coast, from New England to Virginia, and their wonder at the ships sailing up the outlets of their large rivers, filled them with premonitions of the presence of their great Manitou, or Supreme Being, and hence the Iroquois escaped the punishment merited for their perfidy.

Here ends traditional, and veritable history begins as to the Delawares, Mohicans and their tribal relations, coming to the valleys, under consideration in this book. But before following them across the Alleghanies, a few incidents may be in place.

THEIR FIRST ACQUAINTANCE WITH LIQUOR.

An old intelligent Delaware Indian related to Heckewelder, that a great many years previous, when men with white skins had not yet been seen in the land, some Indian runners reported that a large house of many colors was sailing up the coast toward the bay (New York). The chiefs assembled at York Island, and after seeing it stop, the hunters were sent out for game, and the women ordered to prepare victuals, as a sacrifice to the great Manitou. Other runners reported the strange creature to be filled with human beings of a different color from that of the Indians. Soon a man dressed in red came ashore with several of his color, bowed to the chiefs, and having drank some liquid out of a hackback, presented some to the chiefs, who passed it among themselves, and were about to return it untasted, when a chief jumped up, and declaring it an insult to the great man to return the liquid without tasting, swallowed a portion, soon staggered, fell, went to sleep, was laid out for dead by his fellow chiefs, then awoke and induced them to partake, and all became drunk, and so remained for some time, during which the great man and his attendants returned to his house (ship), and when the Indians became sober, he again returned to land with beads, axes, hoes, and other articles as presents, after which he departed, telling them by signs he would return the coming year. On his second visit next season the Indians were much rejoiced, and wore the axes and hoes hanging to their breasts as ornaments, and the stockings given them they had made tobacco-pouches of. The whites then showed them how to cut down large trees with the ax, and to cultivate the ground with the hoe. Having gained the friendship of the Indians, the whites asked for so much ground for a garden spot as the hide of a bullock would cover. This being granted, the whites cut the hide into a thin long rope, not larger than a child's finger, and drawing it out in a circular form, closed the ends, and the hide thus encompassing a large piece of land, they took possession. The Indians were surprised at the cunningness of the whites, but assented to the survey, and they lived contentedly for a long time.

After a while the whites successively asked and obtained more land on each request, until the Indians became convinced that the whites wanted all their land and refused further grants. They referred to the deception of the bullock's hide, and remarked that the land they first conceded to raise *greens on* was planted with *great guns* instead, and strong houses were put up on it. Finding the Lenape and Mahiccani averse to more grants, they forcibly took possession of the whole island (New York Island), and proceeded to the Mengwe country, formed a league with them, and obtained from the treacherous Iroquois or Five Nations, a grant of all the Delaware lands, which they claimed to own by right of conquest when they made women of the Lenape, as heretofore related. This treaty is claimed to have been made by the Hollanders (who settled on Manhattan Island) with the Iroquois or Mengwe.

Then the *Gengees* or Yankees arrived at *Machtitschwanne* (Massachusetts), and possessed themselves of the choice lands, and on protest being made by the Indians, war was made upon them, and such Indian prisoners as were taken, were carried off in ships to sea, and sold as slaves, or drowned, as none ever came back. Those not captured were driven away, one tribe beyond Quebec, others dispersed in small bodies, some to Pennsylvania, while others went to the West and mingled with tribes there.

In Pennsylvania they were disturbed in like manner by the Swedes and Dutch, to whom they had given meat, and land to live upon. Finally the good *miquon* (William Penn) came and brought the Delawares words of peace and good will. They lived on the *Lenape hittuck* (Delaware River) contentedly until he died, when the strangers—land traders and speculators—began by fraud and force to get their lands in that part of the country. To accomplish their object, the strangers sent for the Mengwe (Iroquois) to meet them in council at *Laehauwake* (Easton), and take the Lenape "by the hair and shake them well." The Mengwe came, told the *Lenape* or Delawares, and *Mahiccani* or Mohicans, that they had been made women, had no land, and must be gone out of the country to *Wyoming*, where they might live.

The Delawares, when first known to the whites, were in subjection to the Iroquois or Five Nations, who claimed to own the territory embraced in New York, Pennsylvania and New Jersey, and through the entire western country. The Delawares at that time inhabited a portion of the New Jersey territory and the eastern portion of Pennsylvania, and were held to be in such a state of vassalage to the Five Nations as to be incapable of carrying on war, or of making sales of lands without the consent of their conquerors. Nevertheless they did sell land to the English, which incensed the Iroquois or Five Nations against them. In July, 1742, a council was held at Philadelphia between the governor of the Pennsylvania colony and sundry chiefs of the Six Nations and Delawares, when Cawassatiego, a chief of the Six Nations accused the Delawares of perfidy. His speech is preserved in McIntosh's Book of Indians, and is as follows:

"Cousins: Let the belt of wampum serve to chastise you. You ought to be taken by the hair of the head and shaken severely till you receive your senses and become sober. You don't know what ground you stand on, nor what you are doing. Our brother Onas' (the governor of Pennsylvania) cause is very just and plain, and his intentions are to preserve friendship; on the other hand, your cause is bad, your heart far from being right. We have seen with our eyes a deed signed by nine of our ancestors about fifty years ago for this very land, and a release signed not many years since by some of yourselves. But how come you to take upon yourselves to sell land at all? We conquered you, we made women of you; you know you are women, and can no more sell land than women; nor is it fit you should have the power of selling land, since you would abuse it. This land that you claim, has gone through your guts. You have been furnished with clothes, meat, and drink, by the goods paid for it, and now you want it again, like children, as you are. But what matters! You sell land in the dark. Did you ever tell us that you sold them land? Did we ever receive any part, even the value of a pipe shank, from you for it? This is very different from the conduct our Six Nations observe in the sale of land. On such occasions they give public notice and visit all the Indians of the united nations, and give them all a share of the presents they receive for their lands. But we find you are none of our blood; you act a distinct part, not only in this, but in other matters; your ears are even open to slanderous reports about our brethren. Therefore, for all these reasons, we charge you to remove instantly. We don't give you liberty to think about it. You are women—take the advice of a wise man, and remove immediately. We assign you two places to go: either to Ugoman or Shamokin; you may go to either of these places, and then we shall have you more under our eyes, and shall see how you behave. Don't deliberate, but remove away and take this belt of wampum, which serves to forbid you, your children, and grand-children to the latest posterity, forever meddling in land affairs; neither you nor any who shall descend from you, are ever hereafter to presume to sell any land."

Soured and embittered against their conquerors, many of the Delawares retired to the country watered by the Susquehanna and Alleghany and their tributaries, and between 1742 and 1750 they reached the Tuscarawas and Muskingum. By the year 1768 they had nearly all settled west of the Ohio, and became released from their troublesome relations, the Iroquois, until the breaking out of the American revolution.

CHAPTER IV.

THE FIRST MILITARY EXPEDITION INTO THE VALLEYS IN THE YEAR 1764.

The first English military expedition into Ohio was made in 1764 by Colonel Henry Boquet marching an army of fifteen hundred men into and through what is now Tuscarawas County to the forks of Muskingum, now Coshocton.

Its object was to punish and awe the Indians, and the history of that campaign is full of thrilling interest to the people at this day.

It will be remembered that the French evacuated Fort Pitt as well as all their forts in the Ohio and lake territory in A. D. 1758 by treaty with the English government. The Indians, however, were not satisfied. They were more friendly to the French than to the English rule over their hunting grounds, having received more presents, more ammunition and whisky from the French than they did wherever subject to English domination. They smothered their feelings until about 1762, when the great northwestern war Chief Pontiac had a dream in which the great Spirit appeared to him and said he must arouse the nations and drive the English from the land, and "when you," said the great Spirit to him, "are in distress I will help you." He sent the war belt to all the nations, assembled their warriors before all the British forts, with directions to put on friendly guise, and after getting access to their forts, to slay every man, woman, and child in each garrison and in the territory. There were twelve forts in the Indian territory. Of these, nine were taken by Pontiac's strategy during 1762 and 1763, and the whites not put to death were carried into captivity.

To illustrate the manner and the cunningness of the savages take the fort at Presque Isle, the present locality of Erie, Pennsylvania, as an example: One hundred and fifty Indians appeared in hunting garb with skins to sell. The commander of the fort went out a mile or so to look at the furs. Neither he or his guards ever returned, but the savages, each laden with a package of furs on his back, and his knife and a short rifle hid in his hunting frock, came to the fort, asking admittance to unload the furs the commander had purchased. Of course the gates were opened, the savages entered, and of all the garrison men, women, and children, but two are reported as having escaped. Other forts were taken by other devices, and the only three not taken were Ligonier, Bedford, and Fort Pitt. The white settlers were raided upon and killed, or carried off, and the whole frontier given up for a time to Indian massacre. The indignation of the colonial authorities was aroused. General Bradstreet marched up the lakes with three thousand men. Other forces went out, and the Indians were driven back from the forts they had captured. Pontiac's war of extermination was a failure. Chagrined at the great Spirit for not assisting him, he made peace in 1766, became a drunkard, and wandered about until 1769, when he was killed, near the present St. Louis, by an Illinois Indian in a drunken row, says tradition.

The Delaware, Shawanee, and other Indians of the Ohio territory had been assigned by Pontiac to take Forts Pitt, Ligonier, and Bedford, and after his war was over in 1763 they still menaced these forts, and spread terror throughout western Pennsylvania and Virginia. To punish these savages Colonel Boquet was ordered to march from Philadelphia against the hostile tribes on the Ohio. His force was one thousand five hundred men, three hundred of whom deserted at Carlisle, such was their fear of the savages who had destroyed Braddock's army at Bloody Run nine years before. Boquet was a brave and sagacious chieftain, and he pushed on with his force on Braddock's old trail, through Pennsylvania, until he got to Bushy Run, within four days march of Fort Pitt, in the month of August, 1763, where the combined Indian force of Delawares, Shawanese, Wyandots, &c., attacked and fought him for two days and nights, but were finally defeated, losing sixty of their best warriors and chiefs. The Indian army then raised the investment of Fort Pitt, and retired to their homes on the Tuscarawas, Muskingum, Scioto, &c., while Boquet with his shattered army proceeded to Fort Pitt, and were put to garrison duty, being too much cut up to follow the savages that year into Ohio.

At length, on the 3d of October, 1764, he marched from Fort Pitt with one thousand five hundred regulars and militia to the Muskingum country to punish the Delawares and Shawanese and other tribes.

The order of march was as follows: A corps of Virginia volunteers advanced in front, detaching three scouting parties; one of them, preceded by a guide, marched in the center path which the army was to follow. The other two extended themselves in a line abreast, on the right and left, to scour the woods on the flanks. Under cover of this advance guard, the axmen and two companies of infantry followed in three divisions to clear the side paths and cut a road in which the main army and the convoy marched as follows: The front face of the square, composed of parts of two regiments, marched in single file in the right-hand path, and a Pennsylvania regiment marched in the same manner in the left-hand path. A reserve corps of grenadiers followed in the paths, and they likewise by a second battalion of infantry. All these troops covered the convoy which marched between them in the center path or main road. A company of horsemen and a corps of Virginia volunteers followed, forming the rear guard. The

Pennsylvania volunteers, in single file, flanked the side paths opposite the convoy. The ammunition and tools were placed in the rear of the first column, which were followed by the baggage and tents. The cattle and sheep came after the baggage, in the center road, properly guarded. The provisions came next on pack-horses. The troops were ordered to observe the most profound silence, and the men to march at two yards distance from each other. By marching in this order, if attacked, the whole force could be easily thrown into a hollow square, with the baggage, provisions, &c., in the center.

From the day of starting to the 13th was occupied in reaching camp number twelve, by way of Logstown, Big Beaver, Little Beaver, Yellow, Nimishillen and Sandy creeks.

Colonel Boquet's journal says:

"Saturday, October 13, 1764.—Crossed Nenenchelus (Nimishillen) Creek about fifty feet wide, a little above where it empties itself into a branch of the Muskingum (meaning by this branch what is now Sandy Creek). A little further came to another small stream which was crossed about fifty perches above where it empties into the said Muskingum. Here a high ridge on the right and a creek close on the left forms a narrow defile about seventy perches long. Passing over a very rich bottom came to the main branch of the Muskingum about seventy yards wide, with a good ford a little below, and a little above is *Tuscarawas*, a place exceedingly beautiful in situation, the lands rich on both sides of the river. The country on the north-west side being an entire plain upward of five miles in circumference, and from the ruined houses here appearing, the Indians who inhabited the place and are now with the Delawares are supposed to be about one hundred and fifty warriors." [Supposing each warrior to represent a family of five persons, the town would have numbered seven hundred and fifty Indians.]

"Sunday, October 14, 1764.—The army remained in camp, and two men who had been dispatched with letters returned and reported that within a few miles of this place they had been made prisoners by the Delawares, and carried to one of their towns sixteen miles distant, where they were kept until the savages, knowing of the arrival of the army here, set them at liberty, ordering them to acquaint Colonel Boquet that the head men of the Delawares and Shawanese were coming as soon as possible to treat for peace with him.

"Monday, October 15, 1764.—The army moved two miles and forty perches further down the Muskingum, to camp number thirteen, situated on a very high bank, with the river at the foot of it, which is upward of one hundred yards wide at this place, with fine level country at some distance from its banks, producing stately timber free from underwood and plenty of food for cattle. Six Indians came to inform the colonel that all their chiefs had assembled about eight miles from the camp, and were ready to treat with him of peace, which they were earnestly desirous of obtaining. He returned for answer that he would meet them next day in a bower at some distance from camp. In the meantime he ordered a small stockaded fort to be built to hold provisions for the troops on their return, and to lighten their convoy, as several large bodies of Indians were within a few miles of the camp, whose former instances of treachery—although they now declared they came for peace—made it prudent to trust nothing to their intentions.

"Wednesday, October 17, 1764.—The colonel, with most of the regular troops, Virginia volunteers and Lighthorse, marched from the camp to the bower erected for the congress, and soon after the troops were stationed so as to appear to the best advantage. The Indians arrived and were conducted to the bower. Being seated, they began in a short time to smoke their pipes—the calumet—agreeably to their custom. This ceremony over, they laid down their pipes and opened their pouches wherein were their strings and belts of wampum.

"The Indians present were Seneca Chief Kiyastrula, with fifteen warriors, *Custaloga*, chief of the Wolf-Delaware tribe, Beaver, chief of the Turkey tribe, with twenty warriors, Shawanese Chief *Keiffiwautchtha*, a chief and six warriors."

Kiyafhuta, Turtle Heart, Custaloga, and Beaver were the speakers. The general substance of what they had to offer consisted in excuses for their late treachery and misconduct, throwing the blame on the rashness of their young men and the nations living to the westward of them—suing for peace in the most abject manner, and promising severally to deliver up all their prisoners. After they had concluded the colonel promised to give them an answer the next day, and the army returned to camp. The badness of the weather however prevented his meeting them until the 20th, when he spoke to them.

The boldness with which Colonel Boquet spoke excited the chiefs, but remembering how terribly he had chastised them at the battle of Bushy Run a year previous, they succumbed at once, and the two Delaware chiefs delivered eighteen white prisoners, and eighty-three small sticks expressing the number of other prisoners they still held, and promised to bring them in as soon as possible. *Keiffiwautchtha*, the Shawanese deputy, promised on behalf of his nation to submit to Colonel Boquet's terms. Kiyafhuta addressed the several tribes before their departure, exhorting them to be strong in complying with their engagements, that they might wipe away the reproach of their former breach of faith, and convince the English that they could speak the truth, adding that he would conduct the army to the place appointed for receiving the prisoners. [It will be recollected that the stockade built at camp number thirteen, was two miles and forty perches down the river from the Indian town of Tuscarawas, which was near the present site of Bolivar. The *bower* at which this Indian congress was held was further down the river, and must have been in or near the edge of the Dover plains, that at this spot was consummated an agreement which resulted in the restoration of all the white prisoners held by the Delawares and other tribes in the valley, makes the plains of the Tuscarawas memorable in history.]

"Monday, 22.—The army, attended by the Indian deputies, marched nine miles to camp number fourteen, and crossed Margret's Creek, about fifty feet wide." [The route of this day's march was in a south-west direction from the site of Fort Laurens to Margret's Creek, which is now Sugar Creek, which was crossed in the vicinity of the mouth of what is known as Broad Run, about one mile south of the town of Strasburg; thence up the valley of the latter stream to the place of encampment, which was in the vicinity of the present village of Winfield, in the north-west corner of Dover township.]

"Tuesday, 23.—The army marched sixteen miles one-quarter and seventy-seven perches further to camp number fifteen, and halted there one day." [The route of this day's march was up the Broad Run valley to the head of that stream, where a dividing ridge was crossed in section four, range three, in Sugar Creek township, bringing the army again into the Sugar Creek valley; thence south along the east side of Sugar Creek through Auburn and Bucks townships, passing near to the present site of Ragersville. In the south-western part of Bucks township crossed Sugar Creek; thence over the dividing ridge between the waters of that stream and White Eyes Creek; thence down the valley of White Eyes Creek to a point south of the present village of Chili, in Coshocton County, where camp number fifteen was located.]

"Thursday, 25.—The army marched six miles one half and sixteen perches to camp number sixteen, situated in the forks of the Muskingum." [This being near the present site of Coshocton. Before leaving the encampment where the congress was held, Boquet was informed that there were several marauding bands of Indians along the river valley, and who would likely ambuscade him if he marched down the valley past Three Legstown, at the mouth of Stillwater, and New Comerstown. Hence the route taken as above described.]

"This place (forks of Muskingum) was fixed upon instead of Wakatomica as the most central and convenient place to receive the prisoners, for the principal Indian towns lay around them from seven to twenty miles distant, except the lower Shawnee town situated on the Scioto River about eighty miles, so that from this place the army had it in their power to awe all the enemies' settlements, and destroy their towns, if they should not punctually fulfil the engagements they had entered into. Four redoubts were built here opposite the four angles of the camp. The ground in front was cleared, a storehouse for the provisions was erected, and likewise a house to receive and treat peace with the Indians when they returned. Three houses were separate apartments for the captives of the respective provinces, and proper officers to take charge of them, with a matron to take charge of women and children, so that with the officers' mess-houses, ovens, &c., this camp had the appearance of a little town in which the greatest order and regularity was observed.

"Sunday, October 27, 1764.—A messenger arrived from King Custaloga informing them that he was on his way with the prisoners, and also a messenger from the lower Shawanese towns of the like import. The colonel having reason to suspect the latter nation's backwardness sent one of their own people desiring them to be punctual as to the time fixed—to provide a sufficient quantity of provisions to subsist the prisoners—to bring the letters wrote them last winter by the French commander at Fort Charles, which some of their people had stopped ever since, adding that as their nation had expressed some uneasiness at our not shaking hands with them, they were to know that the English never took their enemies by the hand before peace was concluded.

"The day following the Shawanese messenger returned, saying that when he had proceeded as far as Wakatomica, the chief of the town had undertook to proceed with the message himself, and desired the other to return and acquaint the English that all the prisoners were ready, and he was going to the lower towns to hasten them.

"Monday, October 28, 1764.—Peter, the Caughnawaga chief and twenty Indians arrived from Sandusky with a letter from Colonel Bradstreet. The Caughnawagas reported that the Indians on the lakes had delivered but few of their prisoners; that the Ottowas had killed a great part of theirs, and the other nations had done the same, or had kept them. From this time to November 9 was chiefly spent in sending and receiving messages to and from the Indian towns relative to the prisoners who were now coming into camp in small parties. The colonel kept so steadily to this article of having every prisoner delivered, that when the Delaware kings (Beaver and Custaloga) had brought in all theirs except twelve, which they promised to bring in a few days, he refused to shake hands or have the least talk with them while a single captive remained among them. By the 9th of November most of the prisoners had arrived that could be expected this season, amounting to two hundred and six, besides about one hundred more remaining in possession of the Shawanese, which they promised to deliver in the following spring. Everything being now settled with the Indians the army decamped on Sunday, the 18th of November, from the forks of Muskingum, and marched for Fort Pitt, [up the Tuscarawas valley to its provision stockade, near the present town of Bolivar; thence by way of Sandy valley and Yellow Creek to the Ohio, and up to Fort Pitt,] where it arrived on the 28th of November. The regular troops were sent to garrison the different points of communication, and the provincial troops, with the captives to their several provinces. Here ended the first armed expedition that had ever penetrated the Tuscarawas valley, and as the chronicler says, notwithstanding the difficulties attending it, the troops were never in want of any necessaries, continuing perfectly healthy during the whole campaign, in which no life was lost, except one soldier killed at the Muskingum.

THE WHITE PRISONERS RECOVERED BY COLONEL BOQUET.

The scene of the delivery of these captives to Colonel Boquet is thus narrated by one who was present: "Among them were many who had been seized when very young, and had grown up in the wigwam of the savage. They had contracted the wild habits of their captors, learned their language and forgotten their own, and were bound to them by ties of the strongest affection. Many a mother found a lost child; many were unable to designate their children. There were to be seen husbands hanging round the necks of their newly recovered wives. There were to be seen sisters and brothers unexpectedly coming together after long years of separation. And there were others flying from place to place, inquiring after relatives not found; trembling to receive an answer to questions; distracted with doubts, hopes, and fears on obtaining no account of those they sought for; or stiffened into living monuments of horror and woe on learning their unhappy fate. Among the captives brought in was a woman with a babe three months old. One of the soldiers recognized her as his wife, who had been taken by the Indians six months before. They rushed into each other's arms, and he took her and the child to his tent and had them clothed. But there was still another child missing, and on more children being brought in the woman was sent for. Among them she recognized her own, and was so overcome with joy, that, forgetting her sucking child, she dropped it from her arms, and catching up the other run off with it, unable to give utterance to her joy. The father soon followed her with the babe she had let fall, in no less transport of affection."

The separation between the Indians and their prisoners was equally affecting, and there were as many tears shed by the sons of the forest at the parting, as there were by the captives at meeting their relatives. Mr. Hutchins relates that the Indians visited them from day to day, brought them food and presents, and bestowed upon them all the marks of the most tender affection. Some even followed the army on its return, and employed themselves in hunting and bringing in provisions for the captives on the way. A young chief had formed such an attachment to a young woman among the captives, that he persisted in following her, and afterward paid the penalty of his life for his attachment. Nor was the affection of some of the captive women less strong for the red man. One female who had been captured at the age of fourteen, had become the wife of an Indian, and the mother of several children. When told her that she was to be delivered up to her parents, her grief knew no bounds. "Can I," said she, "enter my parents' dwelling? Will they be kind to my children? No, no; I will not leave my husband;" and she darted off into the woods and was seen no more.

Among the captive children surrendered to Colonel Boquet, was one whom no one claimed, and whose after history is full of romance. In 1756, the wife and child of a Mr. John Grey, living near Carlisle, had been taken by the Indians. Grey died, and by his will gave to his wife one-half his farm and to his daughter the other half, in case they should ever return from captivity. The mother got away from the savages, returned home, and finding her husband's will, proved it and took possession of the farm. In 1764–5, when Colonel Boquet returned with his captives, Mrs. Grey repaired to Philadelphia to search among them for her daughter. Failing to recognize her little Jane, some one induced her to claim the girl before spoken of, for the purpose of holding the other half of the farm. She did so, and brought up the strange child as her own daughter, carefully keeping the secret. The girl grew up as the daughter of John Grey, married a man named Gillespie, and took possession of the farm, which afterward passed through different hands up to the year 1789, when some of the collateral heirs of John Grey, obtaining information about the spurious Jane Grey, commenced suits to recover the land, being four hundred acres of the best land in Mifflin County, Pennsylvania. A legal contest ensued, which lasted in one phase or another for forty-four years, and in 1833 the case was finally disposed of, against the identity of the adopted child, and the property reverted to the heirs of the sisters and brothers of the original John Grey. The above facts are gathered from Sherman Day's History of Pennsylvania.

Of the captives released from bondage in the Tuscarawas valley one hundred and eleven years ago, thirty-two men and boys and fifty-eight females belonged to Virginia, and forty-nine men and boys and sixty-seven females belonged to Pennsylvania. Many of the men took to the woods for a living, and became scouts for Washington's army in the revolution. And as the boys grew up they in turn became scouts and pioneered the way for St. Clair in '91, Wayne in '94, and General Harrison in 1812, in their campaigns against the Indians. Thus did their captivity in this valley have its compensations, for by it they learned the Indian mode of warfare, became familiar with their war-paths and strong-holds, and after assisting to drive out the descendants of their captors, these descendants of the captives, many of them, took up their abode in the Tuscarawas valley, and their posterity are now among its honored citizens in the fourth generation; and as they pursue their daily avocations at the plow or in the workshop, they have little conception of the fact that there is not a crossing place or fishing spot along our river, or a spring among its valleys, or a lookout on the hill-tops, that has not been made sacred by the captivity of their ancestors and the death-screams of white men and women under the tomahawk, scalping-knife, and faggot of the then merciless savages.

Harvey, in his History of Pennsylvania, says a great number of the restored prisoners were sent to Carlisle, Pennsylvania, and Colonel Boquet advertised for those who had lost children to come and reclaim them. One old woman who had lost a child, and failing to recognize it among the returned captives, was lamenting her loss and wringing her hands, telling Colonel Boquet how she had years previous sung a little hymn to her daughter, who was so fond of it. The colonel told her to sing it then, which she did as follows:

> "Alone, yet not alone am I,
> Though in this solitude so drear;
> I feel my Savior always nigh,
> He comes my every hour to cheer."

She had no sooner concluded, than her long-lost daughter, who had failed to know her mother by sight but remembering the hymn, rushed into her mother's arms.

Colonel Boquet's success in conquering the Indians made him a brigadier-general, but he died in 1766, at Pensacola, of fever.

CHAPTER V.

THE GERMANS SETTLE ON THE TUSCARAWAS, 1771-2.

David Zeisberger, who had been preaching to "Lo" for over thirty years in Pennsylvania, Georgia, and New York, suffering great privations, but meeting with some success, became convinced that his converts, to be held faithful, must be removed beyond the evil influences and temptations of the white man's vices. The pious German had established a mission on the Alleghany, where he preached to the sons of the forest every day, and had made such a favorable impression on the chiefs of the "Delawares, that Netawatwes, Pakaake, and Weldpachtschiechen, who ranged from the Susquehanna to the Alleghany, granted us"—says he in his journal—"a portion of land on the Muskingum River, where we might pursue our mission without molestation. When we settled there we found that their promise was fulfilled, and we met with no hinderance in our work. Not long after this Netawatwes with his tribe removed to Goschackgunk. He then ceded to us all the lands in the vicinity of Gekelemukpechunk, in order that we might live separately and apart, and enlarge our settlement. Soon after this Netawatwes requested us to remove to a place close to Goschackgunk, so that his people might have a better opportunity to hear the word of God."

The above is an extract from Zeisberger's unpublished diary, which makes nearly one thousand pages, and is now in the possession of Julius Dexter, Esq., of Cincinnati, who, in making the translation, says "the diary is written in a crabbed German text."

John Heckewelder, the master mind of the two, though not so devout as Zeisberger, in his narrative, says that they made a settlement on Beaver Creek in April, 1770, where the Indians came to hear preaching, and among others who became converts, was a great Indian orator named Glikhican. He was the counselor of Pakaukee—called by Ziesberger Pakaake—chief of the tribe, and his conversion so astounded the other Indians that they called a council, and while discussing the question, messengers arrived from Gekelemukpechunk—and which signifies in English "Stillwater"—with a large black belt of wampum. They brought a message from the Muskingum chiefs to the missionaries at Beaver, stating that a disease had carried off great numbers of Delawares; that it was brought upon them by witchcraft; that the only cure for the contagion was Christianity; that to get rid of the disease, small-pox, it was necessary to become Christians, which they intended to do, and if the missionaries would come to the Muskingum and preach they would be well received, and such Indians as would not embrace their religion should be treated as common enemies. The missionaries however did not go until another invitation was extended to them, with the assurance that they should have all the land they wanted, and which should never be sold from under their feet, as the Iroquois had done to the Delawares.

Zeisberger's first visit to the valley was in March, 1771. From Fort Pitt west was the great trail made by the buffaloes first, and used by the mound builders next, then by the later races of Indians in going to and returning from the Sandusky country and lakes. Zeisberger followed this trail almost due west until he came to the Tuscarawas River, where he left it at the crossing place—near Bolivar of this day—and following the meanderings of the river south and south-eastwardly he reached in about fifteen miles a big spring, three miles from the present New Philadelphia. Along a bluff about twenty feet high, of gravel and sand, which had been the ancient east shore of the river, he found the remains of three ancient earth-works or forts of the mound builders, and opposite thereto in the bottom some fields partially covered by the forest, yet sufficiently visible to satisfy him that they had been once utilized by the ancient race. One was surrounded by a ditch several feet in depth and width, and the excavated earth forming an embankment five to ten feet high, and faint traces of which are yet discernible on the west side of the Tuscarawas. On the north is a mound covering a half to one acre, and ten or more feet high, once used as a sacrificial, or burial place.

Leaving the spring, Zeisberger proceeded on to the forks, where Stillwater Creek enters the Tuscarawas; and then followed the river trail to the Indian capital, adjacent to the present New Comerstown. It was nearly a mile square, contained about one hundred log houses, one of which, belonging to the Delaware chief *Netawatwes*, was shingle roofed, and had board floors, and other indications of partial civilization. This is the chief whom Colonel Boquet in his campaign of 1764 deposed from office for not attending the conference (at the forks of the river, the present site of Coshocton), but the chief continued his functions after Boquet returned to Fort Pitt. Zeisberger remained several days with the chief, and having preached in his house, as is said, the first protestant sermon within the north-west territory, again returned to Pennsylvania.

SETTLEMENT AT SCHOENBRUNN—1772-3.

Early in 1772, with a number of Christian Indians, he again visited the Delaware capital, and desired privilege to establish a mission in the valley. The chief Netawatwes and others, were so pleased (and some of whom believed that the small-pox, which had disappeared, was driven away by his sermon the year before) that the "Big Spring" was suggested as the proper locality, and a grant was made to him, for his mission, of all the land between the mouth of Stillwater and Old Town. Heckewelder says *Tuscarawas* means "old town," but the grant must have extended from the mouth of Old Town Creek, nearly opposite New Philadelphia, to Stillwater Creek. Boquet says he found an old Indian town callen *Tuscarawas* at the river crossing, near the present Bolivar, from which some infer that the grant extended to that town, but such was not the fact. The grant however was extended the same year south, so as to include all the land from Stillwater Creek to within three miles of the Delaware capital—adjoining the present New Comerstown. By the two grants they thus obtained possession of nearly all the bottom lands of the valley in Tuscarawas County.

On the 3d of May, 1772, Zeisberger and twenty-eight persons located at "Big Spring," and called it Schoenbrunn, or "Fine Spring." Here, on lands now owned by Elisha Jacobs, and adjacent thereto, owned by Henry Zimmerman, John B. Reed, and Alexander Brown, they set about erecting houses, clearing land, planting corn, &c.

Early in the same year a large body of Christian Indians, under charge of Rev. John Etwin, had set out from their settlement on the Susquehanna for the Tuscarawas valley. They numbered nearly three hundred persons, had a large number of horses, some seventy head of cattle, plow-irons, harrow teeth, pick-axes, all kinds of farming utensils and tools, iron pots, brass kettles for boiling maple sugar, and provisions for the whole body. They arrived at the settlement on the Big Beaver early in August. Zeisberger had returned from Schoenbrunn to that place to meet them. This whole body of emigrants left the Big Beaver settlement on the 5th of August, accompanied by Etwin, Zeisberger and Heckewelder, and arrived at Schoenbrunn on the 23d of August, 1772. Having decided to make Schoenbrunn a permanent settlement, they sent a delegation to the Indian chiefs at Gekelemukpechunk (in English Stillwater), announcing their arrival. The delegation were received with much friendship by the chiefs in council, and a grand feast was prepared, and the event duly celebrated. Heckewelder, in his narrative, states that visitors arrived daily at Schoenbrunn from Stillwater and other valleys to view the new comers, witness them putting up buildings, plowing the ground, &c., but what most excited their curiosity was the fact of so large a number of Indians living happily together, and devoting themselves to labor in the fields, &c. Encouraged by these friendly visits, the missionaries set to work and built a chapel at Schoenbrunn, of square timber, thirty-six feet by forty feet, shingle roofed, with a cupalo and bell. They also laid out their town regularly, with wide streets, and kept the cattle out by good fences, and adopted a set of rules of government, which are here given verbatim from Heckewelder's narrative:

"1. We will know of no God, nor worship any other but him who has created us, and redeemed us with his most precious blood.

"2. We will rest from all labor on Sundays, and attend the usual meetings on that day for divine service.

"3. We will honor father and mother, and support them in age and distress.

"4. No one shall be permitted to dwell with us, without the consent of our teachers.

"5. No thieves, murderers, drunkards, adulterers, and whoremongers shall be suffered among us.

"6. No one that attendeth dances, sacrifices, or heathenish festivals, can live among us.

"7. No one using *Tschappich* (or witchcraft) in hunting, shall be suffered among us.

"8. We will renounce all juggles, lies, and deceits of Satan.

"9. We will be obedient to our teachers, and to the helpers—national assistants—who are appointed to see that good order be kept both in and out of the town.

"10. We will not be idle and lazy; nor tell lies of one another; nor strike each other; we will live peaceably together.

"11. Whosoever does any harm to another's cattle, goods, or effects, &c., shall pay the damage.

"12. A man shall have only one wife—love her and provide for her, and the children. Likewise a woman shall have but one husband, and be obedient unto him; she shall also take care of the children, and be cleanly in all things.

"13. We will not permit any rum, or spirituous liquors, to be brought into our towns. If strangers or traders happen to bring any, the helpers—national assistants—are to take it into their possession, and take care not to deliver it to them until they set off again.

"14. None of the inhabitants shall run in debt with traders, nor receive goods on commission for traders, without the consent of the national assistants.

"15. No one is to go on a journey or long hunt without informing the minister or stewards of it.

"16. Young people are not to marry without the consent of their parents, and taking their advice.

"17. If the stewards or helpers apply to the inhabitants for assistance, in doing work for the benefit of the place, such as building meeting and school houses, clearing and fencing lands, &c., they are to be obeyed.

"18. All necessary contributions for the public ought cheerfully to be attended to."

The above rules were made and adopted at a time when there was a profound peace; when however, six years afterward (during the revolutionary war), individuals of the Delaware Nation took up the hatchet to join in the conflict, the national assistants proposed and insisted on having the following additional rules added, namely:

"19. No man inclining to go to war—which is the shedding of blood, can remain among us.

"20. Whosoever purchases goods or articles of warriors, *knowing* at the time that such have been stolen or plundered, must leave us. We look upon this as giving encouragement to murder and theft."

No person was allowed to live in the society without first

having promised to conform to the foregoing rules. When any person violated the rules he or she was first admonished, and in case that proved ineffectual the offender was expelled. Other rules were adopted for daily meetings, for government of schools, for attention to visitors, and for rendering assistance to the sick, needy, and distressed, so that the poorest person in the society was dressed, and as well provided for as the most wealthy.

The missionary, Zeisberger, after establishing the emigrants at Schoenbrunn, visited the Shawanese Indians, about fifty miles south of Schoenbrunn, where he preached and was well received. His absence from the Big Beaver settlement soon induced the Christian Indians of that place, with their missionary, Rothe, to quit it and join the settlers on the Tuscarawas. A portion of them traveled across the country by land, and Heckewelder, with the balance, left Beaver on the 13th of April, 1773, in twenty-two canoes, paddled down the Ohio to the mouth of the Muskingum; thence up that and the Tuscarawas River to Schoenbrunn, after encountering many privations. The many converts made from among the Delawares at Schoenbrunn, added to the original emigrants at that place, rendered it necessary to establish a new settlement ten miles down the river, which was begun the same year, 1773. Here they laid out a town in regular order, with wide streets, put up a chapel with cupola and bell, the same as at Schoenbrunn, and gave the place the name of Gnadenhuetten, which it retains to this day. Having need of a resident minister at this settlement, they dispatched some Christian Indians to Bethlehem, Pennsylvania, to bring on the Rev. Mr. Schmick and his wife, who arrived at Gnadenhuetten on the 18th day of August, 1773, and took up their residence in a new house, built expressly for them. Zeisberger, in the fall of this year, again visited the Shawanese Indians, where he was well received, but being a turbulent and warlike tribe, his efforts to civilize them were not so successful as with the Indians around Schoenbrunn. Illustrative of their character, it is related that a horse was stolen from Schoenbrunn. Some time thereafter a Shawanee rode into Schoenbrunn on this horse. The owner, a Christian Indian, seeing the horse claimed him of the Shawanee, averring that he had been stolen from him. The Shawanee insisted that he came by the horse as a gift from an uncle. The Christian Indian cited Zeisberger's law on stolen property, and was about moving away with the horse, when the Shawanee, seizing a bit of burnt coal, made a rude figure on a door, of one man leading a horse, and another man coming up from behind and scalping him. "That," said he, "is Shawanee law." The threat thus conveyed proved effectual, and the Shawanee "border ruffian" was allowed to ride away from Schoenbrunn on his stolen horse.

Thus was commenced on the banks of the Tuscarawas, the first attempt at civil government in the great north-west territory. Post had been at Bolivar ten years before, but no successful attempt had been made to colonize and civilize, as well as christianize, the aboriginies of the Ohio territory, prior to the efforts of Zeisberger. The history of civilization presents no code of government for man, more perfect or more sublime, than a portion of those articles adopted at Schoenbrunn.

One hundred years have come and gone since they were promulgated—Zeisberger's bones lie mixed with the clods of the valley, one mile below—his companions and converts have all passed away—and nothing remains to mark the spot where the first bell sounded in the north-west territory, in Christ's service, save the old spring, and a huge elm tree which was there with Zeisberger, and which now bends with age over the water oozing out of the bank in copious tears of sorrow, but unfit to drink.

The mad locomotive rushes by in gigantic strides, and with deafening screams, as though man, its master, was angered at the thought that he has been for a century expanding the human mind, since Zeisberger and his followers came there, and yet with all his efforts and all his knowledge he can to-day produce no better code of law for human government than the one enunciated by that unarmed man of God, with only the Bible in his hand, in 1772.*

FEAST AT THE NEW COMERSTOWN—REV. DAVID JONES' CRUSADE AGAINST WHISKY—CONVERT KILLBUCK, BARELY SAVED HIS OWN LIFE.

In the year 1773, Rev. David Jones, a Presbyterian minister, was sent out from Philadelphia City to the Scioto and Muskingum valleys, with the view of establishing a mission. On arriving at Schoenbrunn he found Zeisberger had planted his colonies along the Tuscarawas, and as they gave evidence of success, Jones proceeded on south and spent some time among the Shawanese, but found no encouragement for a mission among them. He therefore returned up the Tuscarawas valley to New Comerstown, in the vicinity of the present town of that name. Here the Indians were having a great feast and dance, in which, whisky procured from traders, was the principal performer. Under its influence they refused Jones permission to preach. shut him up in one of their huts, and put a guard around him, and some proposed to kill him, but one of the chiefs, called Gelelemend or Killbuck, interfered and saved his life.

After the Indian feast was over they listened to the preacher, and he having spoken much against the use of whisky, made such an impression on the mind of the Chief

*[*Note.*—Two years ago, being the one hundredth year since the Schoenbrunn settlement, Mr. Jacobs, who owns the spring, deeded it to the Union Bible Society, on condition that the spring and big elm be fenced around. Mr. John Judy, C. H. Mitchener, William C. Williamson, and other citizens then procured a memorial stone, with proper inscriptions, and planted it at the spring, there to point out to those who come at the end of the next hundred years, where Schoenbrunn or "Fine Spring," may be found.]

Killbuck that he became a convert then, and was ever afterward opposed to its use. While Jones remained at "The New Comerstown," Killbuck destroyed all the liquor on hand, and notified the traders that if they brought any more whisky among the Indians they (the traders) would be scalped. This aroused their enmity against the preacher, and threats being again made by some of the drinking Indians against his life, the Chief had him escorted up the river to Gnadenhutten settlement, and from there to Schoenbrunn, from which place the Delawares saw him safe to Fort Pitt, it being mid-winter, and the snow, as Jones states in his journal, some four to five feet deep.

MOCK DEVILS VISIT MR. JONES.

Rev. Jones, while down among the Shawanese, was treated to an exhibition of mock devils which he thus describes:

"Among the diversions of this people may be reckoned their mock devils, three of which I saw myself, and if I had not heard that Mr. Brainerd described such, I should have been more surprised. These they call manitous. Not long before my departure, a young Indian came into the house where I lodged, and told me that the manitous were coming, and if we did not give them something they would bedaub us with all nastiness. Upon which I looked out and saw them near one hundred yards off. All the Indians knew me, and therefore the manitous seeing me I apprehend intended to scare me. Each had a stick in his hand, and one stooped down by a tree as if he was going to shoot at me, but I could see that he had no gun. Afterward he came toward me, with all the pranks imaginable, making as hideous noises as he could possibly invent; each made the same noise. Each had false faces of light wood, and all were dressed in bear-skins, with the black hair on, so that they had no appearance of anything human. The foremost one had a great red face, with a huge, long nose, and prodigious large lips, his head above being covered with bear-skin. As he came near me, he made a wonderful rattling, with a great dry tortoise shell, having an artificial neck and head, and being filled with grains of corn, and other trinkets. The other two had black faces, resembling the countenance of a bear, with very long chins. They came around me with an abundance of pranks, making a noise nothing like the voice of a man. After some time, I asked them what they wanted; but manitous can not speak. They continued their racket, and at last showed me a pipe, by which I understood they wanted tobacco. Upon the reception of any gift, they make some kind of obeisance and depart, dancing the strangest capers that are possible. In short, their looks, voice and actions, are such that I thought if they had got their samples from beneath, the scene could not be much exceeded. This apparel is used also by their pow-wowers in their attempts at conjuration."

EVENTS OF 1774—NEW COMERSTOWN—MISSIONARIES AND INDIANS.

The year 1774 brought trouble to the missionaries and their settlements at Schoenbrunn and Gnadenhutten. A war had begun betwen the white settlers of Virginia and the Mingo, Wyandot and Shawanese tribes, dwelling on the north side of the Ohio. Whenever any of their number were killed they sought revenge upon the first white man who came in their way. Scalping parties came and hovered around the establishments at Schoenbrunn and Gnadenhutten, so that the missionaries were daily in danger of their lives, and dare not leave their houses.

The difficulties between the Virginians and Indians every day became more alarming to the Christian Indians and their missionaries, so to avert war the head men of the

Delawares proceeded to Pittsburgh to meet the deputies of the other nations and the English, in council, with a view of restoring peace. On the 5th of May, 1774, the council met and delivered condolence speeches to the Indians, requesting that Captain White Eyes would carry these speeches to the different nations, and obtain their answers. As these speeches and answers belong to the history of the valleys, they are here given in full, as published by authority of Congress, in the first volume, fourth series, American Archives:

"Pittsburgh, May 5, 1774.—At a condolence held with the Delawares, Six Nations, Shawanese, Munsies, Mohegans and Twigtwees, who are the several nations that have suffered in the late unfortunate disturbances.

"Present: Captain Conolly, commandant, and a number of other gentlemen.

"Six Nations Indians: Guyasutha, White Mingo, and a number of other chiefs, and principal men.

"Delawares: Captains White Eyes, Pipe, Keykewenum, and Samuel Compass, with a number of other Indians of that nation."

The English addressed the Indians thus:

"Brethren: It was with the deepest concern that we informed you two days ago of the late unhappy death of some of your friends, and it adds much to our grief, upon this occasion, when we consider that some of our rash, inconsiderate people, have been accessory thereto. We condole with you, and bewail the misfortunes you have suffered, and as a testimony of our sincerity, we deliver you these strings of wampum. (A string to each nation.)

"Brethren: We wipe the tears from your eyes, and remove the grief which this melancholy circumstance may have impressed upon your hearts, that you may be enabled to look upon your brethren (the English) with the same friendship as usual, and listen to them with the like goodness of heart as formerly, when no evil disturbed your minds. (A string to each nation.)

"Brethren: We now collect the bones of your deceased people, and wrap them up in these goods which we have prepared for that purpose, and we likewise inter them, that every remembrance of uneasiness upon this head may be extinguished, and also buried in oblivion. (Delivered a condolence present.)

"Brethren: We have now conformably with your custom, condoled with you in the usual manner upon such occasions; and we are to request some of your chiefs present, who have the most influence with the distant tribes, to proceed to them with the greatest expedition with what you have now heard, as it is highly necessary that we should be made acquainted, without delay, with the result of their councils upon the present circumstances of affairs, as well as it may be useful for them to be informed of our sentiments thereupon; and that the stroke they have received, is not only contrary to the judgment of every wise man among us, but all authority, which consequently will be exerted to do them justice; therefore these facts ought to have great weight in their determination at this time. And as a further proof of our uprightness toward them two of the gentlemen here present will accompany you in the execution of this good work. (A string of wampum.")

Captain White Eyes, on behalf of the Indians present, made the following answer:

"Brethren: (The English.) We have heard with satisfaction the several speeches you have now delivered to us, and we return our sincere thanks for the friendship and concern you have been pleased to express for us upon this occasion; we can not doubt of your uprightness toward us, and that the mischief done to us, has been done contrary to your intent and desire, which we believe has arose entirely from the evil minded persons who have been the perpetrators of it, therefore it is incumbent upon us to aid you with our best assistance. As the great and good work of peace has been established between us, by the labor and pains of our greatest and wisest men, it ought not to be disturbed by the folly or imprudence of any rash people whatever, who, hereafter, refusing to pay due obedience to good advice, or offering to slip their hand from the chain of friendship, it will be our duty to chastise, should not those examples of violence before their eyes have this effect.

"Brethren: I will carry your message to the other nations; they are intended for myself, as it is a business too serious to be trifled with, or boys to be employed on; it is thé happiness of ourselves, our women and children, and everything dear to us, that we are endeavoring to prescribe. Therefore there can be no doubt that I shall speak my sentiments fully and truly to all nations upon it. (A large string of white wampum.)

May 25. White Eyes after delivering the condolence speeches to the Delawares, at "The New Comerstown," received the following answer, directed to their brethren, the English:

"Brethren: We are glad to receive your messages now delivered to us by Captain White Eyes, upon the late disturbances which have happened between our young men, and we return you thanks for the speedy measures you have taken to speak to us upon it. We are entirely satisfied upon this account, and banish everything which could give us uneasiness from our hearts, as you desire us, and likewise request that you will do the same, that nothing may remain upon either side to discontent us. (A string.)

"Brethren: We have too great a regard for ancient friendship established between you and us, and which has so long existed between our forefathers, to suffer the conduct of foolish men to have any bad effect upon it, or to weaken our good intentions in the least, so as to loosen our hands from the hold we have of it; therefore we do not look toward the evil that has been done with any resentment in our mind, but with a desire to have it buried in oblivion, as well as everything else that has an appearance of disturbing our future tranquility. Be strong, brethren, and think favorably of our peace, as we do, and we shall be too powerful for any bad people, who are not inclined to listen to or preserve it as we do. Brethren, when our wise people concluded the peace that subsists between us, it was mutually agreed between them that the rashness or folly of bad men ought not, nor should not, have any evil effect upon the amity settled between them, and this is still what we adhere to. Brethren, last of all we spoke to our grandchildren, the Shawanese, upon this head, and desire them to keep their young, imprudent men from doing mischief, and this advice we have given them at this time. (A belt.)

"Brethren: From the road which you have cleared between you and us, we now, by this string of wampum, upon our parts, remove every obstacle that may impede our traveling it with satisfaction, and we desire that our young men may be permitted to continue their trade as usual. Those white people who are in our towns, to the number of eleven, you will see in a few days, who are going to Pittsburgh under the protection of your brethren the Delawares and as soon as matters wear a more favorable aspect, we shall expect them to return to our towns. (A string.)

The Shawanese then delivered the following answer to the condolence speakers, and message sent them:

"Brothers: (Captain Conolly, Mr. McKee and Mr. Croghan.) We have received your speeches by White Eyes, and as to what Mr. Croghan and Mr. McKee says, we look upon it all to be lies. Perhaps what you say may be lies also, but as it is the first time you have spoken to us, we also listen to you, and expect that what we may hear from you may be more confined to truth than what we usually hear from white people. It is you who are frequently passing down and up the Ohio, and making settlements upon it, and as you have informed us that your wise people were met together to consult upon this matter, we desire you to be strong, and consider it well.

"Brethren: We see you speak to us at the head of your warriors who have collected together at sundry places upon this river, where we understand they are building forts, and as you have requested us to listen to you, we will do it, but in the same manner that you appear to speak to us. Our people at the Lower Towns have no chiefs among them, but are all warriors, and are also preparing themselves to be in readiness that they may be better able to hear what you have to say. You tell us not to take any notice of what the people have done to us; we desire you likewise not to take any notice of what our young men may now be doing, and as no doubt you can command your warriors, when you desire them to listen to you, we have reason to expect that ours will take the same advice when we require—that is, when we have heard from the governor of Virginia.

"Brethren (of Pennsylvania): It is some years since we had the satisfaction of seeing you at Pittsburgh, when you came there to renew the ancient friendship that subsisted between our forefathers, and it gave us great pleasure to assist you in the great work when the path was opened between you and us, and we now tell you that your traders who have traveled it shall return the same road in peace, and we desire our grandfathers, the Delawares, to be strong in conducting them safe to you. (A string.")

This warlike speech of the Shawanese frustrated the hope of peace with them, which sorely exercised the missionaries.

The following extracts of letters from David Zeisberger, missionary at Schoenbrunn, dated May 24, 1774, depicts their trials:

"In my last I informed you of the critical situation in which we found ourselves here. We then were in hopes that the dark cloud would pass over soon, and peace be re-established, as the *Shawanese*, in the council at Wakatameka, had given seemingly a pretty favorable answer. But it appears now that they were only afraid of the *Delaware* party in the council, for we heard since that a party of twenty warriors were gone to make an incursion where the

Mingoes have been killed. The Chief *Netawatwes* brought this account himself mournfully to Gnadenhutten, desiring some messengers might be sent after one *Killbuck*, who was on the road to Pittsburgh, with the traders. We sent directly two men with a letter to Mr. Anderson, that they may know of it at Pittsburgh. The messengers returned last night, after having delivered their message. The Delawares suppose that the Shawanese will soon move off. I think our greatest danger would be if the white people would make an incursion into the Indians' land; and if they should strike the Dalawares, the war would be general, and we then could not continue here; but we will keep unto the Lord a solemn feast of thanksgiving if he rules things so that we can stay here, for our flight would be subject to many difficulties; and where should such a number of people find a twelve months' subsistence, if they must forsake all that they have planted, for we are more than two hundred souls in this place only, besides the congregation at Gnadenhutten; and to move into the settlements of the white people with our Indians, I can not find advisable. We know how it was in the last war.

"SCHOENBRUNN, May 27, 1774.—We are in great distress, and don't know what to do; our Indians keep watch about us every night, and will not let us go out of town, even not into our cornfields. If there should be more bad news, we will be forced to move from here, for we are in danger from both sides. I heard from some, that if the white brethren should be forced to leave them, the greatest part would return to the Susquehanna. But if only the Delawares continue in their peaceful mind, it may go better than we now think. At the council at *Wakatamaka*, were several head men of the Delawares present, who live at Schoenbrunn and Gnadenhutten, being particularly sent for by *Netawatwes* for to assist them in the good work of preserving peace. The chief addressed the Shawanese and Mingoes present in a fatherly manner, showing unto them the blessing of peace, and folly of war; and told them positively that they need not to expect any help or assistance from the Delawares. The Shawanese gave him in answer, they did believe his words to be good, and they would take notice of them, and desired him to give also a fatherly admonition to their wives to plant corn for them, which he did, but they seemed more inclined to move off than to plant."—*American Archives, fourth series, pages* 285–6.

On the same day that the above letter was written, some whites killed several Indians, a short distance above Wheeling, and those who escaped fled to the Delaware towns for protection, at the same time threatening vengeance.

At a meeting held with the Indians at Pittsburgh, the 29th of June, 1774.

"Present: Captain Aston, Major McCulloch, Captain Crawford, Mr. Valen Crawford, Captain Nevill, Mr. Edward Cook, Mr. John Steveson, Rev. Mr. Whiteaker, Mr. Joseph Wells, Mr. James Innis, Mr. Kneas Mackey, Mr. Joseph Simmons; with a number of the inhabitants and traders.

"Indians: Captain White Eyes, Weyandahila, Captain Johnny, with sundry other young men.

"Captain White Eyes first informed us that he had returned from transacting the business which he had been sent upon by his brethren, the English, and that he now had the satisfaction to tell us that he had succeeded in his negotiations with all those tribes of the several nations of whom he had since seen and conferred with upon the unhappy disturbances which unfortunately arose this spring between the foolish people of both parties; and that he had found all nations fully disposed to adhere to their ancient friendship and the advice of their wise men."

Here he delivered a paper from the chiefs of the Delawares, containing as follows:

"New Comerstown, June 21, 1774.—Brethren: When the late unhappy disturbances happened, you desired us to be strong and to speak to the other tribes of Indians to hold fast the chain of friendship subsisting between the English and them. We now inform you that we sent for our uncles, the Wyandots, and our grandchildren, the Shawanese, and also the Cherokees, and we have desired them to be strong and to inform all other nations, and hold fast on the chain which our grandfathers made, and you may depend our king still continues to go on in that good work.

"As things now seem to have a good prospect, and peace likely to be restored again, brothers, we desire you to be strong; and also, on your parts, to hold fast the chain of friendship, as you may remember when it was made it was agreed that even the loss of ten men on either side should not weaken it. If for the future we are all strong and brighten the chain of friendship, our foolish young men will not have it in their power to disturb it. We can not inform you any more of our grandchildren, the Shawanese, than that they are gone, and intend soon going to Fort Pitt, to hear of the disturbances that had happened between your foolish people and theirs, when you will then hear from their own mouths what they have to say.

"Brothers: As things now seem to be easy, and all the nations have now agreed to hold fast the chain of friendship, and make their young men sit quiet, we desire you to consider of what you have to say when our grandchildren, the Shawanese come to speak to you. The head men of the Shawanese are gone to Waketomica, and intend to send their king up to Fort Pitt, that he may himself hear what his brothers, the English, have to say.

"King Newcomer, Neolige,
"White Eyes, Killbuck,
"Thomas McKee, Wm. Anderson,
"Epaloind, Simon Girty.

"To George Croghan, A. McKee and J. Conolly, Esq."

New Comerstown appears at that day to have been a rendezvous as well for noted white men as Indians. McKee, Anderson and Simon Girty, whose names are attached above, were whites, and we notice the fact that while Zeisberger and Heckewelder at Schoenbrunn and Gnadenhutten were civilizing the Delaware Indians, the other Indians at

New Comerstown were making savages of white men. Girty, McKee and Anderson were of Irish birth, their parents having settled along the Susquehanna at an early day.

Jonathan Alder, who knew Girty, says he was a friend to many prisoners, and that he knew of Girty having purchased several white boys from the Indians, and sent them to the British to be educated.

Heckewelder, in his narrative, gives the following version of the troubles of 1774, in the Tuscarawas valley:

"The year 1774 was a year of trial to the Indian congregations, on account of a war which broke out between the people of Virginia, and the Senecas and Shawanese tribes of Indians, in which, as it became well known, the white people were the aggressors. Of these latter, a number were settled on choice spots of land, on the south side of the Ohio River, while the Indians dwelt on the north side, then their territory. The sale of land below the Kanawah River had opened a wide field for speculation. The whole country on the Ohio River had already drawn the attention of persons from the neighboring provinces, who, generally forming themselves into parties, would rove through the country in search of land, either to settle on or for speculation; and some, careless of watching over their conduct, or destitute of humanity, would join a rabble (a class of people generally met on the frontiers), who maintained that to kill an Indian was the same as killing a bear or a buffalo, and would fire on Indians that came across them by the way; nay, more, would decoy such as lived across the river to come over for the purpose of joining them in hilarity, and when these complied, they fell on them and murdered them."

Heckewelder continues:

"It is indescribable how enraged the relations of the murdered became on seeing such abominable acts committed without cause, and even by some white men who always pretended to be their friends. The cries of the relations of the sufferers soon reached the ears of the respective nations to whom they belonged, and who quickly resolved to take revenge on the long knives; (for, said they) 'they are a barbarous people.' Some, however, considering the difficulty of meeting the perpetrators, proposed killing every white man in their country, until they should believe themselves amply revenged for the valuable lives lost by the long knife men (Virginians). Nothing could equal the rage of the Senecas, in particular, and it was impossible to foresee where the matter would end. Parties after parties came on, the missionaries had to keep within their houses, the enraged Indians insisted that every able man should do his utmost to take revenge. They kept on the look out for traders, to kill them, but these had already generally fled the country, while some were taken under protection by friendly Shawanese Indians, who afterward conducted them safely to Pittsburgh. These good people however, oh! shameful to relate! were, on their return, waylaid by some of those white vagabonds, fired upon, and one man shot in the breast, in which situation he, with his wound bleeding, fortunately reached Schoenbrunn, where it was dressed, and all possible attention paid him.

"A Mr. Jones, who followed trading, and was at the time coming with two men in a canoe up the Muskingum, being ignorant of what had happened, was happily apprised of his danger, and the risk he was running, by an Indian woman, who discovering him, advised him, without a moment's delay, to leave the canoe and take the woods direct for New Comerstown, where he would be safe. On the second day of their traveling in this manner, having accidentally hit upon the path leading to the Shawanese towns, at Waketameki, one of Jones' men, named Campbell, feeling himself so fatigued by traveling in the woods, declared he would not leave the path again, and from which resolution he could not be persuaded. Scarcely had these two men got to the ridge when they heard the scalp yell in the direction they supposed the man to be. The fact was, a large party of Senecas, relations to those who had been murdered on the Ohio, and now on their way to Waketameki, meeting this man, murdered him, and in their rage cut up the body and stuck the pieces on the bushes, marching off in triumph. Captain White Eyes, who lived some distance from the path, hearing the yell, run instantly in that direction, where he found the mangled body, which he collected and buried. The party, however, on returning the next day and finding what had been done, tore up the grave, and scattered the pieces at a greater distance. White Eyes, now on the watch, discovering what they were doing, repaired to the spot a second time, and succeeding in finding every part of the mangled body, carefully dug a grave in a more secure place, and interred the whole.

"Next, a Mr. Duncan, well known to almost every Indian in the parts, was sent out from Pittsburgh, to endeavor to procure from the enemy a cessation of hostilities until government could hold a conference with them. But before he reached Waketameki, having Captain White Eyes for his conductor, he was fired upon, and had a very narrow escape. The enemy now renewed their threats against the Delawares, declaring that if they did not join in the conflict they should pay for it.

"A report being in circulation that the governor of Virginia was marching troops against the enemies' towns on the Scioto and Muskingum, and the inimical Indians having, for the purpose of fighting them, all moved westward of the Christian Indian towns, it was thought a proper time to conduct the missionary Rothe, with his wife and child, to a place of more safety, while the other missionaries were determined to hold out to the last. Accordingly the former were taken to Pittsburgh, from whence they proceeded to Bethlehem; while those remained, together with the Christian Indians, who were holding themselves in readiness to depart and proceed up the river to Cuyahoga should the Virginia troops be beaten, which, however, was not the case, for after the battle at or near the great Kanawah, the enemy sued for peace, promising to deliver up all the prisoners in their possession. In the course of the expedition the Shawanese towns at Waketameki had been destroyed by the white troops, while the orders given by their commanders were, not to pass through any of the Christian Indian towns, nor in any manner to disturb those Indians.

"On the joyful news of peace being concluded between the contending parties, the Christian Indians set apart the 6th day of November as a day of thanksgiving and prayer, which was celebrated with solemnity, offering up thanks and praises to the Lord for his gracious protection.

"The war being now ended, which, although of short duration, was dreadful in its nature for the time it lasted, the general wish of the Christian Indians was that a durable peace might follow.

"In other respects this year (1774) had been remarkable to the Christian Indians. First, the chiefs of the nation, both on the Muskingum and at Cuschcushke, had unitedly agreed and declared that the brethren should have full liberty to preach the gospel to the nation wherever they chose, and this resolution they also made publicly known. And, secondly, these seeing that their friends and relations pursued agriculture, and kept much cattle, they enlarged the tract of land first set apart for them, by moving their people off to a greater distance, and consulting their uncles, the Wyandots, on the subject (they being the nation from whom the Delawares had originally received the land), these set apart, granted, and confirmed all that country lying between Tuscarawas (old town) and the great bend below New Comerstown, a distance of thirty miles on the river, and including the same to the Christian Indians. Two large belts of wampum were on this occasion delivered by the Wyandots and the chiefs of the Delaware nation to the Christian Indians, who in return thanked them for the gift, both verbally and by belts and strings of wampum.

"The peace and rest enjoyed by the Indian congregation

throughout the year 1775 was favorable to visitors, who came in numbers to hear the gospel preached, so that the chapel at Schoenbrunn, although large, was too small to contain them. The heathen preacher, Wangomend, had also in this year come on from Goschgoshink, to see if he could succeed in propagating his foolish doctrines, but the Indian brethren bid him go to their children and learn of them.

"Toward the fall of this year two valuable, worthy, and exemplary national assistants departed this life—the one John Papunhank, a Delaware, and the other Joshua, of the Mohican tribe. Both were, at their respective places, wardens of the congregation, the former at Schoenbrunn, and the latter at Gnadenhutten. Joshua was one of the first Indians baptised by the brethren in 1742."

LEGEND OF THE WHITE WOMAN, AND NEW COMERSTOWN.

"Near the junction of the Killbuck and Walhonding rivers, a few miles north-west of the present Coshocton, lived, as early as 1750, Mary Harris, a white woman. She had been captured in one of the colonies, by the Indians, between 1730 and 1740, and was then a girl verging into womanhood. Her beauty captivated a chief, who made her his wife in the Indian fashion of that day.

"The Indian tribes were being crowded back from the eastern colonies, and the tribe of Custaloga had retired from place to place before the white frontier men, until about 1740 it found a new hunting ground in this valley, where the white woman became one of the inhabitants with her warrior, and where they raised a wigwam which formed the nucleus of an Indian town near the forks of the stream above named. Mary Harris had been sufficiently long with the Indians to become fascinated with their nomadic life and entered into all its romantic avenues, following Eagle Feather, her husband, to all the buffalo, elk and bear hunts in the valley, and whenever he went off with a war party to take a few scalps, she mixed his paint and laid it on, and plumed him for the wars, always putting up with her own hands a sufficiency of dried venison and parched corn for the journey. She was especially careful to polish with soap-stone his 'little hatchet,' always, however, admonishing him not to return without some good long-haired scalps for wigwam parlor ornaments and chignons, such as were worn by the first class of Indian ladies along the Killbuck. So prominent had she become that the town was named 'The White Woman's Town,' and the river from thence to the Muskingum was called in honor of her, 'The White Woman's River.'

"In 1750, when Christopher Gist was on his travels down the valley hunting out the best lands for George Washington's Virginia Land Company, he stopped some time at White Woman's Town, and enjoyed its Indian festivities with Mary Harris, who told him her story; how she liked savage warriors; how she preferred Indian to white life, and said the whites were a wicked race and more cruel than the red man.

"In her wigwam, the white woman was the master spirit, and Eagle Feather was ignored, except when going to war, or when she desired to accompany him on his hunting expeditions, or was about to assist at the burning of some poor captive, on which occasions she was a true squaw to him, and loved him much. All went along as merrily as possible until one day Eagle Feather came home from beyond the Ohio with another white woman, whom he had captured, and who he intended should enjoy the felicities of Indian life on the Killbuck with Mary in her wigwam. She, however, did not see happiness from that stand point, and forthwith the advent of 'The New Comer,' as Mary called her, into that home, made it, as Pomeroy used to say, 'red hot' for Eagle Feather all the time, her puritan idea of the marital overtopping the Indian idea of domestic virtue. Hence, Eagle Feather, whenever he tendered any civilities to the 'new comer,' encountered from Mary all the frowns and hair-raising epithets usually applied by white women to white men of our day under similar surroundings, and he became miserable and unhappy. Failing to appreciate all this storming around the wigwam, he reminded Mary that he could easily kill her; that he had saved her life when captured; had always provided her bear and deer meat to eat, and skins of the finest beasts to lie upon, and in return she had borne him no pappooses, and to provide for her shortcomings in this respect he had brought the 'new comer' home to his wigwam to make all things even again, as a chief who died without young braves to succeed him would soon be forgotten. So saying he took the new captive by the hand, and they departed to the forest to await the operation of his remarks on Mary's mind. Returning at night, and finding her asleep on her buffalo-skins, he lay down beside her as if all were well, at the same time motioning the 'new comer' to take a skin and lie down in the corner.

"He was soon asleep, having in his perturbed state of mind partaken of some whisky saved from the last raid in Virginia. On the following morning he was found with his head split open, and the tomahawk remaining in the skull-crack, while the 'new comer' had fled. Mary, simulating, or being in ignorance of the murder, at once aroused 'The White Woman's Town' with her screams. The warriors were soon out at her wigwam, and comprehending the situation, at once started in pursuit of the fleeing murderess, whom they tracked to the Tuscarawas; thence to an Indian town near by, where they found her. She was claimed as a deserter from 'The White Woman's Town,' and, under the Indian code, liable to be put to death, whether guilty of the murder or not. She was taken back while Gist was at the town, and he relates in his journal that after night a white woman captive who had deserted, was put to death in this manner: 'She was set free and ran off some distance, followed by three Indian warriors, who, overtaking her, struck her on the side of the head with their tomahawks, and otherwise beat and mutilated the body after life was extinct, then left it lying on the ground. Andrew Burney, a blacksmith at 'The White Woman's Town,' obtained and buried the body.

"Mary Harris insisted that the 'new comer' killed her husband with his own hatchet, in revenge for being brought into captivity, while she, as tradition gives it, alleged that Mary did the wicked work out of jealousy, and intended dispatching her also, but she was defeated in her project by the flight of 'new comer.' Be that as it may, Eagle Feather was sent to the spirit-land for introducing polygamy among white ladies in the valley, and as to the 'new comer,' the town to which she fled was thence forward called 'The New Comer's Town' by the Indians as early as 1755. When Netawatwes, chief of the Delawares, took up his abode there about 1760, he retained the name, it corresponding with his own in English. When Colonel Boquet, in 1764, marched down the valley and deposed Netawatwes, he retained the name on his map. When Governor Penn, of Pennsylvania, sent messages to the Indians in 1774, he retained the name in his official paper. When Brodhead, in 1780, marched down to Coshocton, he called it by the same name. In 1827 the good old Nicholas Neighbor, when he laid it off in lots, saw that it would pay him to retain the old name, and did so.

"Mary Harris married again, had children, and removed west about the time Pipe Wolf's tribe removed to Sandusky, in 1778–9. After that she became oblivious in history; but the river from Coshocton to the mouth of Killbuck is still called 'The White Woman's River.'"

THE REVOLUTION—PIPE AND WHITE EYES.

The American colonies having a congress, in 1775, appointed commissioners to convene the chiefs of the western Indians at Pittsburgh, for the purpose of explaining the dispute between the English government and the colonies, and to enlist the tribes on the side of the latter. Heckewelder relates that after the chiefs of the Delawares returned to the Tuscarawas, they proceeded to explain the cause of the dispute to their tribe, and did it as follows:

"Suppose a father had a little son whom he loved and indulged while young, but growing up to be a youth, began to think of having some help from him; and making up a small pack, he bid him carry it for him. The boy cheerfully takes this pack up, following his father with it. The father finding the boy willing and obedient, continues in this way; and as the boy grows stronger, so the father makes the pack in proportion larger; yet as long as the boy is able to carry the pack, he does so without grumbling. At length, however, the boy having arrived at manhood, while the father is making up the pack for him, in comes a person of an evil disposition, and, learning who was to be the carrier of the pack, advises the father to make it heavier, for surely the son is able to carry a larger pack. The father, listening rather to the bad adviser than consulting his own judgment and the feelings of tenderness, follows the advice of the hard-hearted adviser, and makes up a heavy load for his son to carry. The son, now grown up, examining the weight of the load he is to carry, addresses the parent in these words: 'Dear father, this pack is too heavy for me to carry, do pray lighten it; I am willing to do what I can, but am unable to carry this load.' The father's heart having by this time become hardened, and the bad adviser calling to him, whip him if he disobeys, and he refusing to carry the pack, the father orders his son to take up the pack and carry it off or he will whip him, and already takes up a stick to beat him. 'So,' says the son, 'am I to be served thus for not doing what I am unable to do? Well, if entreaties avail nothing with you, father, and it is to be decided by blows, whether or not I am able to carry a pack so heavy, then I have no other choice left me, but that of resisting your unreasonable demand by my strength, and thus, by striking each other, learn who is the strongest.'" Such (Indian reports stated) was a parable given them for the purpose of explaining the nature of the dispute.

They further reported, "that the commissioners had told them that, as the dispute did not concern them, it would be highly wrong in them (the American people) were they to ask the aid of their Indian brethren in bringing the dispute between them and the parent to a close; for, by so doing, they would be made parties to the quarrel, which might involve them in difficulties and dangers, particularly as it could not be foreseen in whose favor the quarrel would terminate. That were they to ask the assistance of their brethren, the Indians, and they together should fail in gaining what they sought for, they would have to suffer with their white brethren; and so, *vice versa*, the case would be were they to join the other side. That therefore they would advise them to sit still until the contest should be over, be friends to both sides, and not take up the hatchet against either; for by taking the hatchet up to strike either side, they must infallibly create to themselves an enemy, who, should it so happen that he became the conqueror, would punish them, take their land from them, &c. And, further, that as, in the course of the war it might happen that their brethren, the Americans, would not have it in their power to supply them with all that they might want, they, not having taken up arms against the British, would consequently be supplied from that side, with such articles as they stood in need of; that their American brethren sought their welfare, and having land enough of their own, did not wish to deprive them of theirs, but sought to secure their constant friendship as brothers, who had sprung up together from one and the same soil; that they wished to make them a great people, and that they would do so to every nation and people that should take the advice herewith given them; yet that they must tell them, that whatever nation should take up the hatchet and strike them, such nation must abide the consequence should they, the American people, become conquerors. Lastly (the reporters added), that in consequence of the good advice given them by their American brethren, the chiefs of the Delawares present at this treaty, had for themselves, and in the name of the whole nation, declared to the commissioners that they would remain neutral during the 'contest between the parent and the son, and not lift up the hatchet against either side.'"

About this time (says Heckewelder), while a number of Senecas were at Pittsburgh, perhaps more for the purpose of learning the disposition of the western nations, particularly that of the Delawares, with regard to the side they should take during the contest, they had an opportunity of hearing Captain White Eyes deliver his sentiments, openly declaring in favor of the American people and their cause, which so chagrined them that they thought proper to offer a check to his proceedings, by giving him, in a haughty tone, a hint, intended to remind him what the Delaware nation was in the eyes of the Six Nations (meaning that it had no will of its own, but was subordinate to the Six Nations), when Captain White Eyes, long since tired of this language, with his usual spirit, and in an air of disdain rose and replied, that "he well knew that the Six Nations considered his nation as a conquered people, and their inferiors. 'You say,' said he, 'that you had conquered me; that you had cut off my legs; had put a petticoat on me, giving me a hoe and corn-pounder in my hands, saying, 'Now, woman, your business henceforward shall be to plant and hoe corn, and pound the same for bread for us men and warriors!' Look (continued White Eyes) at my legs! if, as you say, you had cut them off, they have grown again to their proper size! the petticoat I have thrown away, and put on my proper dress! the corn-hoe and pounder I have exchanged for these fire-arms, and I declare that I am a man!" Then waving his hand in the direction of the Alleghany River, he exclaimed, "and all the country on the other side of that river is mine!"

Perhaps so bold or daring an address was never made to any council of Indians, by an individual chief. But it ought to be noticed, that White Eyes had here spoken on the strength of what the commissioners had said and promised at the treaty. In what they had said he placed full confidence. He took it for granted that the Senecas would join the English against the American people, and therefore lose the land they had so artfully wrested from the Delawares; and, in the firm belief that his nation would keep the peace, he had a right to lay a claim to it. Moreover, his expectation went to this: that should the Six Nations, in consequence of the language he had made use of to them, take up arms against his nation—they being friends of the American people, and at peace with them, they would assist them in fighting for their just rights.

The report of Captain White Eyes' declaration to the Senecas having become known to his nation, some feared the consequence of such daring language, to so proud and powerful a body as the Six Nations, combined, were in comparison to them; while others were satisfied at his proceedings, having long wished to resume their ancient station and character among the Indian nations, so clandestinely wrested from them by the ancestors of these very people. This circumstance was, however, the cause of a division among them, in which the Munsies took the lead. They pretended apprehensions that the Six Nations would resent the liberty White Eyes had taken; and made this a pretense of withdrawing themselves from the councils of the Turtle tribe, and joining themselves to the Wolf tribe.

8

Nor did the Munsey chief, Newalike, rest until he had succeeded in detaching a number of their tribe from the Christian Indians at Schoenbrunn, who had taken it for granted that their chief was secretly acquainted with some evil which would befall the Delaware nation, and therefore wished to remove them from danger. They (the Munsies), retiring nearer to Lake Erie, took care to have the Six Nations informed that they did not approve of what Captain White Eyes had said. And Captain Pipe, at the head of his tribe, was glad to see a breach made, of which White Eyes was to bear the blame. Pipe was an artful, cunning man. Ambitious and fond of power, he endeavored to create a mistrust in the minds of individuals of the nation —persuading them to believe that their chief (White Eyes) had entered into secret engagements with the American people, for the purpose of having their young people enslaved, while they (the chiefs) were to reap the benefit thereof, and be lords over them. Pipe's place of residence was on Waldhonding, about fifteen miles from Goshocking (forks of the Muskingum). Hitherto he had regularly attended the councils at the latter place, but now began to withdraw, probably from a conviction that his intrigues were known, and might one day be held up to him by the chiefs, and he be obliged to render an account of his conduct. The peace chiefs, however, pursued their usual course—their sole object being the welfare of the nation.

SETTLEMENT AT COSHOCTON—1776.

In April, 1776, a third mission settlement was began with eight families, in all thirty-five persons, under their faithful leader, David Zeisberger, and the Rev. John Heckewelder. They laid off a town, within two miles of Goshocking (the present Coshocton), and called it Lichtenau. The word means "The Pasture of Light." The town was laid off in the form of a cross, and stretched along the bank of the river, on one street. The chapel was built equi-distant from the ends of the street. The head chief, Netawatwes, of the Delaware capitol, had abandoned Gekelemukpechunk, when the breach took place among the Delawares, and with those of his tribe who remained true to him, he proceeded to the forks of the Tuscarawas and Walhonding, and built a new capital called, according to Heckewelder, "Goshochking," and according to De Schweinetz, "Goschachgunk." It occupied the lower streets of the present county town of Coshocton. When preaching commenced at Lichtenau, Netawatwes and his family were among the first converts. He had selected the spot for Lichtenau to be erected upon, and recommended it to Zeisberger, as he had a few years before selected "Big Spring"—Schoenbrunn—for a mission. Schoenbrunn, like Lichtenau, was built in the form of a cross, and the latter, like Schoenbrunn, was erected on the site of the remains of earthworks, put there by the ancient mound-builders. Thus the Indian, unconscious of the fact, became the central figure of ages gone, and ages yet to come.

NETAWATWES—CORNSTALK—GEORGE MORGAN—1777.

Netawatwes lived to see both Lichtenau and Schoenbrunn abandoned, and surrendered to heathenism, by reason of the war between christian nations.

Heckewelder says:

"The Chief Netawatwes, together with the chiefs, White Eyes, Gelelemend (alias *Killbuck*), Machingwi Puschiis (alias the *Big Cat*), and others, did everything in their power to preserve peace among the nations, by sending embassies, and exhorting them not to take up the hatchet, or to join either side; to which, however, the Sandusky Wyandots insolently replied: 'that they advised their cousins (the Delawares) to keep shoes in readiness to join the warriors.' This message being returned to them by the Delaware council, with the admonition, 'to sit down and reflect on the misery they had brought upon themselves, by taking an active part in the war between the English and French;' but they thought proper to send a message to the same purport, also to the chiefs of that nation (the Wyandots) living in the vicinity of Detroit, advising that one of these messengers, to be sent with the message, should be selected from among their body. Having accordingly arrived at the Huron village, below Detroit, they were told that no message from the Delaware council could be laid before them, except in the presence of the governor. Conscious as to the powers conferred on them, at the time they were, by the Five Nations, made and declared mediators and peacemakers between the nations, they could not even have a doubt as to the legality of the message; yet, scarcely had these deputies produced their peace belts, when the governor laying hold of them cut them into pieces, and throwing these pieces at the feet of the deputies, commanded them to leave the place within half an hour, or abide the consequences; and Captain White Eyes, who had been the principal bearer of the message, was, after being insulted, told 'that if he sat any value on his head he must be gone instantly.'

"In consequence of this insult to the nation (for the chiefs and council considered it in no other light), they went to Pittsburgh to lay the case before their agent, for the information of Congress, who advised them, together with all peaceably disposed Indians, to come under their protection; but, as sad experience had taught them, by the murder of the Canestoga Indians in the very town of Lancaster, and the narrow escape of the Christian Indians in the city of Philadelphia from being murdered by the Paxton boys, no chief would venture to make this proposal known to his people. As to the safety of the missionaries, government had advised them, through their agent, to take refuge at Pittsburgh; but they chose rather to suffer whatever might befall them, than desert a people committed to their care, and especially when they were most in want of advice and consolation."

Congress having appointed Colonel George Morgan Indian Agent, he that winter visited Schoenbrunn and Gnadenhutten, and had runners sent out to the western Indians with presents to induce them to remain at peace with the colonies, but in that he was unsuccessful, the British having already from Canada been among them, and impressed the western tribes with the belief that the colonists intended to take all the Indians' land, and pointed to the settlements at Schoenbrunn and Gnadenhutten as the rendezvous of the "land stealers," as they called the Americans.

The Delawares, however, still remained friendly, and Heckewelder relates of them that the Delaware chiefs, having at this time in their possession documents and vouchers, both in writing and strings and belts of wampum, of all transactions that had passed between their ancestors and the government of Pennsylvania, from the time William Penn first arrived in the country down to the present time, had hitherto been in the habit of meeting, at least once every year, for the purpose of refreshing their memories on the subject, by hearing the contents; as also, that of instructing one or more promising young men to learn by heart such valuable documents, that they might not be lost to future generations. In assembling for this purpose, they chose to be by themselves in the woods, at a convenient spot, where no person could interrupt them; and when any written documents were produced, they requested one or the other of the missionaries to attend, to read and interpret them.

Heckewelder in his journal says:

"The northern warriors being continually on the watch for such white people who might venture out to the Delaware towns, it was dangerous for any one to attempt such a thing. Yet it so happened that Mr. James O'Hara, who had come out to Schoenbrunn on business, was found out by some of these warriors, eleven of whom were coming on to seize him; but halting on their way at an Indian cabin, nine miles distant, where the man and his sons were equally friends to the Americans, the old man discovering their intentions, privately sent off in the night one of his sons to the writer of this narrative, with the following verbal message: 'My friend! see that our white friend, now at your village, be taken from thence this night, and conducted to a place of safety in the settlement of the white people; and do not neglect to act up to my message. Hear my son farther on the subject!' The son giving the best assurance that at the break of day the party would be here for the purpose of taking, and perhaps murdering Mr. O'Hara, he was informed of it, and forthwith conducted by Anthony, a smart and trusty Indian, through the woods to the Ohio River, and there taken across by white people living on the oppósite shore. The young man who had, agreeable to his father's instructions, immediately returned home, after delivering the message, seeing them sometime after mid-night preparing to set off for the purpose of executing their design, questioned them as to their intentions, and finding that the supposition had been correct, he replied, 'your errand will fail, for the white man you are after is no more there, but returned to Pittsburgh.' On being assured of this, they bent their course another way."

Within a fortnight after the above had taken place, reports in succession were brought to Schoenbrunn that large parties were on their way to murder the missionaries; and the fear of many of the Christian Indians at this place was so great they could not content themselves, unless they had placed them out of all danger. The missionaries, although unwilling to go, and not believing the danger so great as represented, yet had to submit, and were at night taken to Gnadenhutten, from whence, however, Heckewelder returned again in the morning, and there found the Munsey chief, *Newalike*, from Sandusky, pressing those of his tribe to leave the place and save themselves, since 'all living here would soon be murdered, if they remained in the parts;' he thought it his duty to inform the senior missionary, at Lichtenau, thirty miles distant, of the mischief that was intended by the Munsey chief, and others from Sandusky. The missionary without delay having come on, and finding matters worse than he had expected, made known in a public meeting that the place would be evacuated; inviting, at the same time, all such as had a desire to cleave to the Lord, and rely on his help, to get ready to follow their teachers; a last discourse was delivered, and concluded by a fervent prayer. Next the chapel was pulled down, that it might not be made use of for heathenish purposes, and the congregation left the place the same day.

Shoenbrunn had been the largest and handsomest town the Christian Indians had hitherto built, containing upward of sixty dwelling houses, most of which were squared timbers. The street, from east to west, was long and of proper width; from the centre, where the chapel stood, another street run off to the north. The inhabitants had for the greater part become husbandmen. They had large fields under good rail fences, well paled gardens, and fine fruit trees, besides herds of cattle, horses and hogs.

The two congregations, Lichtenau and Gnadenhutten, about twenty-seven miles asunder, had now each one missionary left, and the prospect before them was that of a succession of troubles. These two brethren had, however, made a covenant to remain with their people, and preferred suffering death rather than deserting their posts.

Added to their other troubles came the news of the murder of "Cornstalk," a celebrated Shawanese chief, in the summer of 1777. He had been to the Ohio, and with two companions went over to the garrison at Point Pleasant to talk of peace. The Virginians shut him up in the fort as a hostage for the good behavior of his tribe. Hearing this, his son crossed over and was also shut up with his father. The next day the Indians on the Ohio side killed a white man named Gilmore, and as soon as the garrison heard of it, they rushed to the guard house and shot Cornstalk and his son. Cornstalk was a celebrated warrior, but inclined at times to peace. He had visited Schoenbrunn and Gnadenhutten often, and been impressed with the ideas of Zeisberger, but his tribe were war men. His death greatly exasperated the hostile Indians, and many were the threats to take vengeance on the Moravian settlements. Of Cornstalk, Wilson says that at the battle of Point Pleasant his voice was heard above the din of battle, encouraging the Indians in these words, "Be strong, be strong!" and seeing one of his men skulking, Cornstalk sunk his tomahawk into him. Dr. Doddridge, in his notes, says of Cornstalk, that after the Indians had returned from the battle, Cornstalk called a council at the Chillicothe town, to consult what was to be done next. In this council he reminded the war chiefs of their folly in preventing him from making peace, before the fatal battle of Point Pleasant, and asked, "What shall we do now, the long-knives are coming upon us from two routes; shall we turn out and fight them?" All were silent. He then asked: "Shall we kill all our squaws and children, and then fight until we shall all be killed ourselves?" To this no reply was made. He then rose up and struck his tomahawk in the war post, in the middle of the council house, saying, "Since you are not inclined to fight, I will go and make peace." And accordingly did so.

On the morning of the day of his death, a council was held in the fort at the Point, in which he was present. During the sitting of the council, it is said that he seemed to have a presentiment of his approaching fate. In one of his speeches he remarked to the council, "When I was young, every time I went to war I thought it likely that I might return no more; but I still live, I am now in your hands, and you may kill me if you choose, I can die at once, and it is alike to me, whether I die now or at any other time." When the men presented themselves before the door, for the purpose of killing the Indians, Cornstalk's son manifested signs of fear, on observing which his father said, "Don't be afraid my son, the great Spirit sent you here to die with me, and we must submit to his will. It is all for the best."

It is related by Zeisberger's biographer, that in 1777, when the border war broke out again, the Governor of Detroit sent a hatchet, wrapped in a belt of red and white beads, to the Shawanese, Wyandots, Mingoes, and it was to be offered to the Delawares, and their tribal relatives, and any tribe refusing to accept it, was to be treated as a common enemy. Cornstalk came to the council house at Goshocking, or Goshochgunk, stating that all the Shawanese except his own tribe, accepted the hatchet, and his tribe came and settled at the Delaware capital, he advising the Delawares to hold fast to the chain of peace; they refused the war-belt three times, but at last accepting it, to get rid of the Wyandot messengers, they sent it back to Sandusky as soon as the messengers left their capital.

THE MONSEY CONSPIRACY AT SCHOENBRUNN—1777.

One cause of the troubles of the missions was want of courage, jealousy, and envy among the missionaries. Of Zeisberger it is presumed that not one line can be found among the archives of the missions, in support of an averment that he was either jealous or envious of his brothers, or lacked courage in emergencies. But there is no doubt of the fact that he was hated by one or more of the brethren in secret, because of his paramount influence over the Indians, and his popularity at Bethlehem, and that timidity controlled a portion in times of danger and peril, and hence whenever a crisis arose at the missions over which he had charge, he at least found lukewarmness and indecision where he should have had zealous council and efficient aid. His biographer admits that "there was a want of harmony among the missionaries; they were jealous, one of the other, and the Indians were left as sheep without a shepherd."

The Monsey Indians at Schoenbrunn were seduced to throw off their allegiance as Christian converts. They entered into a plot, concocted by British emissaries, to forsake the mission, join the hostile Indians, and return to heathenism, first capturing and sending away the missionaries. Zeisberger being at Lichtenau was apprised of the conspiracy and hastened to Schoenbrunn, only to find the town in the hands of the conspirators, and the missionaries who were left in charge fled. On the 19th of April, 1777, he called as many of the converts together as could be rallied, and took the road to Lichtenau *via* Gnadenhutten, and Schoenbrunn was given over to the deserters. To show that the Monseys could have been retained in the church by moral courage, it is only necessary to state that they were afterward brought back to the fold by the appeals of Zeisberger to them, when they came raiding around Lichtenau in less than a year after. But in the meantime Schoenbrunn was demolished by the hostile warriors, and when Zeisberger led his converts back in 1779, it was necessary to build a new town on the west side of the river.

This conspiracy, trifling as it turned out to be in results, was but part of an extended effort to subdue the colonies in their effort to attain independence. The hostile Indian warriors, if all mustered at the time, were computed at ten thousand, and to array them all it was only necessary to break up these missions, which acted as breakwaters in dividing the Indian waves that would have swept otherwise over the border States, at a time when the colonies were least able to repel them. Zeisberger's moral courage alone saved the border States from being overrun by the savages in that crisis, and perhaps he thereby saved the Union.

DUNMORE'S WAR—THE WAKATOMICA CAMPAIGN—DRESDEN—LEGEND OF ABRAHAM THOMAS.

In 1774 the Virginia government sent out one thousand men under Governor Lord Dunmore to Ohio, to chastise the Indians. The larger portion proceeded to the Pickaaway country, and defeated the enemy in several skirmishes along the Ohio River, and made peace with them at Chillicothe, the principal town of the Shawanese.

Another portion of the Virginia forces under a Colonel Aymer McDonald, in June, 1774, proceeded from Wheeling west to an Indian town, called by the Shawanese *Wa-ka-tamo-sepe*, near the present site of Dresden. The word was corrupted into *Wakatomeka*, and Wakatomica, and means "a town on the river-side." McDonald's force numbered four hundred, and when near the town it met and dispersed a band of fifty Indians, killing several and losing two, with eight wounded. On reaching the town they found it deserted, the Indians having retreated across the river; and failing to draw McDonald into an ambuscade, they sued for peace, and sent over five chiefs as hostages. He released two to go and bring in all the chiefs to the peace conference, but they did not return, whereupon he burnt the town of Wakatomeka and adjacent cornfields, and other Indian towns on his way, and returned to Virginia with his three chiefs, who were released the same fall by the peace treaty of Lord Dunmore, made at the old Chillicothe town.

Abraham Thomas, when a lad of eighteen, ran away from home in Virginia, and joined the Wakatomeka expedition. In his reminiscences, he says the plan of the expedition was for each man to cross the Ohio with seven days' rations on his back. On the second day out they were joined by Colonel McDonald, who ordered a three days' halt, which greatly incensed the men, as the delay cut up their provisions. A violent storm wet their arms in the night, and the colonel ordered the men to discharge their guns in a hollow log, to deaden the sound. "My rifle would not go off, and I made a noise in beating it with my tomakawk. McDonald came at me with his uplifted cane, on account of fearing that the noise would be heard by the Indians. I arose to my feet, with the rifle barrel in my hand, in self-defense. We looked each other in the eye for some time. At last he dropped his cane and walked off. The men all laughed, and said the boy had scared the colonel. From this encampment we proceeded toward the Indian villages, intending to surprise them, but before reaching them we encountered the Indians in ambush on a second bottom. We marched in three parties, Indian-file columns, and received their fire. The troops deployed to the right and left, and the fight lasted thirty minutes, when the Indians gave way in every direction. While I was ascending a bank with Martin and Fox, all aiming to gain the cover of some large oak trees on the top, they both fell. The first was killed, the last wounded in the breast. Those men were walking in a line with each other, and an Indian chief behind the tree shot them both with one ball. I took no notice whence the ball came, and hastened to the tree. Just as I had gained it the chief fell dead from the other side, and rolled at my feet. It seems a neighbor had seen him fire at Martin and Fox, then dodge behind the tree to load. The Indian had got his ball half down, and peeped out to look at me, when Wilson shot him dead. The Indians retreated toward Wakatomica, flanked by two companies in hot pursuit. We followed in the rear, and as the last Indian was stepping out of the water, Captain Teabaugh brought him to the ground. Night coming on, the division was ordered to encamp in an oak woods. This evening Jack Hayes was spying down the creek and saw an Indian looking at us through the forks of a low tree. He leveled his rifle and shot him between the eyes, and brought him into camp. Captain Cresap* was up the whole

*[*Note* —The Captain Cresap referred to is the same to whom Logan addressed his war-club letter from New Comerstown, a month after Cresap and his men had destroyed Wakatomica town].

night, going the rounds and cautioning his men to keep their arms in a condition for a morning attack. About two hours before day he silently led his men across the creek into the villages, but the Indians fled into an adjoining thicket and dispersed. As we were nearly out of provisions the troops returned to the settlements. The men became exceedingly famished on this march, and I, being young, was so weak that I could not carry any thing. I saw my brother have a good stock of tobacco, and after some beseeching I got a piece, although I had never used it. It revived me, and I was soon able to travel with the rest of them, and was actually the first to reach the Ohio."

CHAPTER VI.

LEGEND OF CORNSTALK AT GNADENHUTTEN.

Early in 1777 the celebrated Shawanee chief, Cornstalk, with one hundred warriors, appeared in the neighborhood of Gnadenhutten and camped. Rev. Smick was in charge of the mission but was absent at the time. Mrs. Smick, not knowing the intentions of the chief, consulted the leading Christian Indians as to what should be done in the emergency. The advice was to invite the chief to the mission house, and send provisions to his warriors, as the sure way of averting their hostile intentions, if any were entertained. Accordingly the great chief was soon invited and escorted to the house of the missionary, but his caution against being surprised and captured by an enemy induced him to take with him a guard of warriors, who were provided for near the house, while Cornstalk became the guest of the lady. His commanding and noble appearance at once made an impression on her, while her womanly person fascinated the chief. He was versed sufficiently in English to talk with her, and, after a repast, he whiled the time away in recounting to her some of his adventures in life, until time to go to his warriors, when he departed, shaking hands and making a kingly bow, she pressing him diplomatically to call again. On the day following Mr. Cornstalk was up early, and repeated his visit about daybreak. The lady was not up, but that made no difference to him. He had called to tell her that a party of Wyandots and Monseys were on the war-path, and were accompanied by a white man, and that they were after *Glikhican*, the Delaware, who they claimed was in the town secreted, and must have him or his scalp. Mrs. Smick, somewhat used to the rough edge of border life, arose, took Cornstalk into another room and showed him Glikhican, whom she had been hiding from his enemies for some days, and her husband intending to send him to Fort Pitt as a place of safety, but all the paths were filled with hostile Indian bands going to and returning from war, and hence he had to be hid. Cornstalk, who was an old acquaintance of the Delaware, after some talk, told her he would see the chief safely on his way. So, taking a woman's gown and bonnet of that day, he gave them to Glikhican, told him to put them on and follow. He shook the lady by the hand and left. That evening he abruptly appeared again, and told her he had sent Glikhican out of danger by a guard of his own warriors, and now, having saved his life, and perhaps hers, he affectionately asked her to leave the mission and go with him to his town on the Scioto and become his wife, as he had little doubt but that her husband was captured or killed. The woman arose within her, and yet artfully concealing her indignation, she begged a short time to make up her mind, and with a little flirtation on her part to please the chief, left him alone; in a few moments he was asleep from the fatigues of the day. But not her. She dispatched a runner to Salem, where Smick had gone for a three days' visit, telling him to hasten and bring back her husband, or Cornstalk would take her off—being then in their house. Smick set out and reached his home before Cornstalk awoke that night. As soon as the great chief became aware of his return he became much dejected, but frankly told the missionary of his new born love for the white woman, and then in a manly way disavowed any intention of offense in proposing to her to become the wife of a chief. Smick, in a true Christian spirit, took him by the hand and leading him to her presence, Cornstalk made the same disavowal to her, and taking from his plume an eagle feather placed it on her head, declaring that he now adopted Mr. Smick into his nation as a brother, and Mrs. Smick as a sister. He then hastily bid them an adieu, and was soon off with his warriors on their journey. He was killed the same summer, as elsewhere related, but before going to the fatal Point Pleasant, he had again visited sister Smick and her husband at Gnadenhutten.

SKETCH OF FORT LAURENS ON THE TUSCARAWAS—NAMES OF OTHER FORTS IN OHIO, &c., &c.

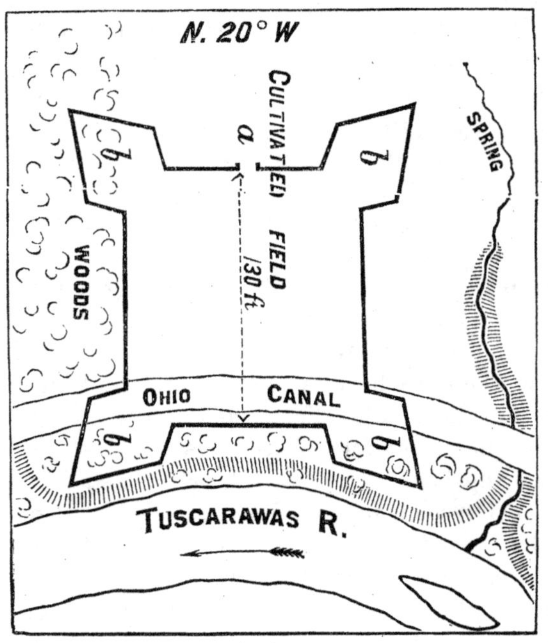

a—gateway ten feet wide. *b b b b*—bastions.

Through the kindness of President Whittlesy, of the Northern Ohio Historical Society, I am enabled to produce the above plan of Fort Laurens, one mile south of Bolivar, Tuscarawas county, surveyed by Charles Whittlesy, January, 1850.

CLEVELAND, OHIO, March 24, 1875.

C. H. MITCHENER, ESQ., New Philadelphia, Ohio:

DEAR SIR:—When I made the accompanying plan of Fort Laurens in January, 1850, that part of the parapet in the cultivated ground was nearly obliterated, but the outline was traceable. The two eastern bastions were very much destroyed by the construction of the Ohio Canal, but the southern curtain, and most of the south-western bastion was then quite perfect along the edge of the woods. Here the base of the parapet was seven feet broad, its height four and a half feet, and the depth of the ditch two and one-half feet, with a breadth of eight feet. It was a regularly laid out work, though small, and was probably picketed along the inner edge of the ditch, connecting the earthwork and stockade.

The ground is an alluvial plain, elevated about twenty feet above the water of the Tuscarawas, and the soil dry and gravelly.

Across the bottom land east of the river is a bluff much higher than the fort, within easy cannon range. It was evidently built for defense against Indians, or parties without artillery.

With this description I trust the engraving will be understood. CHARLES WHITTLESY.

To aid that portion of the western Indians who had joined the American Colonies, as well as to punish those who were continually raiding on the Ohio, and killing the settlers of western Pennsylvania and Virginia, under the instigation of the British at Detroit, Congress, by resolution, early in 1778, appropriated $900,000 to fit out an expedition intended to penetrate the Indian country. General Washington appointed General Lachlan McIntosh, to command the expedition, which rendezvoused at Fort Pitt. From that point it cut a road to the mouth of Beaver River, and built Fort McIntosh. While there the General was advised by Heckewelder's Moravian Indian spies, that the western

9

warriors and hostile Shawanese and Delawares intended to oppose his march west and give him battle at Sugar Creek, near the present town of Dover, Tuscarawas county. He received this word on the 3d of November, 1778, and on the 5th his army was on the march to the Tuscarawas, which by reason of numerous obstacles, such as bad roads, poor horses, &c., he did not reach for fourteen days. In a letter written by him to General Washington in April, 1779, giving an account of what he had done, he details all his troubles about Fort Laurens. Extract:

"Camp (Pittsburgh), April 27, 1779.

"Sir: In obedience to your Excellency's desire, I am to inform you of the situation of the several posts west of the mountains, and will add the reasons for establishing them, which may enable you to judge the better of their propriety.

"When I went there first I found Fort Pitt on the fork of the Ohio, Fort Randolph at the point or mouth of Great Kenhawa, three hundred miles down the Ohio River, and Fort Hand on the Kiskiminatis, fixed stations and garrisoned by Continental troops; and they are still kept up, as there is an independent company raised upon the application of Colonel George Morgan for the sole purpose of maintaining each, and would not weaken the force I had to carry on the expedition. Besides these there were thirty or forty other little stations or forts, at different times garrisoned by militia, between Wheeling and Pittsburgh, upon the waters of the Monongahela, the Kiskiminatis, and in the interior parts of the settlements, which were frequently altered, kept, or evacuated, according to the humors, fears, or interest of the people of most influence, which General Hand was obliged to comply with, as his chief dependence was upon militia. Those I endeavored to break up as soon as I could, without giving too much offense to people whose assistance I so much required, as they were very expensive and of little service, and for that end authorized the lieutenants of Monongahela and Ohio counties to raise a ranging company jointly, of one captain, one lieutenant, one ensign, three sergeants, three corporals, and fifty-four privates, to scout continually the Ohio River from Beaver Creek downward, where the Indians usually crossed to annoy these two counties, and would secure them equally alike; and the lieutenant of Westmoreland County to raise two such companies to secure their frontiers and protect them from scalping parties of the Mingoes or northern Indians, which would render their little force useless and keep our regulars entire for other occasions.

"I found, also, upon inquiry, a number of stores or magazines of provisions, built at public expense by our purchasing commissary, at great distances, difficult of access, and scattered throughout all the counties, which required a number of men at each for commissaries, coopers, packers, guards, &c. These I also discharged and gave the stores up, as, by the report of a court of inquiry, all the provisions in them which were intended for an expedition proved to be spoiled and altogether useless through neglect, and in place of them I had one general storehouse built by a fatigue party, in the fork of the Monongahela River, where all loads from over the mountains are now discharged without crossing any considerable branch of any river, and can be carried from thence at any season, either by land or water, to Big Beaver Creek, to which place I opened a road and built a strong post with barracks and stores, by fatigues of whole line upon the Indian shore of the Ohio River, for the reception of all our stores, clear of all ferries and incumbrances while our troops and supplies were coming up, and in case I was disappointed in both. I had many reasons to apprehend it would secure a footing so far advanced into the enemies' country, and enable me to be better prepared for another attempt, and show them we were in earnest.

"So late as the 3d of November, Mr. Lockhart appeared at Beaver with the cattle extremely poor, after driving them four or five hundred miles, meeting with many obstacles, and could not slaughter them for want of salt. The same day I received a message from the savages, reproaching our tardiness, and threatening that all their nations would join to oppose my progress to Detroit at Sugar Creek, a few miles below Tuscarawas, where they intended giving me battle.

"Immediately upon this intelligence I ordered twelve hundred men to be ready to march, though we had but four weeks' flour, which Mr. Lockhart fortunately brought with him, and left Lieutenant-Colonel Campbell with the rest of the troops at Beaver, to escort and send after me the long-looked for supplies, so repeatedly promised by our deputy quartermaster-general, Mr. Steel, when they arrived, and in the meantime to finish the fort and stores.

"We were fourteen days upon our march, about seventy miles, to Tuscarawas, as our horses and cattle tired every four or five miles from our first setting out, and were met there only by some Cochecking Delawares and Moravians (Indians), who informed me that the Chippewas and Ottawas refused to join the other Indians, upon which their hearts failed them, and none came to oppose our march. But unfortunarely a letter by express from Lieutenant-Colonel Campbell, a little afterward, informed me that no supplies came yet, and we had very little to expect during the winter, nor could he get the staff to account for, or give any reasons for their neglect and deficiencies, which disappointed all my flattering prospects and schemes, and left me no other alternative than either to march back as I came without effecting any valuable purpose, for which the world would justly reflect upon me after so much expense, and confirm the savages in the opinion the enemy inculcates of our weakness, and unite all of them to a man against us, or to build a strong stockade fort upon the Muskingum, and leave as many men as our provisions would allow to secure it until the next season, and to serve as a bridle upon the savages in the heart of their own country; which last I chose, with the unanimous approbation of my principal officers, and we were employed upon it while our provisions lasted.

"I have the honor to be your Excellency's most obedient and humble servant, LACHLAN McINTOSH."

Doctor Philip Dodridge, in his "Notes," published about 1824, says:

"Some time after the completion of the fort the general returned with his army to Fort Pitt, leaving Colonel John Gibson, with a command of one hundred and fifty men to protect the fort until spring. The Indians were soon acquainted with the existence of the fort. The first annoyance the garrison received from the Indians was some time in the month of January. In the night time they caught most of the horses belonging to the fort, and, taking them off some distance in the woods, they took off their bells and formed an ambuscade by the side of a path, leading through high grass of a prairie at a little distance from the fort. In the morning the Indians rattled the horse bells at the further end of the line of the ambuscade. The plan succeeded. A fatigue of sixteen men went out for the horses and fell into the snare. Fourteen were killed on the spot, two were taken prisoners, one of whom was given up at the close of the war, the other was never afterward heard of.

"General Benjamin Biggs, then a captain in the fort, being officer of the day, requested leave of the colonel to go out with the fatigue party which fell into the ambuscade. 'No,' said the colonel, 'this fatigue party does not belong to a captain's command. When I shall have occasion to employ one of that number I shall be thankful for your service, at present you must attend to your duty in the fort.' On what trivial circumstances do life and death sometimes depend.

"In the evening of the day of the ambuscade the whole Indian army, in full war dress and painted, marched in single file through a prairie in view of the fort. Their number, as counted from one of the bastions, was eight hundred and forty-seven. They then took up their encampment on an elevated piece of ground at a small distance from the fort, on the opposite side of the river. From this camp they frequently held conversations with the people of our garrison. In these conversations they seemed to deplore the long continuance of the war and hoped for peace, but were much exasperated at the Americans for attempting to penetrate so far into their country. This great body of Indians continued the investment of the fort as long as they could obtain subsistence, which was about six weeks.

"An old Indian of the name of John Thompson, who was with the American army in the fort, frequently went out among the Indians during their stay at their encampment, with the mutual consent of both parties. A short time before the Indians left the place they sent word to Col. Gibson by the Indian that they were desirous of peace, and if he would send them a barrel of flour they would send in their proposals the next day, but although the colonel complied with their request, they marched off without fulfilling their engagement.

"The commander, supposing the whole number of the Indians had gone off, gave permission to Colonel Clark, of the Pennsylvania line, to escort the invalids, to the number of eleven or twelve, to Fort McIntosh. The whole number of this detachment was fifteen. The wary Indians had left a party behind for the purpose of doing mischief. These attacked this party of invalids and their escort about three miles from the fort, and killed the whole of them, with the exception of four, among whom was the captain, who ran back to the fort. On the same day a detachment went out from the fort, brought in the dead, and buried them with the honors of war in front of the fort gate.

"In three or four days after this disaster a relief of seven hundred men, under General McIntosh, arrived at the fort with a supply of provisions, a great part of which was lost by an untoward accident. When the relief had reached within a hundred yards of the fort, the garrison gave them a salute of a general discharge of musketry, at the report of which the pack-horses took fright, broke loose, and scattered the provisions in every direction through the woods, so that the greater part of it could never be recovered again.

"Among other transactions which took place about this time was that of gathering up the remains of the fourteen men, who had fallen in the ambuscade during the winter, for interment, and which could not be done during the investment of the place by the Indians. They were found mostly devoured by the wolves. The fatigue party dug a pit large enough to contain the remains of all of them, and after depositing them in the pit, merely covering them with a little earth, with a view to have revenge on the wolves for devouring their companions, they covered the pit with slender sticks, rotten wood, and bits of bark, not of sufficient strength to bear the weight of a wolf. On the top of this covering they placed a piece of meat as a bait for the wolves. The next morning seven of them were found in the pit; they were shot, and the pit filled up.

"For about two weeks before the relief arrived, the garrison had been put on the short allowance of half a pound of sour flour, and an equal weight of stinking meat for every two days. The greater part of the last week they had nothing to subsist on but such roots as they could find in the woods and prairies, and raw hides. Two men lost their lives by eating wild parsnip roots by mistake. Four more nearly shared the same fate, but were saved by medical aid.

"On the evening of the arrival of the relief, two days' rations were issued to each man in the fort. These rations were intended as their allowance during their march to Fort McIntosh, but many of the men, supposing them to have been back rations, eat up the whole of their allowance before the next morning. In consequence of this imprudence in eating immoderately, after such extreme starvation from the want of provisions, about forty of the men became faint and sick during the first day's march. On the second day, however, the sufferers were met by a great number of their friends from the settlements to which they belonged, by whom they were amply supplied with provisions."

Major Varnum, sometimes called Vernon, succeeded Colonel Gibson in command at Fort Laurens, and so remained until the abandonment of the works. General McIntosh was relieved at Fort Pitt and Fort McIntosh, and succeeded by Colonel Gibson, who was succeeded by Colonel Brodhead, who, on the 15th of April, 1779, wrote Governor Reed, of Pennsylvania, from Fort Pitt, that his forces "have been divided—one hundred at Fort Laurens, twenty-five at Wheeling, twenty-five at Holliday's Cove, &c."

On the 16th of May he wrote General Armstrong, ridiculing McIntosh for having erected Fort McIntosh at Beaver, and although he was then silent as to Fort Laurens, whatever criticism attached to the one attached to the other, for Laurens was only an out-post to Fort McIntosh.

May 22, 1779, Colonel Brodhead wrote to Colonel George Morgan that he "had got a small supply of salt meat at Carlisle, and sent it to Fort Laurens, otherwise the fort would have had to be abandoned at once."

May 30, 1779, he wrote to Major Frederick Varnum at Fort Laurens, "that Moses Killbuck had just come in from Fort Laurens and told him that the garrison was without subsistence, and the men so low from starvation that many could not keep their feet."

May 31, 1779, he wrote to Colonel Lochry that "Fort Laurens is threatened by a considerable force," and he called for recruits and horses to relieve the fort.

The fort was soon after threatened by about one hundred and ninety British Indians and a few British soldiers, said to be under the leadership of Simon Girty, but the enemy moved off toward the Ohio without making an attack. Had the attack been made at that time, there could have been no other result than surrender and massacre.

August 1, 1779, Colonel Brodhead wrote to Ensign John Beck, then at Fort Laurens, that he "has notice of two squads of Indians, twenty in each squad, going toward the Tuscarawas, and he hopes that the soldiers coming in from Fort Laurens will meet and scourge them."

August 4, 1779, he wrote to General Washington that he "has just learned of two soldiers being killed at Fort Laurens."

These were probably the two referred to by Heckewelder, who, in his narrative, says that in the summer of 1779 the commander at Fort Laurens sent a Mr. Sample, his commissary, with a squad of men to the forks of the Muskingum to purchase corn, and such provisions as could be obtained from the mission at Lichtenau (two miles below the Coshocton of this day), and from the friendly Delawares at Goshocking (Coshocton), where their capital was located. Sample pitched his tent on the opposite side of the river from the Indian village, leaving one soldier to guard his camp and horses, and crossed over to the town. In a short time the scalp yell was heard across the river, and hurrying to the river bank they saw hostile Indians going off with the horses and the scalp of Sample's soldier. On the next day another soldier was fired at and wounded. The Delaware chiefs sent out a force and recovered Sample's horses, and he returned to Fort Laurens with some provisions.

August 6, 1779, Colonel Brodhead wrote to General Sullivan from Fort Pitt, who was then in command in northern Pennsylvania, that he was "daily expecting the garrison from Fort Laurens; when it arrived he would start on his campaign up the Cannewaga," and from the fact that his expedition up the Alleghany did start in a short time, it is certain the garrison left Fort Laurens in August, 1779, but there is no published record of the exact date the fort was abandoned.

From all the facts about this Fort Laurens enterprise, it seems that Varnum's garrison had suffered so many privations that they took what we call at this day "French leave" of the fort, and made their way back to the Ohio as best they could, in their starved condition, after burning everything likely to impede their retreat, or that would be of use to the Indians if captured.

But the fort itself was not destroyed. It remained intact as late as 1782, as is learned from the statement of a young man named Carpenter, who was captured by the Indians in Washington County, Pennsylvania, early that year, and brought by them, with a lot of stolen horses, to one of their camps on the Muskingum, probably Goshocking, as Heckewelder called it, Goshuckgunk as the Indians called it, and Coshocton as we call it. Carpenter made his escape, and ran for his life up the valley trail, past the burned Salem, Gnadenhutten, and Schoenbrunn towns, and reached Fort Laurens, which he found unoccupied, but in good condition. Thence he made his way east to the Ohio over the big trail, and reached home in the fall of 1782.

Henry Jolly, who was one of the Fort Laurens soldiers, says in a statement he published, that "the army marched with such rapidity from Beaver to the Tuscarawas that the Indians were not aware of its approach until the fort was near completion." This is an error. McIntosh, in his letter to Washington, says it took fourteen days to go from Beaver to the Tuscarawas, a distance of seventy miles only, over the great trail, constantly followed by the savages in their raids to and from the Ohio border settlements. Another trail from the lower towns of the Muskingum missions, Lichtenau, Salem, and Gnadenhutten, passed near what is now Uhrichsville, and connected with the big trail at Painted Post, near midway between the Ohio and Tuscarawas, and over which the Christian Indian runners were constantly traveling to and from Fort Pitt with messages. They were as constantly dodging the hostile warriors along this trail; and, with a knowledge of these facts, to suppose that McIntosh with twelve hundred men, marching five miles a day only, was not observed until he got to the Tuscarawas, and nearly finished his fort, is an absurdity on its face.

Mr. Jolly also says, that soon after Fort Laurens was erected, a large force of Indians invested it before the garrison were aware of being surrounded by an Indian army. This is a mistake also. McIntosh had called on the Moravian Indians to meet him at Tuscarawas, with two Indian companies from the missions. He says but about two dozen were there whan he arrived. These operated as scouts to watch the enemies' approach, for that is what he wanted with them; and to suppose that these scouts and the old Indian hunters in McIntosh's army would all lay asleep in the fort, being surrounded, without knowing it until the warriors showed themselves before the fort, is simply ridiculous.

Coincident with McIntosh, the great Delaware chief, White Eyes (and who had been supplanted in the affections of many Delawares by Captain Pipe), had conceived the idea of marching an army to the Tuscarawas and building a fort, to awe Pipe and the British Indians. Squads of hostile warriors had come down the Mohican and Walhonding, and ware roaming over and scourging the settlements, as did the squads under Alaric and Attila, two thousand years before, come down from the Black Forest and scourge people in the declining days of Rome. The Wyandots had an order to bring back to Detroit the scalps of Zeisberger, White Eyes, and Killbuck, and destroy the missions. White Eyes retired to Fort Pitt for safety, and when McIntosh's project was unfolded to him he declared that he would go with the army, and during its march White Eyes died of small-pox, as stated by Heckewelder. Professor DeSchweinitz, in his life of Zeisberger, says White Eyes died November 10, 1778, at "Tuscarawas in the midst of the army of white men." Fort Laurens was erected in close proximity to the ancient Indian town called "Tuscarawas," which Colonel Boquet found abandoned in 1764, but which had over one hundred lodges or houses then still standing. It had been a seat of the Indian empire, where the chiefs of the different nations met and discussed the "public safety," and decided on measures to prevent encroachments of the whites. The great chief, White Eyes, had orated there against white encroachments in by-gone times, and if after guiding an army of white men there to put down his rival, Captain Pipe, and thwart his machinations against the colonies, the great chief died of small-pox in the midst of that army, after it had built the fort, the spot where Fort Laurens stood should be remembered by Americans as the grave of White Eyes, although General McIntosh says his army did not reach the Tuscarawas for nine days after White Eyes died, if DeSchweinitz's date (November 10, 1778), is correct. Captain Pipe, his rival chief, on hearing of his death, declared at Sandusky, in the midst of the British Indians, that White Eyes was a great man, but having sought the ruin of his country, the Great Spirit took him away in order that the Indian nations might be saved. In after times Congress awarded to his widow and family the use of a portion of the four-thousand acre Schoenbrunn tract, below New Philadelphia, and about 1798 she and two daughters came to Zeisberger's mission, at Goshen, and enjoyed it for a time. Her grave is said by some to be at the Goshen cemetery, but other accounts say she and her daughters removed with the Christian Indians west, on the breaking up of Goshen mission, about 1823–4. She is described by those who knew her as a woman of noble and commanding appearance.

Fort Laurens covered about half an acre, and the parapet walls were crowned with pickets made of the split halves of the largest trunks of trees, which accounts in part for the inability of the Indians to capture it, although they had as many warriors besieging it as they had at the siege of Fort Pitt in Pontiac's war of 1763, if we believe Doddridge. Portions of the earth-work can yet be pointed out (1875). In close proximity to this fort, Colonel Boquet, in 1764, erected his stockade fort, which may be designated Fort Tuscarawas, and portions of which were visible when the Ohio Canal was constructed, and the spot is yet discernable. Fort Laurens was the first fort erected west of the Ohio by order of the American Congress. The other forts theretofore, and since erected on Ohio soil, were:

Fort Junandat, Sandusky Bay, by the French, in 1754; Fort Gower, now in Athens County, by Lord Dunmore, in 1774; Fort Harmar, now in Washington County, by the United States, in 1785; Fort Steuben, now Steubenville city, by the United States, in 1784; Fort Washington, now Cincinnati, by the United States, in 1789; Fort Campus Martius, now Marietta, by the United States, in 1791; Fort Dilies, Ohio River, now in Belmont County, by the United States, in 1790; Fort Hamilton, now a city of that name in Butler County, by the United States, in 1791; Fort Jefferson, now in Darke County, by the United States, in 1791; Fort St. Clair, now in Preble County, by the United States in 1791; Fort Recovery, now in Darke County, by the United States, in 1791; Fort Defiance, now in Defiance County, by the United States, in 1794; Fort Deposit, now in Lucas County, by the United States, in 1794; Fort Greenville, now in Darke County, by the United States, in 1794; Fort Laramie, now in Shelby County, by the United States, in 1794; Fort St. Mary's, now in Mercer County, by the United States, in 1794; Fort Piqua, now in Miami County, by the United States, in 1794.

In the war of 1812 the following forts were erected: Fort Miami, on the Maumee, by the British; Forts Sandusky, in Erie County; Stevenson, in Sandusky County; Seneca, in Seneca County; Meigs, in Wood County; Amanda, in Allen County; Ball, in Seneca County; Findlay, in Hancock County; and McArthur, in Hardin County, all in Ohio.

COLONEL JOHN GIBSON, COMMANDER AT FORT LAURENS—HIS FIGHT WITH LITTLE EAGLE.

The man who caused the greatest terror among the hostile Indians west of the Ohio, from 1774 to 1782, was Colonel John Gibson, a native of Lancaster County, Pennsylvania. He was born in 1740 at Lancaster. His first service was in

General Forbes's expedition against the French and Indians, after which he became a trader at Fort Pitt, and at the mouth of Beaver Creek, where he and two others were captured by the Indians, who took him to Virginia, on the Kenhawa, where they intended to burn him, but were prevented by a squaw who adopted him. He remained some time among the Indians, but returned to Fort Pitt in time to take an active part in Dunmore's war of 1774, and at Camp Charlotte, seeing the great Logan, one of whose relatives he had married, he took the liberty of immortalizing Logan by "working up" *that* famous speech. In the revolutionary war he commanded the seventh Virginia regiment, served in New York, New Jersey, and the western department, and visited Schoenbrunn on the Tuscarawas, as a government agent, on his way to carry the great congress six-foot peace belt to the Indians. At Schoenbrunn he remained several days conversing with Zeisberger, observing closely all that passed, witnessing an Indian baptism, on the evening of which he and the holy man sat up until midnight discussing religion.

In 1779 he commanded for a time the garrison at Fort Laurens (near the present Bolivar), and although it was invested by over seven hundred Indian warriors for six weeks, and had but about one hundred defenders fit for duty, such was their fear of Gibson, the "Long Knife," that they never attempted an assault, but running short of provisions they made that the excuse for moving off. Colonel Gibson soon after proceeded to Fort Pitt and assumed command thereof. A party of Delawares and Mingoes, who were of the Indian army investing Fort Laurens, having tried but failed to ambush Colonel Gibson on his way to Fort Pitt, revenged themselves by going to the Ohio border, crossing to the Monongahela country, and killing seven white settlers. Gibson, being apprised of the murders, took a sufficient force from the fort and pursued the savages. Accidentally he met a few Indians under "Little Eagle," Mingo chief, near Cross Creek, who, seeing Gibson, gave the yell and fired at him, the ball perforating his coat but doing no harm. Gibson was so near the chief, that raising his sword he cleaved "Little Eagle's" head from his body in an instant. Two other savages were slain on the spot, the residue fleeing to the forest. Gibson returned to Fort Pitt, and, as tradition says, took "Little Eagle's" head with him, to offset the hole in his coat. He became more than ever the terror of the warriors, by whom he was called "Long Knife," and ere the war closed the term "Long Knives" was applied to the Americans generally. Colonel Gibson's fame by this adventure excited the envy of other officers, and when he projected an expedition against the north-western tribes, the inability of the Government to furnish supplies, and the machinations of leading men against him, caused the total failure of the expedition. When he learned of the expeditionists in Williamson's band, threatening death to the Moravian Indians, he sent a runner to warn them, but it came too late. This excited the borderers against him, and they charged Gibson with treason to them, and when a portion of Williamson's men returned to Fort Pitt to kill the Moravian Indians on "Smoky Island," Gibson's life was endangered to such an extent that he was compelled to keep within the fort. He remained at Fort Pitt during the war. In 1790 he was a member of the Pennsylvania constitutional convention, and in 1800 was made secretary of the Indiana territory. Afterward he retired to private life, and died in 1822, near Braddock's field, Pennsylvania.

NUMBER OF WARRIORS AT FORT LAURENS, AND ELSEWHERE—1779.

Colonel Morgan, Indian agent in 1779, was told by Delaware chiefs that the Indian army investing Fort Laurens in January, 1779, numbered but 180, composed of Wyandots, Shawanese, Mingoès, and Monseys, and four (scallawag) Delawares, with John Montour and his brother.

This is contradicted by the missionaries' record at Lichtenau, for on passing that place they counted about 700 on their way up the Tuscarawas, and on the east bank of the river they paraded opposite the fort to show their strength, when one of the garrison counted 847 painted warriors. The missionary and the soldier could not both have lied five hundred on one subject at the same time when they were fifty miles apart, and strangers to each other.

Moreover, the number of warriors in the northern and western tribes in 1779 were at that time reported upon by Morgan to the government as follows: Delawares and Monseys, 600; Shawanese, 400; Wyandots, 300; Mingoes, 600; Senacas, 650; Mohawks, 100; Cuyugas, 220 (called by Morgan Cuyahogas); Onondagas, 230; Oneidas and Tuscarawas (he meant Tuscaroras), 400; Ottowas, 600; Chippewas (of all the lakes), 5,000; Pottawatomies, 400; Miamies, 300; and smaller tribes, 800; total, 10,000 warriors; which he says they could have concentrated at one point on the frontier in a few weeks, if necessary.

At the second investment of Fort Laurens in the summer of 1779, Morgan says there were present 40 Shawanese, 20 Mingoes, and 20 Delawares, who were induced by Delaware chiefs to move off without firing a gun; thus the Delawares saved Fort Laurens.

BUCKSKIN CURRENCY AT FORT LAURENS.

Heckewelder relates that in 1762, when he and Post were at Post's cabin, he dare not be seen by the Indians while writing or reading a book, they suspecting it had reference to taking their land.

In 1779, they had the same antipathy to paper money, believing that it meant "steal" on its face. Hence, when they sold anything to the Fort Laurens garrison, there being no hard money there, they were paid in buck and doe-skin certificates, which they passed to the traders for whisky, ammunition, &c.

In Colonel Morgan's journal is a certificate of the kind vouched for by Colonel Gibson in these words:

"I do certify that I am indebted to the bearer, Captain Johnny, seven bucks and one doe, for the use of the States, this 12th day of April, 1779.

"Signed, "SAMUEL SAMPLE,
"Assistant Quartermaster."

"The above is due to him for pork, for the use of the garrison at Fort Laurens.

"Signed, "JOHN GIBSON, Colonel."

The ground upon which Fort Laurens was erected, and around which so many historical incidents are located, is now part of the farm of the heirs of Henry Gibler, deceased, in the first and second sections of township ten, range two, about ten miles due north from New Philadelphia.

CHAPTER VII.

HECKEWELDER'S GREAT RIDE.

When Girty, Elliot, and McKee deserted the American cause, and passed from Fort Pitt down the Muskingum, in the winter of 1778, they were followed to Goshocking (Coshocton) by twenty soldier deserters also, who spread terror at the Delaware Indian capital, and at the Moravian mission, Lichtenau, near by. They represented Washington as having been killed, the army dispersed, and the Americans coming west to kill all the Indians.

Captain Pipe called the Delawares to the council house, and in a violent speech urged the Indians to take up the hatchet against the colonies. Even the Indian converts at the mission Lichtenau were aroused, and many clamored for war.

Captain White Eyes replied to Pipe, and pronounced all these stories lies, at the same time asking the Indians to not take the war-path for ten days, and if word did not come in that time showing that these renegades were liars, he would go to war with his nation and be the first to fall. His eloquence stayed the torrent of Indian wrath let loose by Pipe, and all agreed to wait the time asked.

Heckewelder was coming from Bethlehem with his servant, John Martin. They arrived at Fort Pitt jaded and worn, but learning the reports that had come up from the valley, at once started on horseback with peace messages and letters from General Hand, commander at Fort Pitt, to the Delawares, assuring them that all the stories were false, &c. He and John Martin reached Gnadenhutten at midnight of the second day, and learning there that the ten days would be up on the morrow, again mounted, without rest or sleep, and rode into Goshocking the next morning at 10 o'clock. The Delawares were painted and ready for the war-path. His old friends, and even White Eyes, refused to shake hands with him. Seeing the crisis, he stood up in his saddle, his hair flapping in the wind, and waved the peace letters over his head, telling the Indians that all those stories were lies; that instead of Washington being killed, the American army had captured Burgoyne's British army, and that instead of coming west to kill the Indians, the Americans were their true friends, and wanted them not to take any part in the war. White Eyes then spoke and calmed the Delawares, who put off their war plumes, except Pipe and his Monsey band, and thus was peace restored, and Zeisberger and his mission saved for the time from destruction.

This must have taken place early in the fall of 1778, for White Eyes, having had his life threatened by the Pipe party, left the valley for Fort Pitt, joined McIntosh's army and piloted it toward Fort Laurens in November.

COSHOCTON SETTLEMENT ABANDONED—ATTEMPT TO SCALP ZEISBERGER—SETTLEMENT OF SALEM, NEAR PORT WASHINGTON—1780.

The settlers at Lichtenau, near Coshocton, finding that the war parties from the Sandusky country, passed and re-passed their town so often in going to and returning from their depredations at the Ohio River, determined to abandon Lichtenau, and in April, 1779, Zeisberger, with a number of families set out for Schoenbrunn. Mr. Edwards also set out with the former inhabitants of Gnadenhutten for that place, while Heckewelder remained with the balance at Lichtenau, and these three settlements had for a time comparative quiet.

During 1779 a man named McCormick, living at Sandusky, having learned of a plot to capture Zeisberger, or bring in his scalp—and at the head of which plot was Simon Girty—found means to inform Heckewelder at Lichtenau. Zeisberger being then at Lichtenau, on a visit from Schoenbrunn, two guards were selected to conduct him back home *via* Gnadenhutten. When nine miles on the way back, which was, say two-thirds of the distance between the present Coshocton and New Comerstown, all of a sudden Simon Girty and eight Mingoes of the Six Nations appeared before them in the path. Girty exclaimed to his Mingoes, "this is the very man we have come for; now act agreeable to the promise you have made." Two young Delawares, returning from a hunt, suddenly came into the path, and hearing Girty's words, stepped forward to defend Zeisberger and assist his two guards in case of need. Seeing which, and not wanting to raise any alarm among the Delawares, Girty and his band disappeared, and the missionary arrived safely at his town of Schoenbrunn, which he had located anew this year on the west side of the river in sight of old Schoenbrunn.

In March, 1780, Lichtenau was abandoned, and its occupants moved twenty miles up the river and built the town of Salem, near the present Port Washington, erecting among other buildings, a chapel of hewed timber forty feet by thirty-six, with cupola and bell, and in which chapel Heckewelder was married the same year.

After the evacuation of Lichtenau, Pipe and his band of Indians retired to Sandusky, and took up the hatchet against the colonies, under pay from the British commander of Detroit.

GENERAL BRODHEAD'S CAMPAIGN TO COSHOCTON—1781.

General Brodhead, with a military force, was sent out in 1780 to destroy the hostile Indian towns along the Muskingum and tributaries. Arriving in 1781 on the east side of the Tuscarawas, below Salem, he sent for Heckewelder to come over, and bring some articles of provisions. He informed Heckewelder that he was on his way against a band of hostile Indians at the forks of the river (Coshocton), and wished that any of the Christian Indians out hunting in that direction might be called in, as he did not wish to molest them. While at this camp a portion of his troops formed the plan of leaving camp to go up the Tuscarawas and destroy Gnadenhutten and Schoenbrunn. The plan was frustrated, and Brodhead marched on to White Eyes Plain, where an Indian prisoner was taken, and two other Indians shot at but they escaped. He then by a forced march reached and surprised the towns at the forks of the Tuscarawas and Walhonding, but, owing to high water, the Indians on the west side of the river escaped, but all on the east side were captured without firing a shot. Sixteen Indian warriors captured were taken below the town, tomahawked and scalped, by directions of a council of war held in the camp of Brodhead. The next morning an Indian called from the opposite side of the river for the "big captain," saying he wanted peace. Brodhead sent him for his chief, who came over under a promise that he should not be killed. After he got over a notorious Indian fighter, named Louis Wetzell, tomahawked him. The army then commenced their homeward march with some twenty prisoners, but had not gone half a mile when the soldiers killed them all, except a few women and children, who were taken to Fort Pitt, and there exchanged for an equal number of prisoners held by the Indians. This sanguinary march was called "the Coshocton campaign," and many of the men in it, a year later, came out with Williamson and enacted the Gnadenhutten massacre.

Shortly after Brodhead's campaign eighty British Indian warriors arrived near Gnadenhutten and demanded the surrender to them of Killbuck and other chiefs, whom the warriors claimed were hid in the town, and whom they must have "dead or alive," alleging that these chiefs were counseling peace when their nations were at war. Being advised that these chiefs had gone to Fort Pitt they searched the town, and then sent to Schoenbrunn and Salem for the missionaries to come to Gnadenhutten and have a talk about it. The missionaries obeyed, and heard a speech from the head war chief, *Pachgantschillas*, *alias* Bockongahelas, *alias* Shingask, after which the Christian Indians replied, when the war chief proposed and the missionaries agreed to let every one at Gnadenhutten have his free will, either to go with the warriors or stay. The warriors then proceeded to Salem and made the same proposal, adding that those who did not go would be destroyed by those who professed to be their friends. One family agreed to go, and the warriors returned to their homes at Sandusky, where Pipe, McKee, Elliot, and Girty had taken up their residences, and were continually sending out warriors to commit depredations and murders. At Schoenbrunn, this year, the missionary, Senseman, came near being captured by two savages while in his garden. At Gnadenhutten, Edwards and Young were shot at and narrowly escaped.

THE BRITISH CAPTURE SCHOENBRUNN, GNADENHUTTEN, AND SALEM—DRIVE OFF THE INHABITANTS—HECKEWELDER, ZEISBERGER, &C., TRIED AS SPIES BUT ACQUITTED—PROOF OF THEIR GUILT AND PATRIOTISM.

In August, 1781, under directions of the British commandant at Detroit, one hundred and forty Wyandot warriors, forty Monseys, and some straggling Ottawas and Mohicans, all under Pipe, Half King, Wingmund, two Shawanese, Captains John and Thomas Snake, Kuhn, a white man, then a chief, and Captain Elliot with two other white men appeared at Salem and remained a week in council. On the 25th of August they called the missionaries and converted Indians of the three towns to meet at Gnadenhutten and made known their intention of removing them to Sandusky and Detroit. All refused to go, but some of the timid were willing in case all went.

The chiefs assembled and discussed the question of killing the missionary leaders and driving off the balance to Sandusky. The killing was rejected. On the 2d of September, Zeisberger, Senseman, and Heckewelder were taken prisoners, and their watches with other articles taken from them. On the 7th Elliot took Heckewelder from Gnadenhutten to Salem, and on the 8th other missionaries followed. On the 11th all moved off for Sandusky, leaving the three towns forsaken, many cattle and hogs and three hundred acres of corn behind. They arrived at Sandusky October 11, 1781, and were set to building bark huts.

On the 25th of October John Shebash and a party returned to Schoenbrunn to gather corn. On the same day the missionaries, Zeisberger, Edwards, Heckewelder, and Senseman, were taken to Detroit to be tried as spies, having been charged with holding correspondence with the agents of the American colonies, then in rebellion against the British government.

Having arrived at Detroit, Heckewelder, in his narrative, gives the following account of their trial and acquittal:

"It being by this time known in the town that the Moravian missionaries had come in as prisoners, curiosity drew the inhabitants of the place into the street to see what kind of people we were. The few clothes we had on our backs, and these tattered and torn, might have induced them to look contemptuously upon us, but we did not find this to be the case. We observed that we were viewed with commisseration. After standing some time in the street, opposite the dwelling of the commandant, we were brought before him, where, with empty stomachs, shivering with cold, worn down by the journey, and not free from rheumatic pains, we had again to stand until we underwent a strict examination. Being at length dismissed, Mr. Bawbee took us to the house of a private French family, which consisted of Mr. Tybout and wife, both elderly people, and having no children. We were told by Mr. Bawbee, who acted as agent for the Indian department, that we might make ourselves easy for the present; and were not forbidden to walk about. We soon found ourselves in a good birth, for not only our landlord and his wife were obliging and kind to us, but we found many here who befriended us—even among the officers themselves. In other circumstances, than we at the time were, we might have found ourselves contented and happy; but, knowing that our families were not only suffering from hunger and cold, were also kept excited, on our account, between hope and fear, and being so repeatedly told by the savages that we never would be permitted to return to them again, added to which the reports we had heard while at the rapids of the Ohio, was still kept alive by the Indians who were daily coming in; all which produced great anxiety to us. Happy we were, therefore, that the day had come when our conduct while among the Indians was to be inquired into in a public place; and before a council where the accuser and the accused were to meet face to face. These were Captain Pipe and two of his principal counselors, for whom the commandant had been long waiting, and whom were now arrived.

"Accordingly, on the 9th day of November, we were conducted to the council house, where we found the commandant with Mr. Bawbee by his side, together with other gentlemen, and a great number of Indians with the Indian interpreters, seated or standing in their proper places. The Indians of the different tribes were separately seated, some to the right of the commandant, and the Delawares right before him, with Captain Pipe and his counselors in front. We four prisoners were placed by ourselves on a bench to the left; a war chief of each of the two divisions of Indians was holding a stick of three or four feet long with scalps on it, which they had taken in their last excursions against the people of the United States.

"The council being opened by the commandant signifying to Captain Pipe that he might make his report, he rose from his seat, holding a stick with two scalps on it in his left hand, and addressed the commandant in a very remarkable and spirited manner with respect to the present war; and that of their fathers (the British) having drawn their children (the Indians) into it, &c., handing him, at the close of his speech, the scalps. Having seated himself again, a war chief of the other party rose in like manner with his scalp; and after concluding his address, he also handed it to the commandant, who, as before, gave it to the interpreter standing behind him to put aside. This business being finished, the commandant addressed Captain Pipe to the following effect, viz.:

"'Captain Pipe, you have for a long time lodged complaints with me against certain white people among your nation, and whom you call teachers to the believing Indians, who, as you say, are friends to the Americans, and keep up a continual correspondence with them, to the prejudice of your father's (the British) interest. You having so repeatedly accused these teachers, and desiring that I might remove them from among you; I at length commanded you to take them, together with the believing Indians, away from the Muskingum, and bring them into your country; and being since informed that this had been done, I ordered you to bring those teachers, together with some of their principal men, before me that I might see and speak with them; since that time these men, now sitting before you, have come in and surrendered themselves up to me without your being with them. I now ask you, Captain Pipe, if these men are those of whom you so much complained, and whom I ordered you to bring before me?'

"Pipe replying in the affirmative, the commandant continued:

"'Well, both the accuser and the accused being present, it is but fair that the accused hear from the accuser the complaints he has against them; I therefore desire you to repeat what you have told me of these teachers and what you have accused them of.'

"Pipe, standing at the time, now turned to his counselors, telling them to get upon their legs and speak; but finding them panic struck, he appeared to be at a loss how to act. Once more turning to them, he endeavored to make them sensible that this was the time to speak, and that the opportunity now granted them for that purpose would be lost to them forever, if they spoke not. Finally, seeing them hang their heads and remaining mute, he boldly stood up and defended the teachers against the accusations brought against them, saying that 'they were *good* men; and that he wished his father (the commandant) to speak good words to them, to treat them kindly, for they were his friends, and that he would be sorry to see them treated ill and hard.'

"The commandant still persisting in having the call he had made on Pipe, of *repeating* what he had told him of the teachers now present, he, greatly embarrassed and casting another glance at his frightened and dejected counselors, who still were hanging their heads, he did repeat, yet adding:

"'Father, the teachers can not be blamed for this; for living in our country where they had to do whatever we required of them, they were compelled to act as they did. They did not write letters (speeches) for themselves, but for *us*. We are to blame. We caused them to do what they did. We urged them to it, while they refused, telling us that they did not come here for the purpose of meddling with our affairs, but for the spiritual good of the Indians.'

"The commandant then asking him what *he* wished him to do with us, whether he should send us out of the country, or permit us to return again to our families and congregations, he, contrary to what was expected, advised the commandant to suffer us to return to our homes.

"We being now questioned by this general officer with regard to our ordination and vocation, but particularly with regard to our connection with the American congress, and whether we were dependent on that body, we answered that 'the society to which we belonged had for upward of thirty years labored among the North American Indians for the purpose of bringing them over to Christianity; that from the commencement of our missions, missionaries had been continually among them, who were sent by the bishops and directors of our church; that congress indeed knew of our being among the Indians for the purpose already stated; but that they never had, either directly or indirectly, interfered with our missionary concerns, nor prescribed rules for us to act by. That all we knew of the American congress was that they wished all the Indians to be at peace and not take part in the war on either side; but follow the example of their countrymen, the Christian Indians, and join them in becoming an agricultural and a Christian people,' &c.

"The commandant, stepping up to us, declared us acquitted of the charges laid against us, assuring us at the same time that 'he felt great satisfaction and pleasure in seeing our endeavors to civilize and Christianize the Indians, and would cheerfully permit us to return again to our congregation.'

"On the 23d of November, 1781, they returned to Captivestown, on the Sandusky, where they wintered with their converts, suffering from cold and want of provisions to an almost incredible extent.

"There is not a doubt of these missionaries having been hung or shot, had the British governor have known of their correspondence with the American agents.

"On the 20th of November, 1779, Colonel Brodhead, then in command at Fort Pitt, wrote to David Zeisberger at Schoenbrunn, then called New Schoenbrunn, that his Indians 'can have powder, lead, coffee, sugar, salt, and many articles of clothing, at the old rates.' In the same letter he wishes Zeisberger to employ an Indian spy to go to Detroit and find out its strength, provisions, and stores, and promises to pay the spy 'eighty bucks' (dollars), or 'one hundred,' if necessary.

"On the 12th of December, 1779, Colonel Brodhead again wrote Zeisberger that their friend Joshua was willing to undertake 'this business,' and hopes some one will 'be sent at once.'

"On the 13th he wrote from Fort Pitt to General Washington that his principal reliance in getting news from the enemy at Detroit is on the Moravian missionaries, who have intelligent Indians who can get into Detroit without suspicion, &c.

"On the 10th of April, 1780, he wrote to General Gates that 'he had just received letters from the missionaries informing him that the Indian warriors will soon give much trouble on the frontier.'

"On the 19th of April he wrote to Zeisberger that 'he was sorry the cold winter had kept Joshua from visiting Detroit as a spy.'"—(See *Pennsylvania Archives*; also see *Sketch of Joshua, the Mohican Spy*.

Early in the winter the missionaries at Sandusky heard that a party of Virginians, under Captain Benjamin Biggs, had gone out from the Ohio to Schoenbrunn and murdered a number of Christian Indians found there gathering corn.

Captain Biggs had been in 1778 and 1779 one of the defenders of Fort Laurens, and in the fall of 1781 was sent from Wheeling with a party to rout out and kill the Monsey and other Indian warriors who had, after the missionaries were carried off, taken possession of Schoenbrunn and the other forsaken settlements in the valley. When Biggs got to Schoenbrunn he found only some straggling Christian Indians; these he took to Fort Pitt, and they had liberty to go and come as they pleased. Biggs' campaign had drawn no blood in the valley, and this dissatisfied the border settlers along the Ohio who were continually being raided upon by western Indian warriors, and their families murdered or carried into captivity. The abandoned Schoenbrunn, Gnadenhutten, and Salem were during the winter made the resting places of the warriors going to or returning from the Ohio with scalps and prisoners; and small pursuing parties of whites from the east, as well as parties of Christian Indians who had ran back from Sandusky to the warmer Tuscarawas, made the valley one continual scene of excitement and discordant border warfare until the bloody scenes of 1782 began to unfold.

CHAPTER VIII.

LEGEND OF THE BLOODY VALLEY—ORIGIN OF THE MASSACRE OF NINETY-SIX INDIANS, MARCH 7 AND 8, 1782.

The British at Detroit and their auxiliaries, Half King, Pipe, and others at Sandusky, used their influence conjointly in the fall of 1781 to induce the missionaries and their Indian converts to leave the Tuscarawas and join the British. Failing in this, a party of British and Indians came down to the valley, as detailed in a preceding chapter, captured Zeisberger, Heckewelder, and other missionaries, gathered together the converts from Schoenbrunn, Salem, and Gnadenhutten and drove them to the Sandusky country, leaving their cattle, hogs, corn, and other winter provisions behind. A portion of the stock was sent to Detroit and sold, not for the captives, but for the captors. A cold winter setting in, and being without provisions, one hundred or more of the converts asked and obtained leave to go back to the towns in the valley for provisions. At the same time warriors were sent to the Ohio to rob and murder the whites, with intent thereby to exasperate the borderers who were in the American interest, and incite them to cross the Ohio, and pursue the raiders to the Tuscarawas towns, where it was expected they would fall in with the Christian Indians gathering corn and dispatch them. Thus was the Williamson expedition planned in reality by the British at Detroit and Sandusky.

A party of warriors discovering Williamson's expedition organizing on the Ohio, to march to the deserted Tuscarawas towns, immediately thereafter murdered a family named Wallace, and fled toward the Moravian towns on the Tuscarawas. Near to and on the west side of the Ohio River they impaled the body of Mrs. Wallace and one child on trees near the trail by which they knew the settlers' expedition would take on its way to the Indian country. Arriving at Gnadenhutten these warriors found the Christian Indians at work in their cornfields, getting together the grain they soon intended to carry to their starving brethren in the north-west, they informed them of the murders they had committed. The Christians becoming alarmed for their own safety, remonstrated with the warriors for stopping at their town, and warned them off. Before leaving the town the warriors bartered, among other things, the dress they had taken from Mrs. Wallace to some young and thoughtless Indian girls for some provisions. The Christian Indians, upon the departure of their very unwelcome guests, called a council at Salem for the purpose of deliberating upon the proper course to pursue. At this meeting it was agreed to remain and continue gathering the corn, and if the whites from the settlements came in pursuit of the murderers, to trust to the fact of their being known as Christian and peaceable Indians for their safety. As they had by this time secured the crop of corn, it was agreed to begin preparations for the return, and the day of starting was fixed.

While these poor creatures were busily engaged in getting ready to carry succor to their famishing brethren on the Sandusky; feeling perfectly safe, conscious of their innocence of any of the cold-blooded acts that were inflaming the settlements east of the Ohio, the Williamson party was on its march toward their towns. On the very day previous to the one fixed for the departure of the Christian Indians, March 7, 1782, and while they were engaged in bundling up their packs, the white party made their appearance, having laid in the forests the night before, within sight and hearing of Gnadenhutten. On their way to the town a detachment that was to go in from the north met a young half-breed, Joseph Shabosh, who was out early in the morning to catch a horse. Young Shabosh was struck down and scalped while begging for his life on the grounds of his being a Christian and the son of a white man. From the spot of Shabosh's death the detachment went to the river bank, from where they expected to get a view of the town, and on the way passed Jacob, a brother-in-law to Shabosh, who was in the standing corn tying up some sacks recently filled. Although they passed within thirty yards of him he was not discovered. He recognized some of the whites, having seen them in the party that took the Christian Indians from Schoenbrunn the preceding fall to Fort Pitt, whence they were released by the commandant and returned home, he having been one of those taken. Jacob was about to hail a man he knew, when the sharp crack of a rifle checked him, and the next instant he beheld one of his brethren drop in his canoe. This so alarmed Jacob that he fled out of the field and into the forest and did not stop until several miles away, where he remained for twenty-four hours.

The Williamson party seeing a number of the Indians in a cornfield, on the opposite side of the river, sent a detachment of sixteen men, two at a time, in a large sugar trough for want of a canoe over the river, it being very high. They hailed the Indians as friends and shook hands all round, and then advised them to stop work, recross to the town, and prepare to return with the whites to Fort Pitt, declaring that upon reaching there they would be at once supplied with everything they needed. This being pleasing news to the ears of the Indians they at once repaired with the whites to the town.

While these transactions wern going on at Gnadenhutten, John Martin and his son, Christian Indians, were on the west side of the river, observing from an eminence the Indians of the town and the white men walking together and conversing in a friendly manner. Martin sent his son over to the town while he went to Salem to apprise the brethren at that place of what was going on. The Salem Indians sent two of their men with Martin to Gnadenhutten, where the Williamson men appointed a party of their own number to go with these Indians back to Salem, and assist in bringing those at the lower town to Gnadenhutten. When the main body of the Salem Indians arrived at the river bank, opposite Gnadenhutten, they discovered blood in the sand and on a canoe that was lying at the edge of the water. They had already given up their guns, axes, and knives, being assured that the same would all be returned when they arrived at Fort Pitt. Being taken over to the town they found the inhabitants confined, preparatory to the slaughter that was to take place. The whites now ceased calling them friends and Christians, and charged them with being enemies and warriors. In proof of this averment the whites pointed to the pewter-plates, cups, spoons, tea-kettles, pots, basins, &c., and declared it all stolen property from the settlers. They also seized the Indian horses, and pointed to the brands thereon as further evidence that all this property had been stolen from the border families. Finding all this property in their possession, together with the bloody dress that was recognized as having belonged to Mrs. Wallace, they were told to prepare for death, and the execution was fixed for the next day. In refutation of the charges, the Indians accounted for the brands on the horses by offering to produce their own branding irons, which were used for the purpose of enabling them to identify their own horses. In regard to the other property, they insisted that most of it was brought by the missionaries from the Pennsylvania missions, and the balance bought from traders who had from time to time visited the towns. Finding all efforts to save their lives fruitless, they begged for a short time to prepare for death. While at their devotions their captors discussed the manner of putting them to death. Some were in favor of burning them alive, and some of killing first, then burning the bodies after scalping. The commander, Williamson, became powerless in the excited and frenzied condition of his men, to whom had been exhibited the bloody dress of

Mrs. Wallace, which operated on their minds, as history tells us, the bloody robe of Cæsar, when shown to the Romans by Antony, operated on their minds. All Williamson could do was to submit the matter to a vote, as proposed by the most excited of the men. Upon taking a vote, those who were in favor of saving the Indians and taking them to Fort Pitt, were invited to step out to the front, which was responded to by but eighteen out of about one hundred in all (some accounts put the number at three hundred), the residue voting to kill, scalp and burn the captives. It has never been settled whether Williamson voted or not, the presumption being, from the fact of his being commander, that he did not vote. Those of the men who voted against death, then retired from the scene, at the same time calling upon the Almighty to witness that they washed their hands of the crime about to be perpetrated. The victims were then asked if they were ready to die, and the answer being in the affirmative, the work of death commenced. Heckewelder says that the number killed exceeded ninety, all of whom, except four, were killed in the mission houses, they having been tied there—according to Heckwelder's version—and there knocked in the head with a cooper's mallet. One man, he says, taking up the mallet, began with an Indian named Abraham, and continued knocking down until he counted fourteen, he then handed his mallet to one of his fellows, saying, "my arm fails me, go on in the same way; I think I have done pretty well." In another house, where mostly women and children were tied, Judith, an aged and pious widow, was the first victim. After they had finished they retreated a short distance, but on returning to view the dead bodies, and finding one of them named Abel, although scalped and mangled, attempting to raise himself from the floor, they dispatched him, and, having set fire to the house, went off shouting and cursing.

Of the number killed sixty-two were grown persons, one-third of whom were women, the remainder being children. Two youths, who were knocked down and shut up in the first house, escaped death. One named Thomas was knocked down and scalped, but being only stunned, after awhile recovered, and on looking around he saw Abel alive, but scalped, with blood running down his face. The lad quickly laid down as if dead, and had scarcely lain a minute when the party came and finished Abel by chopping his head with a hatchet. Soon after they went away Thomas crept over the dead bodies to the door, and on getting out, hid himself until dark, when he made his way to the path leading to Sandusky. The other lad, who was in the house where the women were, raised a trap-door and got down into the cellar with another boy, where they lay concealed during the time the butchery was going on. After dusk they attempted to get out through a window opening in the foundation of the house. The first succeeded, but the second stuck fast, and was burned alive, the house being set on fire soon after the poor little fellow got fast. The two who escaped afterward made their way to Sandusky, having fallen in with the Schoenbrunn Indians in their flight.

One of Williamson's party saved a little boy eight years old, took him home, and raised him to a man, when he left and returned to his tribe.

In Zeisberger's version of the massacre, as detailed by his biographer, it is reported as occurring on the 8th of March. He says that the victims were tied, some singly, and others two and two, dragged to the appointed house, and then tomahawked and scalped. When the men and boys were all killed, the women were brought out, taken to the other house, and dispatched in the same manner. He states that Christiana, a widow, who was well versed in the English language, appealed to Colonel Williamson as she was being led away, and he replied, "I have no power to help you." She was killed with the others. The massacre being over, Williamson and his men returned home to the Ohio and Monongahela with the scalps and about one hundred horses. In the valley all was desolation. Not a warrior was afterward found to be following Williamson to pick off his men on their way to the Ohio, which they reached on the 10th of March, two days after the massacre, unmolested. Within a radius of twenty-five miles around the three burned towns, not a human being was known to be alive, while but two or three days' march out on the Sandusky there were, perhaps, a thousand warriors, and they knew of Williamson's expedition having marched west from the Ohio, but no warriors intercepted him going or coming. That was part of the British policy matured at Detroit, of having these peaceable Indians massacred by excited American borderers, in order to bring over to the British side all the Indian tribes united against the colonists. How completely it succeeded will be seen.

Simon Girty returned to the Wyandot towns, from which his absence had been short, but sufficiently long to have enabled him, in disguise, to reach the border settlements, and, among his old acquaintances, start and hurry on the expedition against the Moravian towns. On the Sandusky, at the present Fremont, Heckewelder and Zeisberger first heard of the massacre by a convert, who had ran from Captives town to apprise them of the news that had just been brought in by a Wyandot band of warriors, who had crossed the valley with border scalps and stolen horses. This was evidently the party who had killed and impaled the child of Mrs. Wallace, sold her bloody dress at Gnadenhutten to the unsuspecting Indian converts, and then hid in the vicinity until the massacre previously planned was over, when they fled homeward to receive their scalp premiums at Detroit. At the captives' huts, where the residue of convert captives were who had not gone down to the death at Gnadenhutten, the news of the slaughter of their relatives had also come in by Jacob, who had escaped from under the floor of one of the burning houses, and fled to the Sandusky.

Down at the massacre ground the wolves, bears, panthers, and other wild beasts had gathered for a feast, and were fighting for a meal off the dead, but the flesh had been so crisped that they could get but little. It was truly an accursed and desolate country, and the Great Spirit passed up and down the valley uttering the war-whoop, which echoed back and back from tree and dell until it reached the warrior towns of the Shawanese on the Scioto and Miami, the Delawares under Pipe at Sandusky, Monseys under Welendewaeken on the Wabash, and other tribes, calling for a revenge in corresponding magnitude to the murders committed on their kin.

This was the kind of double life that Girty gloried in, first on the border, exciting the whites to kill the Christian Indians and burn their towns in the valley; next at the warrior's towns, inciting them to revenge the deaths of those Christians, and he lost no time in fanning the flame in their camp fires. At all their British camps a unanimous determination existed to take a bloody and two-fold vengeance on the Americans. A vow was made that no white man should ever have that valley for a home, but that it should remain uncontaminated by his presence through all time, and that the boundary line of future treaties with the whites should be the Ohio forever and ever.

To carry out their intentions, large bands of picked warriors started at once to raid afresh on the Pennsylvania, Virginia, and Kentucky borders, and each prisoner was to be taken to the place of the massacre, and there dispatched by the tomahawk and fire brand until the two-fold vengeance had been consummated, as ordered by the Great Spirit, or Manitto.* Here it may be remarked, that revenge is taught by Manitto to be a duty more sacred than all others, and the Indian mind is constantly filled with the

* [*Note.*—The God of the Lenni-Lennape, or Delawares, was "*Kitschi*" (heavenly), "Mannitto" (God)—thus "Kitschimannitto," abbreviated to "Mannitto, and *Manito;* this corrupted to "Manitou," "Manito*a*," or "Manito*n*."

The Algonquins and Chippewas' God is "Kitchi"—Manito*n* and Manit*a*. The Onondaga God is "Nioh."

The Asiatics have a God, "Kitchi Manoa," hence some writers bring the original Indian from Asia.]

idea that if he dies without being revenged, for some wrong committed on his friends or relatives, there is no happiness in the spirit land.

The massacre was a month old, and already the vengeance-taking warriors on the Ohio, and its eastern tributaries in Pennsylvania and Virginia, had sunk their hatchets into the skulls of many white borderers, who fought for life, and were killed in their tracks. These deaths were to be counted as no vengeance until the scalps were carried to the massacre ground, dried, painted red or black on the inside, with the picture of a bullet or a hatchet in another color, to indicate how its owner died. In like manner were the scalps of those whites who should suffer death by fire to be painted, but in lieu of the bullet or hatchet a bunch of faggots were to be represented on the skin side, indicative of the fire-death.

Over on the Monongahela the ninety odd Indian scalps had been exhibited to the settlers by Williamson's men, and this suggested a raid to the Sandusky to punish the tribes who were still hatcheting the white borderers in Pennsylvania and Virginia. On the 25th of April, 1782, General Irvine, who had just assumed command at Fort Pitt (Pittsburgh), wrote to General Washington, that two days before his arrival about three hundred whites from the Monongahela, and among whom were some of Williamson's men, had come, attacked and killed several Christian Indians, who had been captured the preceding fall at Schoenbrunn and brought to Smoky Island, opposite Fort Pitt. This atrocity added fuel to the flame of Indian war, and the government at once set about dispatching a large force, under Colonel Crawford, to chastise western Indians. Crawford's army reached the Tuscarawas about the 26th of May, and camped at the ruins of Schoenbrunn, without having seen an Indian warrior, so desolate had the accursed valley become. In the night two warriors were seen by the officers who were passing on their "grand round" duty around the camp, and who fired, but the warriors disappeared unhurt.

The firing alarmed the camp, and Crawford's men rushed out pell-mell in a panic, as if surrounded by all the Indian hosts, who had come to appease the wrath of the great spirit yelling up and down the haunted valley. There were, however, no Indians about, yet the historian says that even Crawford, when he saw his troopers panic stricken that night, foresaw his coming death, and as he lay there amid the ruins of Schoenbrunn, his imagination conjured up the skeletons of the victims of Williamson's men, filing along the trail on the banks of the Tuscarawas, and led by one Ann Charity. Their skulls were mashed in and the bones of some were charred to a crisp. They were singing the Indian song of sorrow, and calling on—not our God—but their Manitto or Great Spirit, to avenge their death.

Williamson, being second in command, rested in the same tent with Crawford, and shuddered as the latter told what he had seen, then peering out in the darkness he listened, but in vain, for the sound of the gnomes. They had gone on up the trail toward Sandusky. As soon as daylight appeared the two commanders ordered the four hundred troopers into their saddles, and galloped west out of the valley, crossing the Tuscarawas between Stone Creek and Sugar Creek; from thence they plunged into the wilderness toward Sandusky, but on a trail to the left of the one Ann and her spirit comrades had taken. It was now a race between Ann and her skeletons and Crawford, which should reach the huts of the captive Christian Indians first. When he and his troopers arrived within half a mile of the Delaware huts, they were found deserted. Ann had outrun him, and he turned toward the Wyandot town, now called Upper Sandusky. It, too, was deserted. After another mile he called a council of war, and they all determined to retreat in case no Indians were found by nightfall. This was at a spot near a trail leading to Half King's residence, and on June 4, 1782, in the afternoon. Scouts soon came reporting "savages coming," and in a few minutes they were in sight taking shelter in a grove, from which the troopers dislodged them, Crawford losing five killed and nineteen wounded. That night and next day desultory firing was kept up, Crawford intending to attack and disperse the savages in the night, but this was frustrated in the afternoon by the appearance of some British troops brought from Detroit. On his south line also appeared two hundred Shawanese not seen before, the whole body of savages exceeding his own force. A retreat was ordered and kept up through the night. In the morning Crawford was missing.

THE CAPTURE AND DEATH OF COLONEL CRAWFORD.

In the retreat he had become separated from the main body by reason of his horse failing. In the confusion and panic, every man was looking out for himself, so that no other horse could be had. Crawford called for his son John, his nephew William, and his son-in-law William Harrison, who being aids to the colonel, should have been near him in the line of duty, and from one of whom he would have obtained a horse to enable him to push forward and regain his position as commander. But neither answered his call. Doctor Knight, surgeon of the expedition, came galloping up, and both calling for the three men above named and getting no response, Crawford requested Knight to remain with him, which he did. Crawford then denounced the troops for disobeying orders. Hot firing was going on in front, toward the south-west, which indicated that the enemy was between him and the main body of his troops, and he and Knight moved east, reaching the Sandusky about midnight, and by daylight of June 6, they were but eight miles away from the battle-field, by reason of darkness and jaded horses. But by two o'clock in the afternoon they made nine miles, and fell in with Captain Biggs and others during the day, and also a wounded officer, Lieutenant Ashley, whom Biggs was carrying. Camping over night, they had gone a short distance next morning (June 7) when they found a dead deer, and shortly after met a volunteer who had shot it. Making a meal of the deer, all started on their journey. Crawford and Knight by this time were on foot. When near the present site of Leesville, on the south side of the Sandusky, they were confronted by several Indians, who had ambuscaded them. One Indian took Crawford by the hand, and another the hand of Knight. They were then taken to a Delaware camp, half a mile away, where they remained two days with nine other prisoners. The Indians had killed and scalped Biggs and Ashley, and their scalps and two horses were brought into camp. On the 10th of June Crawford was taken to the Half King's Town, and the other prisoners to another town. In the night Crawford had an interview with Simon Girty, who was at Half King's Town, and whom he offered one thousand dollars to save him, he having known Girty before the latter became a British captain. This offer becoming known to Captain Pipe and the other chiefs, they arranged for his death in the shortest possible time. He was taken to the old town on the morning of June 11, with Knight and the other prisoners, with their faces painted black, indicating their fate. Pipe and Wingenund came and shook hands with Crawford, having known him years before. Pipe then painted Crawford's face black with coal and water, and all started on a trail to another Delaware town. Here they halted, and saw five prisoners tomahawked by boys and squaws, and their scalps were thrust into the faces of Knight and Crawford. Here Knight was given over to some Indians to be taken next day to the Shawanese towns. Crawford and Knight were then taken to Pipe's village. In the afternoon, Crawford was taken to a spot where a stake had been set in the ground, and a fire kindled about seven feet away. Around were nearly a hundred Indians, mostly squaws and boys. Girty, Pipe, Wingenund, and a British officer in disguise, were near. Knight was present, tied and guarded, but lived to detail these particulars: Crawford was stripped, his hands bound by a rope fastened to the stake and to his wrists, with play sufficient to enable him to walk around the post, or sit down. He then asked, after they had beat him, if they intended to burn him, and being answered that they did, he remarked that he would bear it patiently. Pipe then made a speech to the Indians, who took their guns and shot powder into Crawford's flesh from his feet to his neck. They then cut off his ears, and thrust burning sticks into his body. The squaws put burning faggots upon his feet, so that he literally walked on fire. In his pain he called on Girty to shoot him, but Girty replied laughingly that he had no gun. Heckewelder says that Crawford also called on Wingenund to save him, but the chief replied that the King of England, if on the ground, could not save him. Being almost dead he fell on his stomach, when he was scalped, and a squaw put coals on his head; then he raised upon his feet again, and began to walk around. Knight was then taken away, but the next morning he was marched by the spot, and told by his Indian guard to look at his "big captain," which he did, and saw only his charred bones in the ashes, around which the Indians had danced all night, wildly singing the scalp song of "Aw-oh-aw-oh-aw-oh."

Knight was taken in charge by a Delaware chief, who was to guard the Doctor to a Shawanese town, more than a day's travel distant. Before starting, Knight was painted black, which meant that he was to suffer torture. The Indian was mounted on a splendid steed, while Knight was compelled to plod along in front of him on foot.

When evening came on they halted for the night, in the vicinity of Kenton, Hardin County, having made considerable more than half the journey. The Indian bound the Doctor, and then ordered him to lay down and sleep, which he pretended to do, but kept awake nearly the whole night watching for the savage to go to sleep so he could make an effort to escape. The chief, however, did not sleep a wink, but closely eyed his prisoner, evidently suspecting the Doctor's intention. Early in the morning the Indian untied Knight and then devoted himself to stirring up the fire, preparatory to cooking some breakfast. While at this, and with his back toward him, the Doctor picked up a stick of wood that lay with one end in the fire, and with it struck the Indian a blow on the side of the head which felled him to the ground, and when in the act of drawing back to strike another blow, the Indian scrambled off on his hands and knees until out of reach of Knight, and then jumped to his feet and ran off into the forest. Knight then snatched up the Indian's gun and aimed to shoot him, but in the excitement broke the lock in cocking it. He then followed some distance, when he gave up the chase and returned to the camping ground, and gathering up the blanket, moccasins, and amunition which belonged to the chief, started on his way for Fort Pitt.

He traveled on all that day and night, stopping at intervals to rest, and until the following evening, when he was compelled to halt from fatigue and hunger. The next morning he threw away the gun, since he was unable to repair it.

His course continued eastward through the present counties of Hardin, Crawford, Richland, Wayne and Tuscarawas, to the Tuscarawas River, which he reached at a point a short distance above the mouth of what is known as Conotten Creek (sometimes called One Leg), where he rested and refreshed himself with various kinds of berries which he found in abundance in the bottoms along the river.

From the Tuscarawas he kept a course almost due east, avoiding all trails and open ground, and arrived at the Ohio River below Fort McIntosh. From here he followed up the river to Fort Pitt, at which place he arrived on the 4th of July, three weeks after making his escape.

On the morning of June 6, Colonel Williamson gathered together all that was left uncaptured or unkilled, of Crawford's army, and retreated back to the Tuscarawas, seeking rest and sleep for his wearied troopers a short distance below Schoenbrunn. But there was no rest for him. In the midst of the desolation a terrific storm arose, revealing by its lightning Ann Charity and the skeleton spirits filing, this time, down the trail, followed by a band of warriors, each dangling from a pole a white man's scalp, all moving toward the massacre ground, while the unearthly scalp yell of the Great Spirit echoed up and down the valley, and silenced for the moment even the thunder of heaven.

Williamson, aroused from the terrific dream, called to horse all his jaded troopers, and at daylight recrossed the Tuscarawas, a short distance above the place of massacre, with all that was intact of Crawford's army, and disappeared along the Stillwater, over the eastern hills, all cursing, as they spurred their horses onward, the day that brought them first to the haunted valley. In the night, before this day of gloom to Williamson, Ann Charity assembled, by her mysterious power, sixty-nine of the massacre victims, around their burnt ruins at Gnadenhutten, and calling them each by christian name as known in life, Isaac Glikhican and Anna Benigna, his wife; Jonah and Amelia, his wife; Christian and Augustina, his wife; John Martin, Samuel Moore, Tobias, Adam and Cornelia, his wife; Henry and Joanna Salome, his wife; Luke and Lucia, his wife; Philip and Lorel, his wife; Lewis and Ruth, his wife; Nicholas and Joanna Sabina, his wife; Israel, Hannah, Abraham, Catharine, Joseph Schebosh, Judith, Mark, John, Christiana, Mary, Abel, Rebecca, Paul, Rachel, Henry, Maria, Susanna, John, Anna, Michael, Joshua, Peter, Bathseba, Gottlieb, Julianna, David, Elizabeth, Martha, Anna Rosina, Salome, Christian, Christiana, Joseph, Leah, Mark, Benigna, Jonathan, Christina, Anthony, Ann Salome, Jonah, Maria Elizabeth, Gottlieb, Benjamin, John Thomas, Sarah, Hannah, and Anna Elizabeth, she presented each with a soldier's scalp, according to Indian custom, to appease the wrath of the great spirit, and fulfill the vow of vengeance so secretly made by her kinsmen up at the Sandusky when they first heard of the massacre. The mashed heads of the Indians and the white men's scalps were then intermingled in the ruins. Revenge had been taken, and that opened the entrance of the Indian heaven to all who had participated in avenging the massacre. All was again a desolate calm in the haunted valley, save and excepting the noise made by the wild denizens of the forest, the wolves, bears, and panthers that had gathered about Gnadenhutten for a feast on the scalps of John Crawford, young William Crawford, William Harrison, Captain Benjamin Biggs, Lieutenant Ashley, and of the other sixty odd officers and soldiers brought down from the Sandusky battle-ground. Over these the beasts fought, ran howling, sprang at each other, and tore the scalps into fragments, for the flesh on the bones of the Christian victims had been so roasted and crisped, as to afford not even a meal to the animals that had come out from their lairs, in the surrounding hills of the Tuscarawas, for a high carnival.

In the midst of this wild tumult Ann Charity disappeared, no one knew where. But she was no myth. She had lived from childhood at the missions in Pennsylvania, and on the Tuscarawas. Gifted with a mysterious mental power, her religion was half heathen, half Christian. She claimed to be able to call up the dead, and when the massacre took place she resolved to try her power, and revenge her friends and kindred. She came down from the Wabash—no one knew her—and was the first to apprise the western Indians of Crawford's army crossing the valley. When all was over, she became again a pious Christian on White River, Indiana, and was there burned as a witch about the year 1806 by order of Tecumseh, the prophet.

In a few days after Williamson crossed the valley, John Slover, Crawford's guide, who had been nearly captured, but escaping his savage pursuers, crossed the Tuscarawas, near the present town of Port Washington, reaching the Ohio in safety. James Paul, another of the body-guard of Crawford, was captured, painted black, but also escaped death by fire, reaching, on his way home, the Sugar Creek, which he followed to its junction with the Tuscarawas, near the present Dover, where he proceeded up the stream, crossed where the Canton fording place was afterward located, and slept at the so-called "Federal Springs," of a later day, where he found a deserted Indian camp, with kegs and empty vessels lying around, which had been captured by the Indians at Fort Laurens three years before, when they stampeded McIntosh's provision train, and on which provisions the savages had many jolly feasts while the garrison were starving. From this point Paul passed over the edge of the plain, whereon is at this day New Philadelphia, and reaching Williamson's trail below Schoenbrunn ruins, he arrived safely at Mingo bottom. But how many more of Crawford's troopers re-crossed the haunted valley history saith not, for until 1785 the savage warriors after scalps, in fulfillment of the vow of vengeance, were its only human inhabitants. In that year an escaped prisoner crossed the river at the massacre town and reached Fort Wheeling, but he reported that he saw no human being in the valley. The bones of the Christian martyrs were scattered around, and the fruit trees planted by the missionaries were in bloom, but the limbs had been broken down by the bears, and the place had become the abode only of rattlesnakes and wild beasts.

At the massacre, the first blood shed was that of a Christian Indian named John Shebosh, who was tomahawked and scalped by Charles Builderback, one of Williamson's men. He was a Virginian, but had settled in Ohio near the mouth of Short Creek. After the massacre he was out with Crawford's army, but escaped the fate of Crawford and returned home. Seven years after, in 1789, he and his wife were captured by Indians near their cabin on the Ohio. When the Indians first attacked her husband and his brother, she hid in the bushes. The brother escaped; but as soon as Charles was tied the Indians hunted, but failing to find her, they told Builderback to call her by name or they would kill him then and there. At his first call she would not answer, but when he called her again, and told her of his fate if she kept silent, the woman came out. The Indians then retreated west with the two captives. Nearing the

Tuscarawas, they separated into two bands, one taking him toward Gnadenhutten, and the other, with Mrs. Builderback, came to the Tuscarawas, higher up the stream, where they encamped at an Indian town, probably "Three-Leg Town," near the present Urichsville. In a short time the other band came up, and an Indian threw into her lap the scalp of her dead husband. The sight so overcame her that she swooned. They laid her against a tree, and when she awoke the scalp was gone. They took her to the Miami Valley, where she remained a captive nine months, but was finally ransomed and sent to her home up the Ohio. In 1791 she married John Green, and moved to Fairfield County, where she died in 1842, near Lancaster, and is said to have given birth to the first white child born in Fairfield County. His captors knew Builderback, and had been watching for him for years, determined to take revenge for the death of Shebosh, their relative, seven years before at Gnadenhutten. Some of his Ohio River friends, who pursued these Indians, found his body a short distance from the spot where he had killed Shebosh. His body was terribly mutilated, and it was evident to his friends that the Indians had intended burning Builderback at the massacre ground, but the pursuers were so close after them that they abandoned burning him alive, and made their escape, after tomahawking and scalping him. He was the last white man known to have been in the massacre who paid the forfeit of his life for his connection therewith. Williamson escaped the vengeance of the Indians, although he had crossed and recrossed the valley four times in one year. He returned to Washington County, Pennsylvania, and was soon sent to guard the Ohio border along the river. On the return of peace he became sheriff of his county, had great influence, and regained all his popularity among the border men. Doddridge says that he was a humane man, but brave and courageous to a fault, and when called on to do any act in discharge of duty, he did it fearlessly as to consequences. Hence, when his men voted nearly unanimously for the massacre of the Indians, he carried out their edict mercilessly, having no power to prevent or avoid killing the Christian Indians. He lived many years afterward, but died in poverty, remembered only as the first and last actor in the tragedy of the bloody valley.

CHAPTER IX.

FIFTY MILES OF RUINS ALONG THE ANCIENT RIVER.

Heckewelder, who was at the Seneca capital in 1762, then inhabited by Delawares, called it "Tuscarawas," the word signifying "old town," or ancient place. Boquet, with his army, was there in 1764, and called it by the same name. So did McIntosh in 1778, when he erected Fort Laurens, in close proximity.

Eight miles north, Rogers, in 1761, found a town which he said was called the "Mingo Cabins." Passing up the river, the Mingoes, Chippewas, Ottawas or Cuyahogas, had a town at or near the mouth of each creek emptying into the Tuscarawas. Rogers spent some time in hunting with the Indians, and relates that eight miles south of Beavertown they shot two elks. They were evidently killed on Sugar Creek, in the vicinity of the present Dover.

From the ancient Seneca capital, on the border of the present Stark County, to Goshockgunk, at the present town of Coshocton, is a distance of fifty odd miles, within which space were "Tuscarawas," Beavertown, the Ottawa town below the fording place, an old town below the mouth of Sugar Creek, Three Legstown, at the mouth of Stillwater, King Beaver's hamlet, near the present Gnadenhutten, Ge-hel-e-muk-pe-chuk, a Delaware capital, fifteen miles south of the "Big Spring, King New Comerstown, at the present town of that name, Old Wyandot town, White Eyes' hamlet, Custaloga's town, White Woman's town, and Goshuckgunk, the present Coshocton, making thirteen, and each in its day the scene of Indian glory, or captive's suffering.

Of Christian towns there were Schoenbrunn, old and new, Gnadenhutten, Lichtenau, Salem, and Post's mission house, each in its day the scene of Christian suffering and heathen persecution.

The struggle had been going on since Gist's visit in 1750 between the pale-faced Christians and the red-faced heathen, the one to obtain, and the other race to retain possession of the valley. The result of the thirty years' conflict was that in 1784, when Virginia ceded the territory to the United States, the two races had whipped and scourged each other out of the valley.

The old Tuscarawas, which had been flowing down the valley, according to the geologist, Newberry, ever since the carboniferous age, and had cut its channel in many places through eighty thousand years of coal formations, was still there, representing God's grand works for the use of man, but there was no man or audience left, for the nineteen towns of red and white men had been demolished, and of their structures there was scarcely one stone left standing upon the other.

Even the fifty yards square of land, stepped off at Post's hamlet, for the use of the white man and his God, and considered then by the Indians ample for his wants, had returned to its forest again.

True, Fort Laurens stood alone like a great ghoul, looking for her defenders, who had ran away in 1779, to come back and take possession anew, but they came not.

Around the ruins of the modern Golgotha, Gnadenhütten, the ashes and bones of the murdered Christians still strewed the ground, and raiding warriors hurried in terror up and down the river trail, either with, or after scalp victims, but that was all of life to be seen along the shores of the ancient river for a distance of fifty miles, with this exception.

LEGEND OF THE BIG SPRING.

In September, 1782, some four hundred warriors from the north-west, on the way to the Ohio, encamped at Schoenbrunn, as Crawford's four hundred troopers had done when going to the north-west in the preceding June. They came back from an unsuccessful raid on Wheeling, as well as along the border, and rested again at Schoenbrunn, as Williamson's routed Crawford army had rested on their way home, the one army having lost Crawford, and the other the celebrated "Big Foot" chief, and the legend is that as the savages stooped to drink at the Zeisberger Spring, the tongues of their victims tied to their necks as trophies of war, uttered unearthly moans, and the water cast back by reflection the visages of those victims into the warriors' faces, which so horrified the superstitious Indians that they mounted in affright, galloping off on the Sandusky trail as Williamson and Crawford's survivors had gone the other way only one hundred days before. The facts were so wonderfully coincident as to appear supernatural. The legend says that a mist suddenly enveloped the spring, from out of which came the God of the Christian, and Mannitto, the God of the heathen, who, viewing the ruins made by their followers, banished each his kind, obliterated each the remaining structures of the other, and decreeing that in the coming time even the spring should shrink from human sight, then each departed to his etherial home to renew their never-ending conflict between Christian and heathen on some other line.

There are men now living who have drank from this historic spring, but after Zeisberger died—after his last Indian had departed, to return no more, the legend was verified—the water of the spring did shrink from human sight and human use, and remains unfit for use to this day.

STORY OF THE WHITE SQUAW'S REVENGE.

At the time Fort Laurens was reduced to a garrison of one hundred men, in January, 1779, it will be recollected that the pack-horses bringing provisions in from Fort McIntosh, were stampeded by joyous firing of guns in the fort, and the horses and provisions, to a great extent, lost. A party of Mingo warriors were at the time coming down the Tuscarawas trail, which crossed the river at what was afterward called the Canton fording place, about one mile north of New Philadelphia of the present time, and near the ford was a large spring, since called the Federal Spring. The Mingoes caught some of the pack-horses laden with provisions and brought them to the spring, where they camped until the provisions were eaten up. Among them was a warrior chief of great stature, who had with him a white squaw, who had been captured in Pennsylvania, and after many hair-breadth escapes, had become the warrior's wife, out of gratitude, if not love, for having saved her life at the time.

When the Mingoes broke camp, this warrior and wife proceeded on a visit to New Schoenbrunn, about one and a half miles south-east of New Philadelphia, where they heard Zeisberger preach, and manifesting some outward feelings of religion, the chief and wife were solicited to join the mission. She assented, but the warrior refused, and she would not join without him. The Indian women about the mission then undertook to gain her over by strategy. At the mission was a creole squaw of great beauty, who gave the missionaries much trouble by her lasciviousness. She possessed such fascinating charms that she was the envious terror of the other women, and turned the heads of such men as visited the mission, and it is in tradition that Zeisberger himself, being then unmarried, was nearly ensnared by her conduct and her wanton approaches, but succeeded like Joseph of old in withstanding the temptress.

The Mingo was told of her, and escorted to her cabin. His white wife was informed of the fact, by the Indian women, they believing that she would abandon him, and become a convert. In jealous rage she avowed the death of both if found together, and repairing with her tomahawk to the woman's cabin, found that they had both left for the woods. She followed their tracks to a high bluff on the edge of the river, a short distance above the Federal Spring, and over which bluff a man named Compton fell in the night time, about twenty years ago, and was killed, the precipice being nearly one hundred feet high, but higher at the time spoken of, in 1779, from the fact that it then descended perpendicular into the river, but since has been excavated for a railway track. On this bluff the jealous white squaw met her chief and paramour face to face. It was but a look of a moment. He sprang up with his knife to strike, but in raising she struck him, and, as he fell back over the ledge, she bounded at the creole beauty, who had thus wronged her, and she, too, went over the precipice, dragging with her the white squaw to a like speedy death. Some Indian converts, who had followed her to the bluff, descended to the river, took the three corpses from the shallow water, carried them to the mission houses at New Schoenbrunn, and related the tragedy. The missionary refused them burial in the Christian grave-yard; directed the bodies to be taken into the forest, and interred beyond the sound of the church bell, that once echoed from Old Schoenbrunn.

The main incidents of the foregoing tragedy were communicated by Captain Killbuck to General Shane, an early settler, who related them to the writer more than a generation by, and it is a curious fact, that in the summer of 1875, a farmer named Hensel, while digging for ore, found on one of his hills, not over a mile and a half from New Schoenbrunn, the skeleton of a giant Indian, with the skull broken in, and by his side the bones of one or two females. They had been hurriedly buried, the remains not being over a couple of feet from the surface, and bore evidence of having been there near an hundred years. It was surmised that they were persons killed in General Wayne's war of 1793–4, but it is more probable that they were the Mingo warrior and his squaws.

In 1781, two years after the mission had been relieved of the evil influences of the artful Indian beauty, David Zeisberger visited Bethlehem, Pennsylvania, and, although sixty years of age, he was attracted by the charms of Susan Lecron, a Christian lady thereat, and married her. She lies burried by his side at Goshen to-day, and there is little doubt but that the pious man took a wife as a shield against temptation in the wilderness, well knowing that notwithstanding the fact that religion is a protector of virtue, there are times, as all sacred and profane history prove, when his physical desires and passions, make of man, if not under the influence of a virtuous wife, only a beast on two legs, after all.

LEGEND OF THE WHITE CAPTIVE AND INDIAN CHIEF AT NEW SCHOENBRUNN.

In the year 1779, a band of Wyandots, on their way home from the Ohio to the Sandusky, stopped at New Schoenbrunn, on the Tuscarawas, about one and a half miles from the present New Philadelphia. They had with them a young white woman, and two scalps, together with plunder they had stolen from some murdered settlers, over on the Monongahela.

It was night when they came in, and having whisky with them, were turbulent and noisy. They called on father Zeisberger, and demanded something to eat, telling him they intended to rest that night with him. He complied with their demand, by having food prepared by the converted Indian women at the mission, and taken out to the warriors.

They had built a fire in the only street or path of the place, and which street was obliterated in constructing the Ohio Canal fifty years afterward. After feasting on the provisions, consisting of corn-bread and meat, and taking their smoke from rude corn-cob pipes, the savages prepared a spot nearly opposite the house of Zeisberger, and began their war-dance, which was kept up for some time, with the usual hootings and yellings of savages, made more savage by the white man's whisky they had brought with them from the border settlements. Presently a drunken chief retired from the dancing ring around the fire into the bushes, but soon returned, half pulling, half carrying the young woman into the ring, and by gestures bade her join in the war-dance. Unable to obey him, through fright and the fatigue of the previous day's march, she fell to the ground, and thus impeded their dance. Enraged with passion the Indian who claimed her as his, first kicked her, then clubbed her, but she remained insensible to his assaults. He then seized her and attempted to force her into the fire, determined to conquer the maiden's stubbornness, as he had understood it, or burn her. Her screams and groans aroused the whole mission with indignation, and about one half the number of the chief's comrades sided with the Christian Indians in giving vent to their feelings at witnessing the scene. The war-dance was broken up, but the chief stood by his victim, with uplifted tomahawk, gesticulating to her to obey him, or he would cleave her skull. At this moment a party of white men arrived at Schoenbrunn, in pursuit of the savages, who all fled, except the chief. He remained stolid for a moment, brandishing his tomahawk in the air, then burying it as he thought in the head of his captive, but, by a timely movement of one of the Christian Indians of the mission with a club, the instrument of death fell from the chief's hand harmless by the side of the woman. In another moment the chief was seized, tied to a tree, and a guard of Christian Indians set to watch him until it should be determined what should be his fate. The missionary,

Zeisberger, took the released captive to his cabin, and soon succeeded in restoring her to consciousness, when she beheld among the men who had pursued the Indians, her own brother. 'He in his rage at the inhuman barbarities inflicted upon his sister, asked that he might be allowed the privilege, single handed, of becoming her avenger. This was accorded him by his comrades, but the missionary here interposed against the shedding of the blood of the chief, as none had been shed, and claiming that all the inhuman conduct of this Indian was the consequence of liquor he had obtained among white men, and that as a Christian convert had saved the captive woman's life, it was his duty as a Christian to prevent the taking of the chief's life, if possible. He then directed all to kneel, and he offered up a prayer of thanks for the rescue of one human being from death, and implored the divine interference to save even this self-determined murderer at the tree. His hearers acquiesced; and the brother, after setting his Indian victim free, returned with his comrades and his sister to their homes in Virginia. In after years, when the mission was broken up and the missionaries became prisoners, and were sent to Detroit, Zeisberger met the chief whose life he had saved, and during the time of his capture and exile from Schoenbrunn, the chief was by him converted to Christianity, and died in the Moravian faith at one of the missions of that sect.

LEGEND OF THE CONNER FAMILY, AND STORY OF TEDPACHXIT.

Richard Conner came from Maryland into the valley of the Muskingum, and was captured by the Shawanese and kept for several years at one of their towns on the Scioto. As a matter of choice between being burned, or becoming a Shawanese, he put on their paint, and married a white woman who had been a prisoner some time, and by whom he had one or more children—all becoming white Indians for the time being.

In the delivery of prisoners, at the close of Dunmore's war, in 1774, Conner and wife were delivered up by the Shawanese, who failed to bring in Conner's son. He and wife were taken to Fort Pitt, where they settled for a time.

In 1775 they came to Schoenbrunn, where she remained, and became a favorite, while Conner went back among the Shawanese to find his boy. During his absence she saw the good being done at Schoenbrunn mission, and on Conner's return without his son, she induced him to join the mission with her. They built a house at Schoenbrunn, and when Colonel John Gibson visited Schoenbrunn, with the committee of congress, and having with them the great congress peace belt, over six feet long, as an emblem of friendship between the colonies and Indian tribes of the Muskingum, they were present at the baptism of one of Conner's children born at Schoenbrunn. Mr. Conner accompanied them down the valley, and succeeded in ransoming his son from the Shawanese, with whisky, it is said, and whom he brought back to Schoenbrunn, to be educated by Zeisberger.

In 1781, when the missions were broken up, the Conner's followed the captives to Sandusky. There they remained after the captives left that country, except the son John, who, it is said, followed Zeisberger in all his wanderings. The elder Conner settled a large tract of land, known afterward as the "Conner farms," and died wealthy, in Michigan, leaving descendants who became prominent citizens in Indiana.

In 1802, when Heckewelder brought the twelve chiefs to Goshen, on their way to the seat of government, John Conner was with them as interpreter. Tedpachxit and the chiefs were introduced by him to President Jefferson, and he returned with them to the Indian country.

Of Tedpachxit, this story is told: He was small, but had been a great warrior, and was as conceited as he was brave.

Stepping up to one of the generals who had been at St. Clair's defeat, he strutted around very pompously, and asked the general these questions: "You not know me? I am Tedpachxit!" The general answered, by asking, "Who the devil is Tedpachxit?" The chief became indignant, and taking from his belt a string with twenty-seven dried human tongues appended, he shook them in the general's face, and walked off saying to himself, "He know me now!"

Tedpachxit was afterward induced to embrace Christianity, and was burnt as a witch by the Prophet Tecsumeh's orders on White River, Indiana, about 1806.

A grandson of Richard Conner, now resides at Indianapolis, and is the head of a large business firm in that city.

THE FIRST SETTLERS IN EASTERN OHIO AND THEIR TROUBLES.

At the old Salt Springs, in the present Trumbull County, the white hunters of the Ohio rendezvoused as early as 1754, to shoot deer, elk and other game, and remained there off and on, living the hunter's life, until between 1770 and 1780, when some enterprising Englishmen from Fort Pitt put up cabins, made salt in the primitive way, and took upon themselves the name of settlers.

In the territory now composing the counties of Mahoning, Columbiana, Jefferson, Stark, Carroll, Harrison, Belmont, Guernsey, and Monroe, were scattered cabins as early as the revolutionary war.

The names of the first settlers in these counties, and along the Ohio River, were in 1785, as follows:

Thomas Tilton, John Nixon, Henry Cassill, John Nowles, John Tilton, John Fitzpatrick, Daniel Menser, Zephenia Dunn, John McDonald, Henry Froggs, Wiland Hoagland, Michael Rawlings, Thomas Dawson, William Shiff, Solomon Delong, Charles Ward, Frederick Lamb, John Rigdon, George Atchinson, Hanes Piley, Walter Cain, Jacob Light,

James Weleams, Jesse Edgerton, Nathaniel Parremore, Jesse Parremore, Jacob Clark, John Custer, James Noyes, Thomas McDonald, John Casstleman, James Clark, Adam House (his x mark), Thomas Johnson, Hanamet Davis, William Wallace, Joseph Reburn, Jonathan Mapins, William Mann, William Kerr, Daniel Duff, Joseph Ross, James Watson, Abertious Bailey, Charles Chambers, Robert Hill, James Paul, William McNees, Archibald Harbson, William Bailey, Jonas Amspoker, Nicholas Decker, John Platt, Benjamin Reed, Joseph Godard, Henry Conrod, William Carpenter, John Godard, George Reno, John Buchanan, Daniel Mathews.

A number had come out with General McIntosh as far as Fort Laurens, in 1778, as axemen, hunters, teamsters, spies, and rangers. After its evacuation in 1779, they remained and took up homes on the different streams emptying into the Ohio and Muskingum.

Colonel Brodhead, then in command at Fort Pitt, conceiving that they were trespassers on the Indian lands, sent out troops to drive them back across the Ohio, and demolish their cabins. Subjoined is one of his letters to General Washington, given as a curious item of the history of those early days of the forefathers in Ohio, who had came from Virginia, Pennsylvania, Maryland, New York, New Jersey, and other old States. Virginia then owned, but had not yet ceded this property to the United States, claiming it as part of that State by her own right of conquest and by Indian treaties:

"PITTSBURGH, October 26, 1779.

"DEAR GENERAL: Immediately after I had closed my last (of the 9th of this instant), I received a letter from Colonel Shepherd, lieutenant of Ohio County, informing me that a certain Decker, Fox & Co., with others, had crossed the Ohio River and committed trespasses on Indian lands, wherefore I ordered sixty rank and file to be equipped, and Captain Clarke, of the Eighth Pennsylvania Regiment, proceeded with this party to Wheeling, with orders to cross the river at that part, and to apprehend some of the principal trespassers and destroy their huts. He returned without finding any of the trespassers, but destroyed some huts. He writes me the inhabitants have made small improvements all the way from the Muskingum River to Fort McIntosh, and thirty miles up some of the branches. I sent a runner to the Delaware Council at Coohocking to inform them of the trespass, and assure them it was committed by some foolish people, and requested them to rely on my doing them justice and punishing the offenders, but as yet have not received an answer.

* * * * * * *

"I have the honor to be, with perfect regard and esteem, your Excellency's most obedient, humble servant,

"D. BRODHEAD.

"His Excellency General WASHINGTON."

In 1785, Colonel Harmar, commandant at Fort McIntosh, also sent out troops to dispossess white settlers from the eastern border counties of Ohio. They banded together to resist the United States troops, and were actually organized with guns and munitions of war. A compromise was effected, whereby they were given time before leaving Ohio to prepare temporary habitations on the Virginia side. They then abandoned their Ohio settlements for a time.

The settlers in eastern Ohio, who were driven back across the Ohio by the government, were principally men whose descendants now fill the valleys of the Tuscarawas and Muskingum, and the eastern Ohio counties.

CONGRESS GIVES THE ABANDONED VALLEY TO THE SOLDIERS OF THE REVOLUTION.

The pious Germans, who had come from beyond the mountains, with the Bible in their hands, to teach the Indian his true salvation, were wandering in the wild northwest, decimated, ragged, and sometimes starving, living a precarious life on wild game, roots, and berries, having at times no roof to shelter them, nor home to call their own, but still trusting to God, in their wretchedness, and praying daily, hourly, nightly, that *he* would not in his anger abandon them, because of their want of success down on the Tuscarawas, but succor and give them strength to continue their efforts in the wilderness, to convert the heathen, and spread the gospel of the King of Kings.

On the other hand, Pipe, Half King, Welendewacken, Wingemund, Black Hoof, Red Hawk, Little Turtle, Blue Jacket, and a host of other Jackets, Hawks, and Turtles, some of whom had taken the missionaries, and guarded them to Detroit, as prisoners, not as apostles, were scampering on fleet horses over Ohio and along the border, utterly regardless of the words they often had heard Zeisberger preach: "All having blood-stained hatchets in their hands, all seeking more scalps, all clamoring for more war, and a partition wall along the Ohio, so high and so strong that no Christian missionary, or other white man, should ever get over it, or under it, or through it into their hunting grounds, to build churches upon the graves of their ancestors, or scare the game away by the ringing of bells, and singing of hymns of praise to the 'Unkown."

And yet, by reason of the deaths of their wisest counselors and chieftains, such as Netawatwees, White Eyes, Cornstalk, King Beaver, Little Eagle, Big Foot, and other chiefs, these red rovers were unable to hold permanent possession, even by tomahawk title, and although they had been successful in driving godly men out of the valleys, they were wholly unable to remain therein themselves.

In the year 1784, Virginia ceded to the United States all her rights in the territory north-west of the Ohio. Congress, in the following year, 1785, ordered a survey of so much territory, as had been ceded by former Indian treaties, for the location of soldier warrants, and by the treaty concluded at Fort McIntosh the same year, the Indian boundary, instead of being the Ohio River, began on the Tuscarawas, near Fort Laurens, thence up said river to the portage, thence down the Cuyahoga to Lake Erie, thence west along the lake shore to the mouth of the Miami or *Omc* River, thence up that river to the portage between the *Omc* and that branch of the Big Miami which runs into the Ohio, thence over the portage to the Big Miami, thence eastwardly to the Tuscarawas at the crossing place above Fort Laurens. All the land in Ohio outside of those lines was thus ceded to the United States, and all within those lines was to be Indian territory, excepting ground for forts, &c. This treaty was signed by the Wyandots and Delawares, and some straggling Indians of other tribes. As soon as it became known to the Shawanese and others that the Ohio River boundary had been surrendered to the whites, they sounded the war-whoop again, declaring that they had been cheated and defrauded.

Congress, standing upon the literal interpretation of the Fort McIntosh treaty, ordered it to be respected, and the surveys to go on. In 1786 the surveys began in ranges, townships, and sections; the first range to run from the Ohio, near the present Steubenville to the lake, and the other ranges to be numbered progressively westwardly, the townships to be numbered from south to north. On the 15th of September, 1786, John Mathews, a nephew of General Putnam, surveyor, and his associates, reached Sandy Creek, and on the 18th were at "Nine Shilling Creek—the present Nimishillen. Here an express rider came in from Beaver, announcing that the Shawanese had taken up arms, were re-assembling at their old towns, and dancing the war-dance, preparatory to moving on the surveyors, and lifting as well their scalps as those of all white men found west of the Ohio.

Mathews' party consisted of fifty men, thirty-six of whom were soldiers. Surveying was suspended, and all retreated to Fort McIntosh. In a short time they moved down to Mingo bottom, and struck west on Crawford's trail toward the Tuscarawas to renew their work. On the 13th of October they left Crawford's trail and moved more north-west, and run about two miles of line. On the 14th and 15th they run about the same, continuing it each clear day up to the 30th, when they lay in camp on account of rain. Besides the surveyors there were twenty-five soldiers as guards. On this day they lost their horses, the same having been stolen by a squad of Indians, who had laid part of the previous night within eighty rods, watching for scalps. The soldiers went to building a block house, which they finished on the 31st of October. From the 1st to the 7th of November, they were on what is now the south boundary of the seventh township of third range in the United States military district. That day they struck Wheeling Creek, and followed it to the Ohio, then crossed and took dinner at Colonel Zanes' house. Then went up the east bank to the house of a Mr. McMahan, then to the house of William Greathouse, sixteen miles, which they reached November 9. November 10 they tarried and heard a sermon from a Methodist minister, located at that early day (1786) on the banks of the Ohio, in Virginia. November 11, Mathews went to a Virginia corn-husking at Harman Greathouse's, where a number of settlers had gathered in. They had rye whisky in plenty, and, the husking being finished, they sang, danced, told stories, quarreled, and all who could walk went home about 10 o'clock in the night. Three, who were too drunk, remained over night, hugging the whisky bottle, and arguing religion. Sunday, November 12, others came in and assisted in drinking up the whisky. November 22, General Tupper, the acting commissioner in General Putnam's absence, left for the east. November 23, Colonel Sprout and a Mr. Simpson left for the east, and the surveying party disbanded for the winter, Mathews remaining at Greathouse's, where the snow was two and a half feet deep on the 5th of December, 1786. On February 4, 1787, he went up to Fort Steuben, the present city of Steubenville, and remained until May as store-keeper of the different surveying parties. On the 8th of May three surveyors came in from the woods and reported three persons killed and three taken prisoners by Indians.

In July Mathews was at Wheeling, and reported Indians in the vicinity, and says that a party of whites killed one and wounded two Indians. On August 4, the people living on the bank of the river heard a person screaming on the Ohio side and begging for life. A party of whites went over and found one man killed and scalped. On the 7th of August left Wheeling for Fort Harmar, and after some days returned to Wheeling. September 21, they started with four men into Ohio, on Williamson's old trail, reached the ridge dividing the waters of Short Creek and Muskingum (Tuscarawas), and dug ginseng four days, then returned to the Ohio, and learned that three men had been killed and one captured by Indians while digging ginseng. On October 11 an old man was killed by Indians near Fort Steuben. On the 7th of April, 1788, Mathews arrived at the mouth of Muskingum with forty-two men, surveyors and guards, where they found Pipe's band of Delawares and Wyandot's holding out the hand of friendship, while other savages continued in the work of mercilessly burying their tomahawks into the heads of men, women and children along the Ohio, from the mouth of the Muskingum to Fort McIntosh.

DEATH OF THE WYANDOT CHIEF, BIG FOOT, IN A FIGHT WITH ANDREW AND ADAM POE.

After the defeat and retreat of Crawford's ill-fated expedition in June, 1782, a picked party of Wyandot warriors, among whom were the celebrated war chief, Big Foot, and his four brothers, followed the trace of the retreating whites until they came to the Tuscarawas, where they diverged and took the old trail leading from Fort Laurens to Fort Pitt. When near the present eastern boundary line of Columbiana County, on what is known as the west fork of Little Beaver Creek, they killed an old man in his cabin, and, taking what plunder they wanted, started on the trail toward the Ohio River. This murder at once aroused several of the border settlers, who, quickly congregating, proceeded after the Indians. In this party of whites were the celebrated brothers, Adam and Andrew Poe, famous for their courage and success as Indian fighters. The whites followed the Indian trail during the night, and on coming to the river, a little after daylight, discovered a raft tied to a sprout at the water's edge. Andrew Poe crept along the bank as stealthily as a cat until he saw a large Indian (Chief Big Foot) and a young warrior, standing with their rifles ready, and listening to the noise made by the party back over the bank. Poe pulled on the chief, but his gun missed fire, and the Indians at that instant discovered him. Seeing that retreat was useless, Poe dropped his gun and sprang upon the larger Indian and threw him to the ground. At this the small Indian ran to the raft and got a tomahawk, and, while Poe and the chief were struggling on the ground, he approached and aimed a blow at Poe's head, but just as he was about to strike he received a well-directed kick in the stomach by Poe's foot, which sent him reeling off and threw the tomahawk some distance away. The young savage soon regained his feet, and getting the tomahawk again, made a stroke for Poe's head, which he parried with his left arm, receiving a severe cut. Poe now exerted himself to the utmost and succeeded in getting away from the chief, and picking up one of their guns shot the young one dead as he was making a third attack with the tomahawk. By this time Big Foot had regained his feet, and jumping upon Poe pushed him down the bank, and in the struggle both were precipitated into the water, where each now made a desperate exertion to drown the other, Poe finally succeeding in getting the chief's head under and holding him there until he supposed him dead. Upon letting go his hold on the Indian's head, the latter raised and they again clinched for another struggle, this time getting into deep water, when both let go and swam for shore, which Big Foot reached first, and picking up a rifle aimed at Poe, who sought to save himself by diving under water. The Indian had got hold of Poe's gun instead of his own, and, it being empty, he proceeded to load as rapidly as possible. At this instant Adam Poe came upon the scene, also with an empty gun, and, seeing his brother in the water unarmed, knew that his life depended upon his loading first. The Indian dropped his ramrod, which gave Poe the advantage, and he fired just as Big Foot was cocking his piece. He then assisted his wounded brother to the shore, and while doing this the chief, who was not killed outright, rolled himself into the current and was seen no more. This was to prevent his scalp being taken by the whites.

While this conflict was progressing the other whites had caught the remaining Indians, and, after a desperate fight, killed all but one warrior, with the loss of three whites and the severe wounding of Andrew Poe.

It is related that the warrior who escaped from this terrific combat, made his way to the Wyandot town near Upper Sandusky, crossing the Tuscarawas on the trail above Fort Laurens, and, before entering the Wyandot town, announced his coming by a series of dismal howls, which indicated that the expedition had been defeated and the chief killed. This solitary survivor remained in the woods a whole day giving vent to his grief by moaning and howling alternately. The whole Wyandot tribe long mourned the loss of Big Foot, who was one of their most revered chiefs.

Subsequent to the closing of active hostilities between the Sandusky Indians and the border settlers, the Wyandots determined on the assassination of Andrew Poe, in revenge for the death of their chief, Big Foot, and detailed one of their most fearless warriors to accomplish the deed. Poe lived near the mouth of Yellow Creek at that time, and on the arrival of the Indian received him with friendship, and showered him with the kindest attentions. Poe's cabin contained but one room, as they were all built in those days, and contained but two beds, one for himself and wife, and a smaller one for his children. In the evening, the Indian intimated a desire to remain all night if Poe and his wife did not object, when they assured him that he was perfectly welcome, and made up a pallet on the floor before the huge log-fire place. Ronyeness, which was the Indian's name, lay awake until he was satisfied that the family were asleep, and the while thought much over the kindness manifested by Poe and his wife toward him. At one time he shuddered to think of the deed he was about to execute, and gave it up, but again the death of his adored chief would come fresh into his mind, when he would again resolve for revenge. Finally, after halting between the two opinions for an hour, he raised and approached Poe's bedside with his tomahawk elevated above his head ready for the fatal blow. At this instant catching a glimpse of the unsuspecting faces of Poe and his wife, his heart failed him, and he could think of nothing but their kindness and confidence. He returned to his resting place and slept until morning, when his host loaded him down with provisions and ammunition, and bade him a warm and brotherly farewell, mentioning that, although they were enemies once, they had burried the tomahawk and should remain as brothers from this time onward.

This Indian was a relation of the chief, Big Foot, and tradition says was the same man who was with him and escaped to tell the tale of the death. He had often attended the Christian Indians' meetings at their town on the Sandusky, and there probably received the germ of their religion, for, after his return from Poe's dwelling, he followed Zeisberger into Canada, and, after wandering with the missionaries several years, he came with them to Goshen in 1798, a convert, and died there. Among the Indian graves at Goshen Cemetery repose the bones of Ronyeness, the warrior who once traveled over one hundred miles to avenge Big Foot by killing Poe, but spared his life through kindness, and finally died a Christian.

LEWIS WETZELL'S ADVENTURE, AND DEATH OF THOMAS MILLS, WHO VALUED HIS HORSE MORE THAN HIS OWN LIFE.

In the retreat of Crawford's men from the Sandusky was one Thomas Mills, who thought more of his horse than his own life. After riding across what is now Crawford, Richland, Wayne, Tuscarawas, Harrison, and Belmont counties, upward of one hundred and fifty miles through wilderness, swamps, and rivers, his noble steed gave out within a few miles of the Ohio, in Belmont County. Mills made his way from that point on foot to Fort Wheeling, and succeeded in getting the famous scout (Lewis Wetzell) to go back with him and look for the horse. Wetzell told him of the danger, and did all that was possible to discourage him, but to no purpose. Mills must have his horse or perish in the attempt to rescue him. They started, and, after nine miles travel, found the horse tied to a tree near a spring. Wetzell, comprehending an ambuscade, motioned to Mills to run, and then made off to save his own life. Mills, instead of running from, ran to his horse, and, in the act of untying him, was shot dead. The Indians, four in number, then pursued Wetzell, and after running half a mile, he turned, shot the nearest Indian, and ran on but a short distance, when the second Indian caught hold of his gun and brought Wetzell to his knees in the scuffle; but he raised, got the muzzle against the savage's neck, and shot him dead. By jumping, Wetzell eluded the remaining two Indians, and loading as he ran, he turned to fire several times at his nearest pursuer, who each time treed. Going on, Wetzell reached a clearing, and, turning in an instant, shot the Indian just as he jumped behined a tree too small to screen him from Wetzell's bullet. The fourth Indian then fled, and Wetzell reached Fort Henry, at Wheeling, unhurt, where he recounted his adventure, and the death of Thomas Mills.

JOHN WETZELL'S PARTY SURPRISED ON WILL'S CREEK BY MONSEYS AND DELAWARES FROM SCHOENBRUNN.

In the spring of 1792, the Indians on the Sandusky, having become very bold since their victory over St. Clair in November preceding, made many raids on the border settlers along the Ohio, stealing horses and whatever else they could get off with, and sometimes killing a white family if in their way. After one of these forays, a party of settlers determined to follow the Indians and recapture several fine horses which had been taken. This party consisted of John Wetzell, one of the celebrated Indian fighting brothers of that name, and six other border men of considerable experience in border warfare. They started from a point nearly opposite Steubenville, and, crossing the Ohio, proceeded northward until they struck the old trail leading from Fort Pitt to the Indian towns on the Sandusky, by way of Fort Laurens, on the Tuscarawas. On reaching the first Indian town on the trail, which was located on Mohican Creek, they found their horses, which they took, and started on their return in the night. Fearing that they might be pursued and overtaken if they returned by the old trail, a southeasterly course was taken, which brought them to the Tuscarawas, in the vicinity of what is now New Comerstown. From there the lower and less traveled trail was followed, which brought the party to Will's Creek, within half a mile of the present town of Cambridge, in Guernsey County, where they arrived in the evening of the second day after recapturing the horses. Here one of the party was attacked with a very severe cramp colic, in consequence of which a halt for the night was made, and a guard placed on the back trail to watch for any pursuers that might be after them. Late in the night, and when all were asleep in the camp, the guard having occasion to go to a little brook which emptied into the creek a short distance below the camp, noticed that the water was muddy, and believing the cause to be Indians coming down in the water to prevent detection, aroused Wetzell and informed him of the discovery. Wetzell went and examined the water, and decided that the muddy streaks in it were the result of raccoons or muskrats moving about in the brook, and then resumed his blankets, after joking the guard as to his unfounded alarm. From this the guard deemed it unnecessary to keep so strict a watch, and remained close to the camp. About half an hour after this transpired a volley was fired into the camp from behind the bank of the brook, and the sick man was riddled with bullets, as he lay on the outside. In an instant a party of savages bounded into the camp, yelling and brandishing their tomahawks in a terrific manner, and at the same instant the white men fled, leaving most of their arms, blankets, &c., in the camp. In the fight that ensued three whites were killed on the ground, and Wetzell and the other succeeded in making their way to Wheeling after great suffering from hunger and fatigue. The bodies of the killed were shortly afterward buried by a party that went out from Wheeling for that purpose. One of the survivors of this party was William McCullough, who settled at Zanesville in 1799, and afterward became a prominent officer in the war of 1812, under General Hull.

The Indians who made this assault were a party of the Monseys, accompanied by some of the old converts of the Moravians who had relapsed into heathenism after the breaking up of the missions in 1782, and who had returned to the Tuscarawas valley because they knew the country so well, and for the purpose of killing all the white people they could find in revenge for the massacre at Gnadenhutten. They had come upon the Wetzell party while returning to the valley from an unsuccessful expedition to the border settlements east of the Ohio, and were not a party of pursuers, as has been stated in some accounts. After the fight they gathered up their plunder, and, with the twice stolen horses, continued their march to their camp near the ruins of Schoenbrunn, on the Tuscarawas. They remained in the valley until called away to join the western tribes in their attempt to repel the invasion of the Maumee country by General Wayne in 1794.

LOGAN'S FAMILY MURDERED—HIS SPEECH AND DEATH.

In the spring of 1774, a party of borderers called the Greathouse men, near the mouth of Yellow Creek, killed the father, brother, and sister of Logan, the Mingo Chief. Logan was absent, but vowed revenge, and never ceased until he had thirty scalps and prisoners. He captured a Major William Robinson, who was taken to the Muskingum Shawanese town, Waketomica, compelled to run the guantlet and ordered to be burned alive. Logan plead eloquently to save his life, and succeeded, after which he took Robinson to New Comerstown, and dictated while Robinson wrote the following letter to Captain Cresap:

"Captain Cresap: What did you kill my people on Yellow Creek for? The white people killed my kin at Conestoga a great while ago, and I thought nothing of that. But you killed my kin again on Yellow Creek, and took my cousin prisoner. Then I thought I must kill too, and I have been three times to war since, but the Indians are not angry, only myself.

"*July* 21, 1774. Captain John Logan."

This letter was tied to a war club and left at a murdered settler's cabin by Logan.

Thomas Jefferson wove from it the celebrated speech which has been read and recited wherever the English language was spoken as a sublime burst of Indian eloquence.

John Gibson met Logan the same fall at Dunmore's treaty. Cresap was also there, without Logan being aware of his presence, and having told Gibson he was not one of the Greathouse party, nor at the massacre of Logan's relatives, Gibson took Logan aside and informed him of the fact. Gibson then wrote down Logan's ideas, omitting Cresap's name; his version was published at Williamsburg, Virginia. The two versions brought on a conflict between Jefferson and his enemies, as to the authenticity of the speech. It led to great feeling among the literati, without settling the matter definitively. In the meantime Logan became famous, and even Campbell, in his "Gertrude of Wyoming," poetized this speech for one of his heroes in after years.

Logan, in the midst of his fame, drowned his grief by drinking liquor, and was finally tomahawked while sitting before his fire with a blanket over his head. Tradition says he hired an Indian friend to kill him. Thus ended Logan.

LOGAN'S SPEECH—JEFFERSON'S VERSION.

"I appeal to any white man to say that he ever entered Logan's cabin but I gave him meat; that he ever came naked but I clothed him.

"In the course of the last war Logan remained in his cabin, an advocate for peace. I had such an affection for the white people that I was pointed at by the rest of my nation. I should have ever lived with them had it not been for Colonel Cresap, who last year cut off, in cold blood, all the relations of Logan; not sparing my women and children. There runs not a drop of my blood in the veins of any human creature. This called upon me for revenge. I have sought it. I have killed many, and fully glutted my vengeance. I am glad there is a prospect of peace, on account of the nation; but I beg that you will not entertain a thought that anything I have said proceeds from fear. Logan disdains the thought. He will not turn on his heel to save his life. Who is there to mourn for Logan? Not one."

The poet versifies it thus—leaving the reader to fill in Cresap's name:

> "Nor man nor child, nor thing of living birth;
> No! not the dog, that watched my household hearth,
> Escaped that night of blood, upon our plains.
> All perished! I alone am left on earth!
> To whom nor relative nor blood remains,
> No! not a kindred drop that runs in human veins."

ADVENTURES OF THE ZANE FAMILY—ELIZABETH THE HEROINE.

Three relatives, Jonathan, Ebenezer, and Silas Zane, removed from Berkley County, Virginia, to the Ohio River, in 1769, and settled at or near Wheeling of the present day. They were fond of roving and adventurous exploits. They soon became acquainted with the territory on both sides of the river, and hunted Indians as their favorite game. Jonathan located the present Wheeling and Zanesville. In 1774 he was one of Dunmore's guides in the campaign against the Indian town of Wakatomaka (near Dresden), acted as a spy for Washington, piloted Colonel Brodhead's expedition up the Alleghany, in 1779, and was wounded in that expedition. In 1782 he was one of Colonel Crawford's guides in the fatal Sandusky expedition, and it is said by one of the prominent men of that time, that Crawford held him in such high esteem that before the army commenced its retreat he consulted Zane, who advised an immediate retreat, and that had Crawford acted at once on the advice of Zane, he and his army would have escaped defeat. After the retreat began, Zane succeeded, by his knowledge of Indian warfare, in avoiding capture, and returned safe to

Wheeling. He was admitted to be the best shot on the border, and on one occasion, meeting a raiding party on the Virginia side, killed five Indians, one after another, with his rifle; four of whom he shot in the river as they were swimming the Ohio, and the fifth after the Indian had gained the Ohio side. He hid behind a fallen tree in the stream, and was in the act of peeping over the trunk, when Zane's quick eye saw the top of his head. In another moment his body floated down stream. Elsewhere in this work it is related that Jonathan Zane and John McIntyre laid out Zanesville, and having made successful investments in the Muskingum country, Zane became very wealthy. He also had large possessions at Wheeling, where he died.

Ebenezer and Silas Zane participated in the border life of Jonathan, and were equally daring and good marksmen.

In the attack on Fort Henry at Wheeling, 1782, Ebenezer, then Colonel Zane, commanded, and with but a handful of men he kept two hundred and sixty Indians and British soldiers at bay for three days, when they finally gave up the attack and moved off. The following is his letter to General Irvine, commandant at Fort Pitt, announcing the result. It is given verbatim from the work of C. W. Butterfield, entitled "Crawford's Expedition Against Sandusky," he having found the letter among General Irvine's correspondence:

"*Weling*, 14th September, 1782.

"Sir: on the Evening of the 11th Instant a Body of the Enemy appeared in Sight of our garrison *the* immediately formed thire Lines Round the garrison paraded British *Cullars* and *demand* the fort to Be *Surrenderred* which was *Refused about twelve o clock att Night* they Rushed hard on the pickets In order to Storm But was repulsed they made two other *attemts* to Storm Before Day to No *purpos*.

"about eight o clock Next morning *thare* come a Negro from them to us and informed us that *thire forse* Consisted of a British Captain and forty Regular Soldiers and two hundred and Sixty Indians *they* Enemy kept a continual fire *they whold* Day *aBout* ten o clock *att* Night they made a *forth* attempt to Storm to no better purpos *then* the former the enemy Continued Round the garrison till the morning of the thirteenth Instant when they Disappeared Our loss is none Daniel Sullivan who arrived here in the first of the action is wounded in the foot.

"I believe they have Drove *they* greatest part of our Stock away and might I think be soon overtaken I am with Due Respect your obedient servt. EBENEZER ZANE."

Colonel Ebenezer Zane had a sister Elizabeth, who figured as a heroine in the Wheeling fight. She afterward married twice, and died near Martinsville, Ohio, leaving a large family of descendants, bearing the names of her respective husbands, McLaughlin and Clark. Her adventure is thus stated:

When the alarm was given by a ranger that the Indians were coming, the fort having for some time been unoccupied by a garrison, and Colonel Zane's house having been used for a magazine, those who retired into the fort had to take with them a supply of ammunition for its defense. The powder became exhausted by reason of the long siege. In this emergency it became necessary to renew the stock from an abundant store in Zane's house. Accordingly, it was proposed that one of the fleetest men should endeavor to reach the house, obtain the powder, and return to the fort. Elizabeth, sister of Colonel Zane, at once volunteered to bring the powder. She was young, active, and athletic, with courage to dare anything. On being told that one of the men would run less risk by reason of his fleetness, she replied, "Should he fall the loss will be more severely felt; you have no men to spare, and a woman will not be missed in defending the fort." She was then told to go, and divesting herself of some heavy clothing, struck out through the gate like a deer. The sight so amazed the savages that they cried, "A squaw, a squaw," and not a shot was fired at her. Arriving at the house, Colonel Zane fastened a tablecloth about her waist, and into it poured a keg of powder, when she again ventured out. The Indians now discovered the object of the "squaw," and bullet after bullet whizzed past her head, several lodging in her clothes. She reached the fort in safety, and the powder she had enabled the brave little band to hold out against the besiegers, who were at last compelled to retire without a scalp or a pound of powder.

SKETCH OF SIMON GIRTY, THE WHITE SAVAGE.

Simon, George, and James Girty were from northwestern Pennsylvania, and in the French war, in 1754, were captured by the Indians. Simon joined the Senecas, James the Shawanese, and George the Wyandots, by whom they were regularly adopted. Simon roamed over what is now eastern Ohio with his tribe, and first became prominent as one of the hostages taken by Boquet in 1764, in the Tuscarawas valley, for the good behavior of the Indians. At the termination of the conference of Boquet and the Indians at Coshocton, Simon was delivered up as a captive, and returned to Fort Pitt. In 1774 he signed the peace message at New Comerstown, and figured in Dunmore's war on the side of the whites. At the beginning of the American revolution he joined the militia at Fort Pitt. Early in 1778, he asked for a captain's commission in the continental service, which being refused him, he deserted to the British, and passing down the Tuscarawas to the present site of Coshocton, with Elliot and McKee, inflamed the Delawares under Pipe to take up the hatchet against the Americans. Passing on to the Shawanese towns at Waketomica and on the Sciota, he aroused portions of the Shawanese to hostilities. Thence making his way toward Detroit he was captured by the Wyandots, but was set at liberty by them when told that he had taken up arms against the Americans. The British governor at Detroit employed him in the Indian service. In September, 1778, the afterward celebrated Simon Kenton, being captured and brought as a prisoner to Wappetomica, in Logan County, was sentenced to be burned at the stake. Girty came to see him, and they having been old acquaintances, and having fought side by side in Dunmore's war, he made the most strenuous efforts to save Kenton's life, and succeeded for the time being, but the Indians a second time condemning Kenton to be burned, Girty's influence a second time saved him, and he was taken to Detroit, from where he effected his escape.

The first we hear of Simon Girty in the Tuscarawas valley after his defection was in 1779, when he headed a party of Mingoes, who attacked a relief squad going from Fort Laurens to Fort Pitt, under one Captain Clark, numbering fourteen men. They were ambushed about three miles east of Fort Laurens, near the present town of Sandyville. Two were killed, four wounded, and one taken prisoner. In the same year he attempted to ambuscade Zeisberger on the Coshocton plains, but was prevented from carrying out his design by some Delaware Indians. In 1780 and 1781, he headed Indian war parties who penetrated the Ohio border, and was one of the principal plotters in breaking up the settlements at Schoenbrunn, Gnadenhutten, Salem, and Coshocton, always evincing great hostility to the missionaries. In the early part of 1782, he was one of the leading spirits in having Heckewelder and Zeisberger tried at Detroit as spies. His machinations also caused the Christian Indians on the Sandusky to be disbanded and scattered. On the approach of Crawford's army to the Sandusky, he assisted in marshaling the Indians and defeating that expedition. It is related that after nightfall of the first day of the fight, when both armies had ceased firing, Girty came forward with a white flag and asked to see Colonel Crawford, who went out to meet him, when Girty told him that the Indians were three times as strong as the whites, and during the night would surround him, except at one spot, where there was a very wet piece of ground, which he pointed out. He advised Crawford that if he wished to save his men, to march through that gap and escape in the night, or they would all be cut off in the morning. Crawford, in the night commenced his retreat in that direction, and the next day his army got into confusion, lost their course, and Crawford taken prisoner, while Williamson, with about three hundred men, made their escape. It is further related that when Crawford was tied to the stake, Girty offered Captain Pipe three hundred and fifty dollars for the victim, for the purpose of making a speculation in saving his life, but that Pipe told him if he uttered another word on the subject he would be tied to the stake and burned with Crawford.

It is further stated that Girty at one time courted one of Crawford's daughters in Pennsylvania. It is elsewhere related that on the night before Crawford's torture he sent for Girty, had an interview, and offered one thousand dollars to save his life, and that Girty promised to do what he could in the matter. But in the midst of Crawford's sufferings he asked Girty to shoot him, and Girty excused himself by laughingly saying he had no gun.

After Crawford's death, the same year, we find Girty at the great Indian council at the old Chilicothe town, organizing an Indian force of six hundred warriors, to march into Kentucky, where, at Bryant's station, they were repulsed, when he retreated to the Blue Licks, and there was overtaken by the Kentuckians, whom he defeated with great slaughter. A treaty of peace being soon after concluded, hostilities between the whites and Indians ceased for a time, and Simon Girty's name was little heard of.

Girty comes to the front again in 1790, assisted the Indians in the campaign against General Harmar, took an active part in the defeat of St. Clair in 1791, and in 1792 and 1793, at all the Indian councils, he earnestly advocated a continuance of the war against the whites. At General Wayne's battle of the Fallen Timbers, in 1794, Girty was present, encouraging the Indians. After peace was made with the hostile tribes, he removed from Girty's Point near the present Napoleon, in Henry County, Ohio, to near Malden, in Canada. He became nearly blind, and took but little part in the war of 1812, and died in Canada in 1818, being over seventy years of age. He left a family, with a name execrated wherever he was known, and yet Jonathan Alder, who was captured by the Indians, and who knew Simon Girty, says this of him: "I knew Simon Girty to purchase, at his own expense, several boys who were prisoners, and take them to the British and have them educated. He was certainly a friend to many prisoners."

Of the brother, Joseph Girty, we have no precise account, other than an attempt to cut off the ears of a prisoner named Oliver M. Spencer.

George Girty led the Indians in their attack on Fort Henry, at Wheeling, in 1782. Other accounts say it was James Girty who commanded the savages there.

CHAPTER X.

TRADITIONS OF THE SENECAS.

The Senecas and Hurons, or Wyandots, originated along the St. Lawrence, where they lived peaceably for a great many years, but were embroiled in war by a Seneca lady, who refused a Wyandot for husband, on the ground that he had taken no scalps in his time. To gain her affections he laid in ambush, killed her brother, and threw his scalp in her lap. Instead of winning her, the two tribes were compelled to take up the hatchet against each other. The Wyandots moved away; the Senecas followed, and wherever they met both were decimated. Through three generations they and their descendants fought, whipping each other along the lakes, over western New York, northern Pennsylvania and Ohio. At length the war ceased, from fear of extermination only; the Wyandots settling in the northwest, while the Senecas settled down in the northeast—both owing allegiance to the Iroquois confederacy. Such is the tradition.

A LEGEND OF SLAUGHTER AT THE SENECA CAPITAL.

A legend exists of a fearful fight that took place between the Senecas and Wyandots, on their return from Braddock's defeat, in 1755. They had fought side by side against the English army, but no sooner had they dispersed toward their homes, than the old unsettled feud between them was renewed. The Senecas took the trail by Beaver, Mingo bottom, and west to Tuscarawas. The Wyandots took the upper trail, striking the ridge between the heads of the Elk Eye Creek (Muskingum) and the Hioga (Cuyahoga), where they camped. It was but a day's journey across the present Stark County, to reach their enemies at the Seneca capital. The warriors there suspected their design, and sent out Ogista, an old sachem, who met the Wyandots on the war-path, stealthily approaching the capital. He sent back a runner to give warning of their coming, and, trusting to his age for protection, boldly penetrated into the midst of the enemy, as a peacemaker. The Senecas, upon being apprised of their proximity, sallied out to fight, but were stopped by Ogista, who was returning with an agreement, made by him and the opposing chief, to the effect that each tribe should pick twenty warriors, willing to suffer death by single combat. When all were slain, they were to be covered, hatchet in hand, in one grave, and henceforth neither Seneca or Wyandot ever again to raise a bloody hand against the other.

Forty braves were soon selected, and each twenty being surrounded, the tribal war-dances were danced, and the death lamentations sung, when the way being cleared, the carnage commenced, which ended as night intervened, there being one martyr left, with none to strike him down. He was the son of Ogista, who had proposed the sacrifice. The aged man received his weapon, and with it cleaved off the head of his offspring, when the bands gathered the dead into a heap, laying their forty hatchets by their sides, and having raised a mound of earth over them, all repaired to the Seneca capital, closing the fearful scene with a feast, in memorium of the compact thus sealed with blood; that the hatchet was then forever buried between the Wyandots and Senecas. Twenty-four years afterward, Fort Laurens was erected in sight of the mound. A friendly Delaware, at the fort, was asked by the commander to explain its origin. He related the above legend. In January, 1779, the fort was invested by one hundred and eighty Wyandots, Mingoes (Senecas), and Monsies, led by John Montour. Under the impression that the Indians had moved off, a squad of seventeen soldiers went out behind the mound to catch the horses and gather wood. They never returned to the fort—having been ambushed and killed by a party of Wyandot and Seneca warriors, who were worshipping the Great Spirit at the grave of their ancestors and relatives.

SKETCH OF CHIEF SHINGASK, OR BOCKONGAHELAS—LEGEND OF HECKEWELDER'S LOVE.

One of the noted war chiefs of the Delawares was Shingask, *alias* Sach-gants-chillas, or Bockongahelas, and called by Judge Burnett, in his notes, Buckingelas, and by other writers, Bockingilla. In 1758, Post met him at Kuskuskee, his town, below Pittsburgh, and took dinner with him. He was so noted, and had committed so many depredations on the border, that the Pennsylvania government offered seven hundred dollars for his head. Fearing capture, he retired west to the "Tuscarawas town," where Heckewelder found him in 1762, a chief, instigating the Indians against the English, and the foremost man to prevent Post and Heckewelder from making a permanent settlement. He entered heartily into Pontiac's conspiracy, and led his warriors—the Turtle tribe of Delawares—in person against Fort Pitt. After the fall of Pontiac he retired to the Miami and Sandusky country, and, in after years, continually annoyed the missionaries. In 1781 he came to Gnadenhutten with his warriors, and demanded the surrender of Killbuck and other converted chiefs. Receiving reply that they had gone to Fort Pitt, he had the town searched from house to house, and made a speech exhorting the converts to remove with him to his own country. On their refusal he proceeded to Salem, made a like speech, but not succeeding, abandoned the valley. The Christian Indians, having treated him to a feast at each town, and shown him the greatest respect, he told them that if any one said he was hostile to the believing Indians they should set it down as a lie, and call the man who so represented him a liar. In Wayne's campaign of 1793, he led his warriors in the last battle, and having many wounded, he applied to the British commander at Fort Miami, near by, for shelter to his wounded men; which being refused, he denounced the British as liars, and urged the Indians to make peace. It is said that it was through his influence that the Greenville treaty was consummated, in 1795. He died at his town, Wapakonneta, in 1804, nearly one hundred years of age.

Thornhaler, in his life of Heckewelder, tells us that the young missionary came to the Tuscarawas, as much to study Indian character as to aid in the mission enterprise with Post. He was young, ardent, adventuresome, and soon after Post left for Pennsylvania he felt the loneliness of his hut and solitary life—there being no habitation nearer than Thomas Calhoon's trading-house, a mile distant, to reach which he had to wade the river, and in doing which he contracted a fever that would have carried him off but for Calhoon, who had him taken to his trading-house, and cared for.

Among the visitors often at the trader's store was the wife of Shingask, chief at the Tuscarawas town. She was a white captive, of great beauty in her youth, and had been educated before becoming a prisoner, and wife of the chief. She, as a matter of course, sympathized with and ministered to the sick man, of her own color and race, and in that way gratitude appeared, and affection responded to it, in all probability. The biographer says that one day, after Heckewelder had gone back to his cabin, Calhoon sent for him, and, on coming over, he was told that a woman had requested him (Calhoon) to bring the missionary away from his hut, as a plot was in existence to scalp him that night.

On the following morning Calhoon sent two men over to the house, who returned, saying that the house had been broken into the night previous, and plundered. Heckewelder never slept there again, but remained with Calhoon. The wife of Shingask soon died at Tuscarawas, and Heckewelder afterward published a glowing account of the funeral ceremonies; for synopsis of which see article on Post's mission in a former chapter.

The legend is that the wife of Shingask was the same person who saved Heckewelder's life by notifying Calhoun of the plot, and that Shingask suspecting her as the informer, and tender friend of Heckewelder, had her put out of the way by the poison of the may-apple, and the imposing funeral ceremony was gotten up to ward off suspicion of having killed the queen. The lady reader will probably infer that the young missionary would not have taken such pains to give in his history such a detailed statement of the funeral, unless there was some matter of the heart connected therewith, on his part.

Heckewelder, soon after being advised by the friendly Indians that he would lose his life in case he remained, speedily returned to Bethlehem, and did not marry for eighteen years after.

DELAWARE BARONS AND LORDS OF THE FOREST.

The Delawares took possession of the ancient seat of power, Tuscarawas, and used it as their capital, conjointly with such Senecas as remained in the valley. Afterward the Delaware capital was removed down to Gekelemukpechuk, near the present New Comerstown, and from there to Goshockgunk.

The chiefs, Beaver, White Eyes, Pipe, Custaloga, Netawatwes, and others, had their hamlets, or "country seats," stationed along the river and its branches, within a day's call of the ancient capital; they nevertheless were frequenters thereat, and with Shingask, *alias* Bockingahelas, as chief ruler at the capital, they there concerted war and peace measures, so far as the same affected the three tribes designated Turtle, Turkey, and Wolf tribes, as well as the subordinated warriors of other tribes owing fealty to the Delawares.

Each chief, having a town, had also his hunting and fishing grounds, and to which he and his retainers repaired in the game and fishing seasons to enjoy life free from care. They also had their annual hunts, when all the clans joined and ranged in common, in pursuit of pleasure, concentrating at a given place or stream, and dividing the product according to rank and station, and it is worthy of remembrance that before the white man came into the valley, these barons and lords of the American forest, were but little behind the Scottish, Irish, and English gentry of coincident time in Europe, in all the essentials of dignity, self-respect, and honor, as they understood the terms.

Heckewelder was at the "Tuscarawas capital," in 1762, and has preserved their manners and customs, of which a portion are here given.

INDIAN FOOD AND COOKERY—1762.

Heckewelder says at that time their principal food consisted of game, fish, corn, potatoes, beans, pumpkins, cucumbers, squashes, melons, cabbages, and turnips, roots of plants, fruits, nuts, and berries.

They take but two meals a day. The hunters or fishermen never go out in the middle of the day, except it be cloudy. Their custom is to go out on an empty stomach as a stimulant to exertion in shooting game or catching fish.

They make a pottage of corn, dry pumpkins, beans, and chestnuts, and fresh or dried meats, pounded, all sweetened with maple sugar or molasses, and well boiled. They also make a good dish of pounded corn and chestnuts, shell-barks and hickory nut kernels, boiled, covering the pots with large pumpkin, cabbage, or other leaves.

They make excellent preserves from cranberries and crab apples, with maple sugar.

Their bread is of two kinds; one made of green, and the other of dry corn. If dry, it is sifted after pounding, kneaded, shaped into cakes six inches in diameter, one inch thick, and baked on clean dry ashes, of dry oak barks. If green, it is mashed, put in broad green corn blades, filled in with a ladle, well wrapped up and baked in ashes.

They make warrior's bread by parching corn, sifting it, pounding into flour, and mixing sugar. A table-spoonful with cold or boiling water is a meal, as it swells in the stomach, and if more than two spoonsful is taken, it is dangerous. Its lightness enables the warrior to go on long journeys and carry his bread with him. Their meat is eaten boiled in pots, or roasted on wooden spits or coals.

INDIAN DRESS AND ORNAMENTS AT THE CAPITAL.

The Indians make beaver and raccoon-skin blankets. Also frocks, shirts, petticoats, leggings, and shoes of deer, bear and other skins. If cold, the fur is placed next to the body; if warm, outside.

With the large rib bones of the elk and buffalo they shave the hair off such skins as they dressed, which was done as clean as with a knife. They also made blankets of feathers of the turkey and goose, which the women arranged interwoven together with thread or twine made from the rind of the wild hemp and nettles.

The dress of the men consists of blankets, plain or ruffled shirts, leggings and moccasins (moxens). The women make petticoats of cloth, red, blue, or black, when it can be had of traders; they adorn with ribbons, beads, silver broaches, arm spangles, round buckles, little thimble-like bells around the ankles to make a noise and attract attention. They paint with vermillion, but not so as to offend their husbands; the loose women and prostitutes paint their faces deeply scarlet.

The men paint their thighs, legs, breasts, and faces, and to appear well, spend some times a whole day in decorating themselves for a night frolic. They pluck out their beards and hair on the head (except a tuft on the crown) with tweezers made of muscle shells, or brass wire. The Indians would all be bearded like white men were it not for their pulling out custom.

INDIAN COURTING IN THE VALLEYS.

An aged Indian, who for many years had spent much of his time among the whites, speaking of marriage to Heckewelder, said: "Indian, when he see industrious squaw which he like, he go to him," (they had no feminine gender in their vocabulary,) "place his two forefingers close aside each other—make him look like one—look squaw in the face, see him smile, which is all, and he say, 'Yes;' so he take him home. No danger he be cross; no, no. Squaw know too well what Indian do if he (she) cross. Throw him (her) away, and take another; squaw have to eat meat—no husband, no meat. Squaw do everything to please husband; he do same to please squaw; live happy."

INDIAN MARRIAGES.

An Indian takes a wife on trial. He builds a house, and provides provisions. She agrees to cook and raise corn and vegetables, while he hunts or fishes. If both perform these duties, they are man and wife. If not, they separate. The woman's labor is light in the house. She has but one pot to clean, and no scrubbing to do, and but little to wash, and that not often. They cut wood, till the ground, sow and reap, pound the corn, bake bread in the ashes, and cook the meat or fish in the pot. If on a journey, the wife carries the baggage, and Heckewelder says he never heard of a wife complaining, for she says the husband must avoid hard labor and stiffening of muscles if he expects to be an expert hunter, so as to provide her meat to eat and furs to wear. The Indian loves to see his wife well clothed, and hence he gives her all the skins he takes. The more he does for her, the more he is esteemed by the community. In selling her furs, if she finds anything at the trader's store which she thinks would please the husband, she buys it for him, even should it take all she has to pay therefor.

KINDNESS TO WIVES.

Heckewelder says: "I have known a man to go forty or fifty miles for a mess of cranberries, to satisfy his wife's longing. In the year 1762, I was witness to a remarkable instance of the disposition of Indians to indulge their wives. There was a famine in the land, and a sick Indian woman expressed a great desire for a mess of Indian corn. Her husband, having heard that a trader at Lower Sandusky had a little, set off on horseback for that place, one hundred miles distant, and returned with as much corn as filled the crown of his hat, for which he gave his horse in exchange, and came home on foot, bringing his saddle back with him."

QUARRELS WITH WIVES.

It very seldom happens that a man condescends to quarrel with his wife, or abuse her, though she has given him just cause. In such a case the man, without replying, or saying a single word, will take his gun and go into the woods, and remain there a week, or perhaps a fortnight, living on the meat he has killed, before he returns home again; well knowing that he can not inflict a greater punishment on his wife, for her conduct to him, than by absenting himself for awhile—for she is not only kept in suspense, uncertain whether he will return again, but is soon reported as a bad and quarrelsome woman. When he at length does return, she endeavors to let him see by her attentions that she has repented, though neither speak to each other a single word on the subject of what has passed.

THE INDIAN'S HEAVEN.

Heckewelder says that in the year 1792 there was an Indian preacher, from the Cuyahoga, traveling about the valley selling a map, which he said the Great Spirit had directed him to make. It was about fifteen inches long, and the same in breadth, and was drawn on a dressed deer-skin. He held it up while preaching, pointing out the spots, lines, and spaces on it. An inside line was the boundary of a square of eight inches, and at two corners the lines were open about half an inch. Across the lines were others an inch in length, intended to represent a barrier, shutting ingress to the square, except at the place appointed in the south-east corner, which he called the "avenue," leading, as he said, to the Indian heaven, and which had been taken possession of by the white people, wherefore the Great Spirit had ordered another avenue at the north-east corner, to enter which a large ditch, leading to a gulf below, had to be crossed, and it was guarded by the Evil Spirit, on the lookout for Indians, and when one was caught he was taken to the regions of the Evil Spirit, where the ground was parched, trees bore no fruit, and the game was almost starved. Here he transformed men into horses, to be ridden by him, and dogs to follow him in his hunts.

On the outside of the interior square was the country given to the Indians to hunt, fish, and dwell on, while in the world. Its eastern side was bounded by the ocean, or great "Salt-water Lake," across which a people of different color had come and taken possession, in the name of friendship, of the Indians' country, and of the south-east avenue leading to the beautiful regions destined for Indians when they leave this world.

To regain their hunting grounds, and the avenue to the beautiful regions beyond, they must make sacrifices, and above all abstain from drinking the deadly *besan* (whisky), which the white strangers had invented and brought with them across the lake. Then the Great Spirit would assist the Indians to drive out their enemies, and recover their heavenly regions.

On the heavenly region part of the map, fat deer and plump turkies were represented to be waiting for the hunters, while in the dreary region they were all skin and bone, scarcely able to move.

The preacher concluded by telling his hearers that the Great Spirit had directed him to prepare a map for every family, provided the price was paid, namely, a buck-skin, or two doe-skins, of the value of one dollar, for each map.*

SKETCH OF BLACK HOOF—ONE HUNDRED AND TWENTY-SEVEN SCALPS.

Black Hoof, a chief of the Shawanese, was known as a great orator as well as warrior. He had come from Florida when young and taken part in all the Indian wars, particularly distingushing himself in taking scalps at Braddock's

*[*Note.*—It is a curious fact in history that this sharp Indian map seller came, at that early day, from the "western reserve," where the inventive genius of their white successors still predominates.

defeat. In all the after wars he bore a conspicuous part, and at all the treaties was a principal orator. In 1795 he became satisfied in the uselessness of further strife, and from that time to his death was friendly to the white settlers. He never would assist in the burning of prisoners. It is said he was a man of rigid virtue and lived forty years with one wife. He lived at Wakatomeka, near the present site of Dresden, on the Muskingum, but removed with his tribe about 1817, and died in 1831, at the great age of one hundred and ten years, at Wapakonnetta, in Auglaize County, Ohio.

He could remember that when a boy he had bathed in the salt-water on the Florida coast. It is related of him that his scalp string had upon it one hundred and twenty-seven scalps, which he had himself taken during his career.

LEGEND OF THREE LEGS TOWN, ON THE STILL-WATER.

On a dividing ridge in Belmont County issues two little streams—one flowing into the Ohio, called Wheeling Creek, the other taking a north-west direction through parts of Harrison and Tuscarawas counties, and emptying into the Tuscarawas River some six miles south-east of New Philadelphia. After wandering a hundred miles south, the waters of these Belmont hills again meet at Marietta, and, mixed with those of the Ohio and Muskingum, all join hands, as it were, and go merrily and muddily down the Ohio and Mississippi, until all are lost in the sea. On one of these small streams, called by the Indians Gehelemukpechuk, by the whites Stillwater, there was an Indian town called "Three Legs Town," as designated on Boquet's map of 1764, and located near its junction with the Tuscarawas.

Tradition says it was so named, after a chief who first resided there by the name of "Three Legs," because of the fact that he had an extra leg. His father was said to be the great Shawanese chief Blackhoof, and his mother a Cherokee of great beauty from the south—the climate having imparted to her all the ingredients of beauty incident to southern white women of a later day. Blackhoof had brought her up into the Sciota country, and while out one day gathering wild plums she was attacked by a wounded buffalo, limping on three legs, but succeeded in escaping from him. In proper time she gave birth to a boy, who, like the beast, had three legs, and when he learned to walk, limped with one leg dangling after him. He was in other respects perfect—inheriting all the genius of Blackhoof himself. The mother thought the more of him because of his misfortune, and instead of putting the monstrosity out of the way, she gave her life to his nurture and bringing up. On reaching the age of manhood, and being unable to follow the chase or go to war, he was offered a chiefship and privilege to select his place of abode in this valley. He chose the mouth of the Gehelemukpechuk (Stillwater), for the reason that immense quantities of fish were caught there—as they are caught there at this day in larger quantities than at other places along the river. Three Legs, being an invalid, could not expect to, nor did he ever, become chief over a large town, but those who had settled near him were old braves who had spent their energies, and sat down at Three Legs town to pass the residue of their lives in fishing, smoking, and giving advice to young warriors.

It happened that after Braddock's defeat, in 1755, a number of the captured English soldiers were brought down by some Shawanese, under Blackhoof, and given over to his son, Three Legs, to be put to death by torture, in their usual mode. The trail from Beaver River, south, passed in sight of the Three Legs town, and hence it was a daily sight to see captives driven or pulled by, on their way to death. Among these was a herculean Highlander, taken at Braddock's fight, who belonged to the Scotch regiment.

His name was Alexander McIntosh, and it is said that he was by blood a relative of Lachlin McIntosh, who became an American general in the revolution, and erected Fort Laurens in 1778.

Young McIntosh, by reason of his great heighth and strength, was reserved from the fiery death of the other prisoners by order of Three Legs, and became his body guard, but was doomed to be a witness to the burning of his fellow prisoners, and told that a similar fate awaited him in case he attempted to escape. The place of burning was at the edge of the plain where a steep bluff bank of rocks ascends some one hundred feet, from the summit of which the whole plain is descernible, forming one of the most picturesque panoramas in the valley. From this eminence prisoners doomed to death were thrown, and whether dead or alive when they reached the base of the precipice, the burning was gone through with. McIntosh surveyed the eminence from below, and saw the first prisoner thrown over, who fell with a thud which knocked the life out of him. His body was thrown on a burning pile of wood. The second victim came down upon his feet, hurt, but able to stand. He was tied to a post and a fire built around him. The Scotchman, unable to listen to his moans, darted at the chief, Three Legs, sitting near, smoking his pipe, and with one blow of the fist prostrated him in death, then seizing his tomahawk hanging in the chief's belt, was but a moment dispatching one of the two Indians attending to the fire, and before another minute elapsed he cut the thongs of his burning fellow captive, pulled him from the fire, and ran some little distance with him, but finding the other Indian had ran in an opposite direction he stopped, and loosened the withes around the legs and arms of his comrade, who at once rose to his feet, and both started up the hill to gain the summit by a circuitous path, in the hope of rescuing their fellow captives. The three savages on the summit, seeing which, and the terrible work of the Highlander below, sprung down from the precipice to the relief of their fallen chief, and this enabled the Scotchman to reach and release his three fellow captives on the summit from the thongs with which they were tied. The four now returned for their comrade, who had been released from the fire, but unable to ascend the path, he was caught by the three savages below and tomahawked. Thus it stood for a minute—four released prisoners against three warriors, the latter having their hatchets, and the former only one, in the Highlander's hands. In another moment they heard the scalp yell of the savage who had run away, and supposing he had other Indians, the four whites reascended the hill and entered the forest, in a run for life—the Highlander keeping in front. After running half a mile they heard their pursuers; the Scotchman telling his unarmed comrades to keep together, while he treed, and awaited the savages. Soon the most fleet one passed him, and at that moment received his quietus—he having come within three feet of the Scotchman without seeing him, and the tomahawk of the latter was buried in his skull. He leaped up, and fell with a terrible scream, dead. The Highlander then rejoined his comrades, and they were not further pursued. Making their way east by the sun, they crossed the Stillwater, following which they reached its source, crossed the dividing ridge, and were on the Ohio in two days, without having eaten anything save roots and bark. From thence they followed the west bank up the river another day, and finally crossed the Ohio by wading it near the present Wellsville where the river was, and is yet, fordable in low water. They then got assistance from a hunter whom they met, and who took them to a settlement on the Monongahela.

Nine years afterward, the Highlander, who had settled in Westmoreland County, joined Boquet's army, and at Coshocton inquired of the Indians what had become of Three Legs and his town up the river—telling them he was once a prisoner there, but escaped. All he could learn was that Three Legs had been killed by a white prisoner, and his town was since deserted. McIntosh returned with the army to Pennsylvania, settled in Fayette County, and again volunteered, in 1778, at Fort Pitt. General Lachlin McIntosh there made his acquaintance, and took him down to Beaver, thence to Fort Laurens, and back to Pittsburgh; after which he was sent to the Tuscarawas as one of Brodhead's Indian killers, in 1780, and at the slaughter of the Coshocton Indians in that campaign the Scotchman was in the fore-front, boasting in his old age of having tomahawked six Indians in one hour, when telling his exploits in Fayette County, where he died, leaving a family.

CHAPTER XI.

FIRST SETTLEMENT IN THE NORTH-WEST TERRITORY, ON THE MUSKINGUM.

As heretofore stated, Congress, in 1785, ordered seven ranges to be surveyed, and, among others, appointed General Putnam surveyor for Massachusetts, who, being at the time otherwise engaged, General Benjamin Tupper came out in 1786 in his place. For the following facts the compiler is indebted to Hon. A. T. Nye, of Marietta:

After the completion of the survey of the seven ranges, General Tupper returned to Massachusetts, and called upon General Rufus Putnam, to whom he communicated a flattering account and description of that part of the north-west territory. As a result of this conference, a notice was published in the public prints, signed by Generals Benjamin Tupper and Rufus Putnam, styled, "Information," which, in substance, called upon all officers and soldiers who had served in the late war, and who were entitled by ordinance of Congress to receive tracts of land in the Ohio country, and on all other good citizens who wished to become adventurers in that region from the State of Massachusetts, for the purpose of forming a company, by the name of the "Ohio Company," to meet, in their respective counties, on a day therein fixed, and appoint delegates to meet at the "Bunch of Grapes" tavern, in Boston.

OHIO COMPANY FORMED IN BOSTON IN 1786.

The meeting of delegates was held at the place appointed, on the first day of March, 1786, and resulted in the formation of the "Ohio Company," and the appointment of Generals Samuel Holden Parsons and Rufus Putnam, and the Rev. Manassah Cutler, as a committee to make application to Congress for a private purchase of lands lying in the "Great Western Territory of the Union."

ONE MILLION AND A HALF ACRES PURCHASED AT THE MOUTH OF THE MUSKINGUM.

After a long negotiation, a contract was made with Congress for the purchase of one million and a half acres of land for said company, at two-thirds of a dollar per acre; which amount, by failure of some of the shareholders to make payment, was reduced to nine hundred and sixty-four thousand two hundred and eighty-five acres, and was located on the Ohio and Muskingum rivers.

The boundaries of the purchase were, namely: "From the seventh range of townships, extending along the Ohio River south-westerly, to the place where the west line of the seventeenth range of townships would intersect that river; thence northerly so far that a line drawn due east to the western boundary of said seventh range of townships would, with the other lines, include one and a half million acres of land, besides the reserves."

Congress *reserved* two full townships for a *university*—sections sixteen for the support of schools and twenty-nine for the support of religion—and also sections eight, eleven, and twenty-six for the future disposition of Congress.

The lands of the company were divided into about one thousand shares, consisting of lots of various sizes, and amounting to about eleven hundred acres to each share.

An advance party, consisting of boat-builders and mechanics, left Danvers, Massachusetts, in December, 1787, under the command of Major Haffield White, and reached "Sumrills," on the Youghiogheny River, in January, and commenced building boats.

The surveyors, and remainder of the pioneers, under the command of Colonel Ebenezer Sproat, left Hartford, Connecticut, in January, and arrived at "Sumrills" about the middle of February, 1788. General Rufus Putnam, who had gone by the way of New York city, on business of the company, rejoined the party at Swatarra Creek, Pennsylvania, on the 24th of January.

PIONEERS ARRIVE AT MUSKINGUM, APRIL 7, 1788.

The boats were soon afterward completed, and left with the pioneers on the 2d day of April, and landed at the mouth of the Muskingum on the 7th day of April, 1788.

They immediately commenced making temporary *huts*, and erected the marque of General Putnam, in which the business of the company was transacted until their *garrison* was completed, a few months afterward.

CAMPUS MARTIUS.

This garrison, or stockade, was located on the brow of the plain, or high ground, nearly a mile up the Muskingum River, and was named "Campus Martius," and included within its limits about one acre of land. At the four corners of the stockade were blockhouses, used for garrison purposes, a school, religious worship, and one by the governor of the North-west Territory.

The first court held in the North-west Territory was in the northwest blockhouse.

MARIETTA.

Between the blockhouses were the houses of the settlers—all inclosed by a picket made of the bodies of trees set in the ground. The picket was about fourteen feet high. A well, furnishing a plentiful supply of water, was dug in the center of the stockade, and walled with brick. At the "Point" (the junction of the Muskingum River with the Ohio), about four acres were inclosed by pickets (stockaded), within which were several dwelling and store-houses, and it covered ground which since then has been a business part of the town.

FORT HARMAR.

On the opposite bank of the Muskingum River, at its mouth, a military post had been called Fort Harmar—built in 1785, and garrisoned by one batallion of the regiment commanded by General Harmar, under Major Doughty. At the time of the arrival of the pioneers, General Harmar was at the fort.

FORT FRY.

At a point on the easterly bank of the Muskingum, about twenty-two miles up the river, and one mile below the present village of Beverly, was built a fortification for defense against the Indians, in 1790, and was occupied by the families of the pioneers, and called Fort Fry. At a point still further up the Muskingum, about forty miles from Marietta, called Big Bottom, a blockhouse was built by the early settlers of that locality.

FARMER'S CASTLE.

At Belpre, about fourteen miles below Marietta, a fortification was also built, called Farmer's Castle, and occupied by the early settlers—their houses being within the pickets. In addition, the settlement had also a blockhouse about two or three miles above Farmer's Castle, called Stone's Station, and some two or three miles below the castle, another blockhouse, called Goodale's Station ; and down the river, below the mouth of the Little Hockhocking, was a station called Newburg.

ARTHUR ST. CLAIR APPOINTED GOVERNOR OF THE NORTH-WEST TERRITORY.

Congress, at its session of 1787–88, appointed Arthur St. Clair, Esq., as governor of the North-west Territory. He was escorted from Pittsburgh by a detachment of troops, under Major Doughty, and arrived at Fort Harmar on the 9th day of July, 1788.

On the 15th day of July, following, a formal reception of the governor was held at a bowery, erected for the occasion, near the stockade. He was escorted by tbe officers of the garrison, and the secretary of the territory—Winthrop Sargent—and was received by General Rufus Putnam, the judges of the territory—General Samuel Holden Parsons and James Whitehall Varnum—and the inhabitants generally. The secretary, Major Sargent, read the ordinance of Congress erecting the North-west Territory, the commissions of the governor, the judges, and his own commission. The first laws for the government of the new territory were adopted from the laws of the States, deemed suitable to the condition of the citizens of the new territory by the governor and judges, and were published at Marietta ; among these, laws for establishing courts of general quarter sessions and county courts of common pleas.

WASHINGTON COUNTY ORGANIZED IN 1788.

By the ordinance of Congress the governor was authorized to make proper divisions of the territory, and by proclamation of the 26th day of July, 1788, he defined the limits of Washington County—named in honor of General Washington—bounded as follows, namely: Beginning on the bank of the Ohio River, where the western boundary line of the State of Pennsylvania crosses it, running with that line to Lake Erie; thence along the shore of the lake to the mouth of Cuyahoga River; thence up the river to the portage, between that and the Tuscarawas branch of the Muskingum River; thence down the branch to the forks at the crossing place above Fort Laurens; thence with a line to be drawn westerly to the portage of that branch of the Big Miami—on which the fort stood that was taken by the French in 1752—until it meets the road from the lower Shawanee town to the Sandusky; thence south to the Scioto River; thence down that river to the mouth; thence up the Ohio River to the place of beginning.

THE FIRST COURT OF COMMON PLEAS IN OHIO

was opened on the 2d day of September, 1788, at Marietta. A procession was formed at the "Point" (the junction of the Muskingum with the Ohio River), of the inhabitants, and the officers from Fort Harmar, who escorted the judges of the court of common pleas, the governor of the territory, and the supreme judges to the hall, appropriated for that purpose, in the north-west blockhouse in "Campus Martius." The procession was headed by the sheriff, with drawn sword and baton of office. After prayer by Rev. Manasseh Cutler the court was then organized by reading the commissions of the judges, the clerk, and sheriff; after which the sheriff proclaimed the court open for the transaction of business.

The judges of the first court of common pleas were: General Rufus Putnam, General Benjamin Tupper, and Colonel Archibald Crary. The clerk was Colonel R. J. Meigs; Colonel Ebenezer Sproat, sheriff. On the 9th day of September following, the court of general quarter sessions was held at "Campus Martius." The commission appointing the judges thereof was read—General Rufus Putnam and General Benjamin Tupper constituted justices of the quorum, and Isaac Pearce, Thomas Lord, and R. J. Meigs, Jr., assistant justices; Colonel R. J. Meigs, Sr., was clerk. The first grand jury of the territory was then impaneled, viz.: William Stacey, foreman, Nathaniel Cushing, Nathan Goodale, Charles Knowles, Anselm Tupper, Jonathan Stone, Oliver Rice, Ezra Lunt, John Mathews, George Ingersoll, Jonathan Devol, Jethro Putnam, Samuel Stebbins, and Jabez True.

ONE HUNDRED AND THIRTY-TWO ACRES OF LAND PLANTED IN 1788.

In the first year of the settlement (1788) about one hundred and thirty-two acres of ground was cleared of the timber and planted in corn, and produced a very good crop. The crop of the succeeding year was badly injured by early frosts; very little was sufficiently matured to be fit for use; but good crops of vegetables were raised.

The loss of the crop of 1789 produced a famine, and the inhabitants were greatly straightened for necessary food, and had to depend upon the partial supply of game which could be killed, until the following spring, when early vegetables were raised. The succeeding year abundant crops were raised.

THE INDIANS DESTROY THE FIRST SETTLEMENT IN MORGAN COUNTY.

In 1790, the first settlement was attempted in the present limits of Morgan County, at a point on the Muskingum called the Big Bottom, near the present Washington County line, by a company of about forty young men from the settlements in the vicinity of Marietta. It was getting late in the fall when the project was started, and on that account was discouraged by many of the older and more experienced border men. The leading spirits in the enterprise were men of great courage and energy, and would not listen to the advice of the old settlers. The company accordingly moved up the Muskingum with a sufficient quantity of provisions, and tools, and ammunition for a stay of several months. Reaching the site of the proposed settlement, the first work done was the erection of a blockhouse, for protection in case of a sudden attack by the Indians. After the completion of the blockhouse, several of the older men of the party paired off and built cabins, leaving about twenty to occupy the blockhouse.

At the time of these operations at Big Bottom, the Indians of the valley were preparing their winter quarters at Waketameki (Dresden), and their other towns further up the valley of the Tuscarawas. While thus engaged, a runner brought information of the new settlement by the whites, and it was at once determined in council that a war party should drive away or kill the whites. Accordingly, at a given time, a band of between fifty and sixty warriors started down the river on the bloody errand. On the afternoon of the second day they came near the place, but not wishing to open an attack until fully apprised of the number and defenses of the settlers, they stationed themselves on a hill on the opposite side of the river, from where they obtained a full view of the whole bottom. Just before dark, on the 2d of Jan. 1791, the Indians proceeded to a point a short distance up the river, where they crossed on the ice. As the shades of twilight disappeared and darkness closed over the valley, the Indians appeared on the ground, and found the whites at supper in the blockhouse. While the major portion of the savages were to attack the main body of whites, a small party proceeded to the cabins to secure their inmates. The whites in one cabin invited the Indians to partake of some supper, when several entered, and others stationed themselves at the door. The Indians inside immediately surrounded the table and informed the whites they were prisoners. Seeing resistance was useless the whites permitted themselves to be bound.

Directly after the surrender of the cabin party, the Indians burst open the blockhouse door, and shot down the inmates who were standing around the fire, the others were at once tomahawked and scalped. The only resistance offered in the blockhouse was by a woman who struck at an Indian with an ax, but missing his skull she cut a gash in his cheek. Another Indian shot her on the spot.

The inmates of the other cabin, hearing the shooting and yelling of the savages, gathered up their arms and trappings, and put for the woods, making good their escape—as the Indians did not offer pursuit. While gathering the plunder in the blockhouse a boy, named Philip Stacey, was found hidden under some bedding. Two Indians at once raised their tomahawks to kill him, when the boy fell at their feet, begging for his life, as he was the only one left. This excited compassion, and he was spared. The Indians now set fire to the buildings, and left the scene. Young Stacey escaped the spring following, and returned to the Marietta settlements. The names of those killed at Big Bottom are given as follows: one of General Putnam's sons, Zebulon Throp, John Stacey, John Camp, James Couch, Joseph Clark, John Farwell, William James, Isaac Meeks and his wife, with two children.

The party who escaped returned the next day with assistance from Marietta, and found the buildings only partly consumed, by reason of the timbers being green, and the bodies of their comrades were lying on the floors in a charred condition—some being beyond recognition. A large hole was dug inside the blockhouse, into which the remains were placed; and over them placed the floor puncheons, and the whole covered with earth.

The Indians raided about the neighborhood for some days, but did not attempt another attack on any of the settlements. They then returned up the valley, and were heard of no more during that winter. Notice was immediately given to all the other settlements—Wolf Creek Mills, Fort Fry, Marietta, Farmers Castle, and Newburg. The settlers immediately commenced to put their blockhouses in a more secure condition, and to add such fortifications as the immediate danger seemed to require. No regular attack was made during the Indian war on any of these garrisons, but they were in constant danger and dread from the prowling bands of Indians who infested the neighborhood of the garrisons. Joseph Rogers, a spy or scout, Robert Warth, Matthew Kerr, a Mr. Carpenter, and a negro boy were killed in the vicinity of Marietta; and a Mr. Davis, a woman named Dunham, and several of the Armstrong family were killed at Belpre, and Major Goodale was captured and carried off from there, by the Indians, to their towns in the north-west, and died among the Indians.

March 15, 1792, Mrs. Brown and two young children, and a young girl aged fourteen, named Perses Dunham, were killed at Newburg. April 24, 1793, Mrs. Armstrong and two young children were killed, and two sons and one daughter taken prisoners opposite Belpre. Last of July, 1795, Mr. Davis, while busy repairing a skiff on the Ohio above Belpre, was killed. In June, 1794, near Sherman Station, on the Muskingum, above Beverly, Abel Sherman was shot through the heart. May 10, 1794, about three hundred yards from Fort Harmar, Robert Warth was killed.

The Indian war continued until the treaty of Greenville, the 3d of August, 1795, a period of nearly five years—during which period the inhabitants were confined to the limits of their fortifications. In 1796, the families of the settlers began to remove to their homes, and commenced clearing their lands and making improvements, and general prosperity began to prevail. Marietta began to improve rapidly. Ship-building was commenced here about 1801, and carried on until the embargo stopped the building of vessels, and all mechanical enterprises connected therewith. The last vessel was taken out in the spring of 1808.

THE FIRST SETTLEMENT AT MARIETTA DESCRIBED BY AN EYE WITNESS.

Hon. William Woodbridge, a United Stateses nator, described the Marietta settlement thus, in a speech made by him in 1844:

"On the 7th of April, 1788, the first and principal detachment of that interesting corps of emigrants landed at the confluence of the Muskingum with the Ohio River. This was directly athwart the old Indian war-path; for it was down the Muskingum and its tributary branches that the Wyandots, the Shawnees, the Ottowas, and all the Indians of the north and north-west were accustomed to march, when from time to time, for almost half a century before, they made those dreadful incursions into western Virginia and western Pennsylvania, which spread desolation, and ruin, and despair throughout all those regions. Having arrived there, they marked out their embryo city, and in honor of the friend of their country, the queen of France, called it Marietta. They surrounded it with palisades and abatis; they erected blockhouses and bastions. On an eminence a little above, and near the Muskingum, they constructed a more regular and scientific fortification. Thus did the settlement of the great State commence. Among these colonists were very many of the most distinguished officers of the revolution, and of all grades. General Rufus Putnam, and General Benjamin Tupper, of the Massachusetts line, were there; General Parsons, of the Connecticut, and General Varnum, of the Rhode Island lines, were there; old Commodore Whipple, of Rhode Island, who fired the first hostile gun from on board a Congress ship, and who, during the whole war, was another Paul Jones, and as active and daring, found his grave there—as did a near relative of General Nathaniel Green; the sons of the 'wolf catcher,' General Israel Putnam, and the descendants of Manasseh Cutler, were there; Colonel Cushing, Colonel Sproat, Colonel Oliver, and Colonel Sargent, and multitudes of others, distinguished alike for their bravery, for their patriotism, and for their skill in war, were there. Some few, very few, still live (1844), and whose names I recognize, who constituted a part of this wonderful band of veteran soldiers. The rest, one after another, have dropped off. Many of the things I have adverted to, I personally saw. I was a child then, but I well recollect the regular morning reveille, and the evening tattoo that helped to give character to the establishment. Even on the Sabbath, the male population were always under arms, and with their chaplain, who was willing to share the lot of his comrades, were accustomed to march in battle array to their blockhouse church."

NAMES OF THE PIONEERS WHO LANDED AT MARIETTA APRIL 7, 1788.

General Rufus Putnam, superintendent of the settlement, and surveyor; Colonel Ebenezer Sproat, Colonel R. J. Meigs, Major Anselm Tupper, and Mr. John Matthews, surveyors; Major Haffield White, steward and quartermaster; Captain Jonathan Devol, Captain Josiah Monroe, Captain Daniel Davis, Captain Jethro Putnam, Captain William Gray, Captain Ezekiel Cooper, Peregrine Foster,

Esq., Jarvis Cutler, Samuel Cushing, Oliver Dodge, Isaac Dodge, Samuel Felshaw, Hezekiah Flint, Hezekiah Flint, Jr., Amos Porter, Josiah Whitridge, John Gardner, Benjamin Griswold, Eleazer Kirtland, Theophilus Leonard, Joseph Lincoln, William Miller, Jabez Barlow, Daniel Bushnell, Ebenezer Corey, Phineas Coburn, Allen Putnam, David Wallace, Joseph Wells, Gilbert Devol, Jr., Henry Maxon, William Maxon, Edward Moulton, Simeon Martin, Benjamin Shaw, Peletiah White, Israel Danton, Josiah White, Jonas Davis, Earl Sproat, Allen Devol.

August 19, 1788 arrived the first families, six in number—General Benjamin Tupper and wife, with three sons and one daughter grown; Colonel Nathaniel Cushing, and wife and children; Major Asa Coburn, and wife and three children; Ichabod Nye, and wife and two children; Andrew Webster and wife; Major Nathan Goodale and wife, and son and daughter; two single men, names unknown, in the employ of General Tupper.

At different periods in 1788, arrived Commodore Abraham Whipple; July 9, Governor Arthur St. Clair; June 16, Dr. Jabez True and Paul Fearing, Esq.; May, Hon. Samuel Holden Parsons, Colonel Ebenezer Battelle, Captain William Dana, Major Jonathan Haskell, Colonel Israel Putnam, Aaron Waldo Putnam, Major Robert Bradford, Jonathan Stone, Colonel Robert Oliver, and Colonel William Stacey; June, Hon. James Mitchell Varnum, Griffin Green, Esq.—one of the directors of the company—Charles Green, Major Dean Tyler, and Colonel Joseph Thompson.

In 1789, there arrived Hon. Joseph Gilman, Benjamin I. Gilman, Rev. Daniel Story—in the spring—Levi Munsall, and William Skinner.

In 1790, there arrived Dudley Woodbridge, Sr., and family, Dudley Woodbridge, Jr., Ebenezer Nye and family, Joshua Shipman and family.

In 1792, there arrived Israel Putnam, Jr., and Ephraim Cutler, later.

The above list does not contain the names of all who came out during that period, as they can not now be ascertained.

ORGANIZATION OF THE STATE OF OHIO.

The six first counties erected in Ohio were Washington, 1788; Hamilton, 1790; Wayne, 1796; Adams and Jefferson, 1797; Ross, 1798; Trumbull, 1800. These counties embraced all the territory of Ohio except so much in the north-west part as was reserved for Indian territory, by previous treaties with the Indians, and military posts.

The population of the North-west Territory having, in 1798, increased to five thousand male adult persons, they became, under the ordinance of 1787, entitled to a territorial legislature. Representatives were accordingly elected—their term being two years. The members of the house of representatives (there being no provision for a senate) were empowered to nominate ten freeholders, each owning five hundred acres, from whom the president appointed five, who constituted the legislative council, instead of a senate, and they to serve five years.

The State of Connecticut, having obtained in the reign of Charles II of England, a grant of land running from Providence Plantations to the Pacific Ocean, it was found that nearly four million acres were embraced in the Ohio territory, and which was called New Connecticut. Of this, Connecticut donated half a million acres in the west portion to certain sufferers by fire, and these became known as "fire lands." Over the balance the State ceded to the United States the jurisdiction, and in 1800 this territory was erected into the county of Trumbull—Connecticut still retaining the right to the soil, which was afterward divided into tracts and sold as part of the "Connecticut Western Reserve."

In 1798, the North-west Territory contained a population of five thousand adult male inhabitants, being the requisite number to entitle the people to elect their legislators, under a property qualification of five hundred acres—as to the legislative council—the representatives to serve two, and the council five years. In 1799, the territorial legislature was elected, organized, and addressed by the governor, after which the necessary laws were enacted—the whole number being thirty-seven. William Henry Harrison, secretary of the territory, was elected delegate to Congress.

In 1802, a convention to form a State constitution was called at Chillicothe, and completed its labors in less than thirty days, and this constitution became the fundamental law, without ratification by the people. It was not abrogated for forty-nine years. The State of Ohio having been formally admitted into the Union, two sessions of the legislature were held in the year 1803, under the State constitution, and the State government regularly organized.

The general assembly continued to meet at Chillicothe, except a year or two that it met at Zanesville, until 1816, when it was removed to Columbus, and that city was made the permanent seat of government.

ORGANIZATION OF THE SIX VALLEY COUNTIES.

The counties through which the Tuscarawas and Muskingum rivers now flow, originally comprised part of Washington county, which was organized July 27, 1788, and embraced about one-half the territory in the present State of Ohio; its boundaries being the Pennsylvania line and Ohio River on the east, and south and south-west the Ohio to the Sciota; thence up that stream to its source; thence to the portage on the Big Miami; thence east to old Fort Laurens, on the Tuscarawas (then called Muskingum); thence north to the Cuyahoga; thence following that stream to Lake Erie; thence east to the Pennsylvania line. Hence the inhabitants of what is now Muskingum County, Morgan County, Coshocton County, Tuscarawas County, and Stark County paid taxes, settled estates, attended courts, &c., at Marietta, until 1804, in which year Muskingum was organized; and thenceforward, until 1808, Stark, Tuscarawas, and Coshocton were part of Muskingum, but in that year Stark and Tuscarawas being organized, Muskingum was shorn of the territory of those two counties. In 1811 Coshocton was organized, and in 1818 the County of Morgan was erected, and the six valley counties, watered by the main streams of the two rivers above named, have remained to the present as originally taken from the one county of Washington; with occasional townships detached from one and added to the other, or attached to a new county formed east or west of the original boundaries.

A RECAPITULATION OF EVENTS IN THE LIVES OF RUFUS PUTNAM AND JOHN HECKEWELDER, FOUNDERS OF THE STATE OF OHIO.

Rufus Putnam was born in Massachusetts in 1738. He received a New England education, after which he went south with a motive to found a settlement. After exploring the lower Mississippi, and finding the natives at that early day averse to English settlements in their country, he returned to New England.

The war of the British government against the American colonies having been precipitated at Boston, he joined the colonies in their struggle against the mother government, and so distinguished himself that he was made a general. After the close of the war, he headed nearly three hundred officers, who had been dropped from the rolls of the army by reason of the peace, and petitioned Congress to grant them a tract of land commensurate with their service, to be located in the western country. Congress deferred action on the petition for the time being.

General Putnam, in 1785, drafted a plan and submitted it to the government, looking to the establishment of a chain of military posts from the Mississippi to the lakes. President Washington, penetrating the sagacious movement of Putnam, favorably recommended it to Congress, and that body directed the work to begin. Fort Harmar, at the mouth of the Muskingum River, was accordingly begun in 1785, but was not finished until 1791.

It was one of the systems recommended by General Putnam in 1785, and in which year he was appointed one of the surveying commissioners to lay off into farm lots, seven ranges of lands in the Ohio territory, immediately west of the Pennsylvania line. This land was designed to be given in part to the officers and soldiers of the army of the revolution for military services, and in part to be sold. The Indians, by treaty, had relinquished their title to the land, but observing the surveying movements, became dissatisfied, declared they had been cheated in the treaty, and commencing hostilities the surveys had for the time to be suspended.

The officers who, with Putnam, had petitioned Congress in 1783, for a large body of land, not getting all they desired from the government, met in Boston in 1786, and with General Putnam as their practical business man, organized the "Ohio Company," determined to emigrate to the Ohio, and make a large and compact settlement at the mouth of the Muskingum. General Putnam engineered the movement, and in April, 1788, forty-eight emigrants reached the Muskingum, laid off Marietta, and a large number of farm lots. The same year eighty-four additional emigrants, mostly from New England, arrived at Marietta, and for self-protection they commenced a stockade fort, to which was given the name of "Campus Martius." In 1789, one hundred and fifty-two additional English emigrants arrived, and in 1790, four hundred French emigrants came. New settlements at Belpre, and Waterford, and other points, had been begun in 1789, but the territorial government having been formed in 1788, with General Arthur St. Clair as governor, Marietta took the lead, and became the seat of territorial power for a time. General Putnam was appointed one of the judges of the United States Court in the territory, and set about with the other judges the business of the organization of courts and the administration of justice. Here we leave him on the bench while the early career of another is traced up, he having from this point to be connected with Putnam in the future history of the valleys.

John Heckewelder was born in Bedford, England, in 1743, of German parents. He received an education for the ministry, and sailed for the new world. On his arrival in the colonies he manifested a desire to mingle in frontier life, and educate the Indian natives. With this motive he left Bethlehem, Pennsylvania, in 1762, with Christian Frederick Post, and in the usual time they reached the head waters of the Muskingum of that day, but Tuscarawas of this day. Post had been to the Tuscarawas in 1761, and erected a small house on the bank of the river, above the present village of Bolivar, which was the first house (except traders' cabins) built in the valleys by a subject of the English government.

A short residence satisfied Heckewelder that he was too early, and being admonished by a friendly Indian chief that if he remained he might lose his scalp, he retired to Pennsylvania, as Putnam afterward did to Massachusetts, to await events.

Ten years later, in 1772, Heckewelder returned to the Tuscarawas with David Zeisberger, and began a settlement for their converted Indians about three miles south-east of the present New Philadelphia, called Schoenbrunn. Heckewelder returned to the east, and in 1773, came back with upward of two hundred emigrants, who were mostly taken in canoes down the Ohio to the mouth of the Muskingum (where Putnam and others, fifteen years later, located Marietta), thence up the Muskingum to Schoenbrunn. They brought clothing, grain, axes, hoes, spades, iron and nails, and farm implements with them, and set about clearing land and building up a town; so that by 1774, they had nearly fifty houses and a church up, and many acres of corn growing, and horses, cattle, and hogs in abundance, for over three hundred people. He afterward assisted in establishing settlements at Gnadenhutten, Litchtenau, and Salem, on the Tuscarawas, where they raised corn and cattle, and converted the heathen. When the war between the colonies and Great Britain commenced, British emmisaries visited these settlements, and, through the influence of Simon Girty, and other renegades, succeeded in arraying a portion of the Delawares, Monseys, and Shawnese, who had not become Christians, to join the British, but those who had been converted, and wore clothes as white men, were for a time the steadfast friends of the colonies, through the untiring efforts of Heckewelder, Zeisberger, and other missionaries, although they were forbidden to take part in war. Seeing this, the British governor at Detroit induced the British Indians to retire from the Tuscarawas to Sandusky, under Captain Pipe, from whence they returned in squads with their friends, the Wyandots, and annoyed the Tuscarawas settlements; as well as the whole Ohio River country. In the fall of 1789, they came down under the British flag, captured and drove to the Sandusky the missionaries and their converts, and had Heckewelder, Zeisberger, and Senseman sent to Detroit to be tried as American spies. They were acquitted twice, but in the meantime about one hundred of the captured Christians returned to their cornfields on the Tuscarawas (at which they had three hundred acres on the stalk) to gather the crop, and while there, in March, 1782, were massacred. This outrage drove the residue of the converts, except a few, into the British hostile ranks; and with these few Zeisberger and the other missionaries attempted settlements in the north-west and Canada, from whence Heckewelder returned to Pennsylvania, and soon took service under the government—in assisting at Indian treaties, and the surveying of the public lands in the valleys of the Tuscarawas and Muskingum. He visited Philadelphia, and was instrumental in procuring the grant from Congress of twelve thousand acres for the missions, to be located in what is now Tuscarawas County.

In December, 1786, Congress instructed Colonel Harmar, who was in command at Fort Harmar, at the mouth of the Muskingum, to invite the exiled missionaries and their Christian converts back to the Tuscarawas, but the Indian chiefs, Half King, Welendawacken, and Pipe, forbade them not to return under pain of death. Heckewelder visited Fort Harmar in 1789, where an Indian treaty was made, and through the influence of General Putnam and himself, Governor St. Clair notified the chiefs he should invite the Christian Indians back to their Tuscarawas settlements at once. The chiefs assented, except Welendawacken, whose capital was at the present Fort Wayne, and who still threatened death to Zeisberger and his converts, in case he returned with them. His hostile attitude dissuaded Zeisberger from making the attempt, and thus the head of the valley was for the time closed against the return of the settlers.

THE INDIAN WAR OF 1791—DEFEAT OF HARMAR AND ST. CLAIR.

When the New England pioneers landed at the mouth of the Muskingum, they were met with apparently open hands by the Indians, and Captain Pipe, with one hundred Wyandots and Delawares, then at the spot, reconnoitering the Yankees, welcomed them to their new homes. Considering his antecedents farther up on the Tuscarawas, where he opposed the missionaries, and harrangued the warriors during the revolution, to drive every white man over the Ohio, this apparent friendship was ominous of future hostility, as he had practiced the same duplicity on former occasions in the upper valley.

The settlers, while they shook hands with the warriors, shook their own heads, as soon as Pipe departed up the trail, and instead of trusting to his words, they went first to work to building defenses, stockades, &c.

Fort Harmar was on the opposite side of the Muskingum from Marietta, and with "Campus Martius" soon erected, together with the stockades, they were shortly in condition to fight or shake hands.

Up in the north-west, Brant had, in 1786, organized the tribes into a western confederation. He was the wiliest chief of his time, and headed the Six Nations, forming as he did the design of erecting the Ohio territory and the other North-west Territory into an Indian barrier between the American and British possessions. In this programme he was promised aid by the British. It was a pleasing idea to the chiefs and warriors of all the tribes, and afforded consolation to the British cabinet for the loss of their colonies.

And, right here, it may be observed that had not Marietta been settled when it was, in the manner it was, and by men from the New England States, this British plan of hemming in the Americans east of the Ohio River would undoubtedly have succeeded, and thus postponed for a generation, at least, the creation of new States in the West.

Even by all their stern and energetic work along the Ohio and Muskingum, these New Englanders were often in despair, and some abandoned all they had brought with them, to get back beyond the mountains, and wait events; if those who remained came out successful, those who had retired could come back—if unsuccessful they need not.

No sooner had Pipe and his warriors made their reconnoissance at the mouth of the Muskingum, in 1788, than they retired from the valley, as they had done years before from the Tuscarawas, to plan and foment raids, and war upon the settlers. Under pretence of negotiating a treaty of peace, they assembled at Duncan's falls on the Muskingum, to meet Governor St. Clair, but instead of making a treaty, their "bad Indians," purposely brought along, fell upon the white sentries, killing two and wounding others. This postponed the treaty—as was intended by those in the secret—several months, meanwhile the Indians prowled around Marietta, and by way of "welcoming the settlers," killed off and destroyed the game on which the pioneers depended for animal food.

In January, 1789, another attempt was made by treaty to quiet the savages, and dissipate their ideas of expelling the whites from Ohio. As soon as signed, the pioneers gave the chiefs a great feast (but had nothing for the rank and file), and all went home up their trails, while the settlers went to surveying and clearing land, under the act of Congress.

This treaty was made at Fort Harmar, opposite Marietta, between the settlers and the Wyandots, Delawares, Chippewas, Ottowas, Miamis, Pottowatamies, Senecas, &c., January 12, 1789. Early that same summer John Matthews, surveyor of the Ohio company, and his party, were attacked on the Virginia side of the Ohio, and seven of his men shot and scalped. The same summer not less than twenty men were killed and scalped on both sides of the Ohio. In 1790, the Indians attacked a number of boats owned by emigrants, and killed or carried off those on board. The raiding parties always had a white man as decoy, who hailed the boats in a friendly manner, thus enticing them near shore, when the killing took place. These white decoys were renegades, like Simon Girty and McKee, who had fled the colonies and were under the British flag.

At length Governor St. Clair unwisely sent a message to the British governor, Hamilton, at Detroit, informing him that Colonel Harmar would go out from the Muskingum to chastise the murdering Indians on the Sandusky and Maumee, and hoped Hamilton would not be offended, as there was no intention to annoy the British posts at Detroit, and elsewhere. Hamilton, although governor of Detroit, was a low, dirty dog, and accordingly showed St. Clair's letter to the chiefs, who applied for and received from him, powder, ball, arms, and whiskey, with which to carry on their murders, down on the Ohio and Muskingum, as well as fight Colonel Harmar.

Colonel Harmar marched an army of over one thousand men into the Indian strongholds of the north-west—the Indians retiring before him. After destroying some towns, he was intercepted by the enraged savages, on his return, and doubled up, driven back, and so utterly routed that there was but little left of his army when he got back to the Ohio. Harmar was disgraced, hundreds of good men cut to pieces, and the border laid open more than ever to Indian depredations.

By September, of 1791, General St. Clair had reorganized another army of twenty-three hundred troops, and started from Cincinnati on Harmar's trail, to inflict punishment on the savages. The war department was inefficient, and its commissariat corrupt—the one failing to send St. Clair supplies, and the other stealing or changing what was sent, so that this courageous old general had not only the savages around him, but want of good ammunition and provisions in his midst. In this dilemma he ordered a retreat, when the Indians, to the number of two thousand warriors, beset him, in what is now Darke County, on the 23d of October, 1791. Three hundred of his militia deserted, adding panic to his cup of calamities. Still he stood his ground until the 4th of November, when a large body of Delawares, Shawanese, and Wyandots drove in his outposts pell-mell on to the main army. He rallied, but the savages being reinforced, pushed his troops into the center of the camp. In vain were efforts made to restore order and rally again. The Indians rushed upon his left line, killed or wounded one-half his artillery officers, captured the guns, slashed and cut hundreds to pieces, and so stampeded the militia that they could not be checked until they ran to Fort Jefferson—twenty-seven miles from the battle-field. The general displayed the most heroic bravery, having four horses shot under him, and as many bullet-holes in his clothes. The fight lasted three hours, and thirteen hundred men were put *hors de combat.*

In 1793, Wayne, in his campaign, camped on St. Clair's battle-field, but his soldiers could not lay down to sleep on account of bones strewing the ground. It is stated that they picked up six hundred skulls, and buried them on the battle ground, which is now marked by a small village, twenty-three miles north of Greenville, the county seat of Darke County.

A hue and cry was raised against St. Clair for this defeat, over the whole country, and people demanded that he be shot by order of court-martial. President Washington refused to listen to the public clamor, and refused even a court of inquiry; knowing well that the blame rested more on the War Department than on St. Clair. He remained governor, but was superseded by General Wilkinson as general, and after the war shut himself up on his farm at Legonier, Pennsylvania, where he died, in disgrace, although innocent of crime or cowardice.

SCENES AROUND MARIETTA IN THE DAYS OF HER DANGER.

After the defeat of General St. Clair, the Delawares, Shawanese, and other warriors came down from the "black forest" of the north-west, yelling the war-whoop along the Mohican, over to, and past the ruins on the Tuscarawas; down the Muskingum, Scioto, and Miami, and over into Kentucky and Virginia. They were plumed with buffalo horns fastened on the head, and costumed with bear-skin breech clouts, while scalps of the slaughtered soldiers dangled from their heels, as they urged their horses onward, looking like so many red demons let loose from the infernal regions. They were jubilant over the recent victories, and re-echoed the old epithet, "No white man shall ever plant corn in Ohio."

Campus Martius became the residence of Governor St. Clair, and son and daughter, General Rufus Putnam and family, General Benjamin Tupper and family, Colonel Oliver and family, Colonel R. J. Meigs and family, R. J. Meigs, Jr., and wife, Colonel Shephard and family, Colonel Ichabod Nye and family, Major Ezra Putnam and family, Major Olney and family, Captain Davis and family, Major Coburn and family, Winthrop Sargent, Thomas Lord, Charles Greene and family, Major Ziegler, Major Haffield White and son, Joshua Shipman and family, James Smith and family, John Russell, Ichibald Lake, Ebenezer Corey and family, James Wells and family, Joseph Wood and family, Robert Allison, Elijah Warren and family, Girshom Flagg and family, widow Kelly and family, and many others, who had taken refuge therein. A portion of the pioneers also resided across the Muskingum in Fort Harmar. One of the pioneers has related that as they looked out over the palisades, or through the port holes, they could see the warriors galloping to and fro with their stained hatchets at arms length, shaking them in defiance at Campus Martius. Although shots were fired at the barbarians, they continued to invest the camp and pick off any one who ventured out to his lot, or garden, or field.

The classic names given to the squares and avenues of the new city stunned these wild red men, and their indignation became intense as they saw portions of their land platted off, and christened with foreign names, such as "Capitoline," "Quadranoua," and the like. The old trail leading down from an ancient mound of the primitive Americans to the edge of the river, they found converted into a broadway, with high embankments. Its classic name "*Sacra via*," given it by some latin scholar, aroused the anger of one of Zeisberger's educated Delawares, who had returned to Indian ways. He was seen to reach down and untie a scalp on the neck of his horse, shake it in the direction of the governor's residence in derision, as evincing a more effective way of speaking "*dead languages*" than the author of "*Sacra via.*"

He was also an artist, and riding up to the guide-board he effaced therefrom the Latin, substituting with war-paint the ominous picture of a scalp, and underneath the word "Gnadenhutten." Heckewelder tells us that the Delawares, though not possessing the white man's art of writing, had certain hieroglyphics by which they described on a piece of bark, or on a large tree, any fact, so that all the nations could understand it.

The warriors lurked in the high grass of the square "Capitolium," to get a good shot at the man who dared desecrate their land with that word. The square "Quadranoua" furnished a covert from which "War Cloud" jumped as he fired at a Putnam pulling his flax, and "Buckshanoath," the Shawanese giant, was discovered in the corn planted by General Putnam, on mound square, and which having been put there in defiance of the injunction, "White man shall plant no corn in Ohio," was levelled to the ground with knives and tomahawks by Buckshanoath's warriors, so great was the Indian wrath.

Outside the garrison were, at the time, some twenty uninhabited log houses, whose occupants fled to the blockhouses as the enemy approached, having been warned thereof by the firing of a small cannon within the fortified camp. Around and about these the savages watched for such pioneers as passed in and out of their camp. When darkness intervened, they made night sleepless with hideous yells, as they cavorted their stolen horses to water in "Duck Creek," which had also received the classical name of "Tiber," after that old Tiber of Rome; or as the barbarians galloped over toward "Capitoline Hill," or up the "*Sacra via,*" in every imitation of their Scythian ancestors, as they once scudded bare-backed along the streets and ways of ancient Rome.

Occasionally, at Marietta, the besieged New Englanders could see from the blockhouse port-holes, smoke on a far-off hill, which they hoped for a moment might be the fore-running signal of assistance looming up from the camp-fires of coming friends, but as it died away, and the mist cleared off, they only saw the savages gathered together, dancing around a fire, in the midst of which was a poor, naked prisoner, caught in some border settler's cabin; and, being tied to a stake, was suffering the slow torture, and whose screams for pity, mercy, and life, could be heard in Campus Martius and Fort Harmar, but without the power of any one there to assist or save him from the fiery death.

Such were the scenes enacted around the city first planted on the Muskingum. Its off-shoots at Belpre, Waterford, and Big Bottom, witnessed similar tragedies throughout these terrible years of misfortune and calamity to the American arms, and border families.

ADVENTURES OF HAMILTON (KERR) CARR, THE INDIAN FIGHTER.

He was born in Pennsylvania, of Irish parents, came to Wheeling when a young man, learned Indian fighting with the Wetzells, removed to Washington County in 1787, and during the Indian wars killed many Indians.

On one occasion, he and Lewis Wetzell, on Wheeling Creek, trailed a party of Indians to their camp, found them sitting around their fire at daylight, and one fellow sitting on a log eating, fell over dead from Kerr's bullet, while Wetzell mortally wounded another. The balance fled, and the fighters went home with one scalp.

In 1784, he was out trapping with Lewis and George Wetzell and John Greene, at the mouth of the Muskingum, and in a day or two missed some of their traps. Suspecting Indians about, they pushed up the Ohio a short distance in a canoe, when George Wetzell was shot dead, and Kerr wounded by Indians on the bank. Greene, who was in the woods, hearing firing, came to the river bank, and when near it, saw an Indian behind a tree loading. He raised his piece, fired, and the Indian dropped down the bank dead. The other Indians hearing the report rushed to where Greene was. Seeing ten or twelve, he jumped into the river, and buried his body under the water among the branches of a dead tree. The Indians came upon the trunk of the tree, peering for him. He saw them but kept his face hid among the leaves, when the Indians failing to find him moved off. He remained in the water until night, then made his escape up the river, and after three days overtook Kerr's party in the canoe, twenty-five miles above the site of Marietta. Kerr's wound kept him at home several months.

In 1785, Kerr and two others went up the Ohio spearing fish. A dozen Indians fired at them, when one man in the boat, named Mills, fell as dead into the bottom of the boat. Kerr and his companion also dropped down, when the Indians rushed into the water to catch the canoe and scalp them. Kerr kept them off with his fish-spear until the canoe got into deep water, when they escaped to Wheeling, and Mills recovered, although he had a dozen wounds on his body. The party had no rifles along, and their escape from the tomahawk was attributed to Kerr's coolness in the moment of danger.

In 1786 he was out with Isaac Williams and a German, at Grave Creek, and espied three Indians in a canoe, and a fourth swimming a horse across the Ohio. Kerr shot the Indian in the stern of the canoe, Williams shot the one in front, when the German, handing Kerr his rifle, the third Indian in the boat was shot and fell into the water, but hung on to the side of the canoe. Kerr reloaded, and was about to fire at a man lying in the bottom of the boat, but discovering him to be a white prisoner, shouted to him to knock off the Indian clinging to the boat. Meanwhile, Kerr shot at the Indian on the horse, who jumped off and swam for the canoe. The white man escaped out of the boat, the Indian got in, crossed to the other shore, and, with a shout of defiance at Kerr, fled into the woods on the back of the captive horse he had been riding, and which had gained the other shore just as he did.

From 1787 to 1791, Kerr was employed as a hunter to furnish the garrison at Fort Harmar with buffalo meat and venison, and to the close of the war he was engaged in every hazardous enterprise, killing several Indians in his combats. After the war closed, he married and settled down as a farmer in Washington County, where he died an old man, much esteemed, leaving numerous descendants, who reside in southeastern Ohio.

LEGEND OF LOUISA ST. CLAIR, THE GOVERNOR'S DAUGHTER.

When General St. Clair came to Marietta, in 1788, as governor of the North-west Territory, he left his family at home in Westmoreland County, Pennsylvania. Louisa, a daughter of eighteen years, educated at Philadelphia, and his son Arthur, came out soon after on a visit, and in 1790 the family moved out, except Mrs. St. Clair, who remained at home some time longer.

The proposed Indian treaty at Duncan's falls, in 1788, being postponed and adjourned to Fort Harmar, the Indians prepared for peace or war, and were hostile to holding a convention to adjust peace measures under the guns of Harmar, and Campus Martius.

Brandt, son of the Six Nation's chief of that name, came down the Tuscarawas and Muskingum trail, with two hundred warriors, camped at Duncan's falls, nine miles below Zanesville, and informed Governor St. Clair, by runner, that they desired the treaty preliminaries to be fixed there.

The governor suspected a plot to get him to the falls, and abduct him, yet nothing had transpired of that import. He sent Brandt's runner back with word that he would soon answer by a ranger. Hamilton Kerr was dispatched to Duncan's falls to reconnoiter, and deliver St. Clair's letter.

A short distance above Waterford, Kerr saw tracks, and keeping the river in sight, crept on a bluff, and raised to his feet, when hearing the laugh of a woman, he came down to the trail, and saw Louisa St. Clair on a pony, dressed Indian style, with a short rifle slung to her body. Stupefied with amazement, the ranger lost his speech, well knowing Louisa, who was the bravest and boldest girl of all at the fort. She had left without knowledge of any one, and calling "Ham"—as he was known by that name—to his senses, told him she was going to Duncan's falls to see Brandt. Expostulation on his part only made her laugh the louder, and she twitted him on his comical dress, head turbaned with red handkerchief, hunting shirt, but no trowsers, the breech-clout taking their place. Taking her pony by the head, he led it up the trail, and at night they suppered on dried deer meat from Ham's pouch; the pony was tied, and Louisa sat against a tree and slept, rifle in hand, while Ham watched her. Next morning they pursued their way, and finally came in sight of the Indian camp. She then took her father's letter from the ranger, and telling him to hide and await her return, dashed off on her pony, and was soon a prisoner. She asked for Brandt, who appeared in war panoply, but was abashed at her gaze. She handed him the letter, remarking that they had met before, he as a student on a visit from college, to Philadelphia, and she as the daughter of General St. Clair, at school. He bowed; being educated, read the letter and became excited. Louisa perceiving this, said she had risked her life to see him, and asked for a guard back to Marietta. Brandt told her he guarded the brave, and would accompany her home. In the evening of the third day they arrived with Ham Kerr at the fort, where she introduced Brandt to her father, relating the incidents. After some hours, he was escorted out of the lines, returned to the falls, and went up the valley with his warriors without a treaty, but crazed in love with Louisa St. Clair.

In January, 1789, he returned, took no part in the Fort Harmar treaty, was at the feast, and asked St. Clair in vain for his daughter's hand.

In the fall of 1791, Brandt led the Chippewas for a time during the battle at St. Clair's defeat, and told his warriors to shoot the general's horse, but not him. St. Clair had four horses shot under him, and as many bullet-holes in his clothes, but escaped unhurt. Louisa's beauty saved her father's life, but sacrificed his fame; and after his downfall she left Marietta with him and the family, loaded down with sorrow for life.

Professor Hildreth thus describes Louisa at Marietta in 1791:

"Louisa was a healthy, vigorous girl, full of life and activity, fond of a frolic, and ready to draw amusement from all and everything around her. She was a fine equestrienne, and would mount the most wild and spirited horse without fear, managing him with ease and gracefulness, dashing through the open woodlands around Campus Martius at full gallop, leaping over logs or any obstruction that fell in her way. She was one of the most expert skaters in the garrison. She was also an expert huntress. Of the rifle she was a perfect mistress, loading and firing with the accuracy of a backwoodsman, killing a squirrel from the highest tree, or cutting off the head of a partridge with wonderful precision. She was fond of roaming in the woods, and often went out alone into the forest near Marietta, fearless of the savages that occasionally lurked in the vicinity. She was as active on foot as on horseback, and could walk with the rapidity of a ranger for miles. Her manners were refined, her person beautiful, with highly cultivated intellectual powers, having been educated with much care at Philadelphia. After the war she returned to her early home amidst the romantic glens of the Legonier valley."

Had St. Clair given his daughter to young Brandt, the alliance would have averted war. His father, Joseph Brandt, highly educated and the most powerful chief of the time, was the originator of the western confederation of Indians in 1786. It is reasonable, therefore, to suppose that had a family connection existed in 1789 with the governor of the North-west territory, neither Harmar or St. Clair would have suffered defeat in 1791, nor would Anthony Wayne have had to whip the confederated nations in 1794.

JOE ROGERS, THE RANGER—A DREAM FORETELLS HIS DEATH.

Joseph Rogers, a Pennsylvanian, who had served in Morgan's rifle corps in the revolution, came to Marietta soon after its settlement to seek a home. In 1791, as the Indian war commenced, he and Edward Henderson were detailed to scout up the Muskingum. On the 13th of March, at night, they were returning to the fort, when two Indians rose and fired, hitting Rogers in the breast, and killing him, within a mile of the fort. They then pursued Henderson down a hill, and at the bottom he met two more Indians who fired, one ball passing through his collar, and the other through a handkerchief bound on his head, ranger fashion. Making a short turn, he eluded his pursuers, reached the garrison, and gave the alarm, when every man's duty was to repair to his post, and the women to the blockhouse. Great consternation prevailed. Every one rushed to the blockhouse, one man carrying his papers, another his arms, a woman her bed and child, and an old gunsmith with his leather apron filled with tools and some smoking tobacco, another woman had a tea-pot, another the Bible, and so on; when all were in, an old mother was missing. They sent for her, and found her fixing up things and sweeping the floor, she telling them she could not think of leaving her house, "even if the Injuns were coming to scalp her," until all was rid up and things in their place. It turned out in the morning that the Indians had retreated. The night before Rogers was shot, he dreamed that he would next day take a scalp or lose one, and on going out in the morning was so dejected that they offered to send a ranger in his place, but he said a dream could not scare him from his duty. For not heeding the dream, Joe Rogers lost his life on the Muskingum.

LEGEND OF A CREDIT MOBILIER AND LOUIS PHILIPPE ON THE MUSKINGUM.

In the year 1790, four hundred French emigrants landed at Marietta from France—principally laborers, artisans, broken gentlemen, and several of royal blood—a marquis, count, &c.; mostly poor, but a few wealthy. They had came to America just as the French revolution was commencing. They were fraudulently induced to come by representations made in Paris, on the part of the Scioto Land Company's agent, who was a brother of Joel Barlow, United States Minister at Paris. The agent had taken their money for land, when in fact the company had no title to land. Finally they settled, and built up Gallipolis, where descendants yet reside. Congress donated them twenty thousand acres of public lands.

Louis Philippe joined the French revolution in that same year of 1790, as a Jacobin (red republican), but having assisted two of his sisters, who had become odious to the government, to escape, he was denounced, fled to the continent, wandered for some time as an exile, came to Philadelphia in 1796, and with two brothers—the Duke de Montpensier and Count Beaujolais—traveled over the United

States, returned to Europe in 1800, became king in 1830, was deposed in 1848, and died an exile in England, in 1850.

While in the United States he visited the west, stopped, as is said, at Coshocton, Zanesville, Marietta, and Gallipolis. No one ever knew exactly his business in traversing the valleys of the Muskingum, but General Cass says that when he was United States Minister at Paris, the king alluded once in conversation to John McIntyre's hotel at Zanesville, and told Cass how well he had been treated there.

There is a tradition that the French marquis who came to Marietta with the four hundred, and who returned to France in 1791, was a blood relation of Philippe, and held valuable papers pertaining to the family interests, which he lost at Marietta, and that Louis's visit to the Muskingum was to find some clue thereto. In the search he was fascinated by one of his countrywomen, among the Gallipolis emigrants—where, is not known—and contracted with her a "left-handed" marriage; the issue of which, under the mother's name, grew to manhood on the Ohio and Muskingum, went to Paris, and in the revolution of 1830 took part in elevating his father to the throne; and after whose fall he returned to the United States, and died at New Orleans, where he disclosed these facts.

The statement that Louis Philippe was once in Coshocton rests upon the fact that when George W. Silliman, attorney at law, Coshocton, and grandson of Major Cass, was bearer of dispatches to the French government, the king told him that he once went to a point in the Northwest Territory, where two rivers came together, and gave such a description of the place, and the landlord of the tavern (Colonel Williams), as to make it pretty certain that this was the place. Colonel Williams, being afterward spoken to on the subject, said that Louis Philippe "had been at his house, and had been rather roughly treated."

Tradition says that the rough treatment was this: He had an altercation with the tavern-keeper, ending in his telling Williams that he was heir to the French throne, and would not, as the coming sovereign, condescend to bandy words with a backwoods plebeian. Williams said in reply, that here in this backwoods of America there were no plebeians; "We are all sovereigns here," said he, "and I'll show you our power," and suiting the action to the word, he kicked Louis Philippe out of the house; at which the "sovereigns," loitering around the tavern, gave three cheers.

It is a historical fact that Louis Philippe and two brothers landed in Philadelphia, October 21, 1796, made a tour of the United States, and sailed from New York for England, where they arrived in January, 1800. Hence, if Colonel Williams did not keep tavern in Coshocton before the year 1800, he kicked some other "sovereign" out of his house.

THE LAST STRUGGLE TO DRIVE THE WHITES FROM OHIO—WAYNE'S VICTORY.

In the spring and summer of 1792, every effort was made by the government that could be conceived, to get the Indian tribes together and conclude a peace. At the instigation of British emissaries they refused to meet, unless assured in advance that the Ohio should be the boundary in future treaties. This would have struck Marietta, the Muskingum, Tuscarawas, and all the Ohio valleys from the map of civilization, and lost to the Ohio Company a million acres bought from Congress at five shillings per acre.

Putnam and the pioneers were therefore deeply interested in the colony. Heckewelder could not survive, if his mission ruins on the Tuscarawas were to be so soon turned over to the wild successors of the mound builders. Yet, strange as the fact was, there were distinguished men in the east willing to make the Ohio the boundary line. They feared the depopulation of the old, and the building up of new States in the west, to take from them the balance of political power.

At length, in September, 1792, General Putnam and John Heckewelder appeared on the Wabash; met the Potawatomies, Wachtenaws, Kickapoos and smaller tribes, and concluded a treaty. This was the first giving way of the Indian barrier. That winter the Shawanese, Six Nations, Wyandots, and Delawares agreed to hold a grand council on the Maumee, which took place in early summer of 1793. The government sent its agents to the mouth of Detroit River to be ready to treat. The Indian council, finding that they could not obtain the Ohio as a boundary line, refused to treat on any other line, broke up, and all the nations prepared for war again. At this council the treaties of Fort McIntosh and Harmar were repudiated as fraudulent, and the gifts proffered by the government were spurned by the Indians with contempt. Their fiat had gone forth: "No white man shall plant corn in Ohio."

After contemplating the probable loss, not only of their lives, but of their million acres, the prayers for help of the pioneer women, and the groans of their anguished husbands, were heard over the Blue Ridge, and above the Alleghanies, and far up into the New England mountains, then a burst of indignation arose, and "Mad Anthony" was ordered from the east to the rescue of the pioneers. He came crushing through the forests like a behemoth.

He left Fort Washington—now Cincinnati—with his legion in October, 1793. He, too, went north-west on Harmar's and St. Clair's trails, building defenses as he moved on. At Greenville, Darke County, he wintered and drilled his men. In June, 1794, he camped on St. Clair's battlefield, and buried the bones of six hundred soldiers, bleaching there since 1791. Here the confederated tribes disputed Wayne's further progress. Being reinforced by eleven hundred Kentuckians, he soon routed the savages, and pushed on to the headquarters of the tribes at the junction of the Auglaize and Maumee rivers. They retreated along the

Maumee forty miles to the rapids, where there was a British fort. Here they prepared for battle. Wayne offered peace without a fight, in case they gave up the Ohio River as a boundary. A portion of the chiefs desired to do so, but the remainder under British influence refused. On the 20th of August he moved on the enemy, who again retreated a short distance and fought him. His whole force being brought into action soon routed them in every direction, leaving the battle-ground strewn with dead Indians, and British soldiers in disguise. General Wayne's loss was thirty-three killed, and one hundred wounded. The Indians in the battle numbered fourteen hundred, while the main body were not in action, being some two miles off, but hearing of the defeat they all scattered to their homes, and Wayne laid waste their towns and corn-fields for fifty miles, thus ending the war.

In this battle were Simon Girty, Elliott, and McKee, who had, ever since their success in breaking up the missions on the Tuscarawas, been the main counsellors and leaders among the Shawanese, Wyandots, and Delawares, and all the time assisted by the British garrisons in the region of the Sandusky and Detroit.

The net result of the Wayne campaign was a treaty of peace, which was made at the present Greenville, Darke County, Ohio, in the following August (1795), between the government, represented by General Wayne, and the Shawanese, Delawares, Wyandots, Ottawas, Pottawatomies, Miamis, and other smaller tribes, at which about two-thirds of the present State of Ohio was ceded to the United States.

The old residenters of the Tuscarawas and Muskingum valleys—the Delawares and Shawanese—bore a conspicuous part in the fore-front of Wayne's war—as they had in all previous wars—to prevent the whites from making homes in these two valleys, so full of romance, so full of tragedies, and so full of the ruins of God's works.

THE WANDERING EXILE RETURNS TO THE VALLEY, FOUNDS GOSHEN, AND DIES IN HIS TRACKS—THE LAST OF THE MISSIONS AND RED MEN.

Zeisberger had been driven away from the valleys in September, 1781, and until October, 1798, a period of seventeen years, he had no real resting place on the earth. What the motive was, of an All-wise and Omnipotent God, in subjecting this holy man to seventeen years of persecution and privation, it is not for man to premise; but on this pious man's return, his frail canoes coasted down the lakes in safety to the Cuyahoga; thence they paddled up that river and down the Tuscarawas to their old home, consuming fifty-one days in the journey, amid perils of the elements above, perils of the waters below, and perils of the land around; all the way some dangerous red light ahead—yet without a serious accident they landed in sight of the old ruins; they laid out Goshen, they proceeded anew to erect a chapel—which they dedicated on Christmas day, 1798, to that same God who had smote Job of old and Zeisberger alike.

One of the first persons baptised at Goshen was the widow of Captain White Eyes; next came a chief of the Delawares, who had succeeded Captain Pipe, and who bore a message from the Delawares on White River, in Indiana, asking that missionaries be sent from Goshen to settle there. Two missionaries and several Christian Indians were sent from Goshen in 1801, and in a short time thereafter Joshua and Ann Charity, aged Indians from Goshen, were denounced by an Indian prophet as witches, and sentenced to be burned, which was done by placing the victims upon a large pile of wood, binding them and tomahawking them; after which, setting fire to the pile, the Indians danced around it until all were consumed—believing that each victim thus sacrificed relieved the tribe of a witch.

This Indian, Joshua, who was sacrificed as a witch, had lost two daughters at the Gnadenhutten massacre in 1782.

Congress having stipulated in its grant of land that all the former inhabitants of the three missions, and their descendants, as well as Killbuck, White Eyes, and their descendants, should have land rent free in these four thousand acre tracts, and all land not thus needed to be let out to white settlers.

In May, 1799, Paul Greer, Peter Edmonds, Ezra and Peter Warner, Jacob Bush, and two others, from Pennsylvania, made settlements, and in the following fall came David and Dorcas Peter, from Bethlehem, being the first white settlers in Tuscarawas County, excepting Heckewelder, Zeisberger, and their co-missionaries.

In November, 1802, twelve Delaware chiefs, on their way to Washington to see Pesident Jefferson, stopped and spent some time with Zeisberger, at Goshen.

In 1803, Loskiel, the great historian of the missions, visited and remained some time at Goshen.

In 1805, the white settlers had so multiplied that a Moravian church was built at a new station near what is now lock numbered seventeen, on the west side of the river, and the same was dedicated by Zeisberger in presence of two hundred people, and called Beersheba.

During this period, missions in other parts of the country becoming demoralized, Zeisberger's health began to fail under the accumulation of his sorrows, and his hearing being impaired, and his eyesight failing, and the infirmities of old age distressing him, he prepared for death, which did not overtake him until 1808, he, however, wishing to be dead.

In 1808, about forty Monsey Indians, heathens, came to Goshen, and in a short time a second party came. Shortly thereafter a boat came up the river, laden with rum, which these Indians getting possession of, carried on such a series of debaucheries around Goshen that the missionaries and their converts fled to the hills for safety, while the white settlers grasped their rifles in self-protection and that of the mission property; Zeisberger aroused himself, called all the Indians together, pointed out the vicious, and ordered them to leave Goshen forever, which a portion of them did, the others remaining.

In October, Rev. Mr. Espick, also a physician, who had settled at New Philadelphia, was called to Goshen to attend Zeisberger, who died on the 17th day of November following, after a service of sixty-two years at various missions. His wife died in ten months after him. In two years after Gelellemund, *alias* Killbuck, finished his career at Goshen.

The war of 1812 having commenced, Goshen declined, and was finally abandoned as a mission in 1824, and its Indians retired to the far west. Thus ended the second advent of the missionaries and the red men in the valleys.

No glittering marble column marks the spot where Zeisberger lies, but a small square block of stone, surmounted with a marble slab, on which is etched his name—all that remains to denote the only place of rest this first and truly pious man ever had in the valley.

His mission, founded at Fairfield, Canada, in 1792, still survives, and it is in tradition that for many years after Zeisberger's death, Indian converts from Fairfield made pilgrimages to Goshen, to clean up his grave and keep green the grass thereon. In 1872, Rev. Reinke, a missionary from Fairfield, with four Indians, William Stonefish, James Snake, Joel Snake, Joshua Jacobs—one of whom was a descendant of a convert slaughtered at the massacre—and also the venerable David Knisely, Rev. E. P. Jacobs, Methodist minister, Rev. Wilhelm, Lutheran minister, John Judy, Esq., and others, visited the graves of Zeisberger and Edwards at Goshen, and assembling around the graves, sung the same hymn that had been translated by Zeisberger for the Indians, and which had been sung sixty-four years before, on the same spot, at the funeral of David Zeisberger himself. These four Indians then visited Schoenbrunn, but hunted in vain for the grave-yard of their convert ancestors, from thirty to forty of whom had been buried there from 1772 to 1779. The spot was pointed out, but the converts' bones had been fertilizing a white man's field for a third of a century. These poor Indians wept at the sight, then shaking from their feet the dust of the valley, departed, never to return again.

FURTHER PUBLIC SERVICES OF PUTNAM AND HECKEWELDER—THEIR DEATHS.

After the return of peace, 1795, General Putnam established a line of packets on the Ohio, from Wheeling to Marietta, surveyed a national road from Wheeling west through the Muskingum County, of to-day, and thus opened up highways by which new settlers reached the valleys in great numbers.

He was, in 1796, appointed surveyor-general of the United States, and directed surveys of one hundred and seventy-four townships, into subdivisions for entry under military warrants and other grants. He came to the Tuscarawas and directed the Schoenbrunn, Gnadenhutten, and Salem tracts, of four thousand each, to be laid off and subdivided into lots, for the use of converted Indians, and for lease to white settlers.

General Putnam, before closing his duties as surveyor-general, visited and slept with Zeisberger at Goshen, then named the little island in the river, after his revered friend, and returned to his home at Marietta, where he was chosen, in 1802, to represent Washington County in the convention to form the first constitution for the State of Ohio, which was completed in thirty days. Being opposed, in 1800, to the election of Thomas Jefferson as president, he retired, after his service in the convention, to private life, and devoted his energies to the encouragement of public improvements, education, and religion, until 1824, when he died, at the age of eighty-six years. He was son of Elisha Putnam; who was son of Edward Putnam—a grandson of John Putnam—who came to America in 1634, and was the founder of the Putnam family on this continent, and whose descendants in the male line numbered one hundred and thirty-four, prior to the birth of General Rufus Putnam, in 1738.

After the return of peace, Heckewelder proceeded to Bethlehem, Pennsylvania, and urged the Pennsylvanians to come and take up homes on the Tuscarawas. He had some years before ceased his functions as a missionary, and became agent for leasing the lands donated in trust to the society, and in due time emigration set into the valley, dotting it over with cabins and clearings of settlers. He had, in 1797, with some emigrants, gathered together the bones of the murdered Indians at Gnadenhutten, and buried the same where the monument now stands. He took up his home there, and entered four thousand acres of land for other parties. He stood at the bedside of Zeisberger when he died, in 1808, at Goshen, and became, on the organization of Tuscarawas County, an associate judge of the court of common pleas. He remained in the valley in which he had lived such an eventful life, until it was settled with an active, vigorous race of white men, and after that returned to Bethlehem, Pennsylvania, where he died, in 1823, wanting eleven months of the age of four score years. Thus ended the careers of these two remarkable men, within a year of each other. They well deserve a monument, as the founders of Ohio.

AN ASSASSIN MAKES THREE ATTEMPTS TO KILL HECKEWELDER.

The following incident occurred while Heckewelder was in charge of the mission at Gnadenhutten, during the American revolution, after the Wyandots had joined the British:

Some Wyandots, returning from the white settlements in Virginia with a prisoner, rested at Gnadenhutten. Among their horses was one that had been stolen from the mission a year before, and which belonged to Heckewelder. The leader of the Wyandots was prevailed on to sell the prisoner to the missionary, Heckewelder, and give up the horse, on the theory that it was a crime to hold stolen property, knowing the fact. He returned with his squad to Sandusky, where his companions told on him. He was ordered by the Indian council to return to Gnadenhutten and get the horse, or the scalp of its owner—the Indians in council adjudging the horse to have been a lawful prize in war when captured in Virginia. A short time after, as Heckewelder was going from Gnadenhutten to Salem, he was shot at from behind a log. In a few days he was traveling the same road, but had two Delaware guides, who discovered an Indian in a tree fork, leveling his gun at the missionary. They frustrated his attempt to shoot. In a few nights the same Indian entered Heckewelder's house with intent to murder him, but he was seized, and when asked his motive for wanting to kill Heckewelder, declared that it was he who had given up Heckewelder's horse, and he was sent back from Sandusky to get the horse, or Heckewelder's scalp. It is not stated in the history of Gnadenhutten what became of the assassin, but he never got back to Sandusky. The white prisoner bought by Heckewelder, and whose life was thereby saved, was sent to Fort Pitt, from whence he reached his home.

AARON BURR AND THE BLENNERHASSETS AT MARIETTA—A BALL IN EARLY TIMES.

Connected with Marietta history is that of Aaron Burr, Harman Blennerhasset, and Margaret, his wife. Burr had honored his country by his military services in the war of independence, and was compensated by being nominated for Vice-President of the United States; having, in the presidential poll, received an equal vote on the same ticket with Thomas Jefferson, the House of Representatives had thrust upon it the duty of electing President and Vice-President. Jefferson succeeded to the first, and Burr to the second, office. His ambition was to be President—failing which he conceived a project of erecting a western republic upon the ruins of Mexico, and becoming president thereof. He had with him many discontented officers, who had been retired to private life poor, at the close of the revolution, and they in turn had soldiers of their old commands, who, having lost their time and property in the war, were ready for any emergency.

The founders of Marietta were in part retired officers, discontented, like those who joined Burr; but instead of overturning Mexico, and recuperating their finances by melting into money the little golden virgins and crosses of the Spanish churches, they chose the plan of buying land on the Ohio, setting up a State government, and selling farms to emigrants at a profit. Still, Burr looked to old friends in Marietta for help and sympathy. Among others, he became acquainted with Harman Blennerhasset and his accomplished wife. Blennerhasset was an educated Irish gentleman, who had built a fantastic mansion on one of Black Hoof's islands in the Ohio, nine miles below Marietta, where he was enjoying a quiet and retired life, in the midst of a score of hilarious good fellows, who were drinking his mountain dew, and entertaining him with "Teddy O'Rourke," and the "Exile of Erin."

Madame Blennerhasset had an outside estate of her own, and being an educated lady, she soon tired of hearing nothing but game and fish, dog and horse talk; hence she wished very often that the island would sink, or Buckshanoth and his warriors come back to the Ohio with their scalping knives.

Burr's project delighted Blennerhasset, and his powers of mind entranced the lady. The island home soon became a commissariat for needy adventurers, while Burr flitted about to Marietta, Chillicothe, Cincinnati, &c., making friends.

In October, Burr sent Blennerhasset to accompany ex-Govenor Alston, of South Carolina, and his wife, Theodosia, Burr's daughter, to Lexington, Louisville, and other down the river towns, leaving Mrs. Blennerhasset at home to direct its management.

Burr had studied at a glance the people he was propitiating and winning over. He knew that the men already on the island would be faithful to him as long as their soup lasted, and the hostess knew well how to make it, hence her place for the time being was at home.

Up at Marietta he contracted with the ship carpenters for fifteen large boats, costing several thousand dollars, and that fact held the New Englanders' heads "level." On their return to the island, Governor Alston and wife were, with Mrs. Blennerhasset and her husband, and Burr, all invited to a ball at Marietta. As the dancing proceeded, and the wine went round, so did Burr; and in a short time he counteracted all the gossip touching himself. It was voted a lie by all, especially the unmarried ladies—Burr being then a widower—and the wives of all who wished Marietta to become a great commercial ship building center, although a thousand miles from the sea.

To put an effectual quietus on all suspicions, Burr, observing Théodosia and Madame Blennerhasset face to face in conversation, clasped his daughter, who had a national reputation for all that was good and virtuous in woman, and imprinted a kiss, while he gave his other arm to Mrs. Blennerhasset, exclaiming as he pressed both, "Man rules the world, and woman man." Then passing round the whirling crowd, he sought two matrons of Marietta at a window, with their puritan eyes gazing at him. But Aaron Burr never shrunk from the gaze of woman, and, making a gracious bow, comprehending at a glance their talk to be about him, he asked each if she had sons. Learning that such was the fact, he added that he had high places for the sons of *courageous mothers*, and further desired to know their wishes. These spartan pioneer women, who had unflinchingly looked out of Campus Martius at Indian war in all its horrors for five years, were just as open to flattery as the sex the world over. They bowed at the words "courageous mothers." Burr passed on through the throng, made the acquaintance of every one, and when the ball closed that night he had but one opponent, and she was a spinster of the post tertiary period, who invidiously remarked that the ex-president of the United States had conquered Marietta with a daughter on one arm and a Pompadour on the other.

On the day of the ball there had been a military training at Marietta, which, in those early times, brought a great crowd to the town. Burr, from his revolutionary experience, was master of the art of war, and he drilled the militia on this occasion so successfully, that it was said he added five hundred recruits to his expedition, having not less than five thousand men in all.

His enemies began to work. The papers soon sounded the alarm of a disunion plot, of which it was hinted Burr was leader. In November, he was summoned into court at Frankfort to answer charges, but no proof being adduced to implicate him in any measure hostile to the Union, he was discharged, and a ball given in his honor. He then completed arrangements for Blennerhasset and his party, to go down the Ohio on the fifteen boats building at Marietta, to meet Burr at the mouth of the Cumberland, and there Burr to take command, and proceed down the Mississippi in quest of "fortune and honor." In the meantime, President Jefferson issued a proclamation, based upon dispatches sent him by General Wilkinson, in command of United States forces at New Orleans, cautioning the people against "unlawful enterprises in the western States."

Blennerhasset came back to his island home, and there unwittingly fell in with a United States detective, who avowed himself one of "Burr's men," and who, after drawing information out of Blennerhasset, proceeded to Marietta, and thence to Chillicothe, and laid all before the Governor of Ohio, who sent a secret message to the Ohio Legislature, then in session, and that body at once passed necessary laws in the premises. The militia were called out, marched to Marietta, captured the fifteen boats, and patrolled the Ohio River. A party proceeded to the island to arrest Blennerhasset, but he and forty companions left in the night for down the river, with directions for Mrs. Blennerhasset to follow soon. She went to Marietta, and while absent, the militia sacked the island home.

Burr was at Nashville—and ignorant of the fact that General Wilkinson had betrayed and exposed him—proceeded on with his flotilla down the Mississippi until near Natchez, where the Governor of Mississippi and militia caused him to surrender. After examination his men were discharged, and Burr finding too many enemies in front, fled into the wilderness. Blennerhasset, on his return homeward, was arrested for treason, and committed to jail in Kentucky. Colonel, afterward General Gaines, arrested Burr in Alabama, who gave bond to appear at Richmond, Virginia, on the 23d of May, 1807, and stand trial for treason. Both he and Blennerhasset were indicted for treason, tried, and acquitted.

Burr retired to England—was expelled from that country, and took up his residence in Sweden. In 1809, he went to Paris, became very poor, returned to New York, where he practiced law. He died in 1833.

Blennerhasset and his wife returned to Marietta, but finding his island home a waste, removed to Mississippi, bought a thousand acre cotton plantation, which completed his ruin, by reason of the embargo on cotton.

These two men caused more sensation, had warmer friends, and more vindictive enemies than any two men of their day. Both became outcasts, though no crime was proven against either. Blennerhasset died on the island of Guernsey in 1822. His wife unsuccessfully demanded damages against the government, and died in New York in 1842, not in want—as some writers have declared—of means or friends, but possessed of both to a moderate extent.

Time, in making all things even, developed the fact that the scandal touching her and Burr's secret intimacy was fictitious, and gotten up by his enemies to destroy his influence among the people. She died a martyr "to state craft."

CHAPTER XII.

THE LAST INDIAN WAR—DEATH OF TECUMSEH.

The impressment of American naturalized citizens on the high seas by British orders, and British intrigues among the frontier Indians, brought on the war of 1812, and in which the white settlers of the Tuscarawas and Muskingum valleys bore an honorable part. But it is not the province of this work to detail other than the Indian incidents of that war.

General Harrison commanded in the north-west, where the prophet, Tecumseh, and his brother, were instigating the Shawanese, Delawares, and other tribes, to engage in war for the recovery of the lands lost by the Indians at the Wayne treaty of 1795. Those of the Indian tribes who opposed his machinations, or favored the Americans, he had burned as witches as fast as caught by his spies.

The atrocities of the prophet finally caused General Harrison to issue and send a "speech" to the Shawanese chiefs, sharply remonstrating against these actions. About this time the British became very active with the Indians, and it soon came to the notice of the Americans. Early in 1808, large numbers of Indians congregated in the vicinity of Fort Wayne, on the Maumee, in obedience to a summons from the prophet. In the following summer the prophet removed to a place called Tippecanoe, on the upper waters of the Wabash, where he was soon surrounded by his deluded followers. Here he remained until 1810, when

Governor Harrison received positive information that the prophet and Tecumseh were inciting the Indians to open a war with the Americans. Traders arriving at Vincennes from the upper country confirmed these reports, and asserted that not less than a thousand warriors were assembled under Tecumseh and the prophet. The government made preparations for a war, but in order to prevent it called upon Tecumseh to meet the governor at Vincennes for a peace conference. Accordingly, in July, 1811, Tecumseh, with three hundred of his warriors, came to Vincennes. Governor Harrison told the Indians what he knew concerning their warlike preparations, and warned them against precipitating a war. Tecumseh boldly denied all, and solemnly pledged the governor that he would return in eighteen days, when he would "wash away all these bad stories." Tecumseh failed to come on the appointed day, but on the 27th of July he appeared with his three hundred warriors, and acted in quite a bold and defiant manner. The conference took place in the presence of the troops and the Indians, who were called out to protect their respective leaders in case of foul play from the opposite side. After several speeches on either side, Tecumseh proposed to let matters rest while he visited the southern tribes to learn their desires. So the meeting broke up without a definite understanding, and Tecumseh went down the Wabash on his proposed visit.

This was his last appearance before the commencement of hostilities. In the meantime the mysterious conduct of the Indians had excited and thoroughly aroused the whites. It is not proposed to detail here the movements of the Indians or the government troops, which culminated in the memorable battle of Tippecanoe, which took place on the 7th of November, 1811, resulting in the defeat of the prophet and his force. Soon after the battle Tecumseh returned from his southern trip, and was much surprised and chagrined at the result of the conflict. He now proposed to Governor

Harrison to be allowed to proceed to Washington, but was not encouraged, and the journey was at once abandoned.

Tecumseh and his brother now applied themselves with all their energy and cunning toward fomenting a general war against the Americans, in which they were abetted and encouraged by the British on the Canada frontier. Matters finally assumed a serious phase, and the ball was opened by the forcible abduction of a party of peacefully disposed Wyandots by a detachment of British and Shawanese, accompanied by Tecumseh, Elliott, and McKee. Sometime afterward a deputation of Indians, with the consent of Governor Harrison, went into the British camps to procure the release and return of all the Indians there who desired to return to their own country. The Wyandots who were held by the British secretly promised the deputation that they would all desert to the Americans at the first opportunity, which they did.

Tecumseh, having returned from a conference with the British agents, Elliott and McKee, sent a message to the prophet to send his women and children westward, and march to attack Vincennes with all the warriors he could command, and that he, Tecumseh, would join him ere long.

In June, 1812, war was declared against England by the United States. Northern Ohio, Lake Erie, Michigan, and Canada comprised the principal theater of the war in the West; and among the noteworthy events were Colonel Croghan's gallant defense of Fort Stephenson, on the present site of Fremont, Ohio; Perry's victory on Lake Erie; Hull's surrender at Detroit; the complete defeat of the British under Proctor, and the Indians under Tecumseh, by General Harrison's army, on the river Thames, in Canada, and the gallant defense of New Orleans by General Jackson.

Tecumseh was engaged in all the fights in the north-west, and at the decisive battle of the Thames he commanded the right wing of the allied British and Indian forces. When the retreat commenced Tecumseh fiercely exerted himself to stem the tide of defeat. And this was his last fight. Refusing to run with the cowardly British, he renewed the contest, and sprang to the front of his savages, and by his appeals encouraged many to stand by him. Finally, the Indians gave way and retreated, when it was found that their brave leader was killed, and around him lay a score of his braves who fell at his side. The old story that Tecumseh was shot by Colonel R. M. Johnson, who commanded the Kentucky troops, has never been definitely settled. He fell in front of where Colonel Johnson was wounded, and that is all that is positively known on the subject. But the Indians soon abandoned all hope of recovering their old valleys. At the close of the war the English granted the family of Tecumseh a pension, as also the prophet, who lived several years afterward. Tecumseh was about forty-five years old when he was killed.

The war on the lakes resulted as disastrously to the British navy as it had to the British army on land, and before the battle of New Orleans was fought, a treaty of peace was signed in December, 1814, between the two governments, but the fact not being known at New Orleans, Packenham moved upon Jackson's army, and was demolished January 8, 1815.

The counties of Tuscarawas and Muskingum furnished in all about five hundred men for the war, and lost but about thirty.

ACCOUNT OF THE ELLIOTT FAMILY OF FIGHTERS.

Colonel Robert Elliott came from Pennsylvania, near the Maryland line. He had been twice married; the last time to a lady named Hughes, by whom he had a daughter, who became the wife of General Irvine, commandant at Fort Pitt; he also had three sons, William, Wilson, and Jesse D. Elliott. The first emigrated to Canada; the second commanded an Ohio company, from Trumbull County, at the seige of Fort Meigs, in the war of 1812; the third was second in command of Perry's fleet on Lake Erie, and his ship coming into action at the opportune moment, contributed to win the victory, Perry's flag-ship having become disabled, and he having to go aboard of Elliott's ship. It is a family legend that William and Wilson Elliott personally encountered each other in a hand to hand fight at Fort Meigs.

Commodore Jesse D. Elliott's son, Washington Elliott, was a Captain in the Mexican war, and a colonel of the regular army in the war of 1861. He was president of the court-martial that tried Captain Jack and his Modocs in 1873.

Colonel Wilson Elliott's son, Jesse D. Elliott, is and has been one of the editors of the Ohio Democrat, at New Philadelphia, Ohio, for thirty years past. Other branches of the Elliott's live at Newark.

The Matthew Elliott, referred to in Heckewelder and Zeisberger's narratives, was of different ancestry.

COLONEL ROBERT ELLIOTT AMBUSHED AND KILLED IN WAYNE'S WAR.

On General Wayne's march from Fort Washington into the Indian country, he so depleted the stores of Forts Hamilton and Jefferson that Colonel Robert Elliott (grandfather of Jesse D. Elliott, Esq., of New Philadelphia, Tuscarawas County), who was acting in the capacity of quartermaster-general, was ordered to replenish those forts with army stores. While attending to this duty, and when on his way from Fort Washington to Fort Hamilton, accompanied by his body servant, a roving band of Indians that had struck out on a spying expedition shortly after Wayne defeated their forces on St. Clair's old battle-field, waylaid and shot the colonel dead from his horse. The servant made good his escape by putting his horse to its utmost speed. He arrived at Fort Hamilton in the night, and soon after him came the faithful charger of his master. On the following morning the commandant at the fort sent a squad of soldiers, accompanied by the servant, out after the body of the colonel, which they found a short distance from the spot where he fell. The savages had stripped it of all valuables and a portion of the clothing. The body was placed in a box taken out for the purpose, and the soldiers started with it for the fort. When about one-third of the way in they were fired upon by the same party of Indians who had shot Elliott, and the servant, who had rode the colonel's horse was killed. The soldiers abandoned the remains and took to the woods, but were rallied by their commander, when they drove off the Indians. In the meantime the savages had broken open the coffin. The remains were then put into the wagon with those of the servant, and taken safely to the fort, and afterward to Cincinnati, where they were buried side by side in the cemetry of the old Presbyterian church at that place. In 1835, his son, Commodore Jesse D. Elliott, of the United States Navy, placed an imposing monument at the grave with the following inscription upon it: "In memory of Robert Elliott, slain by a party of Indians, near this point, while in the service of his country. Placed by his son, Commodore Jesse D. Elliott, United States Navy, 1835. Damon and Fidelity."

Sometime subsequent to the peace that was concluded by the treaty of Greenville, one of the Indians who comprised the murdering party, in relating the exploits he had engaged in during the war, said that he fired the shot that killed the colonel, and that when he attempted to scalp him the wig which Elliott wore came off, and that it created much merriment among the other Indians, one of whom exclaimed, "*damn lie!*"

POPULATION AND GROWTH OF OHIO, BY COUNTIES, SINCE ITS FOUNDING BY PUTNAM AND HECKEWELDER.

	COUNTIES.	AGGREGATE.							
		1870.	1860.	1850.	1840.	1830.	1820.	1810.	1800.
	The State.....	2,665,260	2,339,511	1,980,329	1,519,467	937,903	581,295	230,760	45,365
1	Adams..........	20,750	20,309	18,883	13,183	12,281	10,406	9,434	3,432
2	Allen............	23,623	19,185	12,109	9,079	578	...	...	...
3	Ashland........	21,993	22,951	23,813	...	...	...	...	...
4	Ashtabula......	32,517	31,814	28,767	23,724	14,584	7,375	...	...
5	Athens..........	23,768	21,364	18,215	19,109	9,787	6,338	2,791	...
6	Auglaize	20,041	17,187	11,338	...	...	...	...	...
7	Belmont	39,714	36,398	34,600	30,901	28,027	20,329	11,097	...
8	Brown	30,802	29,958	27,332	22,715	17,867	13,356	...	...
9	Butler...........	39,912	35,840	30,789	28,173	27,142	21,746	11,150	...
10	Carroll..........	14,491	15,738	17,685	18,108	...	...	...	...
11	Champaign ...	24,188	22,698	19,782	16,721	12,131	8,479	6,303	...
12	Clark	32,070	25,300	22,178	16,882	13,114	9,533	...	...
13	Clermont.......	34,268	33,034	30,455	23,106	20,466	15,820	9,996	...
14	Clinton.........	21,914	21,461	18,838	25,719	11,436	8.085	2,674	...
15	Columbiana...	38,299	32,836	33,621	40,378	35,592	22,033	10,878	...
16	Coshocton......	23,600	25,032	25,674	21,590	11,161	7,086	...	...
17	Crawford.......	25,556	23,881	18,177	13,152	4,791	...	...	...
18	Cuyahoga......	132,010	78,033	48,099	26,506	10,373	6,328	1,459	...
19	Darke...........	32,278	26,609	20,276	13,282	6,204	3,717	...	...
20	Defiance	15,719	11,886	6,966	...	...	...	...	...
21	Delaware	25,175	23,902	21,817	22,060	11,504	7,639	2,000	...
22	Erie..............	28,188	24,474	18,568	12,599	...	...	...	...
23	Fairfield........	31,138	30,538	30,264	31,924	24,786	16,633	11,361	...
24	Fayette.........	17,170	15,935	12,726	10,984	8,182	6,316	1,854	...
25	Franklin........	63,019	50,361	42,909	25,049	14,741	10,172	3,486	...
26	Fulton	17,789	14,043	7,781	...	...	...	...	...
27	Gallia...........	25,545	22,043	17,063	13,444	9,733	7,098	4,181	...
28	Geauga	14,190	15,817	17,827	16,297	15,813	7,791	2,917	...
29	Greene..........	28,038	26,197	21,946	17,528	14,801	10,521	5,870	...
30	Guernsey	23,838	24,474	30,438	27,748	18,036	9,292	3,051	...
31	Hamilton	260,370	216,410	156,844	80,145	52,317	31,764	15,258	14,692
32	Hancock........	23,847	22,886	16,751	9,986	813	...	...	...
33	Hardin..........	18,714	13,570	8,521	4,598	210	...	...	...
34	Harrison	18,682	19,110	20,157	20,099	20,916	14,345	...	...
35	Henry...........	14,028	8,901	3,434	2,503	262	...	...	...
36	Highland	29,133	27,773	25,781	22,269	16,345	12,308	5,766	...
37	Hocking........	17,925	17,057	14,119	9,741	4,008	2,130	...	...
38	Holmes........	18,177	20,589	20,452	18,088	9,135	...	...	...
39	Huron	28,532	29,616	26,203	23,933	13,341	6,675	...	...
40	Jackson.	21,759	17,941	12,719	9,744	5,941	3,746	...	...
41	Jefferson... ...	29,188	26,115	29,133	25,030	22,489	18,531	17,260	8,766
42	Knox......	26,333	27,735	28,872	29,579	17,085	8,326	2,149	...
43	Lake............	15,935	15,576	14,654	13,719	...	...	...	...
44	Lawrence... ...	31,380	23,240	15,246	9,738	5,367	3,499	...	...
45	Licking........ ..	35,756	37,011	38,846	35,096	20,869	11,861	3,852	...
46	Logan...	23,028	20,996	19,162	14,015	6,440	3,181	...	...
47	Lorain......... .	30,308	29,744	26,086	18,467	5,696	...	...	...
48	Lucas......	46,722	25,831	12,363	9,382	...	...	...	...
49	Madison....... .	15,633	13,015	10,015	9,025	6,190	4,799	1,603	...
50	Mahoning......	31,001	25,894	23,735	...	...	...	...	...
51	Marion..........	16,184	15,490	12,618	14,765	6,551	...	...	...
52	Medina...... ...	20,092	22,517	24,441	18,352	7,560	3,082	...	...
53	Meigs...........	31,465	26,534	17,971	11,452	6,158	4,480	...	...
54	Mercer...	17,254	14,104	7,712	8,277	1,110	...	...	...
55	Miami..	32,740	29,959	24,999	19,688	12,807	8,851	3,941	...
56	Monroe...	25,779	25,741	28,351	18,521	8,768	4,645	...	...
57	Montgomery..	46,006	52,230	38,218	31,938	24,362	15,999	7,722	...
58	Morgan..	20,363	22,119	28,585	20,852	11,800	5,297	...	...
59	Morrow...	18,583	20,445	20,280	...	...	...	...	...
60	Muskingum...	44,886	44,416	45,049	38,749	29,334	17,824	10,036	...

ROPULATION AND GROWTH OF OHIO—Continued.

	COUNTIES.	AGGREGATE.							
		1870.	1860.	1850.	1840.	1830.	1820.	1810.	1800.
61	Noble	19,949	20,751	....	....	....	....	....	....
62	Ottawa	13,364	7,016	3,308	2,248	....	....	....	....
63	Paulding	8,544	4,945	1,766	1,034	161	....	....	....
64	Perry	18,453	19,678	20,775	19,344	13,970	8,429	....	....
65	Pickaway	24,875	23,469	21,006	19,725	16,001	13,149	7,124	....
66	Pike	15,447	13,643	10,953	7,626	6,024	4,253	....	....
67	Portage	24,584	24,208	24,419	22,965	18,826	10,095	2,995	....
68	Preble	21,809	21,820	21,736	19,482	16,291	10,237	3,304	....
69	Putnam	17,081	12,808	7,221	5,189	230	....	....	....
70	Richland	32,516	31,158	30,879	44,532	24,006	9,169	....	....
71	Ross	37,097	35,071	32,074	27,460	24,068	20,619	15,514	8,540
72	Sandusky	25,503	21,429	14,305	10,182	2,859	852	....	....
73	Scioto	29,302	24,297	18,428	11,192	8,740	5,750	3,399	....
74	Seneca	30,827	30,868	27,104	18,128	5,159	....	....	....
75	Shelby	20,748	17,493	13,958	12,154	3,671	2,106	....	....
76	Stark	52,508	42,978	39,878	34,603	26,588	12,406	2,734	....
77	Summit	34,674	27,344	27,485	22,560	....	....	....	....
78	Trumbull	38,659	30,656	30,490	38,107	26,153	15,542	8,671	1,302
79	Tuscarawas	33,840	32,463	31,761	25,631	14,298	8,328	3,045	....
80	Union	18,730	16,507	12,204	8,422	3,192	1,996	....	....
81	Van Wert	15,823	10,238	4,793	1,577	49	....	....	....
82	Vinton	15,027	13,631	9,353	....	....	....	....	....
83	Warren	26,689	26,902	25,560	23,141	21,468	17,837	9,925	....
84	Washington	40,609	36,268	29,540	20,823	11,731	10,425	5,991	5,427
85	Wayne	35,116	32,483	32,981	35,808	23,333	11,933	....	3,206
86	Williams	20,991	16,633	8,018	4,465	387	....	....	....
87	Wood	24,596	17,886	9,157	5,357	1,102	733	....	....
88	Wyandot	18,553	15,596	11,194	....	....	....	....	....

RISE AND PROGRESS OF PARTIES IN OHIO—NAMES OF, AND VOTES FOR, GOVERNORS AND PRESIDENTS.

In 1803, the first governor, Edward Tiffin, was elected without opposition, receiving 4,564 votes.

In 1807, Return J. Meigs received 6,050 votes, against 4,757 given for Nathaniel Massie, but Meigs soon resigned.

In 1808, Samuel Huntington was elected, receiving 7,293 votes; Thomas Worthington, 5,601, and Thomas Kirker, 3,397.

In 1810, Return J. Meigs was elected, receiving 9,921 votes, and Thomas Worthington, 7,731.

In 1812, Governor Meigs was re-elected, receiving 11,859 votes, against Thomas Scott, 7,903.

In 1814, Thomas Worthington was elected, receiving 15,879 votes, and Othniel Looker, 6,171.

In 1816, Governor Worthington was re-elected, receiving 22,931 votes; James Dunlap, 6,295, and Ethan Allen Brown, 1,607.

In 1818, Ethan Allen Brown was elected, receiving 30,194 votes, and James Dunlap, 8,075.

In 1820, Governor Brown was re-elected, receiving 34,836 votes; Jeremiah Morrow, 9,426, and William Henry Harrison, 4,348.

In 1822, Jeremiah Morrow was elected, receiving 26,659 votes; Allen Trimble, 22,899, and William W. Irwin, 11,050.

In 1824, Governor Morrow was re-elected, receiving 39,526 votes, and Allen Trimble, 37,108.

In 1826, Allen Trimble was elected, receiving 71,475 votes; John Bigger, 4,114; Alexander Campbell, 4,765, and Benjamin Tappan, 4,192.

In 1828, Governor Trimble was re-elected, receiving 53,970 votes, and John W. Campbell, 51,951.

In 1830, Duncan McArthur, whig, was elected, receiving 49,668 votes, and Rovert Lucas, democrat, 49,186.

In 1832, Robert Lucas, democrat, was elected, receiving 71,251 votes, and Darius Lyman, whig, 63,485.

In 1834, Governor Lucas, democrat, was re-elected, receiving 70,738 votes, and James Findlay, whig, 67,414.

In 1836, Joseph Vance, whig, was elected, receiving 92,204 votes, and Eli Baldwin, democrat, 86,158.

In 1838, Wilson Shannon, democrat, was elected, receiving 107,884 votes, and Joseph Vance, whig, 102,146.

In 1840, Thomas Corwin, whig, was elected, receiving 145,442 votes, and Wilson Shannon, democrat, 129,312.

In 1842, Wilson Shannon, was elected, receiving 119,774 votes; Thomas Corwin, whig, 117,902, and Leceister King, free-soil, 5,134.

In 1844, Mordecai Bartley, whig, was elected, receiving 146,333 votes; David Tod, democrat, 145,062, and Leicester King, free-soil, 8,898.

In 1846, William Bebb, whig, was elected, receiving 118,869 votes; David Tod, democrat, 116,484, and Samuel Lewis, free-soil, 10,797.

In 1848, Seabury Ford, whig and free-soil, was elected, receiving 148,250 votes; John B. Weller, democrat, 147,886, and scattering, 939.

In 1850, Reuben Wood, democrat, was elected, receiving 133,093 votes; William Johnson, whig, 121,105, and Edward Smith, free-soil, 13,747.

In 1853, William Medill, democrat, was elected, receiving 147,663 votes; Nelson Berrere, whig, 85,857, and Samuel Lewis, free-soil, 50,346.

In 1855, Salmon P. Chase, republican, was elected, receiving 146,770 votes; William Medill, democrat, 131,019, and Allen Trimble, independent, 24,276.

In 1857, Salmon P. Chase, republican, was re-elected, receiving 160,568 votes; Henry B. Payne, democrat, 159,065, and P. Van Trump, independent, 10,272.

In 1859, William Dennison, Jr., republican, was elected, receiving 184,557 votes, and Rufus P. Ranney, democrat, 171,226.

In 1861, David Tod, republican, was elected, receiving 206,997 votes, and Hugh J. Jewett, democrat, 151,794.

In 1863, John Brough, republican, was elected, receiving 288,374 votes, and C. L. Vallandigham, democrat, 187,492.

In 1865, J. D. Cox, republican, was elected, receiving 233,633 votes, and George W. Morgan, democrat, 193,797.

In 1867, Rutherford B. Hayes, republican, was elected, receiving 243,605 votes, and Allen G. Thurman, democrat, 240,622.

In 1869, Governor Hayes, republican, was re-elected, receiving 235,081 votes; George H. Pendleton, democrat, 227,580, and Samuel Scott, prohibition, 670.

In 1871, Edward F. Noyes, republican, was elected, receiving 238,273 votes; George W. McCook, democrat, 218,105, and G. T. Stewart, prohibition, 4,084.

In 1873, William Allen, democrat, was elected, receiving

214,654 votes; Edward F. Noyes, republican, 213,837; G. T. Stewart, prohibition, 10,278, and Isaac C. Collins, liberal, 10,109.

In 1875, Rutherford B. Hayes, republican, was elected, receiving 297,813 votes, and William Allen, democrat, 292,264.

PRESIDENTIAL VOTES, FROM 1852 TO 1872, IN OHIO.

In 1852, Franklin Pierce, democrat, received 168,933 votes; Winfield Scott, whig, 152,553, and John P. Hale, free-soil, 31,332.

In 1856, James Buchanan, democrat, received 170,874 votes; John C. Fremont, republican, 187,497, and Millard Fillmore, neutral, 28,126.

In 1860, Stephen A. Douglas, democrat, received 187,421 votes; Abraham Lincoln, republican, 221,809; John Bell, 12,193, and John C. Breckenridge, 11,303.

In 1864, George B. McClellan, democrat, received 205,599 votes, and Abraham Lincoln, republican, 265,654.

In 1868, Horatio Seymour, democrat, received 238,621 votes, and Ulysses S. Grant, republican, 280,167.

In 1872, Horace Greeley, democrat and conservative, received 244,321 votes; Ulysses S. Grant, republican, 281,852, and 3,225, scattering.

INCREASE IN WEALTH UNDER A GOLD AND STATE CURRENCY IN 1850, AND A UNITED STATES CURRENCY IN 1874, BY COUNTIES.

COUNTIES.	Assessed value in gold and State currency, 1850.	Assessed value in U. S. currency, 1874.
Adams	$2,806,377	$6,068,892
Allen	1,424,174	10,511,657
Ashland	4,678,991	13,360,031
Ashtabula	5,065,033	16,164,138
Athens	1,949,770	8,625,009
Auglaize	1,480,026	7,469,995
Belmont	7,393,043	21,159,973
Brown	5,444,464	11,313,392
Butler	10,052,631	33,232,416
Carroll	2,994,927	9,044,516
Champaign	5,029,676	21,037,100
Clarke	6,969,483	26,906,543
Clermont	6,622,738	15,032,950
Clinton	4,499,973	14,271,000
Columbiana	7,308,906	23,586,398
Coshocton	5,026,561	13,602,590
Crawford	3,381,915	15,556,810
Cuyahoga	10,750,989	92,130,379
Darke	3,401,797	18,832,790
Fefiance	1,082,492	5,309,808
Delaware	4,144,681	16,522,399
Erie	4,403,642	12,342,669
Fairfield	7,442,964	18,167,540
Fayette	3,204,639	14,249,371
Franklin	11,284,951	49,301,330
Fulton	818,962	5,142,550
Gallia	2,072,587	7,722,774
Geauga	3,354,598	8,234,158
Greene	7,437,116	22,770,701
Guernsey	4,943,753	11,051,107
Hamilton	55,670,631	219,799,383
Hancock	2,404,745	12,245,512
Hardin	1,397,484	8,958,410
Harrison	4,487,746	13,308,320
Henry	519,583	4,337,550
Highland	5,632,719	15,571,616
Hocking	1,281,852	5,735,448
Holmes	3,218,644	8,597,697
Huron	5,509,986	18,155,097
Jackson	1,350,838	5,070,634
Jefferson	7,373,766	20,223,700
Knox	5,750,186	16,864,424
Lake	2,852,533	10,564,986
Lawrence	1,968,224	9,358,202
Licking	9,128,948	26,803,699
Logan	$3,688,523	$13,756,390
Lorain	4,348,158	18,171,040
Lucas	2,350,532	22,980,190
Madison	3,673,279	14,550,960
Mahoning	5,842,882	19,501,206
Marion	2,769,088	12,882,065
Medina	4,105,446	12,933,931
Meigs	2,147,972	9,367,412
Mercer	1,182,511	4,335,160
Miami	6,387,357	21,938,672
Monroe	2,588,563	5,872,469
Montgomery	12,898,485	45,943,420
Morgan	4,702,249	8,510,497
Morrow	3,050,627	12,609,761
Muskingum	10,984,107	25,625,350
Noble	....	6,544,390
Ottawa	487,867	4,986,118
Paulding	308,750	2,439,956
Perry	3,600,499	8,824,774
Pickaway	7,974,047	19,749,552
Pike	2,074,991	5,148,154
Portage	5,926,727	16,726,183
Preble	6,113,291	17,638,435
Putnam	894,772	5,635,902
Richland	5,831,291	22,086,910
Ross	10,232,791	21,894,103
Sandusky	2,397,141	13,265,123
Scioto	3,493,342	12,102,294
Seneca	5,975,268	17,681,776
Shelby	2,575,567	10,174,966
Stark	9,413,008	33,873,980
Summit	6,433,828	22,865,876
Trumbull	7,375,621	20,894,009
Tuscarawas	5,652,775	17,250,954
Union	1,795,249	10,550,280
Van Wert	494,072	6,138,907
Vinton	1,014,694	4,192,616
Warren	8,154,843	21,874,821
Washington	3,982,051	13,877,438
Wayne	6,480,471	24,050,819
Williams	961,353	7,487,383
Wood	1,195,183	9,097,040
Wyandot	1,388,112	10,002,381
Totals	438,598,027	1,580,379,324

COAL, THE GREAT ELEMENT OF FUTURE WEALTH.

In the valleys of the Tuscarawas and Muskingum are the main coal-fields of Ohio. In Tuscarawas County, the State geologists estimate, at a rough calculation, all the workable coal to average 6 feet in thickness over 550 square miles, which, at 6,000,000 tons per mile, gives for 550 square miles, by measurement, 3,300,000,000 tons of coal, which of itself would last the people of Ohio several centuries—as per calculation of Geologist Briggs. Multiply this quantity by each county in the coal area, and it will be safe to say that a hundred centuries can not exhaust the coal-fields of the valleys.

THE FORMATION OF COAL.

The modern geologists' theory is that the materials which were comprised in the formation of coal seams were washed into vast basins by the action of water, which at certain periods would rise to a level with the surface of the land. These sediments, it is claimed, were originally gathered from the land by the constantly changing waters, and subsequently distributed in the basins which were low enough to be reached by the waves and tides of the sea.

The plants which entered principally into the formation of coal were for the most part ferns, for in nearly all coal is found fossils of this plant. Fossils of trees, fishes, mollusks, and corals, also, are found in coal, showing conclusively that the natural products of the land and the living things of the sea, together, enter mainly into the composition of coal.

It is conjectured that at the time the highest coal seam was formed a permanent change affected the topography of our land. This change was the elevation of the high mountain ranges and the draining of the major portion of what is now land. The length of time occupied in producing all the changes on the surface by which the coal seams were formed is entirely incomprehensible to man, and must have continued through countless ages.

In this connection it is well to notice the mountain formations, and the glacial period. The periods subsequent to the carboniferous, or coal period, as known in geology are, permian, triassic, jurassic, cretaceous, tertiary, quarternary, and human. Of these, from the carboniferous to the quarternary, all are wanting in this part of our continent. The most lucid explanation of this great break in the regular formations yet given, is that at the close of the coal period a vast expanse of our continent was raised far above the seas, and from that time the formations were continued only on the water margins, and these have changed from time to time, which will account for the presence of certain deposits in some portions of the continent which are a blank in others. During the progress of this great upheaval of land, much more powerful forces were expended in various localities and along certain lines, which resulted in forming higher elevations, and these, from contact with the ice during the glacial period, were reduced to our present mountain and hill ranges. The forces that culminated in these elevations, stupendous as they must have been, have only been ascribed to some extraordinary volcanic action, or some unaccountable slowly acting but resistless power within the earth.

Succeeding the period which changed the level of this once great plain into hills and valleys, was what is termed the drift period, during which oceans and mountains of ice came down from the north, traces of which are found as far south as Cincinnati. In their course the glaciers plowed down the sides of mountains and hills, dug out the basins of the great lakes, and in breaking up dropped the great bowlders which were frozen in them in the north, and which are found wholly exposed upon the hills and in the valleys at the present day. This period was followed by the submergence of the present lower hills and plains. This in turn was changed by the depression of the island seas, and the gradual drainage caused the alluvial deposits found in all the present valleys. As the waters receded the flow was reduced to lower lands where channels were formed, which, by the long-continued action of the waters, were worn out to great depths, and these channels were again filled up many hundreds of feet by the ebbing and flowing of the waters, until the beds of the streams became elevated above the reach of the tides. Subsequent slight changes have occurred, but they are so well known that their mention is not required in this article.

THE SCRIPTURE NARRATIVES NOT IN CONFLICT WITH THE GEOLOGICAL AGE OF THE COAL FORMATION.

As regards the coming and going of the different seas over the localities in which coal has been formed from their sediments, and the time required to produce coal, being claimed by some writers to be in conflict with the scriptural account of the Mosaic deluge, Dr. Kitto, the great biblical cyclopedian, after discussing the subject, arrives at this conclusion: "There is no limit to Omnipotence, and one miracle is not greater than another. If we suppose the flood to have been miraculously produced, and all the difficulties thus overcome, we can also suppose that it was not only *miraculously terminated*, but every trace and mark of it supernaturally effaced and destroyed."

Professor Lyell, the most eminent geologist of the present age, harmonizes the seeming contradiction between the natural laws governing the structure of the world and the scriptural account of the Noachian deluge, thus: "If we believe the flood to have been a temporary suspension of the ordinary laws of the natural world, requiring a miraculous intervention of Divine power, then it is evident that the credibility of such an event can not be enhanced by any series of inundations, however analogous, of which the geologist may imagine he has discovered the proofs. For my own part, I have always considered the flood as a preternatural event, far beyond the reach of philosophical inquiry, whether as to the *cause* employed to produce it, or the *effects* most likely to result from it."

The Christian believer in the Bible narratives has no contradictions to reconcile between them and geology.

MEMBERS OF THE FIRST CONSTITUTIONAL CONVENTION, NOVEMBER 29, 1802.

Adams County—Joseph Darlington, Israel Donalson, and Thomas Kirker.

Belmont County—James Caldwell and Elijah Woods.

Clermont County—Philip Gatch and James Sargent.

Fairfield County—Henry Abrams and Emanuel Carpenter.

Hamilton County—John W. Browne, Charles Willing Byrd, Francis Dunlavy, William Goforth, John Kitchell, Jeremiah Morrow, John Paul, John Reily, John Smith, and John Wilson.

Jefferson County—Rudolph Bair, George Humphrey, John Milligan, Nathan Updegraff, and Bazaleel Wells.

Ross County—Michael Baldwin, James Grubb, Nathaniel Massie, and Thomas Worthington.

Trumbull County—David Abbott and Samuel Huntington.

Washington County—Ephraim Cutler, Benjamin Ives Gilman, John McIntyre, and Rufus Putnam.

EDWARD TIFFIN, President,
and representative from Ross County.

THOMAS SCOTT, Secretary.

MEMBERS OF THE SECOND CONSTITUTIONAL CONVENTION, MARCH 10, 1851.

S. J. Andrews, William Barbee, Joseph Barnett, David Barnet, William S. Bates, A. I. Bennett, John H. Blair, Jacob Blickensderfer, Van Brown, R. W. Cahill, L. Case, David Chambers, John Chany, H. D. Clark, George Collins, Friend Cook, Otway Curry, G. Volney Dorsey, Thomas W. Ewart, John Ewing, Joseph M. Farr, Elias Florence, Robert Forbes, H. N. Gillett, John Graham, Jacob J. Greene, John L. Green, Henry H. Gregg, W. S. Groesbeck, C. S. Hamilton, D. D. T. Hard, A. Harlan, William Hawkins, James P. Henderson, Peter Hitchcock, J. McCormick, G. W. Holmes, George B. Holt, John J. Hootman, V. B. Horton, Samuel Humphreville, John E. Hunt, B. B. Hunter, John Johnson, J. Daniel Jones, James B. King, S. J. Kirkwood, Thomas J. Larsh, William Lawrence, John Larwill, Robert Leech, D. P. Leadbetter, John Lidey, James Loudon, H. S. Manon, Samson Mason, Matthew H. Mitchell, Isaiah Morris, Charles McCloud, S. F. Norris, Charles J. Orton, W. S. C. Otis, Thomas Patterson, Daniel Peck, Jacob Perkins, Samuel Quigley, R. P. Ranney, Charles Reemelin, Adam N. Riddle, Edward C. Roll, William Sawyer, Sabirt Scott, John Sellers, John A. Smith, George J. Smith, B. P. Smith, Henry Stanbery, B. Stanton, Albert V. Stebbins, E. T. Stickney, Harman Stidger, James Struble, J. R. Swan, L. Swift, James W. Taylor, Norton S. Townshend, Elijah Vance, William M. Warren, Thomas A. Way, J. Milton Williams, Elsey Wilson, James T. Worthington, E. B. Woodbury, H. C. Gray, Edward Archbold, Reuben Hitchcock, F. Case, Joseph Vance, Richard Stillwell, Simeon Nash, Hugh Thompson, and Joseph Thompson.

WILLIAM MEDILL, President.

William H. Gill, Secretary.

MEMBERS OF THE THIRD CONSTITUTIONAL CONVENTION, MAY 14, 1874.

Charles J. Albright, Isaac N. Alexander, S. J. Andrews, Llewellyn Baber, James W. Bannon, David Barnet, Thomas Beer, R. M. Bishop, John H. Blose, Perry Bosworth, Barnabus Burns, Absalom P. Byal, John L. Caldwell, Joseph P. Carbery, Harlow Chapin, Samuel W. Clark, Milton L. Clark, Adam Clay, John B. Coats, Asher Cook, D. D. T. Cowen, Theodore E. Cunningham, R. De Steigner, A. W. Doan, G. Volney Dorsey, Thomas Ewing, M. A. Foran, Julius Freiberg, Mills Gardner, T. J. Godfrey, Jacob J. Greene, Seneca O. Griswold, Harvey Guthrie, John C. Hale, John W. Herron, George William Hill, P. Hitchcock, George Hoadly, Joseph D. Horton, James C. Hostetter, S. Humphreville, Samuel F. Hunt, Lyman J. Jackson, Elias H. Johnson, W. P. Kerr, A. Kraemer, W. V. M. Layton, John K. McBride, John McCauley, John W. McCormick, Ozias Merrill, George D. Miller, John L. Miner, Charles H. Michener, Jacob Mueller, Thomas J. Mullen, Henry S. Neal, William Okey, Henry F. Page, Anson Pease, Charles Phellis, W. H. Phillips, Francis B. Pond, T. W. Powell, Albert M. Pratt, J. W. Reilly, John J. Rickly, C. W. Rowland, Daniel A. Russell, Charles C. Russell, William Sample, W. E. Scofield, Charles H. Scribner, John D. Sears, John Shaw, Emanuel Shultz, John A. Smith, James B. Steedman, T. F. Thompson, Amos Townsend, Thomas P. Townsley, James Tripp, R. S. Tulloss, George M. Tuttle, Asa H. Tyler, James S. Van Valkenburgh, Daniel Van Voorhis, Carolus F. Voorhes, A. C. Voris, W. G. Waddle, Cooper K. Watson, S. P. Weaver, W. H. West, C. A. White, A. White, David M. Wilson, Hamilton B. Woodbury, John H. Young, and William J. Young.

RUFUS KING, President.

Dudley W. Rhodes, Secretary.

The constitution framed in 1874 was rejected as a whole.

In 1875, its most objectionable article was adopted, and the remaining articles will be hereafter adopted, in accordance with the public necessities.

NEWSPAPERS IN THE VALLEYS.

The rise and progress of the public press in the two valleys, as herewith subjoined, is as nearly correct as the same can be given. The newspaper, having become the most potent intellectual engine in the world, to sway the public mind, the historian fails in his duty as compiler of events unless his report of the public press goes side by side with the statistics of population and physical and mental development.

Coshocton County Press.—At Coshocton, the Age, republican in politics, founded in 1824, edited by W. T. Collier, and circulation about 1,200; the Democrat, democratic in politics, founded in 1840, edited by J. C. Fisher, and circulation about 1,000.

Morgan County Press.—At McConnellsville, the Herald, republican in politics, founded in 1842, edited by Kahler & Foulke, and circulation about 1,300; the Democrat, democratic in politics, founded in 1871, edited by F. A. Davis, and circulation about 800.

Muskingum County Press.—At Zanesville, the Courier, republican in politics, founded in 1800, edited by Newman & Dodd, and circulation about 3,100; the Signal, democratic in politics, founded in 1864, edited by James T. Irvine, and circulation about 1,800; the City Times, independent in politics, founded in 1852, edited by W. W. Pyle, and circulation about 800; the Farmers' and Mechanics' Advocate, independent in politics, founded in 1870, edited by J. T. Shryock, and circulation about 1,400; Blandy's Monthly, independent in politics, founded in 1867, and edited by H. & F. Blandy.

Stark County Press.—At Alliance, the Leader, Monitor, Review, Telegraph—four in all—edited by W. H. Phelps,

M. McClellan, S. J. McKee, and J. W. Gillespie, and aggregate circulation of 5,000; at Canton, the Repository, republican in politics, founded in 1815, edited by Josiah Hartzell, and circulation about 2,400; the Stark County Democrat, democratic in politics, founded in 1833, edited by A. McGregor, and circulation about 2,200; the Staats Zeitung, democratic in politics, founded in 1875, edited by N. Montag & Co., and circulation about 1,340; the Times, democratic in politics, edited by M. A. Stewart, and circulation about 1,300; at Massillon, the Independent, republican in politics, founded in 1863, edited by Welker & Taylor, and circulation about 700; the American, independent in politics, edited by S. & J. Hoover, and circulation about 800; at Minerva, the Commercial, republican in politics, founded in 1868, edited by Weaver Brothers, and circulation about 700.

Tuscarawas County Press.—At New Philadelphia, the Ohio Democrat, democratic in politics, founded in 1839, edited by Matthews, Elliott & Co., and circulation about 1,400; the Advocate, republican in politics, founded in 1819, edited by J. L. McIlvaine, and circulation about 1,500; the Beobachter, democratic in politics, founded in 1871, edited by Walter & Minning, and circulation about 1,000; at Dover, the Reporter, independent in politics, founded in 1871, edited by R. Watson, and circulation about 900; at New Comerstown, the Argus, republican in politics, founded in 1870, edited by George McClelland, and circulation about 1,000; at Uhrichsville, the Chronicle, republican in politics, founded in 1865, edited by W. A. Pittinger, and circulation about 1,300.

Washington County Press.—At Marietta, the Mariettian, independent in politics, founded in 1865, published by the Steam Printing Company, and circulation about 1,500; the Register, republican in politics, founded in 1801, edited by E. R. Alderman, and circulation about 2,500; the Times, democratc in politics, founded in 1864, edited by S. McMillen, and circulation about 1,400; the Zeitung, neutral in politics, founded in 1868, edited by Jacob Mueller, and circulation about 800; at Belpre, the Courier, neutral in politics, and edited by T. H. Winchester.

Of non-political, daily, semi-weekly, tri-weekly, weekly, monthly papers, and magazines there are in Ohio	200
Of political papers there are	175
Total	375

200 non-political papers circulate	700,000
90 republican papers circulate	300,000
85 democratic papers circulate	250,000
Total circulation	1,250,000

Of these, three-fourths are weekly issues, one-eighth daily, one-sixteenth tri-weekly and semi-weekly, and one-sixteenth semi-monthly and monthly.

The weekly issues are	937,500
The daily issues are	156,250
The tri-weekly and semi-weekly issues are	78,125
The semi-monthly and monthly issues are	78,125
Total issues	1,250,000

THE FIRST SALT WORKS IN MORGAN AND MUSKINGUM COUNTIES.

Salt Creek empties into the Muskingum at Duncan's Falls, below Zanesville. On this creek the first salt works were erected in the valley, about 1796. Fifty settlers put in $1.50 each. They bought twenty-four kettles at Pittsburgh, which were brought to the falls, by water transportation down the Ohio and up the Muskingum, and thence carried seven miles to the salt licks on pack-horses.

A well was dug fifteen feet deep, to the salt rock. A hollow sycamore, three feet in diameter, was then put down, and bedded into the rock, so as to prevent leakage. The twenty-four kettles were built in two ranges of stone, and a shed erected over them, with a cabin near by. A sweep and pole raised the salt water up the hollow sycamore, to troughs conveying it to the kettles. The owners took turns in work, five men being required to run the works. Every two weeks they changed, and another set of five men took their places. The kettles were kept boiling night and day. A yoke of oxen and one man kept the works in wood. Eight hundred gallons of water were used to make fifty pounds of salt, which consumed twelve hours in the making, and was worth three dollars. Thus, it took in those times six men and a yoke of oxen to earn that sum in twelve hours. The works, however, were a great public convenience, and settlers came forty miles to get salt. This salt company was kept up about three years, and afterward the State became the owner, and leased the works out at a fixed rent, until no person would pay the amount, when these primitive salt works disappeared.

CHAPTER XIII.

EARLY SETTLEMENT OF MORGAN AND MUSKINGUM COUNTIES.

Zanesville was laid out in 1799, by Jonathan Zane and John McIntyre, and the same year houses were erected thereon. Among other early settlers were William McCullough, Henry Crooks, Jamss Duncan, Increase Matthews, Levi Whipple, Edwin Putnam, and some of the Zane family.

As early as 1790, attempts were made to settle in Morgan County, but the ferocity of the Indians compelled the settlers who were not killed to flee for their lives. About the year 1800, peace having been made with the Indians by the Greenville treaty of 1795, settlers came and dotted the county here and there with their cabins; and in due time villages were laid out by original settlers—among whom are to be found the names of Anderson, McConnell, Deaver, Fisher, Hoskins, Sharon, Wharton, Wood, &c.

In 1818, the county of Morgan was formed, aud the county seat established at McConnellsville, the original owner of which was Robert McConnell, one of the influential men of that day in the county.

The editor is indebted to W. G. Moorehead, Esq., for the names of the following early settlers in Muskingum County:

John McIntyre, the founder of Zanesville; Lewis Cass, Elijah Merwin, Wylys Silliman, Samuel W. Culbertson, and Samuel Herrick—the five last being lawyers of wide celebrity. Among the prominent citizens were Judges

Stillwell, Finley, Putnam, and Jeffries; General Van Horn, General Green, Captains Taylor and Cass, Major Cass, Major Pierce, Captain Pierce, George, Richard, and James Reeve; Moses, John, and Isaac Dillon; Joseph Church, James Culbertson, Captain Ross, George Jackson, Daniel Converse, Robert Fulton, Robert Hazlett, Isaac Hazlett, Hugh Hazlett, Alexander McLaughlin, Alexander Adams, Nathan Finley, Colonel John Halle, James Hampson, William Blocksom, Gilbert Blose, Henry Wheeler, James Granger, Henry Granger, Doctors Belknap, Fowler, Safford, Matthews, Rhodes, Conant, Hanna, and Mitchell; Ebenezer Buckingham, Solomon Sturges, J. D. Cushing—one of the first four children born in Ohio; Captain Elijah Ross, William Dennison—father and son; Captain Benoni Pierce—killed at River Raisin in the war of 1812; John Dugan, Nathan, Joseph, John, James, and Absalom Roberts; James Crosby, Joseph Shepherd, Thomas Moorehead, Joseph Robertson, William Pelham, Jeffrey Price, Charles Elliott—author of a work on Romanism; Peter Strickland, David Young, and several families of the Adamses.

Joseph Fisher, Esq., ex-surveyor, furnishes the following list of early settlers of Muskingum County:

"William S. Dennison, whose donation to Granville College gave it its present name, Dennison University, came, when a boy, with his father, from Massachusetts to Muskingum County, about 1810. He is a well-known farmer and stock-raiser; has never aspired to any office, but has, by constant attention to business, acquired a competency.

"Daniel Stillwell, known as Judge Stillwell, in an early day one of the associate judges of the common pleas court of Muskingum County, emigrated from Eastern Pennsylvania, purchased a quarter township of land—four thousand acres—in Madison township, and was a successful farmer. He was the father of Richard Stillwell, for some years judge of the court of common pleas. The old gentleman, in crossing the Muskingum River, some years ago, when too high to be safely forded, had his buggy upset by the current, and he and his granddaughter were drowned. His youngest son, John Stillwell, is now a resident of Tennessee, some fifteen or twenty miles north-west of Nashville.

"George W. Adams, the owner of Adams' mills and of the Ewing mills, is a Virginian by birth, came to Muskingum County from Farquier County, Virginia, with his father, George Adams, early in the present century. His brother Edward and he built a mill near the present Adams mills, about the year 1828 or 1829, and afterward the Ewing mills, near Dresden. They acquired a large landed estate in Muskingum and Coshocton counties. He represented Muskingum County one term in the legislature, as member of the house of representatives, A. D. 1840.

"Jesse John emigrated from eastern Pennsylvania to Blue Rock township, Muskingum County, He was a respectable, influential man in that part of the county. The father of Davis John, who represented this county in the legislature two terms—1843–'44, and 1845–'46.

"Henry Wheeler, aged upward of eighty years, came from western Virginia to Ohio, when a young man; settled in Muskingum County; resides near Adamsville; has been a member of the Baptist church at that place forty-five or fifty years, and was one of the county commissioners at one time.

"Charles R. Copland came from Richmond, Virginia, when a young man. His father was the owner of a quarter township of land—four thousand acres—being partly in Madison and partly in Muskingum townships. He married Evelina Adams, daughter of George Adams, who was also a large land-owner in Madison township. Mr. Copland and his wife are still living in Madison. They are upward of eighty years old.

"George Slack and Jacob Slack, brothers, and living in the same neighborhood in Washington township, Muskingum County, came from Virginia, Loudon County, early in the present century, with their father, John Slack—long since dead. They are between eighty and ninety years old.

"David Richardson and Martin Richardson, brothers, settled in Monroe township, Muskingum County, at an early day. They came from one of the New England States, and were prominent farmers in that part of the county. They died some years ago.

"John Van Voorhis, an early settler of Muskingum County, and a successful farmer in Licking township, came from Pennsylvania, and died a year or so ago, upward of ninety years of age. His son, Daniel Van Voorhis, who was a representative in the legislature one session, and was also a member of the constitutional convention of 1873–'74, still resides in Licking township, near Nashport."

EARLY SETTLERS AND INCIDENTS IN COSHOCTON COUNTY.

Colonel Charles Williams was the first settler in Coshocton County. Born in Washington County, Maryland, in 1764. He married Susannah Carpenter, on the banks of the Ohio River, in the vicinity of Wheeling; emigrated to the salt works, on the Muskingum River, and after remaining there for a time removed to the forks of the Muskingum, and built a cabin on the bank of the river where Coshocton now stands. This was in the year 1800. The next year George and Thomas Carpenter, his brothers-in-law, arrived; also William and Samuel Morrison. These men, making their home with Colonel Williams the first year, raised a crop of corn on "the prairie," four miles up White Woman's Creek. This was probably the first crop of corn raised in the county, and was in the year 1801. The same year (1801) Michael Miller located the second quarter, township four, range six. He lived seven weeks on venison, bear meat and other game, without bread of any kind.

The first lands located were those along the rivers. Among the first sections located were second quarter, township five, range six, Elijah Backus, of Marietta; first quarter, township five, range six, Chandler Price and Benjamin Morgan, of Philadelphia; second quarter, township four, range six, Michael Miller; third quarter, township six, range eight, third quarter, township six, range nine, Cairnoan Medowell, of Philadelphia; third quarter, township five, range six, third quarter, township six, range four, fourth quarter, township six, range five, Martin Baum, of Cincinnati; third quarter, township four, range six, Benjamin Robinson; fourth quarter, township five, range five, Denman and Wells, of Essex County, New Jersey.

John Matthews, surveyor of Marietta, made a number of the early locations for non-residents, receiving a certain part of the land as his compensation. There were thirty-three military sections located in Coshocton County.

Among the early settlers should be mentioned George and Henry Miller, Isaac Hoglin, George McCulloch, Andrew Craig, William Whitten, Elijah Newcomb, Benjamin Robinson, Abraham Sells.

Colonel Williams kept the first tavern, the first store, and the first ferry. The house which he first erected was burned after a few years, with the loss of two children. He rebuilt on the same lot, and here, after the county was organized, court was held. The hardships of frontier life may be illustrated by the fact that Colonel Williams' daughter, at the age of twelve years, would sometimes ride on horseback to the White-eyes Plains (six miles) for a sack of grain; the next day go with the grain to mill at Zanesville, and return the third day.

Major Cass located in the Muskingum valley, fourteen miles north of Coshocton.

From 1805 to 1812 the population of the county increased very rapidly, as is shown by the fact that Coshocton County, embracing at that time part of what is now Holmes County, furnished four companies for the war of 1812: one company of volunteers under the command of Captain Adam Johnston; and three companies of drafted men, under the command of Captains Tanner, Beard and Evans.

Coshocton was laid out in 1802, by Ebenezer Buckingham and John Matthews, of Marietta, under the name of Tuscarawa. The county was organized, and the name of the county seat changed, in April, 1811. The first townships organized were Tuscarawas, Washington, New Castle, Franklin, Oxford, and Linton.

Court was first held in Coshocton County in April, 1811, Little was done at this term, except to order elections for justices of the peace in several of the townships. Court also sat in September, at which time several minor cases were disposed of. The first case in which there were any pleadings filed was at the December term, 1811—Charles Williams *vs.* Adam Marpley; Lewis Cass, attorney for plaintiff; John Howard, attorney for defendant; judge, William Wilson; associates, William Mitchell, Isaac Evans, and Peter Casey; judgment of $9.56 in favor of plaintiff.

Among the first officers of the county were, Cornelius P. Vankirk, sheriff; Adam Johnston, clerk and recorder; Wright Warner, prosecuting attorney; William Lockart, county surveyor, and William Whitten, justice of the peace.

The first resident physician was Dr. Samuel Lee, who located here in 1811. Rev. J. W. Pigman, of the Methodist Episcopal church, who lived in the western part of the county, and Rev. Timothy Harris, of the Congregational church, Utica, used to preach here occasionally about the beginning of the war of 1812. The first Sunday-school was organized in the year 1824, under the superintendence of James Renfrew.

The first mill in the county was built several years before the war of 1812, by Jesse Fulton, one mile south-east of Coshocton, on the farm since known as the Benjamin Rickets place. A mill run by horse power was erected soon after this on lot numbered two hundred and sixteen, corner of Cadiz and Second streets (the Harbaugh lot).

The first brick house in Coshocton was built in 1816, corner of Cadiz and Second streets (the Fritchey house).

Before the construction of the Ohio Canal, goods were

brought from Pittsburgh to Coshocton in keel-boats, *via* Marietta—a slow and laborious method. Letters came from Philadelphia in twenty-five days—postage twenty-five cents.

Coshocton was visited by the "cold plague" in 1814—quite a number of fatal cases occurring in the town and vicinity.

It is said that Louis Philippe, afterward king of France, visited Coshocton in the character of a schoolmaster, during his exile. His aristocratic notions were not in keeping with the republican ideas and rude manners of the frontier, and his stay was very short.

Caldersburgh was laid out in 1816, on the west bank of the Muskingum, by James Calders. A large addition was subsequently laid out north of the old town, and the name changed to Roscoe.

The completion of the canal marks an important epoch in the material prosperity of Coshocton, and other counties in the valley, as it afforded an outlet for the enormous crops of wheat which were raised after the clearing away of the forests.

An incident of those early days may be worth preservation: Five or six runaway slaves, from Virginia, made their way to Coshocton, and were quartered at the house of Pryor Foster, a colored man. Word had reached the citizens beforehand of their escape—a large reward being offered for their capture; but such was the popularity of Foster among the white people, that they were willing to assist in the escape of the refugees. Foster kept them in his house, and stood guard outside all night, to prevent any possible interference. The next morning he took them across the river, and hid them in a cave a mile west of Caldersburgh. The pursuers soon after made their appearance—pretty confident of overtaking the slaves—having traced them in this direction. But no satisfactory information was to be obtained. Some show of violence was also offered, and they rode out of town and gave up the pursuit.

When it was certain that the coast was clear, Foster took them to the White Woman River, and told them to travel up the stream—giving them such further directions as would enable them to reach Lake Erie and Canada.

This occurrence was about the time of the construction of the Ohio Canal. The slaves were afterward captured some distance north-west of Coshocton, and taken back to Virginia.

EARLY SETTLERS AND PROMINENT MEN IN STARK COUNTY.

After the treaty of Greenville, in 1795, the territory now in Stark County attracted many emigrants, down to the period when it was organized into a county, with Canton for the county seat, which was laid out in 1806, by Bazaled Wells, of Steubenville.

From that period the emigrants from Pennsylvania and Maryland flocked in, and in later years the Germans from Europe came, and made it one of the rich and prosperous counties of Ohio.

Among the prominent men of the county forty years ago—and some of whom being of the first settlers—may be mentioned Parker Handy, William Williams, Thomas Blackburn, Jacob Palmer, V. R. Kimball, John Kryder, H. D. Williams, David Stripe, William Dunbar, James Allen, John Saxton, Daniel Gutshall, Peter Kauffman, P. Loutzenheiser, Samuel Hownstine, Samuel Lyons, George N. Webb, George Crouse, George Cribbs, George Roudebush, Richard Sheckles, John Dunbar, Elias D. Albert, Arnold Lynch, William McCormick, William Sarball, Enos Raffensperger, Eli Sala, George B. Hoss, Harmon Stidger, Heram Griswold, John Harries, Samuel Lahm, Lyman Pease, George Slusser, Daniel Diewalt, Thomas H. Webb, Alexander McCulley, John, James, Elias, and Matthew Johnston, Oses Welch, Joseph Watson, Silas Rawson, H.

B. Hurlbutt, Lewis Schaeffer, Abel and James H. Underhill, Robert H. Folger, Daniel Atwater, George Diewalt, John Schlosser, John Myers, William Fogle, William Toffler, John Short, Sr., John C. Rockwell, Henry Kitzmiller, Matthias Sheplar, Peary Stidger, David A. Starkweather, John E. Dunbar, O. T. Browning, Judge Sowers, Peter Croft, William Christmas, John Black, William White, Doctor Rappel, William Bucher, Daniel Raffensperger, Andrew Meyer, Martin Wokedal, Benjamin F. Leiter, William Lemon, Doctor Robert Estep, Joseph Matthews, Sr., John Pirrong, Jonathan G. Lester, William Reed, Samuel Stover, Seraphun Myer, Jacob Schneider, Henry Hawrecht, John Rex, John Clark, Doctor Whiting, C. C. A. Witting, Samuel Petry, William Beals, Samuel Stanker, Joshua Saxton, Joseph Shorb, John Hawk, Samuel Hawk, Samuel Hunt.

Of the above, Matthias Sheplar, David A. Starkweather, and Benjamin F. Leiter, each were members of Congress. John Rex was the father of Hon. George Rex, now one of the supreme judges of Ohio. John Saxton, Esq., James Allen, William Dunbar, Daniel Gutshall, Peter Kauffman, were all able editors. Several of the others named represented the county in the legislature. The physicians named were able men in their profession, known far and wide. The lawyers, Griswold, Starkweather, Carter, Lahm, and Belden, had no superior in eastern Ohio; and of the others it may be said that, as farmers and business men, their influence and examples at an early day made Stark County take rank as one of the first-class counties in the State.

FIRST HOUSES, MILLS, STORE, STILL-HOUSE, ETC.

The first buildings erected in the present county of Tuscarawas were, so far as known, as follows: 1760, Thomas Calhoun, trader's house, on the west bank of the Tuscarawas, near Bolivar; 1761, Christian Post's dwelling house, on the east bank of the Tuscarawas, near Bolivar; 1763,

James O'Harn's trader house, on the east bank of the Tuscarawas, near Bolivar; 1772, David Zeisberger's mission houses, on the east bank of the Tuscarawas, at Schoenbrunn; 1773, John Christian Roth, and others, houses at Gnadenhutten; 1774, James Campbell and others, trader house, at present New Comerstown; 1779, D. Zeisberger and others, houses on the west bank of the Tuscarawas, New Schoenbrunn; 1780, J. Heckewelder and others, houses on the west bank of the Tuscarawas, at Salem; 1796, Charles Stevens, settler, in the present township of Fairfield; 1797, C. Clewell and John Carr and others, at present Gnadenhutten; 1798, Mortimer Benger and others, dwellings at Goshen; 1797, Jacob Bush, Paul Greer, Peter Edmonds, Ezra and Peter Warner, and others of the settlers; 1799, David Peter opened a store at Gnadenhutten for Jacob Recksecker, and H. Bollinger brought teams with goods for the store; 1800, Lewis Huebner, pastor's house and Beesheba church, on the west side of the river, near lock number seventeen; John Kinsey and George Stiffer built near New Philadelphia in 1804; Philip Menech built on the present Gooden farm in 1805; John Hull built the first house in New Philadelphia in 1805; Jacob Uhrich built the first mill (water) at Uhrichville, in 1807; the first horse-mills were put up in 1772, '73 and '74, by the missionaries; the first tavern built in New Philadelphia was by Leninger, in 1807; the first still house in the county was put up by Gabriel Cryder, on the west side of the Tuscarawas, about equi-distant between New Philadelphia and Dover. A Mr. Vanrouff built the first ark, or grain-boat, at the canal at Dover; George Sluthour did the carpenter work. Amos St. Clair built the first bridge across the river, at Dover, in 1826.

FIRST BIRTHS IN OHIO.

John Ludwig Roth, son of Rev. John and Maria Agnes Roth, was born at Gnadenhutten mission, in the present Tuscarawas County, on the fourth day of July, A. D. 1773.

This was the first white child born in the valley, and it is claimed to be the first in Ohio, but the white wife of a French officer gave birth to a child at Fort Junandat, on the Sandusky, as early as 1754, and while Ohio was French territory.

On the 13th of April, 1781, was born at Salem, in the present Tuscarawas County, Maria, daughter of John and Sarah Joanna Heckewelder. Her birth has been stated as occurring on April 6, 1781, but the 13th is correct.

Richard Conner and wife had one or more children born at Schoenbrunn prior to 1781.

Of the several ministers, Mortimer, Smick, Jungman, Edwards, Senseman, and others, none had children in the valley, except as above named.

FIRST CHRISTIAN BURIALS.

Prior to 1775 seventeen interments of Christians had taken place at Schoenbrunn grave-yard, on the farm now owned by Rev. Elisha P. Jacobs, three miles east of New Philadelphia. Between 1774 and 1781 a larger number were there interred, aggregating about forty in all. It was the first burying grounds of Christians in the two valleys, and has long since been obliterated by the plow.

At Guadenhutten grave-yard an equal, if not greater, number of Christians were interred prior to 1782, when the town was burned and inhabitants slaughtered. In October, 1799, John Heckewelder and David Peter, who had came to the burnt town in 1797, gathered up the bones of the slain and buried them in a cellar, on the spot where the monument stands.

In 1801, Rev. William Edwards was buried at Goshen cemetery, as also Zeisberger in 1808, and a number of Christian Indians.

The above three are undoubtedly the most ancient cemeteries in the county, and the first two are the most ancient Christian burying grounds in the State of Ohio.

FIRST PREACHERS IN THE COUNTY.

Of the first preachers in the county mention may be made of David Zeisberger, 1772; Rev. Heckewelder, Smick, Edwards, Roth, Jungman, Huebner and Mortimer; Rev. George Godfrey Miller, of Beersheba church, 1808; Rev. Christian Espech, Lutheran, New Philadelphia, 1811; Rev. Abraham Snyder, Lutheran, 1810; Deacon Elias Crane, 1816; Rev. John Graham, 1817; Rev. Wieland Zarman, 1818; Rev. Michael J. Baumberzoar, 1818; Rev. Thomas B. Clark, and Rev. Jacob Ransberger, in 1819.

THE OLDEST INHABITANTS, MEN AND WOMEN, OF THE TUSCARAWAS VALLEY.

The following are lists of the oldest inhabitants of the valley, who were born prior to the beginning of the present century, and who were, with a few exceptions, ancestors of the persons of the same name now living in Tuscarawas and other counties:

Oldest Inhabitants of Goshen Township.

Born between 1730 and 1740, William Young.

Born between 1750 and 1760, Mrs. Knisely, mother of David; Mrs. Judy, mother of John, Sr.; Mrs. William Young, John Hoopengarner.

Born between 1760 and 1770, Matthias Gossett and wife, Mrs. Lucinda Baltzley, Henry Espich and wife, Philip Fackler, Isaac Cordray, Sr., Valentine Flack, Christian Bachman, Henry Meter, Henry Albright, Philip Jacob Fechtling.

Born between 1770 and 1780, Samuel W. Kendrick, Christian Casebeer and wife, David Stiffler, Sr., and wife, John Judy, Sr., and wife, James Wood, John Frederick, Henry Auchenbaugh, Abraham Kniseley, Sr., and wife, Philip and Jacob Foreman, Mrs. V. Flack, Christian Fuller, George Platz, Mrs. C. Bachman, Casper Engler, Agnes Ellis, John McPherson and wife, Mrs. J. Hoopengarner, Amelia Hummell, Mrs. Henry Albright, John Suttle and wife, John Walby, Edward Dorsey and wife, George Stiffler, Sr., and wife.

Oldest Inhabitants of Dover Township.

Born between 1730 and 1740, Mrs. Finton, mother of William.

Born between 1740 and 1750, Mrs. Brown, grandmother of George W.

Born between 1750 and 1760, George Helwig, Mrs. Crisswell, mother of John; Elijah Critz, Mrs. Critz, mother of Andrew.

Born between 1760 and 1770, Adam Snyder, Mrs. Wallack, Mrs. Lower, Philip Baker, William Finton, Christian Kore, Godfrey Imber.

Born between 1770 and 1780, Richard Burrough, William Gibbs, Sr., George R. Baer and wife, William Henderson, Conrad Lower, John Mumma, Benjamin Wallack, Ludwig Lower, Henry Frinkenbriner, Mrs. William Finton, Paul Grove, Sr., James Harper, Mrs. Kauffman, mother of Jacob; John Hildt, Sr., Mary Burroughs, C. Noftsinger and wife, Mrs. Christian Kore, Elizabeth Harmon, John Chesterman and wife, C. Ritter, Abraham Share, Jacob Blickensderfer.

Oldest Inhabitants of Wayne Township.

Born between 1740 and 1750, William Collett, Mrs. Burrell, mother of Benjamin.

Born between 1750 and 1760, John France.

Born between 1760 and 1770, Henry Myers, Eve Baer, Henry Duncan, John Bess, Sr., and wife, Jacob Bartlett and wife Daniel Bowers, Mrs. Obadiah Patterson, Adam Reamer, Cornelius Hand, Edward Jordan.

Born between 1770 and 1780, John Aultman and wife, Eve Deardorff, George Wallack, John Tyler and wife, John Michael, Benjamin Gorsuch, Henry Knovel, John Lidey, Jacob Knaga, Mrs. Henry Duncan, Mrs. Bayliss Jennings, John Burrell, George Gusler, Jere. Savage and wife, Jonathan Williams, Regena Fulk, Mrs. Philip Bash, Abraham Beninger, Mrs Daniel Bowers, George Rickett and wife, John McQuiston, Sr., and wife, Jacob Snearly, James Mills, Mrs. Adam Reamer, Mrs. David Reshley, Aesop Johnson, John G. Miller, Michael Wallack, John Wright, Sr., Mary Ann Shonk, Elizabeth Swip, Patrick Moore, Michael Kore and wife, John Seloz.

Oldest Inhabitants of Sugar Creek Township.

Born between 1740 and 1750, Michael Dorner, Sr

Born between 1750 and 1760, Mrs. Michael Dorner, Mrs. Bittle, mother of George; Mrs Walter, mother of John; Joseph Kine and wife, John Yotter, David Miller, Jocob Miller, Sr., Mrs. Mafendish, mother of William D.

Born between 1760 and 1770, John Ballman, Daniel Kaiser, Susannah Correll, Peter Harmon and wife, John Miller and wife, Isaac Miller, Mrs. Coblentz, mother of Jacob; Mrs. Jacob Miller, Sr., James Hattery, Joseph Hanlon and wife.

Born between 1770 and 1780, George Richardson and wife, John Walter, Jacob Dietz and wife, Mrs. Daniel Kaiser, John Bricker, Frederick Dorner, Chris. Winklepleck, Peter Hostetter, George Dyce and wife, George Smiley, George Miller, Abram Snyder, Daniel Yotter, Henry Kuntz, Ephriam Middaugh, Jacob Miller, Jr., Mrs. James Hattery, Christian Livengood, Leonard Hyder, Catherine Barnhouse, John Schultze, Jacob Lowe, William D. Mafendish, Mary Noel, Andrew Burkey.

Oldest Inhabitants of Warwick Township.

Born between 1740 and 1750, Barney Reysert, Sr.

Born between 1750 and 1760, William Simmers, Sr., and wife, Godfrey Westhaver, Henry Davis.

Born between 1760 and 1770, Jesse Walton, Samuel Fry, Abraham Fry, Mrs. Benjamin Lane, Jacob Royer and wife, Mrs. Barney Rupert.

Born between 1770 and 1780, Boaz Walton, Jr., John G. Hoffman, Henry Keller, George Metzger, John Knouse, John Demuth, Asa Walton and wife, John Whitehead, Joseph Sturgiss, William Hill, Joseph Madden, John Romig and wife, Joseph Shemal, John Richmond and wife, Richard Taylor, Catherine Whitman.

Oldest Inhabitants of Salem Township.

Born between 1750 and 1760, Peter Good.

Born between 1760 and 1770, Humphrey Corbin.

Born between 1770 and 1780, William Haga and wife, Mrs. Peter Good, Mrs. Frankboner, Mrs. Paine, Burris Moore, Mrs. Barneby Riley, Charles Hill and wife, Jesse Hill and wife.

Oldest Inhabitants of York Township.

Born between 1750 and 1760, Frederick Hummell, Henry Shawver.

Born between 1760 and 1770, Mrs. Frederick Hummell, John Shull, John Pence, William Ross, Eli Barton, George Putt, John Benfer and wife.

Born between 1770 and 1780, William Butt, Mrs. John Shull, Francis Garnant, Henry Ankeny, Samuel Deardorff and wife, Lewis Fox, Mrs Eli Barton, Mrs. George Putt, Christian Beaver, Mary Cummings, George W. Kuhn, William Wolff, Henry Shawver, John Grimes and wife, Jacob Howe, Michael Bedinger.

Oldest Inhabitants of Clay Township.

Born between 1750 and 1760, John Taylor, John P. Sargood, Conrad Roemer,

Born between 1760 and 1770, Adam Stocker, Barbara Wheeland, Mary Genter, Mrs. J. P. Sargood.

Born between 1770 and 1780, Christian Stocker, Mrs. Adam Stocker, Andrew Stocker, Charles L. Stevens, Martin Kiser, John G. Fox, Elizabeth Rebstock, Mrs. Samuel Dingman, Michael Remmell, Henry Kaler.

Oldest Inhabitants of Washington Township.

Born between 1750 and 1760, Matthew Organ, Mrs. George Hussey, Sr.

Born between 1760 and 1770, Jonathan Andrews and wife, Mrs. Matthew Organ, Benjamin G. Duharnell, George Hussey, Jr., Joseph Taylor.

Born between 1770 and 1780, Anannias Randall and wife, Jesse Webb, Isaac Webb, Joseph Miller, James Hamilton, Magdalene Taylor.

Oldest Inhabitants of Perry Township.

Born between 1730 and 1740, Mrs Swain, mother of Joshua, Joseph Johnson, Rebecca Kannon.

Born between 1740 and 1750, John Shaw.

Born between 1750 and 1760, Mrs. Severgood, grandmother of Jacob, Mrs. Morrison, grandmother of Samuel, Peter Hammer, Thomas Archbold, Elisha Kitch and wife.

Born between 1760 and 1770, John Williams, Richard Moore and wife, Ebenezer Kitch.

Born between 1770 and 1780, Shadrack Minster, Mrs. John Williams, Stephen Horn, Moses Horn, Mrs. Parks, Mrs. Robert McCoy, Edward Johnson, Mrs. Schooly, mother of Samuel, Joseph Johnson, Neil Morris, William George, Samuel Boston and wife John Wilson and wife, Gabriel Vansickle and wife, Timora Russell, Mrs. T. Archbold.

Oldest Inhabitants of Rush Township.

Born between 1750 and 1760, Michael Sponsler.

Born between 1760 and 1770, Thomas Gibson, John Fairbrother, Mrs. Ginter, mother of John, Casper Warner, Joshua Davis, William Caples, Sr.

Born between 1770 and 1780, Michael Van Fleary, John Uhrich, Robert Laughlin, Mrs. Thomas Gibson, Thomas Connell, Mrs. Michael Sponsler, Esther Crumm, Peter Bowman and wife, Daniel Enterline, Conrad Westhaver, Mrs. Joshua Davis, Abijah Robinett, James Tracy, John Lambright.

Oldest Inhabitants of Oxford Township.

Born between 1760 and 1770, Samuel Tucker, John Pearce Sr., and wife, Mrs. Gardner, Margaret Tufford.

Born between 1770 and 1780, Sarah Booth, Mrs. Anderson, John Mulvane, Lewis Roberts, William Andrews, Elizabeth Neighbor, William Neighbor, Sr., James Sloane, Mary Ann Salyards, Joseph North.

Oldest Inhabitants of Dohrman Township.

[The territory that comprised this township was subdivided and is now Mill Township, Tuscarawas County, and portions of Harrison and Carroll counties.]

Born between 1730 and 1740, Mrs. Utterbach, grandmother of William.

Born between 1740 and 1750, Stephen Johnson.

Born between 1750 and 1760, Solomon Delong, Adam Gott, George Dickinson, Mrs. Hilton, mother of Leonard; Thomas and William Crumm.

Born between 1760 and 1770, George Snowdigle, Mrs. Solomon Delong, John Hunter, James McKay, Mrs. George Dickinson, John McElroy, Thomas Drummond, John Black Stewart Auld and wife, Andrew Sewell and wife, John Niblack, Sr., and wife, Robert Wilson and wife, William Blackwell, Mrs. Robert Gracy, William Utterbach, Susannah Blackwood, Tarleton B. Willoughby, Mrs. Robert Carson, Elijah Boston and wife, Mrs. John Johnston, Edward Bennett, Susannah Carroll.

Born between 1770 and 1780, John Hooper, John Larry, William Mills, John McBean, Mrs. Moses Rutledge, Mrs. George Snowdigle, Ebenezer Ball, Rebecca Cox, Rezin Pomeroy, Mrs. John McElroy, Nancy McGill, William Corbett, Isaac Eaton, James Aucksom and wife, Samuel Caldwell, Felix Richardson, William Moore and wife, Asa Hamblin, George Hoskins and wife, Harmon

Gitchell, Henry Foster, Thomas Brock, Martha Sterling, Mrs William Welsh, Griffith Cahill and wife, John Howell and wife, Richard French, John Cahill, Sr., John Moore, Arthur Chenoweth and wife.

Oldest Inhabitants of Lawrence Township.

Born between 1740 and 1750, Mrs. Hartser, grandmother of Frederick.

Born between 1750 and 1760, Mrs. Bimeler, mother of Joseph M., Stephen Hoover, John Baker, Mrs. Torner, mother of John.

Born between 1760 and 1770, James Mock, Christopher Platz, Magdalena Auch, Margaret Ackerman, Jacob Heck, John Keller, Sr, John Fashbaugh, William Fashbaugh, Jacob Palmer, Barney Brown, Christopher Singer.

Born between 1770 and 1780, Mrs. Stephen Hoover, Barbara Schock, Godfrey Lent and wife, Casper Fetter and wife, Jacob Shearing, John Miller and wife, Dorothea Dietz, Jacob Kimmerly and wife, Frederick Klotz, Joseph Boyler, Peter Houseman, John Streby and wife, John Mock, John Machin, John Taylor, Mrs. William Fashbaugh, Michael Schaeffer, George Mock and wife, Benjamin Brown and wife, Elizabeth Kullers.

Oldest Inhabitants of Warren and Union Townships.

Born between 1740 and 1750, Mrs. Holmes, mother of Jacob; Conrad Pearch, Mrs. Conover, grandmother of James; Frederick Everhart.

Born between 1750 and 1760 Charles Scott, Joseph Wilson, Joseph Rutter, Sr., Samuel Sample, Sr., Mrs. Frederick Everhart, William Trussell, John Beamer, John Wyandt, Sr.

Born between 1760 and 1770, Joseph Hayes, Frederick Mizer and wife, William Scott and wife, Samuel Russell, Jacob Holmes, Thomas Mills and wife, George Davis, John Witchcraft, Samuel Anderson, Paul Preston, John Dunlap, Michael Smith, Robert Stevenson and wife, Peter Jennings and wife, John Ramsberger and wife, Samuel Lappin and wife, Martin Hoffman, Philip Senter, William McClary, Sr., Thomas McPherson, Reuben Runyan, Peter Beamer, Patrick Reardon, William Sherrard, Abram Richardson, Sr., and wife, Moses Shaw, Benjamin Price, John Tinkey, Charles A. Lindsey and wife, William Sears, George Study.

Born between 1770 and 1780, Samuel Griffin, Henry Machaman and wife, Joseph Miller, Kinsey Cahill, Robert Scott and wife, George Davis, Philip Capel and wife, Mary Huffman, James Russell, David Davis, James Davis, Andrew Miller and wife, George Alfred Andrew Black, Catherine Strause, William Conwell, Elizabeth Marley, Daniel Swally and wife, Joseph Buskirk, William Albaugh, Adam Beamer, Frederick Weaver, James Sellers and wife, Jacob Shaffer, Peter Close, John Cross, Adam Sherrard, Nicholas Skeels, Richard Herron, Philip Miller Isaac Masters, Mary Seran, Obadiah Holmes.

Oldest Inhabitants of Bucks Township.

Born between 1750 and 1760, Mary Seldenright, Jacob Lorrey, Mrs. Bennell, mother of William.

Born between 1760 and 1770, Albright Kintlesberger, Stoddard Anderson,

Mrs. Cummings, mother of Richard, Guy Young, Mrs Helwig, mother of Benjamin, Mrs. Jacob Forney, Israel Penrod and wife, Peter Kern.

Born between 1770 and 1780, David Hoover, Mrs. Guy Young, Valentine Thompson, Mrs. Peter Kern, Joseph Dormer, George Cutshall, John Spangler, Sr., and wife.

Oldest Inhabitants of Fairfield Township.

Born between 1750 and 1760, John Bowman and wife, Thomas Cordroy, Sr.

Born between 1760 and 1770, Jacob Weaver, John McCleary, Mrs. Joseph Herminger, George Kollars, Margaret Long, Matthew Laird, Jacob Smith, Gideon Jennings.

Born between 1770 and 1780, Peter Wolf and wife, John Davy and wife, James McKee and wife, Jacob Waltz and wife, Charles Stevens and wife, Ludwig Snowland, Nathan Corderay, George Strawn.

Oldest Inhabitants of One Leg Township, living in 1830.

[This township was added to Carroll at the erection of that county, in 1833.]

Born between 1730 and 1740, Mrs. Gamble, mother of George.

Born between 1740 and 1750, Mary Waggoner and Mathias Shiltz.

Born between 1750 and 1760, Samuel Snelling, William Reed and wife, Adam Swihart, Sr., Henry Martin, Frederick Walters, Mrs. Warford, grandmother of William.

Born between 1760 and 1770, John Rule, Jacob Crager and wife, Ann Patterson, John Phœnix, William Gamble, Mrs. Laffer, mother of Adam, John Bowers, Sr., George Crumrine, Mary Warner, John Fry and wife, Joseph Jeffries, William Perkins, John Getterell, William Bavard and wife, Mrs Barrack Roby, James Roby and wife, and Benjamin Leggett.

Born between 1770 and 1780, Michael Thompson, George Nicholson, Joseph Boyd, James Palmer, Samuel McKee, Daniel McMillan, John Sterling, Samuel Hyde, William Watkins, Joseph McDaniel and wife, Abram Warner, William Rouse, Michael Quinn, Jesse Clark and wife, Benjamin Knight, George Gamble and wife, William Ball, Daniel Black, Sarah Stoneman, Barney Bower and wife, Alexander Smith and wife, Mrs. Richard Huff, Patrick McMillan, Richard Coleman, William Kyle, Amos Doyle and wife, Henry Ball and wife, Jesse Carter, Eve Glass, Parlan Pyle, Thomas Walker, Barrack Roby, James Parker, Mrs. George Crumrine, and Mrs. William Gamble.

Oldest Inhabitants of Sandy Township.

Born between 1740 and 1750, Walling Miller and wife.

Born between 1750 and 1760, Mrs. M. Burroway, Philip Farber and wife, George Barnett, Catherine Fulk.

Born between 1760 and 1770, Elizabeth Grinder, John Lennox, William Baird, Elizabeth West, Mrs. J. Johnson, Thomas McKnight, Mary Shees, Michael Flicking and wife.

Born between 1770 and 1780, Joseph Sadler, George Barringer and wife, Frederick Holtzhoy, James Bailey, John Burke and wife, Asa Menard and wife, Henry Wingate, Thomas McKnight and wife, William Williams, Joshua Weaver.

SKETCHES OF EARLY SETTLERS, AND ANECDOTES.

CHRISTIAN DEARDORFF

Was one of the first pioneers on Sugar Creek. He came from Maryland, prior to 1807, and settled at what is now Dover, where he took out a ferry license as early as 1809. In company with Bohn and Slingluff he bought land, and laid off farm lots, and platted the town of Dover, which became, and has since retained the name of being, the great wheat market of the county. Mr. Deardorff became one of the associate judges of the court in 1808, and remained in that position until 1824, being the longest period of service of any man who ever held office in the county. A man of the most sterling integrity in all the affairs of life, his name became the synonym of all that was honest and upright. He left a large family of sons to inherit his virtues and his large property, all of whom he made farmers and business men. Being advised to make his son Jesse a professional man, he shook his head, but finally consented to try it; and on Jesse's return from New Athens College in 1841–2, he was asked by the judge what class he graduated in. He replied that he was the best ball-player there. Judge Deardorff died in 1851, and his wife Catherine is yet living in 1875, being perhaps the oldest of the wives of the first pioneers west of the river.

JOHN JUDY.

Among the first white settlers of the county was John Tschudi—in English, Judy—who came to the United States in 1803, and reached Tuscarawas County the same year. He was descended from an ancient Swiss family, the head of which, Von Aegidies Tschudi, was born at Glams in 1505, and who wrote the Chronicles of Switzerland, dating back to A. D. 1000, and coming down to 1470. The subject of this sketch came first to Gnadenhutten, and being single, put up a cabin on a piece of land he had contracted for with John Heckewelder. While making rails, John Knisely, the founder of New Philadelphia, came to the woods where Judy was at work, and bought a large hog of him, and engaged him to come up to town and assist in raising a barn. He did so, and the hog and his work make the first payment on fifty acres he then bought of Knisely, about one mile east of New Philadelphia, and which he owned until he died, having added thereto by other purchases. Martin Keller and Jacob Keller, with their father, had come over with Judy, who was saved from being sold for passage money by their aid. Mr. Judy was a tailor by trade, and made clothes for the Indians; and at some time he put up on Water street the first house erected in New Philadelphia; assisted in cutting out the first road east from the town; and was three days helping to move Godfrey Hoff from town to his settlement, about ten miles up the river, having to make a road, and in some places traveled up the bed of the river.

PHILIP CORRELL.

Among the earliest settlers about New Philadelphia were John, Jacob and Abraham Knisely, Henry Laffer, Major Cribbs, Peter Williams, James Clark, Christian Espich, John Judy, Sr., Henry Minnich, George Lininger, George Steffler, George Stuthour, Abraham Shane, Philip Correll, David Knisely, all of whom are dead except the two last. Mr. Correll informs the writer that in 1811 there were ten or twelve houses in New Philadelphia, and but three or four graves in the cemetery. At Dover there was then but one house in the present town, and that the ferry house. At the Goshen mission there were about thirty families; among whom were Christian and John Henry, sons of the chief Killbuck; Widow White Eyes and two daughters, "Big Foot" and two sons. A party of warriors from Canada came to Goshen, dressed in war costume. Correll and others "went for them," believing there was a premium on scalps. They found the warriors hid in the drift on the island, named by General Putnam "Zeisberger Island," opposite Goshen. After some parley, the Indians surrendered and were brought to jail—which stood where the Auditor's office now is—and remained there hobbled until Colonel Cass came and had them taken away.

In the war of 1812, he says, about two hundred volunteers went from Tuscarawas County to Fort Meigs, the greater number of whom returned safe. He also says several hundred Kentuckians passed through New Philadelphia to the scene of war, and returned home the same way. They had no money, and moved along in scattered parties, the citizens supplying them with provisions while at New Philadelphia, his father feeding twenty to thirty every night. Henry Laffer was detailed as a commissary to take a lot of flour to Mansfield, and young Correll went along as driver of a team. He says that when they got to Wooster there was a panic among the settlers in that country, hearing that the Indians were coming with the British to lay waste the whole of Eastern Ohio. The flour was quickly unloaded at Wooster, and the teams hurried home. On their way back they found the roads lined with the teams of settlers, fleeing east with their families. It turned out that the panic arose from the landing at Cleveland of a large number of paroled soldiers from Hull's surrendered army; whereupon the panic subsided, and the settlers, among whom were some in Tuscarawas County who had fled, returned to their homes, and the county of Tuscarawas escaped the devastations of war.

PETER WILLIAMS

Came to New Philadelphia from Pennsylvania as early as 1808, and was then about twenty years old. He took out license to keep store. In 1811 was appointed county treasurer, being the second in the county. In 1813 he married Maria, daughter of John Knisely, who laid out New Philadelphia, which assured his success in life. He served as treasurer until 1823; and being a shrewd business man, became possessed of good farms and town property, which made him wealthy. Mr. Williams also served as county commissioner, and as associate judge several years. It is related of him that while judge he traveled about some in other counties, and noticing that the judges generally had arm and cushioned or hickory-bottomed split chairs, instead of the old-fashioned straight-backs, hard bottoms, with no arms, as used in Tuscarawas, he determined to effect a reform in this respect. Shortly after his return home he called on Auditor King, told him what fine chairs other counties had provided, and asked King to furnish new chairs for our judges. King, who was a rigid economist, said he guessed the people would prefer to have *new judges* instead of new chairs. The result was that he refused Williams' request, and no new chairs were provided until after Williams retired from the bench, in 1839. Judge Williams had thirteen children, and died in 1868. His wife, Maria, died in 1875, aged seventy-nine years.

JACOB BLICKENSDERFER

Came to Ohio about 1800, and settled as a general business man, able to discharge any duty, being an educated man and having a fine mathematical mind. He served as a county commissioner, president of a bank, took an active part in behalf of the construction of the Ohio Canal through this valley, and in opening up roads through this county, and was always foremost in any improvement going on. He was county auditor from 1818 to 1820, associate judge from 1829 to 1836, and again from 1850 to 1852. He also represented the county in the general assembly, and was a delegate to the constitutional convention in 1851. He was perhaps the most practical man in his day on anything, except making money. Although he purchased largely of lands and other property, and was a man of ordinary economy, he died, after a useful life to his fellow-men, without a sufficiency to discharge his liabilities, which were afterward provided for by his sons out of their means. Failing to leave a fortune to them, as he might have done, they entered upon the career of life the more earnestly, and Professor Jacob Blickensderfer, Jr., to-day stands unsurpassed for his engineering and mathematical attainments, commanding at this time a salary equal to that of a foreign minister or cabinet officer.

JOHN KNISELY AND HENRY LAFFER.

These two men were in the forefront of early civilization in Tuscarawas, and their names are to be found in the list of the first pioneers, in another part of this work.

Knisely came about 1804; bought the thirty-five hundred acre tract on which he laid out New Philadelphia in 1805–6; and to procure the county-seat to be located thereat, donated to the county one hundred and sixty acres and one hundred town lots.

Laffer came about 1806; bought and built at New Philadelphia, and opened a hotel of that day, in 1808–9, which he made headquarters for early settlers.

Both were men of self-will, great energy, ambitious in their way, and each looked upon the other as a rival. One had the more money, and the other the greater brain. The power of the one equalized the power of the other at the start. Just then mischief-makers stepped in. Each had his friends and enemies, who carried stories to irritate. It was whispered to Knisely by one that Laffer had been seen taking his hay. He accosted Laffer in a rough, brusque manner, and taunted him with what he heard. Laffer repelled the imputation, and added that he had never stole hay, or sold the people, or corrupted public officers—alluding to the land and lot donations in the county-seat matter. Knisely repelled the insinuation of bribery; and then said he could prove the charge, having become much heated. They parted enemies. Laffer commenced an action of slander against Knisely for five hundred dollars damages, and caused his arrest on a capias. The trial came on in 1810, Knisely employing Louis Cass and others, and Laffer employing E. Herrick and others, attorneys. The jury found a verdict for defendant, the plaintiff failing to prove that Knisely had spoken the slanderous words.

The blood of these two pioneers was now at a red heat, and Laffer being appointed sheriff of the county, it may be presumed that Knisely feared he would use official influence to injure him. At all events he was ready to continue the war, and sued Laffer for cutting down and carrying away some white-oak, black-oak, and hickory trees from Knisely's woods, claiming two hundred dollars damages. The jury gave him fifty dollars. Thus embittered against each other by bad men, they remained hostile for years, Laffer being all the time honored with office, whilst Knisely was equally respected in private life. After Laffer removed to the Sandy, and laid Sandyville out, he met Knisely one day in the road near the old Canton ford, both being on horseback. "Who stole the hay?" said Laffer. "Not you," replied Knisely; and then he asked, "Who bribed the commissioners, and sold the people?" "Not you," answered Laffer. "That's the truth, and no lie," said an old fisherman sitting close by, and whom they had not seen. His testimony made them laugh, get off their horses, shake hands and bury the hatchet, with a drink of cool water at Federal Springs. From that time until they died they remained friends.

ABRAHAM SHANE

Came to New Philadelphia about 1806, from Pennsylvania, where he was born. He was about twenty-one years of age. One of the first hotels at the county-seat was kept by him. In the war of 1812 he raised two or three companies, and served on the frontier; after which he served as justice, and in other township offices many years, and also served in the general assembly. In the war of the State of Ohio against the United States bank, about 1816, the bank had established a branch in Ohio, and refused to pay any taxes. The State treasurer broke open its vault, and forcibly took therefrom its quota of taxes. For this he was arrested by the bank, and the State sued, the bank claiming that under its charter it could hold property and do business in any State without being amenable to the State laws for taxes. The Ohio assembly sustained its State treasurer, and an excitement was the consequence throughout the State. General Shane raised a squad of men in the Tuscarawas valley to go to Chillicothe and blot the branch bank out of existence; but the United States court sustaining the bank, the State refunded the taxes, and the war ended.

General Shane was at the time, and for a long period before his death, a citizen of Dover, and in the early days shipped flour and other articles in arks down the Tuscarawas and Muskingum, thence to New Orleans. He died much esteemed as one of the most prominent of the early pioneers.

WALTER M. BLAKE

Came to New Philadelphia about 1817, and died in 1865. He was engaged in building the canal, the county courthouse, and served in many civil positions—sheriff, treasurer, county auditor, State senator, associate judge and presidential elector. Was one of the most energetic men of his day and generation, carrying with him to the grave the respect of all men. Was acquainted with all the public men of the State, and was particularly distinguished as the most indefatigable of opponents of all double dealing and chicanery, either in or out of office. This trait, coupled with remarkable sagacity, as well as independence of character, made him some enemies, more than he otherwise would have had, but at the same time it saved him many troubles. Over all things he prized manly firmness and dignity, as well as the remembrance of gratitude for favors received. In this connection he often related an incident which happened in the early days, in the courthouse at New Philadelphia. Judge Alexander Harper had been placed on the bench through the friendship and instrumentality of John M. Goodenow, as the latter claimed. Goodenow and Harper afterward became estranged, for some cause or other, and on the occasion of a trial in which Goodenow took the leading part as attorney, he was ordered, for some remark made, to take his seat, which he did, but immediately arose again and began addressing the jury, but was set down a second time. He then asked Judge Harper if he might say a few words to the jury in the way of repentance. "Certainly," said the judge, supposing an apology was coming. Goodenow raised to his full height, looking at the jury, and pointing with a quivering finger to the judge, said: "Gentlemen of the jury, God made man, and then he repented," alluding in that way to the alleged fact that he had made Harper judge, and now he repented of it.

General Blake, when young, had been in the war of 1812, and afterward a land warrant was issued to him In the Mexican war he raised a company, but failed to get it mustered into the service. In the State militia he became a colonel and general, and in all respects he was a noble specimen of a settler of the early times in the valley. Having never married, his property, some thirty thousand dollars, passed mainly to brothers and sisters.

ALEXANDER M'CONNELL

Came to New Philadelphia about 1810, and worked at his trade. He was of Irish descent, and worked a while at tailoring. Afterward, in the war of 1812, he raised a squad of cavalry for frontier defense, but did not get into action. During the war, three Mohican Indians, armed, came to Goshen Mission, and picked quarters on Zeisberger island. Some whites having been murdered beyond Wooster by Indians, these were suspected. McConnell's cavalry went down, captured and lodged them in jail. They would have been killed by the cavalry, but for McConnell's courage in preventing it. While in jail, a company of forty armed men from the West came to the jail to kill the Indians. McConnell again interfered to save their lives, and, with the assistance of John C. Wright and Sheriff Laffer, succeeded. The Indians were then sent out of the county, and it turned out that they simply visited Goshen to see some Indian relatives, who were converts there. After the war, McConnell had a suit in court, in which the celebrated lawyer, John M. Goodenow appeared against him, and belabored McConnell in his argument. Meeting in Albert's Tavern, McConnell, then in liquor, asked Goodenow if he knew where the lawyers all go when they die. Goodenow confessed his ignorance, and asked to be informed. "Well," said McConnell, "they all go to h—ll." "Ah!" replied Goodenow, "that is better than to go where drunken tailors do." "And where is that?" asked McC. "Why," said Goodenow, "they go to Heckely Barny, five miles below h—ll." "And what is done with them there?" inquired McConnell. "Oh!" said Goodenow, "the devil, finding them saturated with whisky, makes his mince-pies out of them, without having to mix in liquor." Finding himself beaten, McConnell retired.

Mr. McConnell in after times resided in Dover, became a justice, and, by reason of his capacity and integrity, did a heavy business as magistrate. He died in Dover, in 1839.

JOHN COVENTRY

Came to Tuscarawas from Pennsylvania, and settled, about 182–, at New Philadelphia, where he for some time carried on mercantile business with James Patrick, Sr., under the name of Coventry & Patrick. He then turned his attention to farming, which he followed very successfully, adding tract after tract to his first purchase; and at his death, in 1872, he was the owner of about eight hundred acres, estimated in value at one hundred dollars per acre. Close in his business matters, he insisted always in having the last cent due to him; and in settling with men he made it his rule to pay the last fraction of a cent due to them. By virtue of this rigid adherence to upright dealing, he acquired the name of "Honest John." His personal life was unspotted, and by reason of his peculiarities he was known far and wide. He was always opposed to holding public positions, but occasionally the citizens would force him into a township trusteeship, and rather than pay the two dollars fine, he would always discharge the duties, with such rigid honesty as to acquire sufficient unpopularity, designedly, to insure exemption from office for years afterward. The only public position he is known to have held, outside of the township, was on the occasion of hunting for Funston, the murderer of Cartwell, the mailboy. At that time Mr. Covéntry was detailed by Sheriff Blake as one of the posse to make a night raid on a house where Funston was suspected to be. On arriving at the place, and after surrounding the house, Sheriff Blake ordered a search of the house, but without success. Coventry and another were ordered to ascend to the loft, up a ladder, and having got up, the light went out, and some one pulled away the ladder, so that Coventry was in the dark in a strange garret hunting for a murderer, and no means of escape left to either. Pulling out the only weapon he had, a dirk knife, he and his companion groped about, and found nothing but a pair of men's stogies, wet and muddy. By this time Blake had restored order below, put up the ladder, and Coventry descended with his comrade and the stogies, and the posse came away, but not until an unsuccessful attempt was made by a relative of Funston to get possession of the stogies. In the melee Coventry drew his dirk, and threatened death to any one touching the leather foot-gear, which deterred the inmates from any further interference. It afterward turned out that the stogies fitted the footprints in the earth near the spot where Cartwell was shot, and after Funston's arrest they were found to fit him, and belong to him, and that settled his fate. Honest John, in recounting the incident to the writer of this sketch, twenty years ago, said he made up his mind in that dark garret that nobody would ever see him acting as a county officer again, and he kept his word.

GEORGE SLUTHOUR, SR.,

Was born in Pennsylvania between 1780 and 1790, and came to New Philadelphia as early as 1811. Followed the avocation of a carpenter, putting up more of the houses in the early times of New Philadelphia than any other carpenter. He died, universally respected, in 18—, leaving descendants. It is related that when the first bank in new Philadelphia was started, Sluthour had his shop on the south-west corner of the public square, where he was engaged at the house then on the lot, where Bury's store now is. Jacob Blickensderfer was president, and Abraham Shane cashier of the bank. Like all other banks of that day in Ohio, it was honestly run on paper money only, although the bills promised to pay in gold or silver on sight. It was started to build up the town, but met with a sad accident. One day a stranger stepped in with ten thousand dollars of the bills of the bank and demanded the coin. The officers told him to call in again in a short time. This gave them time to hide. They shut the bank and adjourned to Sluthour's shop. He told them he had not many shavings made, and that they had better separate; that he would hide the cashier in the shavings, while the president, having on a pair of leather or buckskin breeches, had better go into the red brush, near the present stable of J. C. Hance, and stay until the stranger left. Thus they kept shady until he was out of town. In a very short time he returned to the bank, and having no specie for him, they let the bank go up higher than a kite, and it never came down. About 1852 or '54, Peter Hines found the bank safe in a garret. It was an old-fashioned hair trunk, lined with newspapers, and behind which he found two Spanish quarters, dated 1796 and 1800, which the writer purchased for a dollar, so that he could boast of having all the specie of the first bank in New Philadelphia when it bursted.

JAMES PATRICK, SR.,

Came to New Philadelphia about ——, and started the Chronicle, the first newspaper in the county, which he controlled, except for a short period, for a quarter of a century. He has held the offices of county recorder, county auditor, associate judge of the common pleas, under State laws, and was appointed government agent to sell the Moravian lands; also filled the office of postmaster, under United States laws, always discharging every trust imposed upon him faithfully. As a politician he was a warm partisan, and at the time of Jackson's election, being postmaster at New Philadelphia, he commented in his paper severely on the conduct of Major Barry, of Kentucky, appointed by Jackson postmaster-general, and who traveled to Washington in a "coach and four," with negroes "before and behind," contrary, as Patrick justly thought, to the ideas of American simplicity in the early times. Some one sent Barry a copy of the paper containing the strictures, and in a few weeks Patrick lost his official head, and was P. M. no more. He relates in his paper of that day how he lost the recorder's office. While a candidate he let this man and that man have a little spare cash on loan, until it got abroad that Patrick was full of money, when dozens rushed to New Philadelphia, and bled him dry. Still they came, and failing to get a loan of a few dollars, the disappointed ones turned on him. To make all things even, and be fair all round, he called in his small loans, and this turned the other set on him, and he was defeated, with a hip, hip, hurrah! by both sets of money-borrowing voters, furnishing a practical illustration of the adage, "a little money is a dangerous thing," to a candidate for office. Judge Patrick is yet living, at the ripe age of — years, surrounded by his daughters and his three sons, whom he made printers, but who, refusing his advice, departed from his ways; and one, Andrew, has become a banker; while the other two, James and Abraham W. Patrick, have become prominent lawyers.

DEATH ROLL OF FOUR HUNDRED EARLY SETTLERS, FARMERS, MECHANICS, AND PROFESSIONAL MEN.

Died in 1820, Christian Blickensderfer, one of the first settlers.

Died in 1821, George Gimlans, one of the pioneers.

Died in 1822, Abraham Mosser, Samuel Slutts, Peter Walter, all belonging to the pioneers.

Died in 1823, Henry Benfer, Jacob Butt, Jeremiah Gard, Jacob Houck, Sr., David Seldenright, Isaac Simmers, Henry Sells, Henry Van Lehn, Joseph Hocksteller, Sylvester Johnston, Frederick Maish, John Rebstock.

Died in 1824, Leonard Baer, William Becher, Sr., Grodfrey Huga, Jr., Philip Minich, William Warford, all original settlers.

Died in 1825, Moses Ayres, one of the first settlers.

Died in 1826, Jacob Benope, Daniel Booth, Aquilla Carr, George W. Canfield, Ernest Deitz, Abraham Forney, Cornelius O'Donnell.

Died in 1827, Henry Baker, Samuel Lappin, father of Judge Lappin James McSweeny, John Switzer, John Welty.

Died in 1828, Henry Sliffe, Michael Ronk, Thornton Whitacre.

Died in 1829, Patrick Bennett, Francis Garnant.

Died in 1830, Conrad Bremer, Christian Baughman, Jacob Correll, Deardorff Isaac, John Fulk, George K. Gray, William Gibbs.

Died in 1831, Philip Baker, Philip Foreman, Annanias Randall.

Died in 1832, David Foreman, Michael Kollar, Lewis Knaus, Nathan McGrew, George Wallick.

Died in 1833, Michael Doll, Jacob Knisely, Henry Keller, Jr.

Died in 1834, Charles Birmbaum, Richard Boon, Nicholas Crites, Jacob Cable, Samuel Deardorff, John Shull, Benjamin Shearer, Abraham Snyder, Henry Stauffer.

Died in 1835, Samuel Casebeer, Justin Clark, Valentine Fleck, Christian Garber, Peter Joss, Henry Saffer, Sr., Isaac B. Lee, John Knisely, Sr., the founder of New Philadelphia.

Died in 1836, Peter Cribbs, Peter Cramer, Casper Engler.

Died in 1837, William Albert, Peter Black, Stokey Craig, Thomas Conwell, Jacob Flickinger.

Died in 1838, John Emerson, Jacob Kuhn, John Moffit, Abraham Mihsch, Leonard Parrish. James H. Stow, Caleb Stark, Merret Seely.

Died in 1839 Richard B. Carr, Henry Davy, Jacob Lanning.

Died in 1840, Benjamin Cable, Jehu Eckman, James E. Hampson, David Harger, David Ramsay, Andrew Seaton, Philip Trupp, William Neighbor, Sr.

Died in 1841, Benjamin Bear, Gabriel Cryder, William Coleman, Frederick C. Pfersick, David Peter, Henry Shaffer, Elisha Stockdale, Samuel Shuster, Godfrey Westhoffen.

Died in 1842, Robert Harmount, Frederick Hummell, Michael T. Kohr, James B. Morrow, Thomas Sargent, William Sproul, Oliver Bosenbury, Peter Walter.

Died in 1843, George Binkley, James Stewart, Sr.

Died in 1844, Jesse Hill, Robert McMurray, Philip Suiter, Milton Smith, William Nebaugh, Richard T. Burrell, Joseph Huff.

Died in 1845, Edwin Booth, John P. Larimer, William S. Myers, Jesse Neighbor, William Slutts, John Silvins, John Benfer, Thomas Bays.

Died in 1846, David Casebeer, Jacob J. Miller, Henry Ankeny, Henry Deardorff, William Gordon, Peter Good, John F. Garnant, George Graham, John P. Heacock.

Died in 1847, Michael Hoff, George Ilyenfritz, Robert M. Kilgore, Jacob Kollar, Nathan Leggett, James McCue, William Silvins, Henry Albright, Abraham Forney, Henry Murphy, Charles Meldean, Abraham Overholtz.

Died in 1848, George Bugher, Sr., Ira Bates, Robert M. Dawson, John Graham, Thomas Price.

Died in 1849, John D. Cummins, Henry Fackler, George H. Fogle, Henry Keller, Samuel C. Wright, John Davy, Jacob Uhrich, George Sees, Medad Vinton

Died in 1850, William Gordon, George Gonter, George W. Kuhn, Lepold Fox, Robert Hursey, Henry Laffer, Jr.

Died in 1851, Matthew Croft, Christian Deardorff, James B. Gray, Benjamin Gorsuch, Edward Lafferty, Samuel McGragor, Abraham Shane. Peter Widener, Michael Uhrich.

Died in 1852, Jacob Foreman, Jacob Frisbly, Joshua Simmons, T. Sargent.

Died in 1653, Peter Houseman, Martin Keller, Rezin Pumphrey, James B. Parrish, David Rassler, David Riggle, Henry Shaffer, Christian Stocker.

Died in 1854, Philip Dotes, George Fernsell, Oliver Rosenbury, Paul Roberts, George Sluthour, Elijah Welty, John Ripley.

Died in 1855, Charles Van Buskirk, Michael Swagler.

Died in 1856, Philip Gharky, Nathaniel Gilmore, John Hummell, Jacob Blickensderfer, John Tucker.

Died in 1857, Jonathan Chandler, Charles Hagan, David Kitch, George Mezer.

Died in 1858, Henry Cramer, William Butt, Jacob Kitch.

Died in 1859, John Hoagland, John Baltzly, Henry Kail, Daniel McGregor. James Nugen, John Sheets, Samuel Thomas, Plin Vinton, John Welch, Samuel Wright.

Died in 1860, John Garver, James Gribble, Jacob Kuldenback, Alfred Pumphrey.

Died in 1861, Andrew Creter, Bazill D. Downey, John Domer, Samuel Fry, James Forbes, Benjamin Blickensderfer, Henry Machamun, Walling Miller, Robert B. Wilson.

Died in 1862, Daniel Ashbaugh, Francis Gilmore, John Butt, Robert Baker, Beriah Jones, Martin Keller, John Mitchell.

Died in 1863, Daniel Anderson, Prettyman Conwell, John Domer, John Hildt, Sr., Philip Bremer, M. H. Bartilson.

Died in 1864, James Eakey, John Farber, Conrad Gentsch, William Hodge, Andrew Bremer, John Brisben, Ezra Brainard, Peter Hoopingamer, Charles M. Sherrod, Ralph Winspear.

Died in 1865, William Couts, Sr., Jacob Casebeer, George H. Dent, Walter

M. Blake, George Hoopingamer, Abijah Robinett, James Rutter, A. W. Sargent, George Welty.

Died in 1866, John Brady, John Langhead.

Died in 1867, Harlan Beal, Edward Boyd, George Hursey, Gersham Kilgore, Philip Knappenberger, John Sparks.

Died in 1868, Joseph Demuth, Peter Williams, Francis Scott, Valentine Fleck, George Chadwell, Peter Helmrich, Joseph Stout, George Stoody, John Laffer, C. F. Espich.

Died in 1869, Henry Cramer, D. W. Stambaugh, John Gray, Hebbard Hill, Robert Seaman, John Dearth, Peter Suawk, Abraham Nebert, Daniel Bear.

Died in 1870, Thomas Hardesty, Solomon Hoover, Nelson Hogland, John Minnich, Jacob Miller, Jacob Myers, Daniel Hoopengarner, Jacob Romig, Philip Rank, Robert McCoy, Michael J. Bennett, Andrew Peters.

Died in 1871, John Dickson, Adam Fackler, Ephraim Sparks, Joseph Keplinger, John Hensel, John Coventry, Peter Edmonds, Thomas Williams, John Lower.

Died in 1872, John M. Roberts, Robert H. Nugull, Martin Mumma, John Heller, Sr., Matthew Grace, David Sells, Joseph Helmich, Joseph Fox, Charles Koms.

Died in 1873, William Neighbors, John Allshouse, Israel Ricksecker, Benjamin Walton, Henry Zimmerman, John Belch, Adam Berkley, John Tomer, Jesse O. Piper, Lems Peter, Robert McConnell, Elijah Hank.

Died in 1874, Andrew Lytle, Martin Kitch, Christian Gross, Thomas Fox, Peter Leutherman, William Reidenbach, Frederich Crater, John Walter, Daniel Christy, Joseph Slingluff, Vance P. Bonham.

Died in 1875, Francis Render, Edward Edwards, Benjamin Warfel, John Andrews, Joshua Blickensderfer.

SKETCH OF ZOAR—BIMELER'S MODEL WILL.

About the year 1817 a colony of religious Germans settled in Lawrence township, and named it Zoar. In Europe they were known as "Separatists," having seceded from the main church of their community, and on account of the persecutions entailed upon them, left for the United States. On board ship they made the acquaintance of a passenger named Joseph M. Baumler, of intelligence and education, and, being young, was smitten, as is said, with one of the young females, whom he married, and united his fortunes with the society.

They were poor, and were assisted to the West by the Quakers, and other philanthropic sects. Baumler became manager, and negotiated with Jonathan Dayton, of New Jersey, for four hundred acres of land, on credit, to which they made additions from time to time, and paid for the whole by their united labor, thrown into a common fund. At first they had rude bark and log huts, but in time built comfortable houses, kept up a store, hotel, and shops for mechanics, besides farming, mining and milling.

Mr. Baumler's name being pronounced in English Bimeler, he assumed that name, and was afterward known as Joseph M. Bimeler. At an early day he organized the colony into a close corporation under the laws of Ohio, of which he remained the master mind until within a few years of his death, which happened August 27, 1853, his wife Dorotha having died September 16, 1852. He was assisted by trustees, chosen by the members annually, the females having the voting power the same as males.

The colony was divided into families, for convenience, with a chosen head for each, who became measurably responsible for the good conduct and morals of those under his or her charge.

In 1830, Joseph M. Bimeler's family consisted at one time of three males and four females. Stephen Hoover's family consisted of two males and twelve females. Joanna Mock's family consisted of fifteen females, and no males. Christian Platz's family had in it nine males and one female. George Goesele's family consisted of two males and two females. Barbara Shock had in her family seven females, and no male. Maria Sink had two females only. Magdalena Auck had three females only. John Breymeyer had in his family seven males and one female. Margaret Ackerman had in her family one male and fourteen females. Casper Fetter had in his family eight males and two females. Jacob Shearing had in his family eight males and two females. John Miller had in his family ten males and three females. Dorethea Dietz had in her family fourteen females, and no males. Maria Kuehule had in her family fourteen females, and no males. Jacob Kimmerly had in his family four males and two females. Christian Mitchely had in his family one male and two females. George Groetzinger had in his family five males and two females. Frederick Klotz had in his family three males only. Godfrey Lentz had in his family four males and four females. Making in all 67 males, and 106 females. Of the males, 17 were under 21; 13 between 20 and 30 years; 15 between 30 and 40; 10 were between 40 and 50; 10 between 50 and 60; 1 between 60 and 70; and 1 between 70 and 80 years of age. Of the females, 18 under 20; 22 between 20 and 30; 24 between 30 and 40; 20 between 40 and 50; 17 between 50 and 60; 4 between 60 and 70; and one between 70 and 80.

As the society became prosperous, attempts were made to divide the property by seceding members, but all failed. When a member secedes, is expelled, or dies, his rights merge in the surviving members, and by reason whereof the society can never be broken up, unless by common consent, and the dissolving corporation acts.

It has existed about fifty-seven years, and the society owns 6,989 acres of land, the real value of which is about $500,000, or an average of $70 per acre. Its personality, moneys, and credits do not exceed $200,000.

In its history of nearly three score years, no instance is known of a member in good standing, ever having violated a law of the State.

In the course of a long life of business, a large amount of property became legally the property of Joseph M. Bimeler, but ten days before his death he willed it all to the society, heeding in all probability the Bible admonition that it is harder for a rich man to enter the kingdom of heaven, than for a camel to pass through the eye of a needle.

The following is a copy of his will, inserted here for the benefit of all heads of corporations, and others whom it may concern, in preparing for the life to come:

"I, Joseph Michael Bimeler, of Zoar, Tuscarawas County, and State of Ohio, being weak in body, but of sound and disposing mind, memory and understanding, do make and publish this as my last will and testament. That is to say: I give and bequeath all my property, real, personal and mixed, of whatever kind, be the same in lands, tenements, trusts or otherwise, bonds, notes, claims, book accounts, or other evidences of debt of whatever nature, to the Society of Separatists of Zoar, and its assigns, forever; hereby declaring that all the property I ever held, real and personal, within the county of Tuscarawas, has been the property of said Society, and was held by me in trust for said Society, to which I now return it.

"And I do hereby appoint John G. Grozinger, Jacob Silvan and Jacob Ackerman, trustees of said Society, as my executors, to carry this, my last will, into effect.

"In testimony whereof, I have hereunto set my hand and affixed my seal, this sixteenth day of August, A. D. one thousand eight hundred and fifty-three.

"JOSEPH M. BIMELER. [*Seal.*]

"Signed, sealed and declared by the above named J. M. Bimeler, as his last will and testament, in presence of us (the words 'and its assigns forever,' interlined before signing).

"JACOB BLICKENSDERFER,
"JOSEPH C. HANCE."

In 1832, the cholera year, a man was put off a boat with the disease, and was buried in the Zoar cemetery. Soon after another was dropped from a boat on the towing path to die. The society took him in, cared for him, and buried him in a Christian manner. In a short time appeared a woman claiming that he was her husband and had a large sum of money on his person, which she wished to recover. She was informed that all he had about him was buried with him, as they would not disturb his apparel or anything in it. She then went away, and came back with a stranger whom she had hired for one hundred dollars to dig up the body and recover the money. Permission being given, he and the woman repaired with two of the members to the cemetery and disinterring the body found in the dead man's clothes several hundred dollars of paper money and coin. They then re-interred the remains, and arriving at the hotel she counted the money, gave the hired man his hundred dollars, and offered pay to the society, but it was refused. She then went away with the man and money. That night the cholera broke out in Zoar, and became so virulent that it is said upward of twenty, one account says fifty odd members, or nearly one-third the population of Zoar were carried off. It is also said that the money-digger and woman were both attacked, a few miles from Zoar, with the disease, and both died.

LARGEST LAND-HOLDERS IN TUSCARAWAS COUNTY.

The following is a list of persons owning three hundred acres, or upward, of land in the townships indicated, and probable worth, the real value being estimated at treble the tax value. Parties owning about three hundred acres, or upward, in

Auburn Township.—John Laderick, 393 acres, $40,000; David Swihart, 420 acres, $40,000; Ulrich Garber, 320 acres, $20,000; Daniel Zimmerman, 380 acres, $40,000.

Bucks Township.—Philip Mizer, 480 acres, $40,000; Joseph Trently, 330 acres, $30,000.

Clay Township.—R. Seaman's heirs, 1,100 acres, $70,000; Benedict Gross, 453 acres, $50,000; David Graim, 320 acres, $40,000; Harrison Kail, 360 acres, $25,000; H. Wyant, 350 acres, $40,000; James Patrick, Sr., 300 acres, $30,000.

Dover Township.—David Casebeer, 500 acres, $40,000; George W. Slungluff, 350 acres, $50,000; Michael Bair, 340 acres, $35,000; Daniel Calendine, 320 acres, $30,000; Joseph Krantz, 380 acres, $30,000; Wesley Miner, 380 acres, $30,000; John Overholt, 400 acres, $40,000; Isaac Swihart, 300 acres, $30,000; Joseph Slingluff's heirs, 300 acres, $35,000; Tuscarawas Coal and Iron Company, 439 acres, $100,000; Augustus Wilhelmi, 363 acres, $50,000.

Fairfield Township.—Conrad Goodering, 310 acres, $35,000; Joseph Kollar, 316 acres, $25,000; Joseph Jenkins, 350 acres,

$26,000; D. McConnell, 420 acres, $35,000; Wilson Minnis, 300 acres, $20,000; William Waddington, 330 acres, $30,000; James Moffat, 413 acres, $35,000; Tuscarawas Coal and Iron Company, 1,196 acres, $200,000.

Franklin Township.—Charles Myers, 390 acres, $40,000; James Patterson, 550 acres, $60,000; F. Hartline, 323 acres, $30,000; James A. Saxton, 520 acres, $50,000.

Goshen Township.—Abraham Bourquin, 370 acres, $50,000; Alvin Vinton, 697 acres, $100,000; John W. Coventry, 550 acres, $60,000; R. & T. G. Gartrell, 300 acres, $25,000; John B. Read, 470 acres, $60,000; James Waddington, 470 acres, $50,000; W. Wallace, 330 acres, $30,000; Valentine Wills, 580 acres, $75,000; Isaac H. Kurtz, 403 acres, $50,000; David Rummell, 319 acres, $30,000; S. G. Crites, 300 acres, $30,000.

Jefferson Township—John Blouse, 360 acres, $30,000; Joseph Murphy, 323 acres, $30,000; John Hawk, Jr., 425 acres, $30,000.

Laurence Township.—Henry Gibler's heirs, 380 acres, $35,000; John Labold, 608 acres, $60,000; George F. Fisher, 300 acres, $50,000; Frederick Labold, 352 acres, $40,000; Zoar Separatists, 5,789 acres, $600,000.

Mill Township.—Thomas O'Donnell, 350 acres, $30,000; John J. O'Donnell, 416 acres, $40,000; J. E. Fredenburr, 430 acres, $35,000; Fleming Bukey, 440 acres, $45,000; George and J. B. Dawson, 360 acres, $35,000; A. G. Gatchell, 350 acres, $35,000; J. W. Gatchell, 310 acres, $20,000; Francis Scott, 328 acres, $25,000; William Welch, 300 acres, $22,000; Thomas J. Forbes, 313 acres, $30,000.

Oxford Township—John Booth, 1,310 acres, $85,000; D. Mulvaine & Sons, 750 acres, $55,000; Morris Creter, 520 acres, $55,000; John Knight, 500 acres, $60,000; Lorenzo C. Davis, 412 acres, $45,000; Elias Knisely, 387 acres, $36,000; John McDonald, 381 acres, $20,000; R. H. Nugen heirs, 783 acres, $60,000.

Perry Township.—William Barnhill, 340 acres, $27,000; Harrison Miller farm, 360 acres, $22,000.

Rush Township.—Jacob Houk, 390 acres, $25,000; N. B. Kennedy, 320 acres, $20,000; H. R. Ripley, 340 acres, $23,000; James Sproul, Jr., 390 acres, $27,000; Robert Sproul, 400 acres, $30,000; Joseph Harmon, 300 acres, $20,000; H. Ripley, 320 acres, $20,000.

Sandy Township.—John Baily, Sr., 548 acres, $50,000; Michael Evans, 300 acres, $30,000; Reagen W. Myers, 400 acres, $50,000;

Joseph Leins, 300 acres, $23,000; John Knotts, 430 acres, $40,000; George Lechner, 300 acres, $27,000; Joseph Laughlin, 325 acres, $30,000; William Swaney, 360 acres, $40,000; John Farber, Jr., 300 acres, $30,000.

Sugar Creek Township.—Joseph Silvins, 500 acres, $40,000; M. Deitz, 487 acres, $45,000; Daniel Coblenz, 303 acres, $30,000; Daniel J. Miller, 310 acres, $30,000; Joseph Yodder, 380 acres, $36,000.

Salem Township.—J. & J. Bremer, 400 acres, $70,000; Conrad Bremer, 348 acres, $40,000; Leonard Hart, 326 acres, $30,000; Hebbard Hill's heirs, 320 acres, $40,000; Robert Lyons, 360 acres, $30,000; D. Mulvain, 350 acres, $30,000; D. Nelson, 300 acres, $30,000; J. A. Roenbaugh, 300 acres, $30,000; W. Robertson & Co., 580 acres, $170,000; Adam Stocker, 600 acres, $60,000; Paul Weatherby farm, 400 acres, $25,000; J. A. Wyant, 300 acres, $30,000.

Union Township.—William Brock, 340 acres, $20,000; Leslie McCullough, 340 acres, $20,000; H. J. Oliver, 384 acres, $20,000; J. Pyle, 462 acres, $25,000; William Rutlidge, 400 acres, $25,000.

Warren Township.—William Carnes, 450 acres, $30,000; Jacob Riggle, 435 acres, $25,000; David Machaman, 300 acres, $23,000; J. M. Mills, 300 acres, $25,000; A. Machaman, 440 acres, $30,000; Richard McClelland, 360 acres, $30,000; William Strawn, 450 acres, $33,000; George Steece farm, 330 acres, $24,000; Micajah Seran, 360 acres, $28,000; William R. Kennedy, 300 acres, $25,000.

Warwick Township.—John Edie, Sr., 340 acres, $25,000; John Knause, 360 acres, $27,000; Godfrey Everett. 640 acres, $48,000; John Minnich farm, 350 acres, $40,000.

Washington Township.—H. C. Asher, 300 acres, $20,000; Isaac Blair, 320 acres, $20,000; Solomon Corley, 300 acres, $15,000; Lee Hudson, 300 acres, $20,000; Daniel Keese, 350 acres, $24,000; Benjamin Murphy, 300 acres, $15,000; John McCollough, 300 acres, $20,000; James H. Quigley, 590 acres, $40,000; James Taylor, 620 acres, $40,000.

Wayne Township.—Peter Fleck, 300 acres, $30,000; Amos Johnson farm, 300 acres, $25,000; Frederick Rirchenbach, 310 acres, $25,000; Caleb Jones, 390 acres, $35,000.

York Township.—George Ankeny, 620 acres, $50,000; George Fachler, 300 acres, $30,000; N. Winkler, 380 acres, $35,000.

A number of land-owners have land in different townships in smaller quantities than three hundred acres aggregating over three hundred, but this list includes only such men as own three hundred acres in any township.

LIST OF COUNTY OFFICERS FROM 1808 TO 1875.

ASSOCIATE JUDGES.

The following is a list of the associate judges of the court of common pleas of Tuscarawas county from its organization to 1852, when the new constitution abolished that office:

Johh Heckewelder from 1808 to 1810; Aquilla Carr, 1808 to 1811; Christian Deardorff, 1808 to 1824; Godfrey Haga, Jr., 1810 to 1813; Conrad Roth, 1811 to 1812; Robert S. Caples, 1812 to 1818; Joseph Wampler, part of 1813; Henry Laffer, 1813 to 1829; Nicholas Neighbor, 1818 to 1832; Thomas Cummings, 1824 to 1833; Jacob Blickensderfer, 1829 to 1836; Peter Williams, 1832 to 1839; Rezin Pritchard, 1833 to 1840; Israel S. Lappin, 1836 to 1852; Walter M. Blake, 1839 to 1846; Isaac N. Roberts, 1840 to 1847; James Patrick, Sr., 1846 to 1852; Morris Creter, 1847 to 1852; Jacob Blickensderfer, 1850 to 1852.

LIST OF FIRST PRACTICING ATTORNEYS IN TUSCARAWAS.

Sampson S. King, 1808; Lewis Cass, 1808; Fisher A. Blocksom, 1808; E. W. Herrick, 1810; Robert Bay, 1810; John C. Wright, 1812; Alexander Harker, 1812; Samuel W. Culbertson, 1812; D. Redeck, 1816; M. D. Pettibone, 1817; John M. Goodenow, 1817; Walter B. Beebe, 1818; Ephraim Root; Wright & Collier, 1818; Wright Warner, 1818; S. Johnson, 1819; John C. Stockton; J. W. Lathrop, 1819; Samuel W. Bell, 1819; John Harris, 1820.

COUNTY COMMISSIONERS.

The following is a list of the men who have served as commissioners of Tuscarawas county since its organization, in 1808:

John Junkins, Michael Uhrich, Philip Minnich, Booz Walton, Isaac Deardorff, Gabriel Cryder, Samuel Lappin, Jacob Blickensderfer, George Davis, Michael Smith, William Summers, Peter Williams, James Rippeth, Jacob Uhrich, William Albert, William Rouse, Michael Doll, Abram Knisely, Benjamin Ream, John M. Patton, Samuel Miller, Andrew Creter, Charles Korns, George Welty, John Wallace, John Dearth, George K. Fankboner, Thomas Bayes, Milton Smith, Lewis Conwell, Henry Lupher, Cyrus C. Carroll, David Gram, George Wallack, Jacob Houk, George Fernsel, Robert Seaman, John Shank, Joseph Kollar, Samuel Schweitzer, John C. Zutavern, Daniel Swaim, George Troelich, Joseph Kinsey, Martin Kugler, William Rankin, Matthias Rudolph.

COUNTY AUDITORS.

The following named men have served as auditor since the organization of the county, in 1808:

Godfrey Hoga, Jr., from 1808 to 1809; Christian Espich, 1809 to 1813; James Clark, 1813 to 1818; Jacob Blickensderfer, 1818 to 1820; Sylvester Johnson, 1820 to 1822; James Patrick, Sr., 1822 to 1823; Walter M. Blake, 1823 to 1825; Thornton Whitaker, 1825 to 1826; Azor Abell, 1826 to 1832; Joseph Talbott, 1832 to 1836; Thomas King, 1836 to 1840; John Everhard, 1840 to 1847; David Judy, 1847 to 1851; John Hildt, 1851 to 1855; Philip Uhrich, 1855 to 1859; Benjamin F. Helwig, 1859 to 1863; Jesse D. Elliott, 1863 to 1867; Oliver H. Hoover, 1867 to 1871; Philip Getzman, 1871 to 1873; Solomon Ashbaugh, 1873 to 1877.

COUNTY TREASURERS.

The following is a list of the men who have served as county treasurers since the organization of the county in 1808:

David Peter, from 1808 to 1811; Peter Williams, 1811 to 1823; Gabriel Cryder, 1823 to 1836; Jacob Overholtz, 1836 to 1842; Joseph Demuth, 1842 to 1846; Edward Peter, 1846 to 1850; John Buthler, 1850 to 1853; Simpson Harmount, 1853 to 1858; Levi Sargent, 1858 to 1860; Henry Anderman, 1860 to 1864; Martin Hagan, 1864 to 1866; Nicholas Montag, 1866 to 1870; William H. Crisswell, 1870 to 1874; Josiah Murphy, 1874 to 1878.

COUNTY CLERKS.

The following is a list of the men who have served as clerks of the court since the organization of the county in 1808:

James Clark, from 1808 to 1818; George W. Canfield, 1818 to 1826; Charles S. Frailey, 1826 to 1827; James W. English, 1827 to 1843; Charles H. Mitchener, 1843 to 1851; Joseph Walton, 1851 to 1852, Emerson Goodrich, 1852 to 1855; Hosea T. Stockwell, 1855 to 1858; John D. Langhead, 1858 to 1864; Peter Kunz, 1864 to 1867; James M. Kennedy, 1867 to 1873; Daniel C. McGregor, 1873 to 1875; Thomas C. Ferrell, 1875; Jacob De Greif, 1875 to 1878.

PROBATE JUDGES.

The office of probate judge was established by the constitution of 1851, since which time the following named men have served:

James Moffitt, from 1852 to 1855; John H. Barnhill, 1855 to 1861; Oliver P. Taylor, 1861 to 1867; Abraham W. Patrick, 1867 to 1870; William B. Brown, 1870 to 1876.

COUNTY SHERIFFS.

The following is a list of the sheriffs since the organization of the county in 1808:

Henry Davis, from 1808 to 1810; Henry Laffer, 1810 to 1813; Henry Shetler, 1813 to 1817; Frederick Maish, 1817 to 1819; Thornton Whitacre, 1819 to 1823; Walter M. Blake, 1823 to 1827; John Butt, 1827 to 1832; Jacob Knisely, 1832 to 1833; Jacob Kitch, 1833 to 1838; Elisha James, 1838 to 1842; John English, 1842 to 1846; Levi Sargent, 1846 to 1850; Philip Uhrich, 1850 to 1852; Dorsey Wilson, 1852 to 1854; Charles H. Mathews, 1854 to 1856; John W. Lytle, 1856 to 1860; Philip Getzman, 1860 to 1864; Simon Fackler, 1864 to 1866; Charles Howard, 1866 to 1868; John Howard, 1868 to 1869; James Truman, 1860 to 1870; Jacob De Griff, 1870 to 1874; Robert Price, 1874 to 1878.

PROSECUTING ATTORNEYS.

The following is a list of the men who served this county as prosecuting attorney, from the organization to the present:

Edward Herrick, from 1808 to 1810; Alexander Harper, 1810 to 1811; Robert Bay, 1811 to 1814; Wright Warner, 1814 to 1816; William B. Raymond, 1816 to 1818; John C. Stockton, 1818 to ——; Sylvester Johnson, 1818 to 1820; Wright Warner, 1820 to 1825; Booz M. Atherton, 1825 to 1831; Francis D. Leonard, 1831 to 1836; John D. Cummins, 1836 to 1842; Joseph C. Hance, 1842 to 1844; Isaac Hartman, 1844 to 1846; Lorenzo C. Davis, 1846 to 1848; John A. Bingham, 1848 to 1850; James B. Gray, 1850 to 1852; William Helmich, 1852 to 1854; Matthias H. Bartilson, 1854 to 1858; Abraham W. Patrick, 1858 to 1862; David W. Stambaugh, 1862 to 1864; Alexander L. Neely, 1864 to 1866; James Patrick, Jr., 1866 to 1870; John J. Robinson, 1870 to 1874; John W. Allbaugh, 1874 to 1878.

COUNTY RECORDERS.

The following are the names of the recorders who have held office since the organization of the county:

James Clark, from 1808 to 1818; George W. Canfield, 1818 to 1826; James Patrick, Sr., 1826 to 1836; Bower Seaton, 1836 to 1845; Joel Warner, 1845 to 1851; Simon Bugher, 1851 to 1854; Matthias S. Nabor, 1854 to 1861; Asbury Insley, 1861 to 1867; John Mygrantz, 1867 to 1873; Peter W. Himes, 1873 to 1879.

A FIGHT WITH ELKS ON THE (MUSKINGUM) TUSCARAWAS IN 1761.

It is well known that some of the Indians called the Muskingum "Elk Eye," while others called it "Moosekingdom," from the fact that the elk or moose inhabited these valleys at one time, and by reason thereof they became the important hunting grounds of the red men in

Ohio, and on that account were deemed of such value that the aborigines fought a generation before surrendering their elk country to the white man.

When Gist passed down the Tuscarawas in 1750 he was fed on elk steak, and in 1755 Smith speaks of them as making excellent meat, the Indians preferring it to venison. A full-sized elk or moose was six feet high and seven in length, and weighed from eight hundred to one thousand pounds, the large, spreading horns often weighing seventy pounds, and protruding upward and outward from the head several feet, so that when the animal was running its nose was thrust forward, to have the horns fall along the back, thus protecting the body to a certain extent from thorns and briars, and preventing the horns from catching in the limbs overhead. They were very fleet, and it is said could travel two hundred miles in a day. When suddenly aroused or frightened the horns were kept erect, as a defensive weapon, and woe to the hunter who came in contact with an enraged animal. In the rutting season the males became furious, fighting each other, or even man, as they rushed with a noisy roar through the woods in pursuit of a female, who likewise became furious in defense of her calves, two of which were born yearly, in May. The elks fed on grass, the bark of the maple, buttonwood, and twigs, and lived to the age of twenty years. They were hunted in March and September by the Indians, and were most easily overtaken in times of deep snow. They were sometimes caught by slip-nooses attached to saplings bent down in the path the animal frequented in going to and from the river.

In January, 1761, Major Robert Rogers and his hunter, while visiting the Seneca capital, near Bolivar, went out hunting on one of the streams emptying into the Tuscarawas. They were old hunters, and one moonlight night stationed themselves by the creek and began imitating the noise of the bull elk or moose, knowing that he would come rushing, if in the vicinity of the sound, to the spot, to give battle to the intruding bull who dared to venture near his females (the elk being more jealous than man). In a short time they heard the twigs and limbs cracking on the opposite side of the creek, and prepared to get a shot as he approached. Bounding down the declivity and into the water came the male, female and calves. The hunters fired, hit the calves but missed the parents, who in a moment were upon them, and the rifles empty. There was no time to run or tree, so taking out their knives they roared and rushed, each man plunging his knife at what he wanted—the heart of his animal; but before either could reach it they each were tramped down by the fore feet of the elks, who struck in unison.

As quick as thought the elks receded a few feet, to give play to their horns, and catching the hunters thereon tossed them both into the air, but among the spreading limbs of beech tree, to which each adroitly clung in an instant, and soon climbed out of reach. The infuriated animals pawed, raised on their hind legs and bellowed, but all to no purpose, and after some time, hearing a noise over the creek, they bounded across and were soon out of view. The hunters got in next day, bruised but not hurt, each having his elk calf for his adventure.

WOLVES AND WOLF HUNTERS OF THE VALLEYS.

The early pioneers were greatly annoyed by the wolves, and they embraced every opportunity to get a shot at the beasts, first to save hogs, sheep, and calves; and second to get the scalp premium paid by the State, as a mark of hunter's merit. Whoever killed a wolf, by presenting the scalp, and making affidavit before the clerk of the court, within twenty days, stating age and sex, and that the affiant killed it in the county, got an order on the treasury.

Between 1808 and 1843, four hundred affidavits were filed, after which the scalp law ceased.

Premiums were also paid for a few years upon the scalps of panthers, and wild cats, or catamounts, but they were rarely killed.

John Mizer, in his time killed 47 wolves; Adam Reemer, 35; Jacob Hoopengarner, 20; Henry Willard, 15; George Miller, 13; John Purdee, 16; Jonathan Andrews, 10; Christian Yotter, 11; Christian Royer, 9; Jacob Troyer, 8; Benjamin Johnson, 8; Jacob Mizer, 7; Benjamin Wallick, 7; Abijah Robinet, 7; William Fler, 6; John Sommers, 6; Henry Kail, 6; Abram Harshberger, 6; Samuel Huff, 5; John Goodage, 5; John Bevers, 5; David Neeshaum, 5; Samuel Deardorff, 5; and scattering hunters 139, making in all 400.

Many traditions have passed down to this day, at the firesides, of the adventures of the wolf hunters.

In 1810, it is related that on Laurel Creek, in the present Rush township, there was a wolf den in a cave, where numbers lived securely, no hunter being bold enough to enter. On one occasion, a hired man of John Perdue, going along the creek on a Saturday night, to a neighbor's house, to fiddle for the dancers, was attacked by a pack of wolves, who surrounded and were about to make a meal of him. He had no weapon but his fiddle, and as he was *looking* for a hollow tree *butt to shelter* himself from their front and rear snaps, he kept them at bay for a time by drawing the bow over the strings, making the most *unearthly* noise possible, which, scaring them off some yards, he commenced climbing a sapling, when a wolf seized him by the foot. It was life or death with him then, and, making a last effort, he shook the wolf off, and reached a height out of their way. They then began circling him, barking in concert as they ran around his tree, every third or fourth round one would break out of the circle, and leaping up against the tree, endeavoring to reach him. Having continued in this way for some time in their war-dance, the pack suddenly scampered off, to the great relief of the treed man. He soon heard dogs bark, and then the report of a rifle; he yelled, and attracted the party, who came to his relief and escorted him home. The next day the settlers surrounded the hill where the den was located, smoked the cave so strongly that the wolves came out one by one, and were shot, to the number of seven. The entrance was shut up with large stones, and the settlers were troubled no more by the pack.

On Huff's run, in 1815, one of the Huffs heard a noise at his stable in the night. Quickly getting his gun he crept out and found five wolves tearing a hog to pieces. He shot one, and the four left. He lay in wait and soon the four returned when he shot a second, and lay in wait until morning but no more came back. The next night he put the bait hog out, and waited. Soon came a pack of half a dozen, of which he shot three before morning. He put the five in one affidavit and got twelve dollars, about the price of his hog.

HENRY WILLARD'S FIGHT WITH A BEAR.

Henry Willard emigrated to Tuscarawas County shortly after the year 1800, and settled in the present Lawrence Township. He was a hunter, and the county records attest that he killed, and received premiums for, fifteen wolf scalps in his time.

On one occasion in the winter, when the snow was several inches deep, he started across the country to Killbuck Creek, near the present Wooster, where there was to be on Christmas day a great shooting match. In the afternoon he was on the west line of the county, and the walking hard, a crust having formed on the heaviest snowfall, on top of which there were some two inches of snow of the night before. Ascending a ridge he stopped to rest, setting his rifle against the body of a dead tree; and spying a bear track which approached the tree and turned off at right angles, he was curious to see if it was fresh, and finding that the bear track turned off down the hill he followed it a rod or so, and then went back to get his rifle, satisfied that it was the track of a bear made that morning. Hearing a noise, he looked toward the dead tree and saw a bear descending it, and in a moment bruin was at the butt, standing guard over Willard's rifle. As Willard eyed him he set himself on his haunches, and seizing the rifle with his paws, began to wallop it against the tree, then cast it from him down the hillside some feet, and started for Willard, who had unsheathed his knife and was waiting for the charge. As the bear raised to embrace the hunter, he received the knife in his abdomen, the blood spouting on the snow. Feeling the wound, bruin grappled Willard, squeezed him, and began to gnaw his neck, then falling, pulled him down, holding Willard with a death grip. He soon ceased biting, and in the effort to get the knife from Willard they both rolled in the snow, some feet down the hillside, and by chance the hunter's knife hand became disengaged, and he pulled upward, making a gash in the stomach and flank which let out part of the animal's entrails. The bear and the hunter had in the scuffle rolled against a sapling, and for an instant both were still, the bear having Willard's arm in his mouth, and Willard working the knife around as well as he could in the belly. Suddenly the bear rose, still holding the hunter, but letting go his armhold, he gnawing the face of Willard, who at once made a lunge with the knife in his released hand, and all was over. The bear's hold relaxed; he attempted to get the knife out of his body, but fell forward and expired. It was now sunset, and Willard, seeing that he could not reach Killbuck Creek that night, made a fire, and by its light skinned the bear, roasted and ate some bear steak, went to sleep, and in the morning returned to his home, traveling some nine miles in the cold, with his face hacked and his right arm useless, but no bones broken. His boys went out and brought in the hide, which was long shown to neighbors as evidence of the most desperate fight he had ever been in.

Old John Baker, west of Dover had a similar encounter with a bear, which tore his flesh and face so horribly that he was not recognizable for some time. He survived the bear, however.

Another instance is related of a young man in the county being killed by a bear in a deep ravine, and his body could not be found for many years, when the bones turned up in burning the remains of a hollow tree, in a clearing.

JOHN MIZER'S CONFLICT WITH A CATAMOUNT.

Old John Mizer, who was one of the early settlers of what is now Bucks township, went out on Buckhorn Creek to secure a wolf scalp. Having fixed the bait, which consisted of a skinned rabbit covered with blood, he was about to hide near by when his practiced ear detected the tread of an animal behind him. Upon turning to look for the expected wolf he beheld a large catamount, which, seeing him, instantly treed; Mizer shot, and ere the report left his rifle the beast pounced upon him, sinking its claws into his back. With great presence of mind the old hunter instantly backed against a tree and pressed the catamount hard against it, at the same time dropping his gun and drawing his hunting knife, which he plunged into the beast's side several times in quick succession. At this unexpected turn of affairs the catamount let go, and endeavored to get out of its close quarters. By the repeated blows from the knife its entrails were soon cut out and it dropped dead at Mizer's feet. The animal proved to be one of the largest of its species and measured over three feet in length. The body weighed about one hundred pounds, as he tested on reaching home with it. Mizer's back wounds troubled him for some time but nothing serious came of them, and he was soon out again after more wolf scalps.

JOHN HENRY'S PANTHER FIGHT.

In December, 1809, John Henry, a son of the old chief Killbuck, who lived at the Goshen Mission town, went to a deer lick, in the present Warwick Township, to watch for and kill a large buck which he had seen frequently, but had never succeeded in getting a shot at. Upon arriving at the lick, Henry posted himself in the fork of a tree, a short distance from the path which the deer trod in going to and from the lick. After half an hour spent in patiently watching for the least sign of coming deer, the veritable buck, followed by two does, came walking leisurely down the path, with their noses elevated, and sniffing the air in all directions to find the location of a foe they detected. Just before coming opposite to the tree in which Henry sat concealed, the buck stopped short and turned half round, which movement started the does on the back track. As the buck threw his head around to look after his retreating companions, the bullet from Henry's rifle penetrated his heart, and he fell dead in his tracks. An instant after the report of the gun a terrible scream came from a tree which stood only a few feet to the right of Henry's tree, and there sprang a large panther down upon the dead deer. To reload the rifle was short work for Henry. He took careful aim at the animal, which lay motionless upon the buck, looking him fair in the face. The powder missed fire, and in the haste to recock the gun the flint became dislodged and went tumbling to the ground. Having started out for only an hour or two, Henry had not taken the precaution to carry an extra flint. Here was a crisis not easily bridged by the boldest and most experienced of hunters, but Henry at once determined upon his course of action. Grasping his rifle in his left hand, and placing his hunting-knife between his teeth, Henry descended the tree to recover the flint, if possible. The panther remained crouching upon the buck, switching his tail in nervous agitation, apparently at the hunter's delay in coming within its reach. Cautiously the Indian dropped down the tree, a foot or less at a time, ready at the slightest movement of the panther to drop the gun and grasp the knife to defend himself if attacked. Down, down he came, every inch bringing him nearer to the claws of the ferocious beast, until at length his feet touched the ground. To snatch up the flint was the work of an instant, but before he could fasten it in the lips of the gun-cock the panther uttered another scream and sprang for him. Henry jumped around the tree just in time to allow only one of the paws of the animal to graze his side, stripping his shirt and leggings to his moccasins. He clubbed the gun, and before the panther could recover for another spring, struck it a hard blow on the side of the head, which stunned it. In another moment the knife was plunged to its heart, where he left it in his haste to spring away to avoid the claws of the panther, with which it tore up the dead leaves and twigs in its death throes. Before the animal ceased its struggles Henry had replaced the flint, and then, to make death doubly sure, fired a bullet into its brain. He then skinned the buck, hung part of the carcass upon a sapling, and started home with the hind quarters and the scalp of the panther.

The next day, being the 9th of December, 1809, Henry took the scalp to the county seat, where he made affidavit before James Clark, clerk of the court, who certified to the fact, upon which he received the premium ordered to be paid for panther scalps by the county commissioners, which was one dollar and fifty cents.

STORY OF A PIONEER AND THE MAD WOMAN.

Adam Reamer, who lived in what is Wayne township, was born between 1760 and 1770, and was one of the first Tuscarawas pioneers in 1810–11, and killed in his day many wolves. He obtained premiums for thirty-five, and has handed down this legend to modern times. He was out on the French hills hunting about 1811, and passing a cabin was asked to assist in holding a mad woman, who had been wolf bitten. Her husband had shot a cub wolf, running with its mother. He fired at her, but the ball passed through her ear and killed the cub. He carried it home and gave the dead cub to his young wife, throwing it in her lap, and saying its hide would make lining for a baby cradle, which in those days was a sugar trough. Some weeks thereafter, she saw, while sitting at the cabin door, a wolf coming in full speed along the path. She screamed and bounded into the cabin, followed by the wolf. Her husband, making an ax handle near by, hearing the scream, and supposing she had seen a snake, rushed to the door with the ax helve, just as the wolf was coming out. One stroke felled it, and he soon killed the beast, but was horror-struck to see its mouth filled with saliva, and a half-healed bullet hole in its ear. His wife then told him the wolf had bitten her. They applied all the remedies and preventives then known among the settlers for hydrophobia, and no troublesome indications of madness appeared. But the bullet hole in the ear of the dead wolf satisfied him that she was the mother of the cub whose skin had been cured and pegged on the wall, waiting for the time to be made into a baby bed. Informing his wife of his suspicion, she was terrified with ominous forebodings. He endeavored to appease her by taking away the cub's pelt, and burying it from her sight. The circumstance soon passed out of mind at their new home in the wilderness, surrounded by live wolves, bears, and panthers, and in due time the woman gave birth to her first boy, who soon died, but the mother had terrible dreams that she had contracted hydrophobia, which she actually did in a short time, and it was just as she had become most furious when Reamer called at the cabin. The poor mother, after suffering intensely, and becoming so strong that two men could scarcely hold her in bed, died in a spasm. She was buried temporarily in a shallow grave near the cabin, for want of a grave-yard in the neighborhood. The husband in a short time met the old hunter, and told him that he had cut a tree down over the grave to keep the wolves out of it, but that the howling of the animals around his cabin at night so terrified him that he would leave the country, and he did. Reamer, passing by the deserted cabin soon after the young settler had left, went to the grave, only to find that the wolves and forest animals had disinterred the body of the mad woman, and eaten the flesh from her bones. The country for twenty miles around was warned, and little else was done for a time but to hunt down and slaughter wolves.

These incidents illustrate the dangers attendant upon the lives of the early settlers, and from which the present generation are exempt. In those days there were few burglars among men, but every wolf was a thief and marauder in its day, and caused or committed some ravage on the pioneers.

It may be remarked that old Adam Reamer was past sixty when he killed his last wolf, and died over three score and ten, leaving descendants.

CANALS IN OHIO.

The two canals in most useful existence at this time are the Ohio Canal, from Cleveland to Portsmouth, 307 miles, and Miami Canal, from Cincinnati to Defiance, 178 miles.

The first cost $5,000,000, and the second $3,750,000.

The Ohio Canal was begun in 1825, and finished in 1832. The cost of repairs have been partly paid out of tolls and rents, and partly by taxation. The interest on the original cost has been paid partly from canal revenues and partly from taxation.

Congress donated one million acres to Ohio, to aid in canals, which was in part applied thereto.

When the present lease shall have terminated, in 1881,

the lessees will have kept the canals in repair (except as to unavoidable expenses arising from destruction by the elements), and also have paid into the revenue fund of the State $200,000.

The increase in the value of property since their construction, along their lines of communication, demonstrate that they have more than twice paid the original cost of construction, and that the increased valuation of property along their lines, by being put upon the duplicate, have more than paid the canal taxes levied upon counties through which the canals were not located.

The incisive and incessant efforts of railway corporations either to control or destroy the usefulness of the great arteries of cheap transportation in New York, induced that State to take active measures to protect and improve her canals, and the consequence is shown in the facts following:

INCREASE OF OHIO COMPARED WITH HER RIVAL STATES.

It will be seen by the census that our own State, and our great rivals on each side, have increased, between 1850 and 1870, as follows:

Population.

	1850.	*1870.*
New York	3,097,000	4,382,000
Ohio	1,980,000	2,665,000

Property.

	1850.	*1870.*
New York	1,080,000,000	6,500,000,000
Ohio	504,000,000	2,235,000,000

Value of Manufactures.

	1850.	*1870.*
New York	100,000,000	367,000,000
Ohio	29,000,000	141,000,000

Aggregate Taxation.

	1860.	*1870.*
New York	15,000,000	48,000,000
Pennsylvania	9,000,000	24,000,000
Ohio	10,000,000	23,000,000
Indiana	4,000,000	10,000,000
Illinois	6,000,000	22,000,000

These figures show that while Ohio has increased, it is not in the same ratio, either in population, wealth, mining or manufactures; while in taxation her rate of increase of burthens upon the people is equal to that State in ratio. This fact has, in twenty years, caused Ohio to fall behind her rival neighbor about two hundred per cent. in all the elements of wealth growing out of protection to mining, manufacturing, and farming industries.

The portentious fact stares the people of Ohio in the face, that while she is the second mineral State (Pennsylvania alone excelling her), her increase is but three hundred per cent., while the State of New York has increased five hundred per cent. in the same time, by expanding her mining and manufacturing interests along her lines of water communication; in widening, deepening and enlarging the same; not to destroy railway corporations, but to enable the people engaged in mining and manufacturing, as well as in agricultural pursuits, to compete with these corporations in the one great desideratum—cheap transportation to a market.

The remedy is a change in the organic law similar to the provisions in the New York constitution, which prohibits sale or destruction, and provides for the continual improvement of the water lines of the State.

RAILROADS IN OHIO.

The number of miles of railways in Ohio are nearly 5,000. These have been constructed by private capital and credit, amounting by average to $30,000 per mile, or $150,000,000, less taxation on exceptional or special counties, townships, cities, and towns to the amount of $10,000,000.

Under the laws taxing railway corporations there have been collected since 1846, from railways, and applied to general tax fund, an amount exceeding $10,000,000.

The whole sum raised by taxation, in special localities,

has therefore been repaid, not to the communities taxed, but to the State treasury for the benefit of the whole people of the State.

The enhanced value of property in counties permeated by railroads, by reason of their construction, is equal to a gross sum that would yield an interest equal to the tax paid by railroads. Thus the tax paid being $10,000,000, that sum is equal to six per cent. on a principal of $1,000,000,000, which is the estimated enhanced value given to the property in Ohio, by the construction of 5,000 miles of railway therein, or about $4 per acre, over the State, in counties having no railroads, as well as counties through which they have been constructed.

In about forty counties, no county or municipal tax has been collected from communities for railroads. Hence, in the counties and municipalities paying no tax for railroads, the same resulting benefits have accrued to the tax-payers that accrued to the counties and municipalities taxed, so far as general increase of wealth is concerned over the State.

The amount of stock paid in on construction of 5,500 miles of railroad in Ohio is, in round numbers, $150,000,000. Their indebtedness is $151,000,000. Their average earnings aggregate $40,000,000, of which three-fourths is consumed in operating the roads, leaving $10,000,000 as net earnings, applied to interest, dividends, &c.; of these $40,000,000 earnings, about three-fifths are distributed along the lines among the people, for work, and labor, and materials.

The fifty odd railroads in Ohio carry annually 30,000,000 tons of freight, and 15,000,000 passengers, to and fro. The saving of time and expenses of transportation compared with the old common carrier system, is equal to $5 per head per annum, by average, or about $150,000,000.

Table of Railroads, June 30, 1874, in Ohio.

Number.	Name.	Length of Track Laid.	
		Main line and branches.	Sidings and other tracks.
1	Ashtabula, Youngstown & Pittsburgh Railroad	62.60	5.20
2	Atlantic & Great Western Railroad	308.00	42.23
3	Baltimore, Pittsburgh & Chicago Railway (Ohio Div.)	94.80	3.45
4	Central Ohio Railroad	† 137.00	30.36
5	Chicago & Canada Southern Railway	1.50	50.00
6	Cincinnati & Baltimore Railway	5.60	9.08
7	Cincinnati, Hamilton & Dayton Railroad	59.927	61.218
8	Cincinnati, Hamilton & Indianapolis Railroad	19.00	0.907
9	Cincinnati & Indiana Railroad	20.50	9.60
10	Cincinnati & Muskingum Valley Railway	148.44	13.84
11	Cincinnati, Richmond & Chicago Railroad	36.00	2.69
12	Cincinnati, Sandusky & Cleveland Railroad	168.50	15.96
13	Cincinnati & Springfield Railway	48.80	9.26
14	Cincinnati & Whitewater Valley Railroad	2.10	0.40
15	Cleveland, Columbus, Cincinnati & Indianapolis R'y	307.75	87.62
16	Cleveland & Mahoning Valley Railway	123.35	94.472
17	Cleveland, Mt. Vernon & Delaware Railroad	147.66	14.70
18	Cleveland & Newburgh Railroad	3.333	....
19	Cleveland & Pittsburgh Railway	184.77	56.00
20	Columbus, Chicago & Indiana Central Railway	135.90	24.20
21	Columbus & Hocking Valley Railroad	89.00	22.03
22	Columbus, Springfield & Cincinnati Railroad	44.37	2.00
23	Columbus & Xenia Railroad	54.42	13.72
24	Dayton & Michigan Railroad	140.714	20.188
25	Dayton & Union Railroad	31.74	1.79
26	Gallipolis, McArthur & Columbus Railroad	2.34	....
27	Harrison Branch Railroad	7.203	0.491
28	Iron Railroad	16.50	2.50
29	Lake Erie & Louisville Railway	87.66	3.79
30	Lake Shore & Michigan Southern Railway	377.61	304.56
31	Cleveland, Tuscarawas Valley & Wheeling Railroad.	101.14	22.60
32	Lawrence Railroad	12.70	0.80
33	Little Miami Railroad	136.97	46.27
34	Mahoning Coal Railroad	41.58	3.60
35	Mansfield, Coldwater & Lake Michigan Railroad	64.485	1.832
36	Marietta & Cincinnati Railroad	276.80	59.37
37	Marietta, Pittsburgh & Cleveland Railway	102.50	6.50
38	Massillon & Cleveland Railroad	12.50	1.20
39	Newark, Somerset & Straitsville Railroad	44.00	4.06
40	North Columbus Railway	3.81	0.25
41	Ohio & Mississippi Railway	19.53	7.30
42	Ohio & Toledo Railroad	10.50	....
43	Painesville & Youngstown Railroad	50.30	2.10
44	Pittsburgh, Cincinnati & St. Louis Railway	† 157.50	39.50
45	Pittsburgh, Ft. Wayne & Chicago Railway	251.90	56.10
46	Rocky River Railroad	5.53	0.36
47	Sandusky, Mansfield & Newark Railroad	116.25	17.09
48	Toledo, Canada Southern & Detroit Railway	7.00	2.00
49	Toledo & Maumee Narrow Guage Railroad	7.00	0.518
50	Toledo, Tiffin & Eastern Railroad	43.06	3.54
51	Toledo, Wabash & Western Railway	75.50	14.30
		4,407.442	1,142.046
	†Deduct Newark to Col., owned jointly, counted in both	33.00	
	Total	4,374,442	

TRIAL AND EXECUTION OF JOHN FUNSTON FOR MURDER.

The first and only capital execution that has taken place in Tuscarawas County, was that of John Funston, who was found guilty of shooting William Cartwell, a mail-boy, in Oxford Township, on the 9th day of September, 1825, under the following circumstances: Cartwell was carrying the horse-mail from Westchester to Coshocton, and while going through the woods, on the Coshocton road, was shot. A man named Johnson, out hunting, heard the crack of a rifle, and, coming out in the road, found Cartwell dead and the mailbag rifled. He gave the alarm, and was soon after arrested and brought to the New Philadelphia jail (then standing on the site of the present auditor's office), charged with the murder. A man's footprints on the ground near the murder spot were measured, but disagreed in size when compared with Johnson's footprints. The murder of young Cartwell caused the most intense excitement, and every effort to catch the right man was resorted to. Johnson, in jail, told the sheriff that he had got a glimpse of the murderer as he (Johnson) came out of the woods into the road, and that if he ever saw him in a crowd he could point him out. The entire able-bodied male portion of the community in the south part of the county were requested to meet on a certain day at the jail, and allow Johnson to look at them. About three hundred appeared, and were ranked along Broadway, and Johnson was brought out and passed between the ranks. After scanning many men very closely, he pointed to John Funston, in the crowd, saying "That is the man." Funston replied, "You are a liar!" but at once all eyes being turned on him, he showed fear, and began to exhibit outward evidence against himself. He was put in jail; and the crowd went home, satisfied that the murderer was caught. After trial and conviction he confessed the crime, and Johnson was set at liberty. Sheriff Blake's return on the execution tells the finale, thus:

"1825, December 28th, received this writ; and on the 30th day of December, A. D. 1825, between the hours of 12 o'clock, noon, and 2 o'clock P. M., I executed this writ by hanging the within named John Funston, until he was dead. No fees charged.

"WALTER M. BLAKE, Sheriff."

The execution took place at, or on, what is now block No. 3, West Philadelphia. The military were called out, and men, women and children attended from every township, as well as other counties. Some estimates give the number present at five thousand persons.

The traveler on the Marietta and Pittsburg railway will see on his through ticket "Post Boy Station," south of New Comerstown. It is so called from the fact that the post boy Cartwell was murdered there fifty years ago.

FRONT MEN OF THE TUSCARAWAS AND MUSKINGUM VALLEYS AND THEIR TRIBUTARIES.

GOVERNORS.

R. J. Meigs, Duncan McArthur, Wilson Shannon, William Medill, William Dennison, Jr.

UNITED STATES SENATORS FROM EASTERN OHIO.

Thomas Ewing, of Fairfield County, United States Senator from 1831 to 1837, and 1850 to 1851; Return Jonathan Meigs, of Washington, United States Senator from 1808 to 1810; Benjamin Ruggles, of Belmont, United States Senator from 1815 to 1833; Benjamin Tappin, of Jefferson, United States Senator from 1839 to 1845.

JUDGES OF THE SUPREME COURT, FROM EASTERN OHIO.

Return Jonathan Meigs, of Washington County; William Sprigg, Jefferson; William W. Irvin, Fairfield; Charles R. Sherman, Fairfield; John M. Goodenow, Jefferson; John C. Wright, Jefferson; William Kennon, Belmont; Charles C. Converse, Muskingum; Hocking H. Hunter, Fairfield; George W. McIlvain, Tuscarawas.

MEMBERS OF CONGRESS.

Charles J. Albright, Guernsey, 1855 to 1857; James Alexander, Jr., Belmont, 1837 to 1839; Edward Ball, Muskingum, 1853 to 1857; Levi Barber, Washington, 1821 to 1823; J. M. Bell, Guernsey, 1833 to 1835; John A. Bingham, Harrison, 1855 to 1863, and 1865 to 1873; Joseph Burns, Coshocton, 1857 to 1859; Joseph Cable, Carroll, 1849 to 1853; James Caldwell, Belmont, 1813 to 1817; D. K. Cartter, Stark, 1849 to 1853; David Chambers, Muskingum, 1821 to 1823; John Chaney, Fairfield, 1833 to 1839; Benjamin S. Cowen, Belmont, 1841 to 1843; John D. Cummins, Tuscarawas, 1845 to 1849; William T. Cutler, Washington, 1861 to 1863; Lorenzo Danford, Belmont, 1873 to 1877; John Davenport, Belmont, 1827 to 1829; Daniel Duncan, Licking, 1847 to 1849; Ephraim R. Eckley, Carroll, 1863 to 1869; Thomas O. Edwards, Fairfield, 1847 to 1849; Nathan Evans, Guernsey, 1847 to 1851; Paul Fearing, Washington, 1801 to 1803; William E. Fenck, Perry, 1863 to 1867 and 1874; James M. Gaylord, Morgan, 1851 to 1853; John M. Goodenow, Jefferson, 1829 to 1830; Alexander Harper, Muskingum, 1837 to 1839, and 1843 to 1847; William Helmich, Tuscarawas, 1859 to 1861; Samuel Herrich, Muskingum, 1817 to 1821; Moses Hoagland, Holmes, 1849 to 1851; Elias Howell, Licking, 1835 to 1837; William W. Irvin, Fairfield, 1829 to 1833; David Jennings, Belmont, 1825 to 1826; John Johnson, Coshocton, 1851 to 1853; Perley B. Johnson, Morgan, 1843 to 1845; William Kennon, Belmont, 1829 to 1833, and 1835 to 1837; William Kennon, Jr., Belmont, 1847 to 1849; Daniel Kilgore, Harrison, 1834 to 1838; Samuel Lahm, Stark, 1847 to 1849; William

Lawrence, Guernsey, 1857 to 1859; Daniel P. Leadbetter, Holmes, 1837 to 1841; Humphrey H. Leavitt, Jefferson, 1830 to 1834; Benjamin F. Leiter, Stark, 1855 to 1859; Charles D. Martin, Fairfield, 1859 to 1861; James Mathews, Coshocton, 1841 to 1845; Joshua Mathiot, Licking, 1841 to 1843; William C. McCauslin, Jefferson, 1843 to 1845; William Medill, Fairfield, 1839 to 1843; Robert Mitchell, Muskingum, 1833 to 1835; Robert H. Nugen, Tuscarawas, 1861 to 1863; John O'Neill, Muskingum, 1863 to 1865; Isaac Parrish, Guernsey and Morgan, 1839 to 1841, and 1847 to 1849; John Patterson, Belmont, 1823 to 1825; Thomas Ritchie, Perry, 1847 to 1849, and 1853 to 1855; Thomas Shannon, Belmont, 1826 to 1827; Wilson Shannon, Belmont, 1853 to 1857; Matthias Shepler, Stark, 1837 to 1839; Milton J. Southard, Muskingum, 1873 to 1877; William P. Sprague, Morgan, 1871 1875; David Spangler, Coshocton, 1833 to 1837; William Stansberry, Licking, 1829 to 1833; David A. Starkweather, Stark, 1839 to 1841, and 1845 to 1847; Samuel Stokely, Jefferson, 1841 to 1843; Andrew Stuart, Jefferson, 1853 to 1855; Henry Swearingen, Jefferson, 1838 to 1841; Jonathan Taylor, Licking, 1839 to 1841; Thomas C. Theaker, Belmont, 1859 to 1861; C. B. Tompkins, Morgan, 1857 to 1861; P. Van Trump, Fairfield, 1867 to 1873; Joseph W. White, 1863 to 1875; William A. Whittles, Washington, 1849 to 1851; William Wilson, Licking, 1823 to 1829; John C. Wright, Jefferson, 1821 to 1829.

DEVELOPMENT OF INTELLIGENCE IN OHIO.

THE NEWSPAPER AND PERIODICAL PRESS.

There are upwards of three hundred and fifty newspapers and and periodicals issued in Ohio.

Of these, one-half are religious, literary, scientific, agricultural, and non-political; the residue, ninety odd are Republican, and eighty odd Democratic publications.

The daily issues approximate 156,000; the weekly issues approximate 937,000; the semi and tri-weekly approximate 70,000; the semi-monthly and monthly, about 86,000. Total estimated issues, 1,249,000.

It is rather an under than an over estimate to count each copy issued as having two readers, but upon that hypothesis the subjoined statement is made, with some exceptional instances.

The names, editors as known, and number of readers as estimated, are classified:

CINCINNATI.

Commercial, M. Halstead, independent, estimated readers over 120,000; Enquirer, Faren & McLean, democratic, 100,000; Gazette, Gazette Company, republican, 80,000; Star, Star Publishing Company, independent, 40,000; Times, Times Publishing Company, republican, 30,000; Free Press, C. C. Houthumb, German, 15,000; Volksblatt, Hof & Hassaurek, republican, 20,000; Volksfriend, Limburg & Haake, democratic, 24,000; fifty-three others, non-political, 400,000. Aggregate readers, 829,000.

CLEVELAND.

Herald, Fairbanks, Benedict & Co., republican, readers, 50,000; Leader, Leader Company, republican, 36,000; Plaindealer, W. W. Armstrong, democratic, 25,000; Wachter, A. Thieme, independent, 8,000; Columbia, F. Donner, democratic, 8,000; Anzeiger, Bohn, Kinger & Co., republican, 6,000; Die Biene, William Muller, democratic, 6,000; twenty-six, non-political, 200,000. Aggregate readers, 339,000.

COLUMBUS.

Journal, J. M. Comly, republican, readers, over 12,000; Dispatch, Dispatch Company, neutral, 6,000; Westbote, Reinhard & Fieser, democratic, 10,000; Statesman, Myers & Mark, democratic, 8,000; fifteen, non-political, 72,000. Aggregate readers, 98,000.

DAYTON.

Journal, W. D. Bickham, republican, readers, over 12,000; Empire, J. G. Doren & Co., democratic, 10,000; Democrat, J. McLain Smith, democratic, 8,000; Sunday-school Herald, 100,000; ten non-political, 40,000. Aggregate readers, 170,000.

TOLEDO.

Commercial, C. Wagner, readers, 10,000; Blade, J. P. Jones, 25,000; Experiment, J. Vortride, 3,000; thirteen other publications, 40,000. Aggregate readers, 78,000.

ZANESVILLE.

Courier, Newman & Dodd, republican, readers, 6,000; Signal, James J. Irvin, democratic, 4,000; Advocate, J. T. Shryock, independent, 2,800; Post, A. Schneider, German, 2,000; other non-political publications, 30,000. Aggregate readers, 44,800.

Akron, J. F. Rowe, S. A. Lane, C. R. Knight, J. J. Wright—papers, Argus, Beacon, Times, Germania, Commercial. Aggregate readers, 15,000.

Alliance, W. H. Phelps, M. McClellan, S. G. McKee, J. W. Gillespie; papers—Leader, Monitor, Review, Telegraph. Aggregate, readers, 10,000.

L. J. Sprenkle, B. F. Nelson, Ashland, Times, Union, and Press, 10,000; James Reed & Son, Sperry & Hawley, G. W. Hill, Ashtabula, News, Telegraph, 3,000; C. E. Jennings, R. W. Jones, Athens, Journal, Messenger, 6,000; McClellan & Price, Barnesville, Enterprise, 5,000; C. A. Browning, D. O. Cowen & Co., D. Hillin, Batavia, Courier, Sun, and Advance, 6,000; J. S. T. Clarkson, J. B. Longley, Bellaire, Commercial, Independent, 2,500; Thomas Hubbard, J. H. Fleehart, J. Q. Campbell, Bellefontaine, Examiner, Press, republican, 5,000; E. J. Hammer, Bluffton Gazette, neutral 1,200; J. S. Morley, Andover, Enterprise, 1,000; G. W. Osborne, Antwerp, Gazette, 1,000; Potto & Faus, Bellville Weekly, co-operative, 1,400; T. H. Winchester, Belpre Courier, neutral, 1,000; W. H. Pearce, Berea, Advertiser, neutral, 1,400; D. W. Fisher, Bloomville Banner, co-operative, 1,000; S. B. Davis, Bluffton Standard, co-operative, 1,600; J. D. Baker, Bowling Green, democratic, 1,800; A. W. Rudolph & Co., Bowling Green Sentinel, republican, 2,400; R. N. Patterson, Bryan Democrat, democratic, 2,000; D. B. Ainzer, Bryan Press, republican, 2,200; J. R. Clymer, Bucyrus Forum, democratic, 5,000; J. Hopley, Bucyrus Journal, republican, 3,000; J. B. Coffin, Burton Leader, 1,000; W. B. Hearn, Cadiz Republican, republican, 2,400; W. H. Arnold, Cadiz Sentinel, democratic, 2,000; John M. Amos, Caldwell Citizen, democratic, 2,000; W. H. Cooley, Caldwell Republican, republican, 2,800; Taylor & Taylor, Cambridge Times, republican, 4,200; J. Kirkpatrick, Cambridge Jeffersonian, democratic, 3,400; L. G. Haines, Cambridge News, independent, 2,800; R. E. Watson, Canal Dover Reporter, co-operative, 1,800; A. J. Baughman, Canal Fulton Herald, 1,000; C. M. Gould, Canal Winchester Times, co-operative, 1,000; W. S. Peterson, Canfield News, democratic, 2,800; Mrs. M. C. W. Dawson, Canfield Golden Mean, temperance, 1,500; M. A. Stewart, Canton Times, democratic, 2,300; N. Montag & Son, Canton Staats Zeitung, democratic, 2,300; W. T. Bascom, Canton Repository, republican, 4,800; A. McGregor & Son, Canton Democrat, democratic, 4,400; W. S. McKellar, Cardington Independent, co-operative, 1,000; Frank T. Tripp, Carey Times, co-operative, 800; J. V. Lawler, Carrollton, Carroll Chronicle, 1,600; S. J. Cameron & Co., Carrollton, Carroll Free Press, republican, 1,800; A. P. J. Snyder, Celina Standard, democratic, 1,000; D. J. Callen, Celina Democrat, democratic, 2,000; J. J. Stranaham, Chagrin Falls Exponent, co-operative, 1,600; J. O. Converse, Chardon Republican, republican, 2,800; James Chambers, Chardon Times, 2,000; A. Mayo, Chillicothe Advertiser, democratic, 2,400; F. E. Armstrong, Chillicothe Register, independent, 3,400; Raper & Wolfe, Chillicothe Gazette, republican, 3,000; John P. Burns, Chillicothe Post, democratic, 2,400; A. R. Van Cleaf, Circleville Democrat, democratic, 3,200; L. C. Darst, Circleville Herald, independent, 2,800; Alfred Williams, Circleville Union, republican, 2,400; George E. Sweetland, Clyde Review, co-operative, 1,000; E. S. Holloway, Columbiana (New Lisbon) Register, co-operative, 1,600; Reig & Stonen, Conneaut Reporter, republican, 2,600; T. W. Collier, Coshocton Age, republican, 2,400; J. C. Fisher, Coshocton Democrat, democratic, 2,000; W. A. Browne, Covington Gazette, independent, 1,400; A. Billow, Crestline Gazette, co-operative, 1,600; A. N. Jenner, Crestline Democrat, co-operative, 1,400; E. O. Knox, Cuyahoga Falls Reporter, co-operative, 1,400; White & Blymer, Defiance Democrat, democratic, 2,400; F. B. Ainger, Defiance, Express, 1,600; A. Thomas & Sons, Delaware Gazette, republican, 3,000; R. F. Hurlbutt, Delaware Herald, democratic, 2,000; Hunt & Springstead, Dresden Herald, co-operative, 1,000; L. G. Gould, Eaton Democrat, democratic, 1,600; W. F. Albright & Co., Eaton Register, Republican, 2,400; F. S. Reefy, Elyria Constitution, democratic 2,000; George G. Washburn, Elyria Independent, republican, 2,000; H. A. Fisher, Elyria Republican, republican, 2,400; J. K. Barnd, Findlay Patron, agricultural, 10,000; L. Glessner, Findlay Courier, democratic, 2,800; De Wolf Brothers, Findlay Jeffersonian, republican, 3,800; F. Wilmer, Fremont Courier, democratic, 2,200; J. M. Osborn, Fremont Messenger, democratic, 2,500; A. H. Balsley, Fremont Journal, republican, 3,200; J. L. Vance, Gallipolis Bulletin, 1,400; W. H. Nash, Gallipolis Journal, republican, 2,400; G. D. Hebard, Gallipolis Ledger, 1,000; L. B. Leeds, Georgetown News, democratic, 2,000; T. H. Hodder, Butler County Democrat, democratic, 2,800; Frederick Egry, Butler County Telegraph, republican, 2,000; J. C. Springer, Hillsborough Gazette, 2,000; J. L. Boardman, Hillsborough News, republican, 2,300; H. M. Adams, Ironton Journal, republican, 2,000; Albert Lawson, Ironton Commercial, independent, 1,600; G. R. Scriven, Ironton Democrat, co-operative, 2,000; E. S. Wilson, Ironton Register, republican, 2,600; Irvan Dungan, Ironton Herald, democratic, 1,700; D. Mackley, Ironton Standard, republican, 2,800; D. S. Fisher, Kenton (Hardin County) Democrat, democratic, 2,400; A. W. Miller, Kenton Republican, republican, 1,800; W. C. Howells, Ashtabula, Jefferson Sentinel, republican, 2,000; A. Griswold, Lancaster Gazette, republican, 3,000; Thomas Wetzler, Lancaster Eagle, democratic, 3,500; Edward Warwick, Lebanon Patriot, democratic, 2,000; W. C. McClintock, Lebanon Star, republican, 2,000; H. B. Kelly, Lima (Allen County) Democrat, democratic, 1,600; Edmiston & Sherman, Lima Gazette, republican, 2,300; Lewis Green, Logan Sentinel, democratic, 2,000; F. Montgomery, Logan Republican, republican, 1,600; M. L. Bryan, London Democrat, democratic, 2,000; G. E. Ross, London Times, republican, 2,000; E. Mettles, Mechanicsburg News, 1,000; A. J. Baughman, Medina Democrat, 1,800; J. H. Greene, Medina Gazette, republican, 2,800; Blossom Brothers, Miamisburg Bulletin, independent, 1,000; Bechan & Seter, Middleport (Meigs County) News, republican, 1,200; E. S. Harkrader, Middletown Journal, neutral, 1,400; A. H. Balsley, Milan Advertiser, 1,000; James A. Estill, Millersburg (Holmes County) Farmer, democratic, 4,000; White & Cunningham, Millersburg Republican, republican, 2,600; Wearer Brothers, Minerva Commercial, republican, 1,000; J. F. Clough, Monroeville Spectator, independent, 1,200; J. W. Griffith, Mount Gilead Sentinel, republican, 2,000; W. G. Beebe, Mount Gilead Register, democratic, 1,400; L. Harper, Mount Vernon Democratic Banner, democratic, 2,600; J. H. & E. C. Hamilton, Mount Vernon Republican, republican, 2,300; S. & J. Hoover, Massillon American, independent, 1,600; Welker & Taylor, Massillon Independent, republican, 1,600; J. W. Bowen, McArthur Enquirer, democratic, 2,400; John T. Rapper, McArthur Record, republican, 1,200; F. A. Davis, McConnellsville Democrat, democratic, 1,600; J. R. Foulke & Co., McConnellsville Herald, republican, 2,500; D. Lee & Sons, Madison Gazette, co-operative, 1,400; Thomas P. Foster, Manchester Gazette, republican, 1,000; Mrs. R. F. Lockhart, Mansfield Flag, independent, 1,500; John B. Netscher, Mansfield Courier, 1,200; L. D. Myers & Co., Mansfield Herald, republican, 3,600; Liberal Printing Company, Mansfield Liberal, co-operative, 2,400; J. Y. Glessner, Mansfield Banner, democratic, 3,500; E. R. Alderman, Marietta Register, republican, 5,000; S. McMillen, Marietta Times, democratic, 2,800; Jacob Mueller, Marietta Zeitung, 1,000; Newcomer & Williston, Marion Mirror, democratic, 2,400; George Crawford & Co., Marion Independent, republican, 1,400; Charles M. Kenton, Marysville Journal, 1,900; J. H. Shearer, Marysville Tribune, republican, 2,800; Orwig & Wisler, Napoleon Northwest, democratic, 2,200; J. S. Fouke, Napoleon Signal, republican, 1,200; Morgan & Kingsbury, Newark Advocate, democratic, 5,000; Clark & Underwood, Newark American, republican, 2,500; Milton R. Scott, Newark Banner, co-operative, 1,000; Buchanan & McClelland, New Comerstown Argus, co-operative, 1,000; Duffy & Meloy, New Lexington Herald, democratic, 1,000; J. F. McMahon, New Lexington Tribune, republican, 2,000; R. W. Taylor, Jr., New Lisbon Buckeye State, 2,000; J. K. Krew, New Lisbon Journal, independent, 2,000; G. B. Vallandigham, New Lisbon Patriot, democratic, 2,200; Walter & Minnig, New Philadelphia Beobachter, democratic, 1,800; Mathews, Elliott & Co., New Philadelphia Democrat, democratic, 2,800; J. L. McIlvaine, New Philadelphia Advocate, republican, 3,000; W. W. Redfield, Norwalk Experiment, democratic, 2,000; Pratt & Hammer, Norwalk Chronicle, republican, 2,000; Wickham & Gibbs, Norwalk Reflector, republican, 2,200; J. H. Battle & Co., Oberlin News, republican, 4,000; George D. Kender, Ottawa News, democratic, 2,200; W. C. Chambers & Son, Painesville Journal, independent, 3,000; E. W. Clark, Painesville Advertiser, 2,000; Merrill & Scoville, Painesville Telegraph, republican, 3,000; C. W. Potter & Son, Paulding Democrat, co-operative, 2,000; N. H. Callard & Son, Perrysburg Granger, co-operative, 2,000; James Timmons, Perrysburg Journal, republican, 1,400; D. M. Fleming, Piqua Journal, republican, 1,400; J. C. Cole, Piqua Democrat, democratic, 1,100; O. B.

Chapman, Pomeroy Telegraph, republican, 3,000; Joseph Jessing, Pomeroy Wassenfreund, 1,500; Stalter & Taylor, Port Clinton News, democratic, 1,400; James Maxwell, Port Clinton Reporter, co-operative, 1,200; Julius Bock, Portsmouth Correspondent, independent, 2,400; D. D. W. Davis, Portsmouth Gazette, 2,400; C. E. Erwin, Portsmouth Republican, republican, 3,000; James B. Newman, Portsmouth Times, democratic, 3,000; McFarland & Elick, Portsmouth Tribune, republican, 2,600; L. W. Hall & Son, Ravenna Democrat, republican, 3,800; M. J. Chase, Ripley Times, 1,800; A. Hunt, St. Clairsville Chronicle, 2,600; C. N. Gaumer, St. Clairsville Gazette, democratic, 2,300; J. F. Mack & Bro., Sandusky Register, republican, 5,600; Ernst & Son, Sandusky Democrat, democratic, 2,500; Kinney & Brother, Sandusky Journal, republican, 1,600; Trego & Binkley, Sidney Journal, republican, 2,000; J. S. Van Valkenburg, Sidney (Shelby County) Democrat, democratic, 2,000; C. M. Nichols, Springfield Republic, republican, 6,000; Elifritz & Francis, Springfield Transcript, democratic, 2,000; McFadden & Hunter, Steubenville Gazette, democratic, 3,200; P. B. Conn, Steubenville Herald, republican, 8,000; J. K. Huddle, Tiffin Star, 8,000; George Homan, Tiffin Presse, 1,800; Armstrong & Myers, Tiffin Advertiser, democratic, 2,600; Locke & Brothers, Tiffin Tribune, 4,000; W. H. & C. Bidlack, Troy Bulletin, 1,200; J. W. Defrees, Troy Union, republican, 1,200; W. A. Pittinger, Uhrichsville Chronicle, republican, 2,200; P. Cuneo, Upper Sandusky Republican, republican, 1,600; Charles L. Zahn, Upper Sandusky Democrat, democratic, 2,000; Buckeye Democrat Company, Urbana, Buckeye Democrat, 2,500; J. Saxton & W. A. Brand, Urbana Gazette, republican, 3,200; J. H. Foster, Van Wert Bulletin, republican, 2,000; J. A McConahay, Van Wert Press, 1,200; W. H. Clymer, Van Wert Times, democratic, 1,800; John A. Clark, Wadsworth Enterprise, independent, 2,000; Andrews & McMurray, Wapakoneta Democrat, 2,200; J. Powell, Wapakoneta Republican, 1,400; M. Borchard & Son, Warren Constitution, democratic, 1,400; William Ritezell, Warren Chronicle, republican, 3,000; William Millikan & Co., Washington Herald, republican, 2,600; F. M. Jones, Washington News, co-operative, 1,800; Simmons & Beasley, Washington State Register, 1,600; W. H. Handy & Co., Wauseon Democrat, 1,500; Smith & Sherwood, Wauseon Republican, 1,800; S. F. Wetmore & Brother, Waverly Republican, 1,200; John A. Jones, Waverly Watchman, 2,500; J. W. Eyler, West Union Defender, democratic, 1,800; S Burnell, West Union Scion, republican, 1,700; Browning & Way, Wilmington Republican, republican, 2,100; W. H. P. Denny, Wilmington Journal, republican, 1,800; J. B. Driggs, Woodsfield Democrat, democratic, 2,000; Jere Williams, Woodsfield Spirit of Democracy, 1,000; McClure & Sanborn, Wooster Republican, 2,800; E. B. Eshelman, Wooster Democrat, 4,000; Patton & Findley, Xenia Gazette, republican, 3,000; J. Fahey, Xenia News, co-operative, 2,000; Stine & Marshall, Xenia Torchlight, republican, 3,600; Youngstown Printing Company, Youngstown Register, republican, 3,000; S. L. Everett, Youngstown Vindicator, democratic, 1,600; A. D. Fassett, Youngstown Miner, 1,000.

Each of the 350 papers and periodical editors write by average per issue on ten different subjects. Thirty dailies, 300 times per year, consume 90,000 editorials; and 320 weekly and other periodicals, consume 167,000 editorials.

One-half of the whole are non-political, and one-half political editorials. Of this one-half, a moiety are the offspring of party feeling, and govern the mass of voters, whether right or wrong.

But as both can not be right, it follows that the people pronounce indirectly upon the same annually through the ballot-box; their judgment that whichever party may have been defeated, have propagated about sixty thousand lies to carrry the election.

This is the remedy of civil government for purification, without resorting to the bayonet, as in other countries; and thus the work goes on from year to year and decade to decade, the ballot-box annually becoming the lever of public opinion in making statesmen out of pigmies, and reducing statesmen to pigmies, in a political point of view.

On the other hand, the public press builds up the fabric of government, assists religion, prevents sectarianism, and promotes the general welfare so thoroughly that no man, woman or child can be wronged in Ohio, without punishment to the wrong-doer.

The editors engaged in this momentous labor devote their lives to the public good, yet generally receive as compensation more "kicks than coppers;" and when they die, it is, with a few exceptions, without remembrance, or tomb-stones, from the public.

www.ingramcontent.com/pod-product-compliance
Lightning Source LLC
LaVergne TN
LVHW010140110826
845151LV00002B/389

* 9 7 8 1 4 2 5 5 3 8 7 6 7 *